500 MORE FAT-FREE RECIPES

500 MORE FAT-FREE RECIPES

SARAH SCHLESINGER

Villard

New York

All rights reserved under International and Pan-American Copyright
Conventions. Published in the United States by Villard Books, a division of
Random House, Inc., New York, and simultaneously in Canada by
Random House of Canada Limited, Toronto.

VILLARD BOOKS is a registered trademark of Random House, Inc.

Library of Congress Cataloging-in-Publication Data
Schlesinger, Sarah.
500 more fat-free recipes / Sarah Schlesinger.
p.   cm.
Includes index.
ISBN 0-679-44518-8
1. Low-fat diet—Recipes.   I. Title.
RM237.7.S35   1998
641.5′638—dc21   97-15131

Random House website address: http://www.randomhouse.com/

Printed in the United States of America on acid-free paper

24689753

First Edition

Book design by Chris Welsh

To Sam Gossage, the co-creator of this book, whose good heart is the source and center of my happiness

Thanks to Robert Cornfield, David Rosenthal, Annik La Farge, Ruth Fecych, Benjamin Dreyer, Brian McLendon, and the enthusiastic cooks and tasters who shared in the process of creating this book.

CONTENTS

∾

INTRODUCTION

❦

The idea of eating a primarily fat-free diet has extended far beyond the fad stage in American life. Our family has been eating a primarily fat-free diet for the past six years and during that period, we have witnessed a literal revolution in the way millions of Americans think about the fat content of the food they consume.

We began eating a fat-free diet when, several years after multiple-bypass surgery, my husband, Sam, was told that his arteries had become obstructed again. He could not have further bypass surgery. He was given few alternatives beyond letting nature take its course as his arteries continued to become more and more blocked. We turned, as we had since he began his battle against heart disease twenty years ago, to diet as a way to fight back. Thankfully, Dr. Dean Ornish had just published his program for reversing heart disease, which stressed an extremely low-fat diet as a primary strategy for battling diseases of the heart and arteries.

Although we had been eating more and more conservative quantities of saturated fat over the years, following the Ornish program led us to far more extreme reductions of the fat in our diets. We realized that we would be eating this way for the rest of our lives and that we would have to cook at home much of the time due to the amount of fat present in most restaurant cooking and packaged foods. We found few existing fat-free recipes and soon decided to create our own. Our experimentation with fat-free cooking led to the 500 recipes that made up *500 Fat-Free Recipes* (Villard, 1994). That book, which has become a classic bestselling guide for fat-free cooking, provided 500 ways to make quick, easy, nutritionally correct dishes with 1 gram of fat or less per serving.

Thankfully, since that book was published, packaged food manufacturers have responded to the huge consumer interest in eating fat-free products by placing many new fat-free choices on supermarket shelves. However, most of these continue to be in the categories of dairy products, snacks, and desserts. While there has been some movement on the part of the restaurant industry to make fat-free foods an accessible choice on menus, there is still much work to be done before eating out in America ceases to be a fat-free eater's nightmare.

When we finished our first 500 recipes, we thought we would have enough choices to keep us content indefinitely. However, the reality is that fat-free eating demands options for three meals a day, three hundred and sixty-five days a year. No sooner had the first book been published when we began developing new fat-free dishes.

Within these pages you will find 500 more simple-to-prepare fat-free recipes featuring fruit, vegetables, whole grains, cereals, and beans with 1 gram of fat or less per serving. We hope that they will make your fat-free eating a little simpler and a lot more satisfying.

▪ FACTS ABOUT FAT ▪

▪ The average American diet includes nearly 40% of its calories from fat. Most health professionals recommend that we get less than 30% of our total daily calories from fat and many are currently suggesting that we should go as low as 10%.

▪ Fats have 9 calories per gram while carbohydrates and proteins have only 4. We load up on fat calories because fat tastes so good, and because most fat-laden foods are also low in fiber, they don't make us feel full. Since we eat large portions of these foods in order to satisfy our cravings, eating fat causes us to consume a lot of extra calories.

▪ When we eat more food than our bodies need, our livers convert the extra calories to fat. Too much body fat can contribute to indigestion, bloating, and sluggishness; it can also impact appearance. Low-fat vegetarian diets are linked to lower rates of heart disease and stroke, as well as breast, prostate, colon, lung, and ovarian cancers. They may also reduce the incidence of osteoporosis, adult-onset diabetes, hypertension, and obesity.

▪ Low-fat vegetarian diets are essential for anyone who is overweight or has high blood cholesterol, high blood pressure, diabetes, chronic constipation, or gallbladder disease. They are also important for anyone with increased risk of heart attack, diabetes, or cancer of the prostate, breast, uterus, colon, or gallbladder.

▪ Cutting back on fat can result in an increased desire for it because fat cravings may actually be triggered by the same mechanism that causes drug addiction. However, most people are able to reduce their cravings for fat in 7 to 10 days.

▪ To figure your own daily 10% fat allowance, multiply your daily calorie intake by .1. Then divide that figure by 9 for the number of fat grams that you should eat every day.

▪ Facts About Saturated, ▪ Unsaturated, and Monounsaturated Fats

▪ All foods contain a mixture of the three different types of fats: saturated, polyunsaturated, and monounsaturated.

▪ Saturated fats are found in all food sources of fat, but in large quantities in meat, eggs, and the tropical oils such as coconut, palm, and palm kernel oils. When we take in more calories than we need, saturated fats raise blood cholesterol more than the other types of fats do. Saturated fats are solid at room temperature.

▪ Polyunsaturated fats are also found in all sources of fat, particularly in vegetable oils. They are liquid at room temperature. Replacing saturated fats with polyunsaturated fats lowers blood-cholesterol levels slightly but raises triglycerides, the fats that are made by the liver when we take in more calories than our bodies need. Large doses of polyunsaturated fat can also increase our chances of developing cancers of the uterus, breast, prostate, colon, and gallbladder. They can suppress immunity so we are at increased risk of developing infections, and they can cause gallstones.

Avoid margarine and commercially prepared bakery products because their polyunsaturated fats are often partially hydrogenated, which means they can raise cholesterol even more than saturated fat.

▪ Monounsaturated fats are also found in every source of fat in nature. Almonds and olives are particularly rich sources. As is true of polyunsaturated fats, substituting monounsaturated fats for saturated fats can help lower blood cholesterol a little bit. When we substitute polyunsaturated for saturated fats, we lower our good HDL as well as our bad LDL, but substituting monounsaturated fats for saturated fats lowers blood levels of the bad LDL cholesterol without also lowering the good HDL. Remember, however, that monounsaturated oils are still fats, and a tablespoon of any oil contains 120 calories and 14 grams of fat. It isn't necessary to eat extra fat of any kind. We eat all the fats our bodies need when we eat plenty of fruits, vegetables, whole grains, and beans.

▪ Omega-3 polyunsaturated fats are subclassified into omega-3s and omega-6s. The only essential nutrients related to fats are two fatty acids— linolenic and linoleic acids—which our bodies can't make. These two essential fatty acids are usually found as omega-3 and omega-6 fatty acids.

▪ The omega-3 acids are found in cold-water fish and vegetable sources such as golden flaxseed. The omega-6 acids are found in whole grains such as cereals.

▪ Omega-3s can also lower cholesterol when we reduce our total intake of all fats. They help to prevent blood clots, which completely obstruct the flow of blood to cause a heart attack. While omega-3s offer added protection against clotting, it's even more important to restrict dietary fat. The maximum anticlotting benefit can be attained by eating fish twice a week. People who eat fish twice a week have a reduced incidence of heart attacks, but those who eat fish more often than that do not have any further reduction. One baby aspirin every other day provides the same anticlotting benefit.

▪ Tropical oils such as palm, palm kernel, and coconut oils are loaded with saturated fats. The main sources of tropical oils are bakery products such as cookies, crackers, breads, and rolls, and prepared, canned, and frozen foods such as breaded fish and prepared vegetables.

▪ Hydrogenated oils (trans-fats) are used in commercial baked goods because consumer demand pushed manufacturers to reduce their use of tropical oils. While tropical oils have a long shelf life, other vegetable oils do not. Consequently, bakers add hydrogen ions to the polyunsaturated fats to create partially hydrogenated trans-fat vegetable oils, which stay fresh. Hydrogenation changes an oil by making it more saturated. United States Department of Agriculture studies have revealed that trans-fats not only raise LDL cholesterol as much as saturated fats do, but they lower the good HDL cholesterol that helps to prevent heart attacks, thereby giving it the potential to raise blood-cholesterol levels. If a manufacturer claims to be using vegetable oil in a product, check the ingredient list. If the oil appears in the product as a hydrogenated fat, be aware that the product contains saturated fat.

∎ Artificial fats or fat substitutes include three types: those made from animal protein, those made from starch, and those made from a sugar-and-fatty-acid molecule that cannot be absorbed. Animal protein fat substitutes are manufactured from egg white and milk powder. They are used in many different products, such as ice cream and frozen yogurt. Artificial fats called polydextrose and maltdextrin are found in drinks, desserts, and various diet foods. The third type is made by combining sugars and fatty acids into a molecule that cannot be absorbed into the bloodstream. Olestra is of the third type and was approved by the Food and Drug Administration in January 1996.

∎ FACTS ABOUT CHOLESTEROL ∎

∎ Cholesterol is a substance that is produced by the body and used in the production of body tissues. We also get cholesterol from consuming foods that contain cholesterol. When the body is fed more cholesterol than it can handle, it stores the excess cholesterol in the arteries. This stored cholesterol is suspected of being a major factor in the development of heart disease.

∎ Cholesterol is only found in animal foods, such as poultry, seafood, meat, dairy products, egg yolks, and animal fats (butter, chicken fat, and lard). However, there are a number of plant foods such as nuts, nut butters, coconuts, olives, avocados, margarines, and vegetable oils that are high in fat although they are cholesterol-free. Any fat with a high percentage of saturated fat can also potentially raise your blood-cholesterol level.

▪ Total cholesterol contains both good HDL cholesterol and harmful LDL cholesterol. People who have high blood levels of HDL cholesterol and low blood levels of LDL cholesterol have the lowest risk of heart attacks. The LDL carries cholesterol in the bloodstream onto artery walls to form plaques. HDL carries cholesterol from the bloodstream to the liver, where it is converted to bile and eliminated from the body. Low-fat diets may cause HDL cholesterol to go down, but they don't increase the risk of developing a heart attack. A low-fat diet lowers both the good HDL and the bad LDL cholesterol. The decrease of HDL in the blood is good because it shows the HDL is being removed to the liver at a faster rate.

▪ FACTS ABOUT FIBER ▪

▪ A low-fat diet that is also high in fiber is an important defensive strategy against heart disease and several forms of cancer. Fiber is the indigestible parts of plant food, such as pectin, cellulose, and bran. Suggested fiber intake is between 25 and 30 grams a day.

▪ Water-soluble fiber may significantly lower blood-cholesterol levels. This type of fiber is abundant in many plant foods, including oats, apples, figs, prunes, carrots, plums, squash, barley, kidney beans, split peas, and chickpeas.

▪ Insoluble fiber is found in whole grains such as cornmeal and whole wheat flour (especially wheat bran), and in fruits and vegetables such as broccoli, cabbage, raspberries, and strawberries. This type of fiber seems to improve intestinal function, and many researchers feel that it may help in preventing some types of cancer. It is important to have both types of fiber in the diet.

▪ Fiber can be added to meals by choosing whole-grain breads, crackers, pasta, and whole-grain breakfast cereals. Make bread crumbs from whole-grain breads and add peas, beans, and lentils to soups, stews, and salads. Leave the skin on fruits and vegetables and add grated vegetables to sauces and casseroles. Use pureed vegetables to thicken soups and stews, and make tossed salads using vegetables of all colors. Eat fresh or dried fruit for snacks and desserts. Use brown rice and experiment with other grains like barley. Add cooked grains to soups and casseroles; replace half the flour in baked goods with whole wheat flour.

▪ FACTS ABOUT SODIUM ▪

▪ Sodium is a mineral that occurs naturally in many foods. Most of the sodium in the American diet comes from table salt and the sodium added to processed foods and beverages. It is added for flavor and as a preservative and is sometimes called sodium citrate, sodium nitrate, and sodium phosphate. Too much sodium can contribute to high blood pressure. Daily intake should be limited to 2,400 to 3,000 milligrams of sodium. Reducing salt is particularly important if you have high blood pressure, kidney disease, or heart failure. Choose reduced-sodium or salt-free canned foods if they are available or rinse canned foods such as beans to remove salt. Choose reduced-sodium soy sauce and other condiments.

▪ FACTS ABOUT FAT-FREE FOODS ▪

▪ All whole foods contain fat, sometimes in very small quantities. The U.S. Food and Drug Administration has defined "fat free" as a food that contains less than 0.5 gram of fat per serving. In this book, we have defined "fat free" as a recipe that contains less than 1 gram of fat per serving.

▪ Most commercially manufactured desserts and snack foods made with artificial fats have lots of calories and very little fiber. Portion sizes are often extremely small.

▪ Some plant foods are relatively high in fat, so, while large amounts of them do not actually contain cholesterol, they still contribute too much fat to the diet and may raise cholesterol levels in the blood. These include nuts, nut butters, coconut, olives, avocados, margarine, and vegetable oils.

▪ Advertisers may stress the advantages of their products being cholesterol-free, failing to mention the possible high fat content of the ingredients.

▪ The foods that are highest in saturated fat are butter, whole-milk dairy products, meat, poultry, eggs, and the recipes and products that contain them such as mayonnaise, cheese, puddings, and chocolate products.

▪ Foods such as crackers may contain very high amounts of (often saturated) fat. Other potential sources of hidden fats are some cereals, nondairy coffee creamers, whipped toppings, packaged popcorn, and dry bread crumbs.

▪ PREPARING FAT-FREE FOOD ▪
AT HOME

Because an extraordinary amount of fat in processed and packaged foods is "hidden" the only way to eat a total diet that is nutritious and low in fat is to cook many of the dishes you consume each day at home—an awesome task in a too-busy world. This cookbook provides you with 500 easy and delicious ways to create dishes that have 1 gram or less per serving of fat.

Fat-Free Cooking Tips

▪ Fat is not actually a flavor, but rather a flavor carrier and an ingredient that gives food a creamy texture. We have compensated for the loss of fat as a flavoring agent by highlighting the natural flavor of foods using herbs and spices, and combining sweet ingredients with spicy ingredients. Heighten the flavor of your own cooking by stocking a ready supply of bottled sauces and seasonings, including a variety of interesting mustards, Worcestershire sauce, horseradish, steak sauce, catsup, fat-free salad dressings, Thai fish sauce, flavored vinegars, hoisin sauce, hot pepper sauces, teriyaki sauce, soy sauce, and oyster sauce. Check labels to be sure you are buying fat-free products.

▪ Use tomato products when steaming, simmering, and sautéeing. Keep your pantry stocked with low-sodium tomato paste, tomato puree, tomato juice, and canned tomatoes.

▪ Use wine, fruit juices, and tomato or other vegetable juices for steaming, simmering, and sautéing.

▪ Try adding fruit juice to vegetables near the end of the cooking time.

▪ Use fat-free canned chicken and vegetable broth. You can intensify the flavor of these broths by boiling them to reduce them by half.

▪ Strain liquids used for steaming vegetables or soaking dried mushrooms and recycle them for soup or cooking rice.

▪ Use steaming as a nonfat cooking method. Place a half inch to an inch of water in a pot and bring it to a boil. Add food in a steamer basket over the water and cover tightly. Cook until food is tender-crisp, checking to be sure the liquid doesn't boil away.

▪ Simmer long-cooking foods gently in water, nonfat stocks, or other liquids. Cover food with liquid, bring it to a boil, reduce heat, and simmer. The pot can be covered or uncovered, but check that the liquid doesn't simmer away.

▪ Sauté food by cooking it rapidly in a small amount of boiling liquid. Place ¼ to ½ cup liquid in a skillet and bring it to a boil. Add the food and stir frequently. Add liquid if needed to keep food from sticking. At the end of the cooking time, the liquid should all be evaporated. Use this technique for softening onions, celery, or bell peppers and sautéing other quick-cooking vegetables.

▪ Thicken soups and stews by replacing butter and flour with vegetable purees or buttermilk.

▪ Replace oil in salad dressings with either corn syrup or honey if you want the dressing to cling to salad ingredients.

▪ Broil, bake, roast, and grill without fat. Experiment with broiling or roasting vegetables instead of steaming.

▪ Experiment with herbs you haven't tried before. Buy fresh herbs when they are available at your supermarket or specialty store. Try toasting whole spices and grinding them yourself instead of buying ground spices.

▪ Try creating salad dressings using nonfat yogurt or tofu as a base. Add flavored vinegars, mustard, honey, fresh parsley, and other herbs.

▪ Try tossing steamed vegetables with balsamic vinegar, rice vinegar, or sherry vinegar.

▪ Add grated citrus fruit peel to stews and fruit salads.

▪ Add a few drops of lemon or lime juice before serving stews and soups.

▪ When making fat-free baked goods, don't overmix batters or overcook.

▪ Replace cream in recipes with skim milk thickened with cornstarch. Dissolve 2 tablespoons cornstarch in ¼ cup cold water. Then add dissolved cornstarch to 1 cup of milk.

▪ Don't let nonfat yogurt boil or it will curdle. Nonfat sour cream and milk may curdle if boiled with lemon juice, vinegar, tomato juice, or other acids.

▪ Empty your cabinet shelves and refrigerator of tempting, fat-laden foods.

▪ Map meal plans out in advance.

▪ Build your diet mainly around fruits, vegetables, beans, and grains. Include at least one serving of skim milk or skim-milk products every day.

Equipping a Fat-Free Kitchen

Look for:

- Top-quality nonstick cookware. Buy cookware that is ovenproof, heavy, and has a highly durable coating with a textured bottom surface. Important pieces to collect include a 10-inch or 12-inch skillet, pots, a roasting pan, and a baking pan. Brand names to look for in nonstick coatings include Autograph and Silverstone Select or Super-Select. Ridged surfaces prevent sticking and allow easier deglazing. Wide pans have more surface and cook foods faster.
- A collapsible metal steamer or a bamboo steamer.
- An electric steamer or rice cooker.
- Food processor and/or blender for pureeing, chopping, grating, and blending.
- An electronic kitchen scale.
- A wire whisk with a dozen or more stainless steel wires that are not too rigid or too flexible.
- Pepper mill.
- Parchment paper for lining baking sheets and cake pans.
- Large cutting board.
- A big, sharp chef's knife and a small paring knife.
- Microwave oven.
- Pressure cooker.

Ingredient Glossary

Here is a shopping guide for the ingredients used in *500 More Fat-Free Recipes.*

Amaretto An almond-flavored liqueur.

Angel Food Cake Mix Angel food cakes, which are free of fat and cholesterol, are a dessert staple on a fat-free diet. If you don't have time to make angel food cake from scratch, there are a number of dry mixes on the market to choose from.

Apple Juice Concentrate Apple and other juice concentrates can be used to sweeten some dishes. They can be found in the freezer section of your supermarket or packaged in a box in the canned and bottled juice section.

Applesauce   Buy natural applesauce without added sugar. Applesauce can be substituted for butter and margarine in many recipes to reduce fat, calories, and cholesterol. Applesauce provides moisture and stability when used as a fat alternative in baked goods. It performs best when it is used in recipes containing other wet ingredients such as skim milk or fresh fruit. Replace ½ cup butter with ½ cup natural applesauce.

Artichoke Hearts   Canned artichoke hearts are baby artichokes with tender leaves and bottom in which the bristly choke is undeveloped and therefore edible. Buy only artichoke hearts packed in water. They can be stored unopened on a cool, dry pantry shelf for a year.

Bagels   Look for "water" bagels and avoid those made with egg. Check labels on packaged bagels for fat content.

Baking Powder   Baking powder is a combination of an acid, an alkali, and a starch that keeps the other ingredients stable and dry. The powder reacts with liquid by foaming and the resulting bubbles can aerate and raise dough. Buy double-acting, low-sodium baking powder. Don't expose it to steam, humid air, wet spoons, or moisture. Store it in a tightly sealed container for no more than six months. To test the strength of baking powder, place 1 teaspoon powder into ½ cup hot water. If the mixture fails to fizz and bubble, the baking powder is no longer potent.

Baking Soda   This plain white powder is an alkali, one of the ingredients in baking powder. It is also called bicarbonate of soda. When kept dry and well covered, it can be stored for as long as three months.

Bamboo Shoots   The tender-crisp ivory-colored shoots of a particular, edible species of bamboo plant are cut as soon as they appear above ground. Canned shoots are available in most supermarkets in the Asian foods section.

Barley   A hearty grain with a chewy texture and nutty taste. It looks like rice and puffs up when cooked. The soluble fiber in barley is believed to be just as effective as oats in lowering cholesterol levels. Barley is commercially hulled to shorten the cooking time. Pearled barley is the most common variety.

Bean Sprouts   Sprouts are infant plants that grow out of beans in a moist, warm environment. Look for moist and crisp-looking sprouts with a fresh scent. The shorter the tendrils, the younger and tenderer the sprout. Fresh sprouts will keep for 7 to 10 days in a plastic bag in the refrigerator. They should be kept moist, but don't allow a lot of free water to build up on the inside of the bag. Canned bean sprouts are also available.

Canned Beans   Cannellini beans, pinto beans, kidney beans, Great Northern beans, navy beans, black beans, chickpeas, black-eyed peas, and lentils are used in the recipes. Read labels on canned beans carefully. Most beans contain some natural fat, which will be indicated on the label. However, avoid those that have meats like bacon or pork added. Look for low-sodium products and/or drain them and rinse well before adding to a recipe. Rinsing can reduce the sodium in canned beans by half. If you begin with dry beans, 1 cup of dried beans (8 ounces) is equal to 2 to 2½ cups cooked beans. Before cooking, wash and pick over beans, discarding stones and cracked or shriveled beans.

Beer   Beer and/or nonalcoholic beer are used as flavorings in some recipes.

Bread   Buy French, Italian, whole-wheat, and rye breads that are made without fat. Major bread manufacturers are now producing fat-free breads.

Broccoflower   A light green vegetable resembling cauliflower, it's a cross between broccoli and cauliflower.

Bulgur   Bulgur is made from whole wheat kernels. The wheat kernels are parboiled, dried, and partially debranned, then cracked into coarse fragments to make bulgur.

Butter Substitutes   Natural nonfat, low-calorie, low-sodium, instant butter-flavored granule substitutes contain no cholesterol. They can be turned into a liquid by adding water or may be sprinkled in dry form directly on hot, moist foods. In liquid form, they can be used with baked potatoes and pancakes and in sauces and soups. They are available in ½-ounce packets and in jars. One-half teaspoon of these granules equals the taste of 2 teaspoons butter; 8 teaspoons mixed with ½ cup hot water equals ½ cup or 8 tablespoons liquid butter.

Buttermilk   If you don't have access to nonfat buttermilk, you can substitute equal parts nonfat yogurt and skim milk, or mix a tablespoon of white vinegar or lemon juice with one cup of skim milk. Let the mixture sit for five minutes before using.

Candied Ginger   Sometimes called "crystallized ginger," this is a form of ginger that has been cooked in a sugar syrup and coated with coarse sugar. It can be found in many supermarkets and in Asian markets.

Cereals Shop for fat-free granolas. Most whole-grain cereals contain some fat per serving because whole grains include the wholesome germ—the inner portion of the grain that is an important source of essential fatty acids and vitamin E. The best cereals are 100% whole grain and contain no added sugar, salt, or fat. They should provide at least 4 grams of fiber per 2-ounce serving.

Chicken Broth Look for fat-free, low-sodium canned chicken broth. If you cannot find fat-free broth, refrigerate low-sodium canned broth in a glass or plastic container overnight (or place in freezer for 30 minutes) until fat congeals and rises to the top. Skim fat off before using. You can also make your own broth and skim the fat off before using. If you make a large quantity, you can freeze it in cubes for easy use. Homemade broth will have the richest flavor if it is reduced by one third.

Chutney Chutney is a spicy condiment that contains fruit, vinegar, sugar, and spices. Its texture can range from chunky to smooth and the degree of spiciness from mild to hot. Mango chutney, which is readily available in most supermarkets, is suggested in some of the recipes.

Cocoa Powder made from dried, roasted cocoa beans.

Cointreau A clear liqueur infused with orange flavor.

Cookies Commercially made fat-free cookies can be used for crumb crusts. More and more varieties of fat-free cookies are appearing on supermarket shelves. You can choose among fudge cookies, oatmeal cookies, or fruit-flavored cookies such as apple, date, apricot, and raspberry. Select a cookie for your crumb crusts that will best complement the filling you are using.

Corn Chips You can either create your own fat-free corn chips by cutting fat-free tortillas into smaller sections and baking them or by buying commercially prepared fat-free, baked corn chips.

Cornmeal Cornmeal is ground yellow or white corn kernels. Yellow cornmeal has more vitamin A. Cornmeal can be used to make polenta, an Italian pudding or mush that can be eaten hot or cold with sauce and other ingredients sprinkled over it.

Cornstarch This silky white powder is a thickener for sauces, puddings, and pie fillings.

Cottage Cheese Avoid high sodium count by buying dry-curd cottage cheese, which is made without the dressing or creaming mixture.

Couscous A precooked, cracked-wheat product that is an alternative to rice, couscous is made from white durum wheat from which the bran and germ have been removed. Once cooked it has a very light, airy quality and a silky texture. Couscous can be found with other grains such as rice or in the imported food aisle.

Crackers   A variety of nonfat crackers can be found in most supermarkets.

Curry Powder   Curry powder is a blend of different herbs and spices that vary according to the country of origin. Varieties can differ in intensity of flavor, so use carefully. Curry flavor becomes stronger in a dish that is refrigerated and then reheated.

Dijon Mustard   Dijon is a strong French mustard readily available in supermarkets. Avoid varieties with added oil or eggs. Store in the refrigerator.

Dressings   Many fat-free, commercially prepared dressings are now on the market. Some are packaged in dried form to be mixed as needed. Fat-free Italian dressing is used in recipes that might otherwise require large amounts of oil.

Eggs and Egg Substitute   The recipes call for egg whites, but not for egg yolks, which are extremely high in cholesterol. Egg whites contain half the protein found in an egg and no fat or cholesterol. Three tablespoons of egg white can be substituted for a whole egg. When buying commercial egg substitutes, shop for fat-free brands. Some brands contain vegetable oil. Eight ounces (1 cup) of a commercial egg substitute replaces 4 whole eggs and 8 egg whites. Two ounces (¼ cup) egg substitute is equivalent to 1 medium egg.

English Muffins   Check package labels to be sure you are buying nonfat English muffins.

Evaporated Skim Milk   Evaporated skim milk can add much of the richness of cream to recipes with almost none of the fat. This is a heat-sterilized, concentrated skim milk with half the water removed. The consistency of evaporated skim milk resembles whole milk. Once a can of evaporated skim milk has been opened, the contents should be refrigerated, tightly sealed, and used within five days.

Extracts   The intense flavor of extracts is produced by dissolving the essential oils of foods in alcohol. Shop for natural extracts including vanilla, almond, maple, chocolate, and rum. Amaretto (almond-flavored) liqueur is occasionally used in the recipes. Imitation extracts are made from chemicals that taste similar to their natural counterparts.

Fruit   When fresh fruit is not available, consider substituting frozen or canned fruit, but buy fruit packed in juice or water. Canned fruits used in the recipes include pineapples (crushed and chunk), mandarin oranges, pears, peaches, and apricots.

Garam Masala   Garam masala is the Indian term for "warm," and this blend of dry-roasted, ground spices may include black pepper, cinnamon, cloves, coriander, cumin, cardamom, dried chiles, fennel, mace, nutmeg, and other spices. You can mix your own garam masala, or buy it in many supermarkets or Indian markets.

Garlic   Buy fresh garlic, chopped garlic packed without oil, and minced dried garlic. When buying fresh garlic, look for bulbs with large cloves. Store garlic in a cool, dry place. Roast fresh garlic in its skin to bring the flavor out before adding to a dish instead of sautéing. Before adding minced garlic to a dish, try microwaving it with a bit of lemon juice for 30 seconds.

Gelatin   Gelatin is a dry, powdered protein made from animal by-products. Buy unflavored gelatin.

Gingerroot   Fresh gingerroot, which adds a distinctive, spicy flavor to many dishes, can be found in the produce department of many supermarkets. To use, peel the tan skin and thinly slice the root. You can freeze leftover gingerroot wrapped in plastic freezer wrap until ready to use.

Herbs   Dried herbs are called for in this book because fresh herbs are not always available. However, always substitute fresh herbs anytime you have access to them. A half teaspoon of dried herbs equals 1 tablespoon of fresh herbs. Dried herbs should be replaced once a year. You can intensify their flavor by crushing or rubbing them between your fingers. Store dried herbs in airtight containers in a dark and cool place. Herbs used in these recipes include basil, oregano, dill, rosemary, and sage.

Herb Teas   Herb teas in a wide variety of flavors can be found in supermarkets in the coffee and tea aisle.

Hominy   Hominy is dried corn that has had its hull and germ removed with lye or soda. Hominy grits are ground hominy grains. They are white, about the size of toast crumbs. They have a thick, chewy texture when cooked.

Honey   Honey is sweeter than granulated sugar and easier to digest. Its flavor and sweetness vary, depending on what kind of nectar the bees were eating when they made the honey.

Horseradish   Prepared horseradish is mixed with vinegar and packed in jars. You can store it in the refrigerator for three to four months, but it will lose pungency as it ages. Fresh horseradish is a woody-looking root with a fiery flavor. It can be stored in the refrigerator for three weeks.

Jams and Jellies   Buy jams, jellies, and marmalades that are sugar-free and made with fruit and fruit juices, referred to as "sugarless all-fruit jam" in these recipes.

Ketchup   Shop for low-sodium ketchup.

Lemon Juice and Lime Juice   Lemon and lime juices are most flavorful when they are freshly squeezed. Store fresh lemons and limes in the refrigerator, or if using within a few days, at room temperature.

Lemon Peel   Either grate the peel of fresh lemons or buy grated lemon peel in the spice section of your supermarket.

Lemongrass   An herb widely used in the cuisine of Thailand, its distinctive aroma and flavor comes from an oil also found in the peel of lemons.

Maple Syrup   Pure maple syrup is more expensive than pancake syrups made by mixing artificial maple flavoring with corn syrup. However, the taste of pure maple syrup is well worth the difference in price. Once opened, the syrup should be refrigerated. It will last a year in the refrigerator. Cold pure maple syrup does not pour easily, so you should leave it at room temperature for an hour before serving.

Mayonnaise Dressings   A number of fat-free mayonnaise products are available in which the fat has been replaced with starch and emulsifiers. Served plain, these dressings may not have the flavor of regular mayonnaise, but they work well when combined with seasonings and other ingredients. Be aware of the rather high sodium content of these products.

Milk   Buy fresh skim milk, nonfat buttermilk, and instant nonfat dry milk.

Molasses   Molasses consists of the plant juices pressed from sugar cane that are purified and concentrated by boiling. After opening, you can store molasses for another twelve months on the shelf.

Mushrooms   Buy young, pale, cultivated button mushrooms. Brush them and wipe them with a damp cloth. If you need to wash them, be sure to dry them thoroughly. When serving them raw, sprinkle with lemon juice or white wine to keep them light in color.

Nonfat Dry Milk Powder   Adding this powder to cream soups, sauces, and puddings adds richness and nutritional value. One cup of skim milk and ⅓ cup of nonfat dry milk powder can replace cream in many recipes.

Noodles   Shop for cholesterol-free noodles made with egg whites only.

Oats   Shop for old-fashioned rolled oats or quick oats. Avoid instant oat products.

Olive Oil Spray   Buy nonstick olive oil spray for spraying baking pans or other utensil surfaces while cooking. You can also buy an inexpensive plastic spray bottle and fill it with olive oil or canola oil.

Orange Juice Concentrate   Orange juice concentrate can be used to sweeten some dishes. It can be found in the freezer section of your supermarket.

Orange Peel   Either grate the peel of fresh oranges or buy grated orange peel in the spice section of your supermarket.

Orzo   Orzo is a tiny pasta that resembles elongated rice or barley.

Parsley   Because fresh parsley is now widely available, we have specified its use in the recipes. Parsley may be either curly or flat. Flat parsley is often called Italian parsley, and many cooks feel its taste is superior.

Pasta   A cup of cooked macaroni or spaghetti (about 2 ounces dry) has barely a trace of fat or cholesterol. Most of the 210 calories in a cup of cooked pasta come from complex carbohydrates. Stored in a cool, dry place, dried pasta keeps indefinitely. Fresh pasta should be stored in the refrigerator until ready to cook. It should be used within two or three days of purchase or according to the date on the package. It can also be stored in the freezer and thawed before cooking. Dried and fresh pastas are both made from flour and water or flour and eggs. If you are watching your cholesterol, avoid pasta made with whole eggs. However, there are now a number of fresh and dried pastas made with flour and egg whites. Durum wheat, the hardest, or semolina, the coarsest grind of durum, makes the most flavorful and resilient pasta. Pasta made from softer flours tends to turn soggy quickly. For main-dish recipes allow 2 ounces of pasta per person.

Pepper Sauce   Tabasco-type sauces are very hot purees of red chiles, vinegar, and numerous seasonings. They are bright red when fresh. They will last up to a year at room temperature. When pepper sauce turns brown, throw it out.

Pickle Relish   Sweet pickle relish is called for in several of the recipes. Look for brands that have no added salt.

Pickles   Although pickles are high in sodium, small quantities of dill pickles and pickle relish are used in the recipes to add flavor.

Pita Bread   Buy whole-wheat, nonfat pita breads (also called pocket breads). Store in the refrigerator wrapped in tightly closed plastic bags.

Prunes   Prunes have become an important part of fat-free cooking since the discovery that they can replace fat in baking. Prunes are very high in pectin, which forms a protective coating around the air in baked goods, giving the foods the volume and lift usually provided by fat. Pectin can also enhance and trap flavor. Prunes are high in sorbitol, a humectant that attracts and binds moisture, keeping baked foods moist. Butter and shortening keep food moist because they do not evaporate. You can either make your own puree from whole prunes, buy commercially prepared baby-food pureed prunes, or buy prune butter, which is located in either the jam/jelly or baking section of your supermarket. To make your own, place 1 cup whole pitted prunes and ¼ cup water in a food processor or blender and puree.

Rice

Arborio Rice: This is a short-grained Italian rice.

Basmati Rice: The word *basmati* means "queen of fragrance," and this Indian rice has a nutlike aroma.

Brown Rice: Brown rice is processed to remove the tough outer hull but not the bran. It is sometimes parboiled, a process that hardens the grains, ensuring that they remain separated when cooked. It is available in both long-grain and short-grain varieties. The long-grain kind tends to result in a less gummy cooked rice. Brown rice has a superior nutritional profile compared to white rice because it is still covered with bran. However, it has a higher natural fat content.

White Rice: Regular white rice has been milled to remove the hull, germ, and most of the bran. It is available in both long and short grain.

Wild Rice: Actually the seed of aquatic grass that grows in marshes, wild rice takes longer to cook than cultivated rice. It is dark greenish-brown in color and has a distinctive, nutty flavor. It is rich in fiber, vitamins, and minerals.

Salsas   These relishes made from chopped vegetables and spices can be found in the condiments aisle or with the international foods in your supermarket. Some fresh-vegetable salsas are also kept in the refrigerator case alongside fresh tortillas.

Sherry   This still wine from the south of Spain is now made and consumed throughout the world. It is widely valued for cooking.

Sour Cream   Shop for nonfat sour cream. If you find that your nonfat sour cream separates when added to hot sauces, try another brand.

Soy Sauce   Light soy sauce contains from 33 to 46 percent less sodium than regular soy sauce, with little or no difference in flavor. Store in the refrigerator.

Spices   Keep dried spices in an airtight container. Don't expose them to extremely high heat or intense light. Dried spices are best if used within six months to a year, so it is wise to date containers at the time you purchase or store them. During the summer months, store ground cayenne pepper, paprika, chili powder, and crushed red pepper in the refrigerator.

Sugar   Table sugar is sucrose, a highly refined product made from sugar beets or sugar cane. It is nearly 100 percent pure and almost indestructible. Powdered or confectioners' sugar (in a range of textures from coarse to superfine) and brown sugar are variations on granulated sugar and share its very long shelf life. Brown sugar contains granulated sugar coated with refined, colored, molasses-flavored syrup. Light brown sugar has less molasses flavor than dark brown sugar. Store granulated sugar in an airtight container at room temperature. Powdered sugar and brown sugar should be stored in an airtight plastic bag inside a glass jar.

Sugar Substitutes   If you choose to buy sugar substitutes, be aware of their particular chemical compositions and any resulting health implications.

Tofu   Tofu is made from fermented soybeans. It is valued in Asian cuisine for its nutritious qualities and its ability to assume the flavors of other foods.

Tomatillos   Tomatillos are used extensively in Mexican cooking. They are from the same family as the ubiquitous tomato and not only appear in cooked dishes but are featured raw in salads. Tomatillos can be found in markets specializing in Latin American food products.

Tomato Products   When buying canned tomatoes, tomato puree, and tomato paste, look for low-sodium products. Italian plum tomatoes are the best substitute for fresh tomatoes. Do not keep unopened canned tomato products for more than six months. Store them on a cool, dry shelf. After opening, canned tomato products should be stored in clean, covered glass containers. They tend to take on a metallic flavor if left in their cans.

You can keep them in the refrigerator for a week. Leftover tomato paste and tomato sauce can be frozen for up to two months in airtight containers. Drop leftover tomato paste by the tablespoon-full on a sheet of wax paper and freeze. When frozen, store in a plastic freezer bag until needed.

Tortillas Both flour and corn tortillas are available. Corn tortillas usually do not contain oil or shortening. Tortillas can be warmed in the microwave by wrapping them in a damp paper towel and microwaving for 1 minute on HIGH.

Vegetables Fresh vegetables are used in the recipes whenever possible. When shopping for canned vegetables look for those with no added sodium. If you use frozen vegetables, look for those with no added salt or fat.

Vegetable Broth Commercially prepared nonfat vegetable broth can be found at your supermarket. You can also make vegetable broth from leftover raw and cooked vegetables. Freeze it in cubes for easy access.

Vegetable Juices Mixed vegetable juice and tomato juice are used in the recipes. Look for low-sodium juices.

Vegetable Spray Buy nonstick vegetable spray with the lowest fat count possible in case you need it to spray baking pans or other cooking surfaces. You can also buy an inexpensive plastic spray bottle and fill it with olive oil or canola oil.

Vinegars Vinegars are very sour liquids fermented from a distilled alcohol, often wine or apple cider. Vinegar tightly capped keeps up to one year at room temperature, or until sediment appears at the bottom of the bottle.

Balsamic Vinegar: Balsamic vinegar adds an elegant, complex sweet-and-sour taste to food. It is aged in Italy in wooden casks for about 4 years with the skins from grapes used to make red wine, which gives it a wine-like sweetness.

Cider Vinegar: This is made from apple cider.

Rice Wine Vinegar: Japanese or Chinese vinegars made from fermented rice are milder than most Western vinegars. They can be found in many supermarkets and in Asian markets.

Wine Vinegar: Buy red and white wine vinegars.

Water Chestnuts The canned variety of water chestnut, which is round and woody and about the size of a cherry tomato, can be refrigerated, covered in liquid, for one week after opening.

Wine   Dry white wine, red wine, and sherry are used as flavoring in some of the recipes. Nonalcoholic wines can be substituted if desired.

Wonton Wrappers   Wonton wrappers can be used not only for wontons and dumplings but as a quick and easy way to prepare dishes often made with fresh pasta dough like ravioli and tortellini. They can also be baked and used as a substitute for crackers. Some are made with fat, so watch the package labels. They can be found in the produce or frozen-food section of supermarkets and in Asian groceries.

Yogurt   Buy only nonfat plain yogurt, which has less than 1 gram of fat per serving. If you want flavored yogurt you can cut calories by adding your own fruit and a small amount of honey to nonfat plain yogurt.

Adapting Your Own Recipes

You can expand your collection of fat-free menu choices by adapting many of your favorite recipes to meet your fat-free eating profile. Begin with recipes that include key ingredients that are now part of your eating plan such as beans, grains, fruits, and vegetables.

▪ Cut out oil, butter, and margarine. Replace oil or butter with fat-free salad dressings. Sauté in nonfat chicken or vegetable broth, wine, or fruit juice.

▪ When baking, replace fat with applesauce, bananas, or prune puree, using the recipes in this book as a model.

▪ Replace nuts with dried fruits or cereal nuggets.

▪ Replace ground meat in casseroles with lentils, chickpeas, brown or wild rice, or chopped shiitake mushrooms.

▪ Replace high-fat cheeses with yogurt cheese. To make it, place yogurt in a funnel lined with cheesecloth or a coffee filter and let it drain into a jar in the refrigerator for eight hours or overnight. The remaining cheese can be used in muffin and quickbread recipes in place of the called-for liquid fat.

▪ Increase the amount and variety of spices in your recipes to make up for the flavor lost when you remove the fat.

▪ Replace eggs with egg whites or egg substitute. Use egg substitutes when replacing eggs in pudding or quiche. Because they have been pasteurized, egg substitutes are also safe to use in eggnog or salad dressings. Use egg whites when egg needs to be whipped. One large egg equals 3 tablespoons egg white or egg substitute; 1 large egg white equals 2 tablespoons egg substitute.

To adapt pancake recipes:

▪ Replace each tablespoon of oil in the batter with three-fourths as much nonfat buttermilk, nonfat yogurt, applesauce, or mashed banana. (Replace 2 tablespoons of fat with 1½ tablespoons of your chosen fat substitute.) Replace each whole egg with 3 tablespoons of egg white or fat-free egg substitute.

To adapt muffin and quickbread recipes:

▪ Replace oil with three-fourths as much applesauce, mashed banana, pureed fruit, or prune puree. If the recipe uses butter or margarine, replace it with half as much fat substitute. If the recipe seems dry, add more fat substitute. Replace each egg with 3 tablespoons of egg white or fat-free egg substitute.
▪ Bake fat-free muffins and quickbreads at 350°F and reduce baking time by 3 or 4 minutes to avoid overbaking and dryness.

To adapt cheesecake recipes:

▪ Substitute nonfat cream cheese for full-fat cream cheese on a one-to-one basis, or substitute one-half nonfat cream cheese and one-half nonfat ricotta cheese for full-fat cream cheese. Add a tablespoon of flour for each 8 ounces of nonfat cheese to compensate for the fact that it contains more water than full-fat cheese.

To adapt recipes containing cheese:

▪ Replace full-fat cheese with nonfat cheese. When preparing cheese sauces and other smooth, creamy cheese dishes, a finely shredded nonfat cheese will melt better than more coarsely shredded cheese. Processed nonfat cheeses also melt well, but tend to be higher in sodium. Nonfat ricotta cheese works better than nonfat cottage cheese in cooked dishes.

To adapt recipes containing chocolate:

▪ Replace high-fat baking chocolate with cocoa powder. Use 3 table-spoons of cocoa powder plus 2 teaspoons of water or another liquid to re-place each ounce of baking chocolate in cakes, brownies, and puddings. Dutch processed cocoa will offer the deepest, darkest flavor. Be sure cocoa has no more than half a gram of fat per tablespoon. Replace the fat in chocolate recipes with prune puree.

To adapt cream-cheese frosting recipes:

▪ Replace full-fat cream cheese with nonfat cream cheese mixed with 1½ tablespoons of instant nonfat vanilla pudding mix.

To adapt pasta sauces made with egg yolks and cream:

▪ Replace cream with evaporated skim milk. Replace egg yolks with 1 ta-blespoon of fat-free egg substitute.

To adapt creamy soups:

▪ Replace cream with evaporated skim milk on a one-to-one basis. When making a creamy vegetable soup, puree some of the cooked vegetables and broth and return to the soup to thicken it. You can also add a pureed boiled potato to a creamy soup for added texture.

▪ NUTRITIONAL ANALYSIS ▪

The analyses that follow each recipe are designed to give you a basic nutri-tional profile of the foods included. Each analysis includes calories; fat (in grams); cholesterol (in milligrams); protein (in grams); carbohydrates (in grams); and sodium (in milligrams). Numbers in the analyses are rounded off to the nearest digit.

Analyses are based on a single serving. You can adjust serving sizes to suit your needs. When the ingredient listing gives more than one choice, the first ingredient listed is the one analyzed. Optional ingredients are not included in the analyses.

Due to inevitable variations in specific ingredients you may select, nutritional analyses should be considered approximate.

Be sure to check the sodium counts on individual recipes if you are on a controlled sodium diet, because many fat-free products such as mayonnaise and cheese have very high sodium contents.

The recipes were analyzed by computer using software whose primary sources of information are USDA handbooks of food composition.

FRUIT RECIPES

❧

Fresh Fruit Supreme · Persian Applesauce · Lemon-Ginger Bananas · Blackberries with Fresh Peaches · Blueberry-Banana Salad · Blueberries with Creamy Peach Topping · Double Berry Salad · Spiced Cantaloupe · Cardamom-Ginger Cantaloupe · Broiled Berries · Sherried Cantaloupe-Blueberry Salad · Cherry-Tangerine Salad · Cinnamon-Sugar Grapefruit · Cucumber-Citrus Salad · Sugar Grapes · Kiwi-Mandarin-Grape Salad · Three-Melon Toss · Maple-Topped Tangerine-Kiwi Salad · Honey-Lime Honeydew · Mango with Cinnamon and Pineapple · Nectarine-Strawberry Toss · Papaya-Berry Delight · Peach-Watermelon Salad · Raspberries with Orange-Yogurt Sauce · Raspberries Cointreau · Raspberry-Orange Medley · Cocoa-Dipped Strawberries · Gingered Strawberry-Orange Salad · Honeydew-Strawberry Salad · Strawberry-Spinach Salad · Candied Ginger Fruit · Tropical Salad with Orange-Honey Dressing · Fruit Salad with Poppy-Seed Dressing · Apple-Pear Bake · Cinnamon-Clove Baked Apples · Spiced Apples · Cinnamon Apple Wedges and Frozen Yogurt · Apricot-Pineapple Baked Apples ·

Simple Applesauce ▪ Apricot-Cinnamon Compote ▪ Orange-Lime Bananas ▪ Cinnamon–Broiled Bananas ▪ Carrot Pudding with Simmered Fruit ▪ Cranberry-Apple Dessert ▪ Mango Pudding ▪ Grilled Nectarines with Berry Sauce ▪ Nectarine-Cantaloupe Kabobs ▪ Cinnamon Oranges ▪ Papaya-Mango Kabobs ▪ Curried Peaches and Pineapple ▪ Poached Peaches with Vanilla Frozen Yogurt ▪ Peach Pudding ▪ Lemon-Poached Pears in Wine Sauce ▪ Spiced Poached Pears ▪ Spiced Pears and Raisins ▪ Curried Pear Compote ▪ Pear-Ricotta Pita ▪ Pineapple Pudding ▪ Strawberry Kabobs ▪ Spiced Rhubarb ▪ Rhubarb Dessert ▪ Strawberry Soufflés ▪ Honey-Baked Dried Fruit

❧ *Fresh Fruit Supreme* ❧

A wonderful, wholesome way to wake up with the delicious bounty of fresh fruit.

PREPARATION TIME: *5 minutes*   •   YIELD: *4 servings*

1 medium banana, peeled and thinly sliced	1 tablespoon lemon juice
1 medium peach, pitted and diced	½ cup orange juice
1 medium apple, cored and diced	1 cup nonfat plain yogurt
	½ cup Post Grape-Nuts cereal

1. Combine banana, peach, and apple. Sprinkle with the lemon juice and divide among individual serving bowls.
2. Stir orange juice and yogurt together.
3. Top the fruit with the yogurt mixture, sprinkle with Grape-Nuts, and serve at once.

Calories Per Serving: 153	Carbohydrates: 34 g
Fat: 0 g	Dietary Fiber: 3 g
Cholesterol: 1 mg	Sodium: 130 mg
Protein: 6 g	

❧ *Persian Applesauce* ❧

The delicate flavor of rose water is a traditional favorite in Middle and Far East cuisines. Rose water is available at specialty food stores and in pharmacies.

PREPARATION TIME: *10 minutes*   •   YIELD: *4 servings*

4 medium apples, peeled, cored, and quartered	1½ tablespoons rose water
3 tablespoons sugar	2 tablespoons lemon juice
	½ teaspoon dried mint

1. Place the apples, sugar, rose water, and lemon juice in a food processor or blender and process until apples are coarsely chopped.
2. Transfer to individual bowls, sprinkle with mint, and serve.

Calories Per Serving: 112	Carbohydrates: 29 g
Fat: 0 g	Dietary Fiber: 2 g
Cholesterol: 0 mg	Sodium: 0 mg
Protein: 0 g	

❧ Lemon-Ginger Bananas ❧

Ginger and lemon juice accent sliced bananas. Bananas are rich in potassium and vitamin C.

PREPARATION TIME: 10 minutes plus 1 hour chilling time •
COOKING TIME: 3 minutes • YIELD: 4 servings

4 medium bananas	*¼ cup water*
½ teaspoon ground ginger	*2 tablespoons lemon juice*
¼ cup sugar	

1. Peel and slice the bananas.
2. Place a layer of bananas in the bottom of a glass serving dish. Sprinkle with half the ginger. Add a second layer of bananas and sprinkle it with the remaining ginger.
3. Combine the sugar and water in a small saucepan, bring to a boil, reduce heat, and simmer until sugar dissolves, about 3 minutes. Stir in lemon juice and pour syrup over the bananas.
4. Chill for 1 hour before serving.

Calories Per Serving: 156	Carbohydrates: 40 g
Fat: 1 g	Dietary Fiber: 2 g
Cholesterol: 0 mg	Sodium: 2 mg
Protein: 1 g	

❧ *Blackberries with Fresh Peaches* ❧

Make this salad when both peaches and blackberries are in season. Fresh blackberries are best when used immediately, while peaches can be stored in the refrigerator in a plastic bag for up to five days.

PREPARATION TIME: 5 minutes • *YIELD: 4 servings*

3 cups peeled and sliced peaches	*1 tablespoon brown sugar*
1 cup blackberries	*1 teaspoon lemon juice*

1. Combine the peaches and blackberries.
2. Sprinkle with brown sugar and lemon juice, and serve.

Calories Per Serving: 98	Carbohydrates: 25 g
Fat: 0 g	Dietary Fiber: 5 g
Cholesterol: 0 mg	Sodium: 1 mg
Protein: 1 g	

❧ *Blueberry-Banana Salad* ❧

Blueberries and bananas are combined with mini marshmallows, sour cream, yogurt, honey, and mandarin oranges. Shop for blueberries that are firm, uniform in size, and indigo blue with a silvery frost.

PREPARATION TIME: 10 minutes plus 1 hour chilling time • *YIELD: 6 servings*

2 medium bananas, sliced	*¼ cup nonfat plain yogurt*
1 cup fresh blueberries	*1 tablespoon honey*
½ cup miniature marshmallows	*1 cup mandarin oranges, drained*
¼ cup nonfat sour cream	

1. Combine bananas, blueberries, and marshmallows in a large bowl.
2. In a separate bowl, mix sour cream, yogurt, and honey, and stir into the fruit mixture.
3. Add oranges, toss gently, and refrigerate for 1 hour before serving.

Calories Per Serving: 184

Carbohydrates: 46 g

Fat: 0 mg

Dietary Fiber: 2 g

Cholesterol: 0 mg

Sodium: 25 mg

Protein: 3 g

❧ *Blueberries with Creamy Peach Topping* ❧

A peach dressing covers fresh blueberries for a tempting summertime treat. Blueberries can be stored in a moisture-proof container in the refrigerator for up to five days.

PREPARATION TIME: 10 minutes plus 1 hour chilling time • YIELD: 6 servings

1 cup nonfat ricotta cheese

1 teaspoon fresh grated lemon peel

¼ cup sugarless all-fruit peach jam

4 cups fresh blueberries

½ teaspoon vanilla extract

1. Combine ricotta cheese, jam, vanilla extract, and lemon peel in a blender or food processor. Process until ingredients are well mixed. Chill for 1 hour.
2. Divide the berries among individual serving bowls, top with the dressing, and serve.

Calories Per Serving: 100

Carbohydrates: 20 g

Fat: 0 g

Dietary Fiber: 3 g

Cholesterol: 4 mg

Sodium: 23 mg

Protein: 6 g

❧ *Double Berry Salad* ❧

Strawberries are served with blueberries and topped with a creamy honey- and mint-flavored dressing. Strawberries have grown wild in both America and Europe for centuries and are an excellent source of vitamin C.

PREPARATION TIME: 10 minutes • YIELD: 4 servings

2 cups hulled and halved fresh strawberries
½ teaspoon dried mint
1 teaspoon honey

¼ cup nonfat sour cream
¼ cup nonfat plain yogurt
2 cups fresh blueberries

1. Place ½ cup strawberries, mint, honey, sour cream, and yogurt in a blender or food processor and blend until smooth.
2. Toss dressing, remaining strawberries, and blueberries in a large bowl. Serve at once.

Calories Per Serving: 151
Fat: 0 g
Cholesterol: 0 mg
Protein: 4 g

Carbohydrates: 37 g
Dietary Fiber: 1 g
Sodium: 22 mg

❧ Spiced Cantaloupe ❧

Cantaloupe chunks are flavored with powdered sugar and ginger.

PREPARATION TIME: *15 minutes plus 1 hour chilling time* • YIELD: *6 servings*

1 tablespoon powdered sugar
½ teaspoon ground ginger

8 cups cantaloupe chunks

1. Combine powdered sugar and ginger.
2. Toss sugar mixture with cantaloupe chunks.
3. Chill for 1 hour before serving.

Calories Per Serving: 79
Fat: 1 g
Cholesterol: 0 mg
Protein: 2 g

Carbohydrates: 19 g
Dietary Fiber: 1 g
Sodium: 19 mg

❧ *Cardamom-Ginger Cantaloupe* ❧

Cantaloupe is chilled in a dressing spiced with cardamom and ginger.

PREPARATION TIME: 10 minutes plus 2 hours chilling time • YIELD: 8 servings

8 cups cantaloupe chunks
3 tablespoons honey
2½ tablespoons lime juice

2½ tablespoons orange juice
¼ teaspoon ground cardamom
⅛ teaspoon ground ginger

1. Place cantaloupe chunks in a large serving bowl.
2. In a separate bowl, combine honey, lime juice, orange juice, cardamom, and ginger.
3. Spoon dressing over cantaloupe and chill for 2 hours before serving.

Calories Per Serving: 138
Fat: 0 g
Cholesterol: 0 mg
Protein: 2 g

Carbohydrates: 35 g
Dietary Fiber: 3 g
Sodium: 49 mg

❧ *Broiled Berries* ❧

Succulent summer berries are broiled with lemon peel and cinnamon.

*PREPARATION TIME: 15 minutes • COOKING TIME: 3 minutes •
YIELD: 4 servings*

2 cups blueberries
1 cup raspberries
2 cups strawberries
1 teaspoon grated lemon peel

¼ teaspoon ground cinnamon
¼ teaspoon ground nutmeg
½ cup nonfat plain yogurt
4 teaspoons brown sugar

1. Preheat broiler.
2. Combine blueberries, raspberries, and strawberries, and divide the mixture among 4 glass custard baking dishes.

3. Stir lemon peel, cinnamon, and nutmeg into the yogurt. Top each dish of fruit with a tablespoon of yogurt and then a teaspoon of brown sugar.
4. Place dishes under the broiler until the sugar melts, about 3 minutes, and serve.

Calories Per Serving: 106	Carbohydrates: 25 g
Fat: 1 g	Dietary Fiber: 5 g
Cholesterol: 1 mg	Sodium: 26 mg
Protein: 3 g	

❧ *Sherried Cantaloupe-Blueberry Salad* ❧

Sherry is the special ingredient in the mint-flavored dressing that tops this salad of blueberries, raisins, and cantaloupe.

PREPARATION TIME: 15 minutes plus 1 hour chilling time • YIELD: 4 servings

1½ cups blueberries	*2 tablespoons orange juice*
½ cup seedless raisins	*½ cup nonfat plain yogurt*
4 cups cantaloupe balls	*1 tablespoon sherry*
1 teaspoon sugar	*1 teaspoon dried mint*

1. Combine blueberries, raisins, and cantaloupe in a large bowl.
2. In a separate bowl, whisk together the sugar, orange juice, yogurt, and sherry.
3. Spoon the dressing over the fruit, divide among individual serving plates, and sprinkle with mint. Chill for 1 hour before serving.

Calories Per Serving: 114	Carbohydrates: 25 g
Fat: 1 g	Dietary Fiber: 3 g
Cholesterol: 1 mg	Sodium: 37 mg
Protein: 4 g	

❧ *Cherry-Tangerine Salad* ❧

Cherries, pineapple, tangerines, and cantaloupe are tossed in a dressing of orange juice, lime juice, yogurt, and mayonnaise.

PREPARATION TIME: 10 minutes • *YIELD: 6 servings*

½ cup nonfat plain yogurt
3 tablespoons orange juice
2 tablespoons nonfat mayonnaise
1 tablespoon lime juice
1 tablespoon sugar
2 cups canned sweet cherries, with their juice

2 cups pineapple chunks, fresh or juice packed, drained
1 tangerine, peeled and broken into sections
3 cups cantaloupe chunks
1 teaspoon grated orange peel

1. Place yogurt, orange juice, mayonnaise, lime juice, and sugar in a blender or food processor, and blend until smooth.
2. Toss cherries, their juice, pineapple chunks, tangerine sections, and cantaloupe chunks in a large bowl. Top with dressing, sprinkle with orange peel, and serve.

Calories Per Serving: 164
Fat: 0 g
Cholesterol: 0 mg
Protein: 3 g

Carbohydrates: 41 g
Dietary Fiber: 3 g
Sodium: 62 mg

❧ *Cinnamon-Sugar Grapefruit* ❧

A refreshing way to greet the morning—a tangy blend of tart grapefruit and sugar and cinnamon.

PREPARATION TIME: 5 minutes • *COOKING TIME: 3 minutes* •
YIELD: 4 servings

2 ruby red grapefruits, halved
2 tablespoons brown sugar

½ teaspoon ground cinnamon
½ teaspoon ground nutmeg

1. Preheat broiler.
2. Combine brown sugar, cinnamon, and nutmeg.
3. Top each grapefruit half with one-fourth of the brown sugar, cinnamon, and nutmeg, and place under the broiler until sugar begins to melt, about 3 minutes. Serve at once.

Calories Per Serving: 64

Carbohydrates: 16 g

Fat: 0 g

Dietary Fiber: 2 g

Cholesterol: 0 mg

Sodium: 3 mg

Protein: 1 g

❧ *Cucumber-Citrus Salad* ❧

This salad of cucumber, oranges, and bell pepper is served with a cottage cheese dressing. Be sure to select firm cucumbers with smooth, brightly colored skins.

PREPARATION TIME: *10 minutes* • YIELD: *6 servings*

*2 medium cucumbers, peeled and
thinly sliced*
*2 navel oranges, peeled and broken
into sections*
*½ cup cored and minced red bell
pepper*

2 tablespoons chopped fresh parsley
⅛ teaspoon white pepper
1 cup nonfat cottage cheese
¼ cup skim milk

1. Toss cucumbers, orange sections, bell pepper, and parsley in a large bowl. Sprinkle with white pepper.
2. Combine cottage cheese and milk in a blender or food processor. Process until just smooth.
3. Top salad with dressing and serve.

Calories Per Serving: 75

Carbohydrates: 10 g

Fat: 0 g

Dietary Fiber: 3 g

Cholesterol: 5 mg

Sodium: 79 mg

Protein: 9 g

❧ Sugar Grapes ❧

Seedless red grapes are topped with yogurt and brown sugar. Red grapes should be plump and deeply colored. Fresh grapes contain small amounts of vitamin A and a variety of minerals.

PREPARATION TIME: 10 minutes plus 2 hours chilling time ▪ *YIELD: 8 servings*

4 cups halved seedless red grapes
2 cups nonfat plain yogurt, drained

½ cup brown sugar

1. Divide grapes among 8 dessert dishes.
2. Top each with yogurt and a tablespoon of brown sugar. Chill for 2 hours before serving.

Calories Per Serving: 124
Fat: 0 g
Cholesterol: 1 mg
Protein: 3 g

Carbohydrates: 29 g
Dietary Fiber: 1 g
Sodium: 47 mg

❧ Kiwi-Mandarin-Grape Salad ❧

Kiwis are tossed with red grapes and orange slices. Kiwis are grown in both California and New Zealand. Their little black seeds are edible.

PREPARATION TIME: 10 minutes ▪ *YIELD: 4 servings*

6 kiwifruits, peeled and sliced
2 cups seedless red grapes
1 cup canned mandarin orange slices, drained

1 cup nonfat plain yogurt
1 tablespoon thawed frozen orange juice concentrate
1 tablespoon honey

1. Toss kiwi, grapes, and orange slices in a large bowl.
2. Combine yogurt, orange juice, and honey. Whisk briskly.
3. Pour dressing over fruit, toss to coat, and serve at once.

Calories Per Serving: 191

Carbohydrates: 44 g

Fat: 1 g

Dietary Fiber: 5 g

Cholesterol: 1 mg

Sodium: 44 mg

Protein: 5 g

❧ *Three-Melon Toss* ❧

Three kinds of melon are mixed with onion, vinegar, and basil. This salad is a perfect side dish with spicy Thai, Indian, or Chinese entrées.

PREPARATION TIME: 20 minutes plus melon chilling time ▪ *YIELD: 4 servings*

1 cup honeydew balls, chilled

½ cup diced red onion

1 cup cantaloupe balls, chilled

4 tablespoons cider vinegar

2 cups seeded watermelon balls, chilled

1 tablespoon dried basil

½ teaspoon ground black pepper

1. Gently toss the chilled melon balls and the onion in a large bowl.
2. Combine the vinegar, basil, and black pepper, and pour over the melon.
3. Toss very gently and serve.

Calories Per Serving: 55

Carbohydrates: 14 g

Fat: 0 g

Dietary Fiber: 1 g

Cholesterol: 0 mg

Sodium: 4 mg

Protein: 1 g

❧ *Maple-Topped Tangerine-Kiwi Salad*

Maple syrup and orange juice are spooned over a trio of fruits and chilled.

PREPARATION TIME: 15 minutes plus 1 hour chilling time ▪ *YIELD: 4 servings*

¼ cup maple syrup

3 kiwifruits, peeled and sliced

¼ cup orange juice

2 medium bananas, peeled and sliced

3 tangerines, peeled, sectioned, and seeded

1. Combine the syrup and the orange juice.
2. Toss the tangerines, kiwi, and bananas.
3. Divide fruit among 4 bowls.
4. Spoon syrup-juice combination over each bowl and chill for 1 hour before serving.

Calories Per Serving: 200   Carbohydrates: 49 g
Fat: 1 g   Dietary Fiber: 3 g
Cholesterol: 0 mg   Sodium: 4 mg
Protein: 3 g

ℰ *Honey-Lime Honeydew* ℰ

Chunks of juicy honeydew are chilled in a dressing of honey, lime juice, coriander, and nutmeg. Coriander has been one of the world's most popular herbs for centuries.

PREPARATION TIME: 20 minutes plus 1 hour chilling time • *YIELD: 6 servings*

8 cups honeydew chunks   *¼ teaspoon ground coriander*
2 tablespoons lime juice   *¼ teaspoon ground nutmeg*
2 tablespoons honey

1. Toss the honeydew chunks with lime juice, honey, coriander, and nutmeg.
2. Chill for 1 hour before serving.

Calories Per Serving: 147   Carbohydrates: 36 g
Fat: 1 g   Dietary Fiber: 2 g
Cholesterol: 0 mg   Sodium: 29 mg
Protein: 3 g

❧ *Mango with Cinnamon and Pineapple* ❧

Mango is combined with crushed pineapple and spiced with cinnamon. Look for mangoes with an unblemished yellowish skin tinged with red.

PREPARATION TIME: 10 minutes plus 2 hours chilling time • YIELD: 4 servings

2 mangoes, peeled, seeded, and cut
 into chunks
¾ cup nonfat cottage cheese
¼ cup nonfat plain yogurt
⅓ cup crushed juice-packed canned
 pineapple, drained

3 tablespoons honey
⅛ teaspoon ground allspice
1 teaspoon lime juice
¼ teaspoon ground cinnamon

1. Combine mangoes, cottage cheese, yogurt, pineapple, honey, allspice, and lime juice. Chill for 2 hours.
2. Remove from refrigerator, sprinkle with cinnamon, and serve.

Calories Per Serving: 193
Fat: 0 g
Cholesterol: 1 mg
Protein: 3 g

Carbohydrates: 46 g
Dietary Fiber: 4 g
Sodium: 36 mg

❧ *Nectarine-Strawberry Toss* ❧

Strawberries, green grapes, and nectarines are poached in syrup, tossed with mandarin oranges, and chilled. This is delicious served over angel food cake.

PREPARATION TIME: 20 minutes plus 2 hours chilling time •
COOKING TIME: 12 minutes • YIELD: 8 servings

1 cup sugar
1 cup water
2½ cups canned mandarin orange sections, drained, juice reserved

1 pound nectarines, halved and pitted
2 cups whole strawberries
1 cup green seedless grapes

1. Combine sugar, water, and reserved mandarin orange juice in a saucepan. Bring to a boil over medium heat and stir until sugar is dissolved. Simmer for 3 minutes.
2. Add nectarines and continue to simmer for an additional 30 seconds. Add the strawberries and simmer for 15 seconds more. Stir in the grapes and continue to simmer for 15 additional seconds.
3. Remove the nectarines, strawberries, and grapes from the saucepan, and toss gently with the mandarin orange sections.
4. Boil the cooking liquid until it is reduced by half, remove from heat, and let stand until cool.
5. Spoon the syrup over the fruit and chill for 2 hours before serving.

Calories Per Serving: 211

Fat: 1 g

Cholesterol: 0 mg

Protein: 2 g

Carbohydrates: 50 g

Dietary Fiber: 5 g

Sodium: 11 mg

✎ *Papaya-Berry Delight* ✎

Papaya, orange juice, and honey are blended and served over strawberries in this delightful snack. Look for richly colored papayas that give slightly to pressure.

PREPARATION TIME: 10 minutes • YIELD: 4 servings

1 papaya, peeled, seeded, and cut into chunks

1 tablespoon orange juice

1 tablespoon honey

3 cups whole strawberries

1. In a blender or food processor, blend papaya, orange juice, and honey until smooth.
2. Divide berries among 4 individual serving bowls, spoon papaya dressing over fruit, and serve.

Calories Per Serving: 97

Fat: 1 g

Cholesterol: 0 mg

Protein: 1 g

Carbohydrates: 24 g

Dietary Fiber: 6 g

Sodium: 1 mg

❧ *Peach-Watermelon Salad* ❧

Peaches are surrounded by blueberries, watermelon balls, and bananas. Look for intensely fragrant peaches that are slightly soft, and avoid those with signs of green.

PREPARATION TIME: 10 minutes plus 2 hours chilling time • *YIELD: 12 servings*

2 cups sliced peaches

2 cups blueberries

5 cups seeded watermelon balls

2 bananas, sliced

¾ cup orange juice

¼ cup lemon juice

1 tablespoon honey

1. Combine all the fruit in a large bowl.
2. In a separate bowl, whisk together the orange juice, lemon juice, and honey.
3. Pour the juice mixture over the fruit and allow to chill in the refrigerator for 2 hours before serving.

Calories Per Serving: 76

Fat: 0 g

Cholesterol: 0 mg

Protein: 1 g

Carbohydrates: 18 g

Dietary Fiber: 2 g

Sodium: 6 mg

❧ *Raspberries with Orange-Yogurt Sauce* ❧

Raspberries are topped with an orange-yogurt sauce for a sweet, simple salad. Do not wash the berries until you are ready to use them.

PREPARATION TIME: 10 minutes • *YIELD: 4 servings*

2½ cups whole fresh or thawed frozen
  raspberries
1 cup fresh or thawed frozen halved
  strawberries

2 tablespoons brown sugar
2 tablespoons orange juice
1 cup nonfat plain yogurt

1. Combine raspberries and strawberries in a large bowl. Sprinkle with brown sugar and toss gently.
2. Whisk together the orange juice and yogurt.
3. Top fruit with dressing and serve.

Calories Per Serving: 110
Fat: 0 g
Cholesterol: 1 mg
Protein: 3 g

Carbohydrates: 25 g
Dietary Fiber: 2 g
Sodium: 38 mg

❧ *Raspberries Cointreau* ❧

Raspberries and Cointreau, an orange-flavored French liqueur, are blended to create this delicious sauce. Raspberries contain iron, potassium, and vitamins A and C. Serve over frozen desserts.

PREPARATION TIME: 10 minutes ▪ *YIELD: 8 servings*

2 10-ounce packages frozen unsweet-
  ened raspberries, thawed and
  drained

⅔ cup sugar
2 tablespoons Cointreau

1. Place the raspberries in a blender or food processor and puree. Remove from blender and strain the puree.
2. Stir in the sugar and Cointreau and mix to blend thoroughly.

Calories Per Serving: 149
Fat: 0 g
Cholesterol: 0 mg
Protein: 1 g

Carbohydrates: 37 g
Dietary Fiber: 3 g
Sodium: 1 mg

❧ *Raspberry-Orange Medley* ❧

Spreadable fruit and orange juice are combined with raspberries and mandarin oranges. Layer with fat-free frozen yogurt in parfait glasses.

Preparation Time: 15 minutes plus 40 minutes cooling time ▪
Cooking Time: 7 minutes ▪ Yield: 8 servings

½ cup sugarless all-fruit blackberry
   jelly
½ cup plus 1 tablespoon orange juice
1½ cups canned mandarin orange
   sections, drained, juice reserved

2 tablespoons cornstarch
2 cups whole raspberries
1½ cups fat-free frozen yogurt

1. Combine jelly with orange juice in a saucepan. Cook, stirring occasionally, until jelly is dissolved, about 5 minutes. Remove from heat.
2. Combine reserved mandarin orange juice and cornstarch, and mix until well blended. Stir cornstarch mixture into jelly mixture and return to heat.
3. Bring to a boil and cook, stirring frequently, until thickened, about 1 minute. Remove from heat and allow to cool for 10 minutes.
4. Gently mix orange sections and raspberries into the sauce and allow to cool to room temperature before serving.
5. Serve in parfait glasses layered with fat-free frozen yogurt.

Calories Per Serving: 133
Fat: 0 g
Cholesterol: 2 mg
Protein: 4 g

Carbohydrates: 29 g
Dietary Fiber: 1 g
Sodium: 52 mg

❧ *Cocoa-Dipped Strawberries* ❧

This low-fat version of chocolate-covered strawberries is made with cocoa powder, from which the cocoa butter (fat) has been removed.

Preparation Time: 10 minutes ▪ Yield: 10 servings

4 tablespoons unsweetened cocoa	½ teaspoon vanilla extract
powder	5 tablespoons skim milk
2 cups powdered sugar	6 cups whole strawberries, rinsed

1. Combine cocoa powder, powdered sugar, vanilla extract, and milk. Mix well.
2. Dip berries in the cocoa mixture and set out on a serving plate. Serve with party picks.

Calories Per Serving: 115
Fat: 1 g
Cholesterol: 0 mg
Protein: 1 g

Carbohydrates: 28 g
Dietary Fiber: 2 g
Sodium: 5 mg

✎ Gingered Strawberry-Orange Salad ✎

A mixture of seasonal fruit is tossed with ginger-flavored syrup.

PREPARATION TIME: 25 minutes plus 1 hour chilling time ∙
COOKING TIME: 15 minutes ∙ YIELD: 12 servings

5¼-inch-thick slice fresh gingerroot,	3 cups honeydew balls
cut into thin strips	2 cups seedless red grapes
1 teaspoon lemon juice	2 medium bananas, cut into chunks
¾ cup cold water	1 navel orange, peeled and chopped
1½ cups sugar	1 pear, cored and cut into chunks
2 cups whole strawberries	

1. Cover gingerroot with lemon juice and ½ cup of the water in a small saucepan. Bring to a boil, reduce heat, and simmer for 5 minutes.
2. Strain gingerroot, rinse in cold water, and set aside.
3. Combine sugar and remaining ¼ cup water in another saucepan. Bring to a boil and stir until the sugar dissolves. Add the gingerroot to the syrup, return to a boil, reduce heat, and simmer for 5 minutes. Remove from heat and refrigerate for 1 hour.
4. Combine strawberries, honeydew balls, grapes, banana chunks, orange pieces, and pear chunks.
5. Toss with chilled syrup before serving.

Calories Per Serving: 222

Carbohydrates: 56 g

Fat: 1 g

Dietary Fiber: 3 g

Cholesterol: 0 mg

Sodium: 6 mg

Protein: 2 g

❧ *Honeydew-Strawberry Salad* ❧

Honeydew and strawberries are topped with a yogurt dressing featuring allspice, whose name comes from its flavor, a combination of cinnamon, nutmeg, and cloves.

PREPARATION TIME: 15 minutes • YIELD: 8 servings

4 cups honeydew chunks

2 cups halved strawberries

2 kiwifruits, peeled and sliced

2 medium bananas, sliced

1 cup nonfat plain yogurt

1 tablespoon honey

¼ teaspoon ground allspice

2 tablespoons chopped mint

1. Combine the honeydew, strawberries, kiwifruits, and bananas in a large bowl.
2. In a separate bowl, whisk together the yogurt, honey, and allspice.
3. Divide the fruit among 8 individual plates. Top each with dressing, sprinkle with mint, and serve.

Calories Per Serving: 106

Carbohydrates: 25 g

Fat: 1 g

Dietary Fiber: 3 g

Cholesterol: 1 mg

Sodium: 30 mg

Protein: 3 g

❧ *Strawberry-Spinach Salad* ❧

A variety of flavors and textures come together in this fruit salad. Choose spinach that is crisp and dark with a fresh fragrance.

PREPARATION TIME: 10 minutes • YIELD: 4 servings

2 medium bananas, sliced
3 tablespoons lemon juice
1 cup sliced strawberries
2 cups spinach, chopped

2 kiwifruits, peeled and sliced
1 teaspoon grated lemon peel
¼ cup nonfat plain yogurt
4 teaspoons honey

1. Place the sliced bananas in a large bowl. Drizzle 1 tablespoon lemon juice over the bananas and toss to coat.
2. Mix in the strawberries, spinach, and kiwi.
3. In a separate bowl, whisk together the remaining lemon juice, lemon peel, yogurt, and honey.
4. Pour the dressing over the fruit, toss gently to coat, and serve.

Calories Per Serving: 100
Fat: 1 g
Cholesterol: 0 mg
Protein: 3 g

Carbohydrates: 24 g
Dietary Fiber: 3 g
Sodium: 40 mg

❧ Candied Ginger Fruit ❧

Pineapple chunks and orange slices are tossed with bananas and grapes then spiced with candied ginger. Candied (or crystallized) ginger has been cooked in sugar syrup. If you can't find it in your local supermarket, look in an Asian market.

PREPARATION TIME: 15 minutes plus 1 hour chilling time • YIELD: 6 servings

2 cups fresh or canned juice-packed
    pineapple chunks, drained
2 navel oranges, peeled and sliced

2 firm bananas, peeled and sliced
1 cup seedless green grapes
4 slices candied ginger, chopped

1. Toss pineapple chunks, orange slices, bananas, and green grapes with chopped ginger.
2. Chill for 1 hour before serving.

Calories Per Serving: 117

Fat: 0 g

Cholesterol: 0 mg

Protein: 1 g

Carbohydrates: 30 g

Dietary Fiber: 2 g

Sodium: 2 mg

℘ *Tropical Salad with Orange-Honey Dressing* ℘

For centuries, the pineapple has been a symbol of hospitality. In this recipe, pineapple and fresh papaya are tossed with fresh orange sections.

PREPARATION TIME: 10 minutes • *YIELD: 8 servings*

3 tablespoons honey

¾ cup nonfat plain yogurt

2 tablespoons orange juice

4 cups fresh or canned juice-packed pineapple chunks, drained

1 papaya, peeled, seeded, and cut into chunks

1 navel orange, peeled, broken into sections, and cut into 1-inch pieces

1 tablespoon lime juice

1. Whisk together 1 tablespoon honey, the yogurt, and the orange juice.
2. Combine pineapple chunks, papaya chunks, and orange pieces in a large bowl. Drizzle remaining honey and lime juice over the fruit and toss gently.
3. Top with dressing and serve.

Calories Per Serving: 128

Fat: 0 g

Cholesterol: 0 mg

Protein: 2 g

Carbohydrates: 31 g

Dietary Fiber: 3 g

Sodium: 21 mg

℘ *Fruit Salad with Poppy-Seed Dressing* ℘

Poppy seeds add a crunchy texture and nutty flavor to this fruit salad. They can be stored in an airtight container in the refrigerator for up to 6 months.

PREPARATION TIME: 10 minutes • *YIELD: 10 servings*

2 bananas, sliced

2 cups fresh diced pineapple

2 cups fresh sliced strawberries

3 kiwifruits, peeled and chopped

4 ounces nonfat cream cheese, softened to room temperature

¼ cup nonfat plain yogurt

¼ cup skim milk

3 tablespoons honey

1 teaspoon poppy seeds

1. Place bananas, pineapple, strawberries, and kiwifruits in a large bowl. Toss to mix.
2. Combine cream cheese, yogurt, milk, and honey in a blender or food processor and blend until smooth. Gently stir in poppy seeds.
3. Divide fruit among 10 individual bowls, top with dressing, and serve at once.

Calories Per Serving: 124

Fat: 1 g

Cholesterol: 2 mg

Protein: 4 g

Carbohydrates: 28 g

Dietary Fiber: 3 g

Sodium: 86 mg

❧ *Apple-Pear Bake* ❧

This delicious apple dish needs no crust.

PREPARATION TIME: *15 minutes plus 10 minutes cooling time* ▪
COOKING TIME: *40 minutes* ▪ YIELD: *8 servings*

½ cup nonfat granola

1 cup chopped apple

1 cup chopped pear

1 tablespoon lemon juice

½ cup honey

¾ teaspoon ground cinnamon

¼ teaspoon ground nutmeg

2 egg whites

⅓ cup whole-wheat pastry flour

½ teaspoon baking soda

⅓ cup nonfat plain yogurt

1. Place granola in a blender or food processor and process until it has the consistency of coarse salt.
2. Preheat oven to 325 degrees.

3. Combine apple, pear, lemon juice, honey, cinnamon, and nutmeg in a saucepan. Simmer gently for 10 minutes. Remove from heat and allow to cool for 10 minutes.
4. Stir in egg whites, flour, baking soda, and half the ground granola. Add the yogurt and mix well.
5. Transfer to a glass pie plate, sprinkle additional nutmeg and remaining granola on top, and bake until lightly browned, about 30 minutes.
6. Allow to cool for 5 minutes before serving in individual bowls.

Calories Per Serving: 141   Carbohydrates: 33 g
Fat: 0 g   Dietary Fiber: 2 g
Cholesterol: 0 mg   Sodium: 141 mg
Protein: 3 g

❧ *Cinnamon-Clove Baked Apples* ❧

Warm baked apples topped with vanilla frozen yogurt are an excellent winter dessert. Look for firm, well-colored apples with a fresh fragrance.

PREPARATION TIME: 15 minutes • *COOKING TIME: 30 minutes* •
YIELD: 4 servings

¼ cup brown sugar
½ teaspoon ground cinnamon
¼ teaspoon ground allspice
¼ teaspoon ground cloves

2 tablespoons chopped walnuts
  (optional)
4 medium tart apples
¾ cup boiling water
1 pint nonfat vanilla frozen yogurt

1. Preheat oven to 375 degrees.
2. Combine brown sugar, cinnamon, allspice, cloves, and walnuts.
3. Core apples, leaving bottoms intact. Fill the cavities with the brown sugar mixture.
4. Place the apples upright in the baking dish and pour the water around them. Bake until tender, about 30 minutes.
5. Transfer the apples to individual serving plates and serve with frozen yogurt.

Calories Per Serving: 199

Carbohydrates: 46 g

Fat: 0 g

Dietary Fiber: 2 g

Cholesterol: 3 mg

Sodium: 76 mg

Protein: 6 g

❧ *Spiced Apples* ❧

These sweet and spicy apples, cooked in red wine, make a perfect fall dessert.

PREPARATION TIME: 15 minutes • COOKING TIME: 30 minutes •
YIELD: 4 servings

4 medium tart apples

⅓ cup brown sugar

1 cup red wine

¼ teaspoon ground cinnamon

½ cup orange juice

1. Preheat oven to 375 degrees.
2. Peel, halve, and core the apples. Place them cut side down in a baking dish.
3. Combine wine, orange juice, brown sugar, and cinnamon, and pour over the apples.
4. Bake, basting several times, until the apples are just tender, about 30 minutes.
5. Transfer to individual bowls and serve.

Calories Per Serving: 195

Carbohydrates: 40 g

Fat: 0 g

Dietary Fiber: 2 g

Cholesterol: 0 mg

Sodium: 6 mg

Protein: 1 g

❧ *Cinnamon Apple Wedges and Frozen Yogurt* ❧

Apple wedges are simmered with cloves and sugar, then topped with cinnamon and frozen yogurt.

PREPARATION TIME: 10 minutes • COOKING TIME: 5 minutes •
YIELD: 6 servings

4 medium tart apples	*¼ teaspoon ground cinnamon*
⅔ cup water	*1 pint nonfat vanilla frozen yogurt*
⅓ cup brown sugar	

1. Peel apples and cut each into 6 wedges.
2. Bring water and brown sugar to a boil in a saucepan. Add the fruit, return to a boil, reduce heat, and simmer until it is just tender, about 5 minutes.
3. Transfer wedges to individual serving plates, sprinkle with cinnamon, top with frozen yogurt, and serve.

Calories Per Serving: 38	Carbohydrates: 38 g
Fat: 0 g	Dietary Fiber: 1 g
Cholesterol: 2 mg	Sodium: 49 mg
Protein: 4 g	

❧ *Apricot-Pineapple Baked Apples* ❧

Apples are stuffed with a mixture of honey, crushed pineapple, dried apricots, then sprinkled with cinnamon before baking.

PREPARATION TIME: 15 minutes • COOKING TIME: 30 minutes •
YIELD: 4 servings

4 medium tart apples	*2 tablespoons chopped dried apricots*
1 tablespoon honey	*3 cups apple juice*
⅓ cup crushed water-packed canned pineapple, drained	*1 cup nonfat vanilla frozen yogurt*

1. Preheat oven to 375 degrees.
2. Core apples but leave bottoms intact.
3. Combine honey, pineapple, and apricots. Fill the apple cavities with the mixture.
4. Arrange apples in a shallow baking dish and surround them with apple juice. Bake, basting several times, until apples are just tender, about 30 minutes.
5. Allow to cool, transfer to individual serving plates, top with frozen yogurt, and serve.

Calories Per Serving: 213   Carbohydrates: 52 g
Fat: 1 g   Dietary Fiber: 5 g
Cholesterol: 0 mg   Sodium: 3 mg
Protein: 2 g

❧ *Simple Applesauce* ❧

This wholesome applesauce can be served either warm or cold.

PREPARATION TIME: 15 minutes • *COOKING TIME: 10 minutes* •
YIELD: 8 servings

10 medium tart apples, peeled, cored,   1 cup apple juice
and cut into small chunks

1. Place apples and apple juice in a large pot. Bring to a simmer, cover, and cook gently until apples are just tender, about 10 minutes.
2. Transfer to a food processor or blender and blend until the desired consistency is attained. Serve at once.

Calories Per Serving: 168   Carbohydrates: 43 g
Fat: 1 g   Dietary Fiber: 3 g
Cholesterol: 0 mg   Sodium: 9 mg
Protein: 0 g

❧ *Apricot-Cinnamon Compote* ❧

This dried-fruit compote is quick and easy to prepare. Other dried fruits can be substituted for those listed.

PREPARATION TIME: 10 minutes • *COOKING TIME: 25 minutes* •
YIELD: 6 servings

½ cup dried apricot halves
½ cup pitted prunes
½ cup dried peaches, chopped
3 cups water

¼ cup sugar
1 tablespoon lemon juice
1 teaspoon ground cinnamon

1. Combine all ingredients and bring to a boil over medium heat.
2. Reduce heat and simmer uncovered for 20 minutes.
3. Serve warm.

Calories Per Serving: 247
Fat: 0 g
Cholesterol: 0 mg
Protein: 1 g

Carbohydrates: 46 g
Dietary Fiber: 2 g
Sodium: 7 mg

❧ *Orange-Lime Bananas* ❧

Bananas are simmered in orange juice and sugar, then sprinkled with lime juice.

PREPARATION TIME: 10 minutes • *COOKING TIME: 2 minutes* •
YIELD: 2 servings

2 medium bananas
¼ cup orange juice

2 tablespoons brown sugar
½ tablespoon lime juice

1. Peel bananas. Cut them in half crosswise. Cut each half in half lengthwise.

2. Combine orange juice and brown sugar. Bring to a boil in a nonstick skillet. Add bananas and cook for 1 minute. Turn bananas and cook for 1 additional minute.
3. Transfer bananas to individual serving plates, top with any juices remaining in the skillet, sprinkle with lime juice, and serve.

Calories Per Serving: 179   Carbohydrates: 44 g
Fat: 1 g   Dietary Fiber: 2 g
Cholesterol: 0 mg   Sodium: 7 mg
Protein: 1 g

৩ *Cinnamon-Broiled Bananas* ৩

This simple banana dish can be served as a side dish or enjoyed for dessert. Ripe bananas can be stored in the refrigerator for several days. The peel will turn brown, but the insides will remain unchanged.

PREPARATION TIME: 10 minutes ▪ *COOKING TIME: 3 minutes* ▪
YIELD: 6 servings

½ cup brown sugar   *6 bananas*
½ teaspoon ground cinnamon

1. Preheat the broiler.
2. Combine the brown sugar and cinnamon.
3. Peel bananas. Cut each in half crosswise. Cut each half in half lengthwise. Arrange the bananas on a nonstick baking sheet. Sprinkle with the sugar mixture and broil until sugar begins to bubble, about 3 minutes. Serve hot.

Calories Per Serving: 151   Carbohydrates: 39 g
Fat: 1 g   Dietary Fiber: 2 g
Cholesterol: 0 mg   Sodium: 6 mg
Protein: 1 g

❧ *Carrot Pudding with Simmered Fruit* ❧

Maple syrup, gingerroot, and cinnamon flavor this pudding, which is served with a fruit topping.

PREPARATION TIME: 20 minutes plus 30 minutes cooling time •
COOKING TIME: 1 hour, 30 minutes • *YIELD: 8 servings*

¾ cup skim milk
¼ cup cornstarch
½ teaspoon low-sodium baking
 powder
½ cup maple syrup
¾ cup grated carrots
3 cups nonfat bread crumbs
3 teaspoons minced fresh gingerroot

2 teaspoons ground cinnamon
¼ teaspoon ground nutmeg
¾ cup chopped dried peaches
1 medium orange, peeled, sectioned,
 and chopped
1 medium apple, cored and chopped
½ cup chopped dried apricots
2 cups apple juice

1. Preheat oven to 350 degrees.
2. Whisk together milk, cornstarch, and baking powder. Stir in syrup, carrots, bread crumbs, 2 teaspoons gingerroot, cinnamon, nutmeg, and peaches. Mix well.
3. Transfer batter to a nonstick 9 × 5-inch baking dish, cover with foil, and bake until set, about 1 hour. Allow to cool for 30 minutes, and cut into 8 slices.
4. Combine orange, apple, apricots, remaining gingerroot, and apple juice in a saucepan. Bring to a boil over medium heat, reduce heat, and simmer, stirring occasionally until apricots are tender and the liquid begins to thicken, about 30 minutes.
5. Serve pudding in individual bowls topped with the fruit.

Calories Per Serving: 229
Fat: 0 g
Cholesterol: 0 mg
Protein: 3 g

Carbohydrates: 54 g
Dietary Fiber: 3 g
Sodium: 111 mg

❦ *Cranberry-Apple Dessert* ❦

Fresh cranberries are grown in huge sandy bogs and harvested between Labor Day and Halloween.

PREPARATION TIME: 20 minutes plus 2 hours chilling time •
COOKING TIME: 18 minutes • *YIELD: 6 servings*

3 cups whole fresh cranberries	2 tablespoons cornstarch
1½ cups water	2 tablespoons apple juice
⅔ cup brown sugar	1 cup nonfat vanilla frozen yogurt

1. Bring cranberries and water to a boil in a saucepan. Reduce heat and simmer over medium heat for 15 minutes.
2. Strain cranberries and discard solids. Stir brown sugar into the cranberry liquid.
3. Gradually stir cornstarch into apple juice until cornstarch dissolves. Combine cranberry and apple juice mixtures in a saucepan. Bring to a boil, stirring constantly. Reduce heat, and stir and cook for 2 minutes.
4. Divide among 6 individual custard cups and chill. Top with frozen yogurt before serving.

Calories Per Serving: 156	Carbohydrates: 38 g
Fat: 0 g	Dietary Fiber: 2 g
Cholesterol: 1 mg	Sodium: 26 mg
Protein: 2 g	

❦ *Mango Pudding* ❦

This chilled mango dessert is flavored with lemon and brown sugar. Fresh mangoes are rich in vitamins A, C, and D.

PREPARATION TIME: 15 minutes plus 2 hours chilling time •
COOKING TIME: 2 minutes • *YIELD: 6 servings*

2 medium mangoes	¼ cup cornstarch
1 teaspoon lemon juice	3 tablespoons brown sugar
1 cup skim milk	

1. Peel the mangoes, remove their seeds, and cut the fruit into chunks. Place the mangoes and lemon juice in a blender or food processor and blend until smooth.
2. Whisk together the milk, cornstarch, and brown sugar until thoroughly dissolved. Stir in the mangoes. Transfer mixture to a saucepan. Bring to a boil, stirring constantly. Reduce heat, and cook and stir for 2 minutes.
3. Pour pudding into a shallow serving bowl and chill for 2 hours before serving.

Calories Per Serving: 106   Carbohydrates: 25 g
Fat: 0 g   Dietary Fiber: 2 g
Cholesterol: 1 mg   Sodium: 25 mg
Protein: 2 g

❧ *Grilled Nectarines with Berry Sauce* ☙

Grilled fruit is an elegant dessert for a summer meal.

PREPARATION TIME: 10 minutes • *COOKING TIME: 10 minutes* •
YIELD: 4 servings

¼ cup brown sugar   *¾ cup fresh raspberries*
½ teaspoon ground cinnamon   *1 teaspoon lemon juice*
¼ teaspoon ground nutmeg   *1 teaspoon honey*
½ teaspoon vanilla extract   *1 teaspoon grated lemon peel*
2 fresh nectarines, halved and pitted

1. Whisk together the brown sugar, cinnamon, nutmeg, and vanilla extract.
2. Place the nectarine halves cut side up on a sheet of aluminum foil. Top each half with the sugar mixture, fold the foil over, and seal. Grill over hot coals or under a broiler, turning once, until heated through, about 5 minutes each side.
3. Combine the raspberries, lemon juice, and honey in a blender or food processor, and blend until smooth. Divide the berry sauce among the nectarine halves, garnish with lemon peel, and serve.

Calories Per Serving: 96

Carbohydrates: 24 g

Fat: 0 g

Dietary Fiber: 2 g

Cholesterol: 0 mg

Sodium: 7 mg

Protein: 1 g

❧ *Nectarine-Cantaloupe Kabobs* ☙

Prepare these grilled kabobs indoors under your broiler or outdoors on your barbecue.

PREPARATION TIME: 15 minutes plus 30 minutes marinating time　•
COOKING TIME: 5 minutes　•　YIELD: 8 servings

1 cup orange juice

¼ cup lemon juice

½ cup sugar

6 medium nectarines, peeled and cut
   into chunks

3 medium bananas, peeled and
   thickly sliced

2 cups 1-inch fresh pineapple cubes

2 cups cantaloupe chunks

1. Combine orange juice, lemon juice, and sugar.
2. Place nectarines, bananas, pineapple, and cantaloupe chunks in a bowl. Pour orange juice mixture over the fruit and marinate for 30 minutes.
3. Thread marinated fruit on skewers.
4. Grill or broil for 5 minutes, basting with marinade. Serve at once.

Calories Per Serving: 219

Carbohydrates: 54 g

Fat: 1 g

Dietary Fiber: 4 g

Cholesterol: 0 mg

Sodium: 10 mg

Protein: 2 g

❧ *Cinnamon Oranges* ☙

Oranges are tossed with a cinnamon-accented syrup.

PREPARATION TIME: 15 minutes plus 1 hour chilling time　•
COOKING TIME: 10 minutes　•　YIELD: 6 servings

1 cup orange juice
1 cup water
½ cup sugar

½ teaspoon ground cinnamon
6 medium navel oranges, peeled and
    sectioned

1. Combine orange juice, water, sugar, and cinnamon in a saucepan. Bring to a boil over medium heat.
2. Reduce heat and simmer, stirring occasionally, until reduced by half.
3. Remove from heat and allow syrup to cool for 10 minutes.
4. Toss oranges with syrup and chill for 1 hour before serving.

Calories Per Serving: 151
Fat: 0 g
Cholesterol: 0 mg
Protein: 2 g

Carbohydrates: 38 g
Dietary Fiber: 10 g
Sodium: 4 mg

❧ *Papaya-Mango Kabobs* ❧

These grilled kabobs with a lime-honey marinade make a refreshing side dish or dessert.

PREPARATION TIME: *20 minutes* • COOKING TIME: *5 minutes* •
YIELD: *4 servings*

2 firm medium bananas, cut into
    1-inch pieces
1 cup fresh or canned, juice-packed
    pineapple chunks, drained
1 medium papaya, peeled, seeded,
    and cut into 1-inch cubes

1 medium mango, peeled, seeded,
    and cut into 1-inch pieces
2 tablespoons lime juice
1 tablespoon lemon juice
¼ cup honey

1. Arrange the chunks of banana, pineapple, papaya, and mango on skewers.
2. Combine the lime juice, lemon juice, and honey.
3. Brush the juice-honey mixture on the fruit and broil for 3 minutes. Turn the kabobs, baste, and broil for an additional 2 minutes. Serve at once.

Calories Per Serving: 235
Fat: 1 g
Cholesterol: 0 mg
Protein: 2 g

Carbohydrates: 60 g
Dietary Fiber: 5 g
Sodium: 10 mg

❧ *Curried Peaches and Pineapple* ❧

Fruit and curry powder are perfectly paired in this melange of fruit. Serve warm with Indian-inspired main dishes.

PREPARATION TIME: 15 minutes • *COOKING TIME: 15 minutes* •
YIELD: 4 servings

½ cup orange juice
½ teaspoon curry powder
¼ teaspoon ground ginger
1 pear, peeled, cored, and cut into
  chunks
½ cup seedless raisins

½ cup dried apricots, chopped
1 cup canned water-packed sliced
  peaches
1 cup canned water-packed pineapple
  chunks

1. Heat orange juice, curry powder, and ginger in a large saucepan.
2. Stir in pear, raisins, and apricots.
3. Cover and simmer gently for 10 minutes.
4. Add peaches and pineapple and continue to simmer for 3 additional minutes. Serve warm.

Calories Per Serving: 436
Fat: 0 g
Cholesterol: 0 mg
Protein: 3 g

Carbohydrates: 112 g
Dietary Fiber: 5 g
Sodium: 11 mg

❧ *Poached Peaches with Vanilla Frozen Yogurt* ❧

Poaching produces a delicate flavor in peaches. After chilling, they are topped with frozen yogurt.

PREPARATION TIME: *15 minutes plus 1 hour chilling time* •
COOKING TIME: *11 minutes* • YIELD: *8 servings*

6 cups water
1½ cups sugar
1 tablespoon vanilla extract

8 medium peaches
1 cup nonfat vanilla frozen yogurt

1. Combine water, sugar, and vanilla extract in a large saucepan. Simmer until sugar is dissolved, about 3 minutes.
2. Add peaches and return to gentle simmer until they are soft. Remove peaches and allow to cool until they can be handled. Peel and slice them and chill for 1 hour before serving.
3. Top with frozen yogurt and serve.

Calories Per Serving: 215
Fat: 0 g
Cholesterol: 0 mg
Protein: 1 g

Carbohydrates: 54 g
Dietary Fiber: 1 g
Sodium: 20 mg

❧ *Peach Pudding* ❧

Pudding is thickened by finely ground rice.

PREPARATION TIME: *15 minutes plus 30 minutes cooling time* •
COOKING TIME: *5 minutes* • YIELD: *8 servings*

¼ cup uncooked white rice
¼ cup water
3 tablespoons cornstarch

4 cups juice-packed canned peach
  halves, drained
2½ cups skim milk
2 teaspoons almond extract

1. Place rice in a blender or food processor and blend until the texture of salt.
2. Transfer rice to a small bowl, add water, and stir in cornstarch until it is dissolved.
3. Place peach halves in blender or food processor and blend until smooth. Pour in enough milk to total 4 cups liquid. Transfer to a saucepan.
4. Stir rice mixture into the peach mixture. Bring to a boil, stirring constantly; reduce heat, cook, and stir for 4 minutes. Remove from heat and stir in almond extract.
5. Pour pudding into individual serving bowls and chill in the refrigerator for 1 hour before serving.

Calories Per Serving: 130 Carbohydrates: 28 g
Fat: 1 g Dietary Fiber: 2 g
Cholesterol: 1 mg Sodium: 44 mg
Protein: 4 g

❧ *Lemon-Poached Pears in Wine Sauce* ❦

Whole pears are poached in red wine, lemon juice, sugar, lemon peel, and cinnamon. Look for pears that are firm for cooking.

PREPARATION TIME: 15 minutes plus 20 minutes cooling time ·
COOKING TIME: 15 minutes · *YIELD: 6 servings*

2 tablespoons lemon juice *Two ½ × 2-inch strips lemon peel*
4 cups red wine *½ teaspoon ground cinnamon*
1 cup water *6 medium pears, cored and halved*
1½ cups sugar

1. Place lemon juice, wine, water, sugar, lemon peel, and cinnamon in a large saucepan. Bring to a boil, reduce heat, and simmer until sugar dissolves, about 5 minutes.
2. Add pears and continue to simmer gently until pears are done through, about 10 minutes. Remove from heat and allow to cool in the cooking liquid for 20 minutes.
3. Remove the pears from the liquid to serve.

Calories Per Serving: 392   Carbohydrates: 75 g
Fat: 1 g   Dietary Fiber: 4 g
Cholesterol: 0 mg   Sodium: 104 mg
Protein: 1 g

❧ *Spiced Poached Pears* ❧

Aniseed, a spice that plays an important part in the cooking of Southeast Asia, is the special ingredient in these simmered pears.

PREPARATION TIME: *10 minutes plus 1 hour chilling time* ▪
COOKING TIME: *8 minutes* ▪ YIELD: *4 servings*

½ cup water   4 medium pears, peeled, cored, and
¼ cup sugar   quartered
1 teaspoon lemon juice   ½ cup nonfat vanilla frozen yogurt
¼ teaspoon aniseed, crushed

1. Bring water, sugar, lemon juice, and aniseed to a boil in a saucepan, stirring occasionally.
2. Add pears. Return to a boil, reduce heat, and simmer until pears are just tender, about 6 minutes.
3. Top each serving with a dollop of frozen yogurt, and serve.

Calories Per Serving: 138   Carbohydrates: 35 g
Fat: 1 g   Dietary Fiber: 4 g
Cholesterol: 0 mg   Sodium: 2 mg
Protein: 1 g

❧ *Spiced Pears and Raisins* ❧

Fresh pears are poached with apple juice, raisins, cinnamon, cloves, and orange peel. Look for pears that are fragrant and free of blemishes and soft spots.

PREPARATION TIME: *10 minutes* ▪ COOKING TIME: *8 minutes* ▪
YIELD: *4 servings*

2 cups apple juice
½ cup raisins
½ teaspoon ground cinnamon
¼ teaspoon ground cloves

3 tablespoons grated orange peel
4 medium pears, cored and halved
1 cup nonfat vanilla frozen yogurt

1. Bring apple juice, raisins, cinnamon, cloves, and orange peel to a boil in a saucepan. Add pear halves. Return to a boil, reduce heat, and simmer gently until pears are done, about 6 minutes.
2. Allow to cool. Transfer to individual plates, top with frozen yogurt, and serve.

Calories Per Serving: 260
Fat: 1 g
Cholesterol: 1 mg
Protein: 4 g

Carbohydrates: 64 g
Dietary Fiber: 6 g
Sodium: 41 mg

✿ *Curried Pear Compote* ✿

This curried fruit melange is cooked slowly, so the fruit retains its shape.

PREPARATION TIME: 20 minutes • COOKING TIME: 1 hour •
YIELD: 10 servings

2 cups water-packed canned pineapple chunks, drained, liquid reserved
2 medium pears, cut in half lengthwise, cored, and sliced
1 medium apple, cored and sliced

2 cups dried apricot halves, cut in half
2 cups pitted prunes, cut in half
¼ cup brown sugar
2 teaspoons curry powder
¾ cup nonfat vanilla yogurt

1. Preheat oven to 350 degrees.
2. Combine pineapple chunks, pear and apple slices, apricots, and prunes in a large bowl.
3. In another bowl mix pineapple liquid, brown sugar, and curry powder. Stir until thoroughly mixed and pour over fruit. Toss to coat all ingredients.

4. Transfer to baking dish and bake, covered, for 1 hour.
5. Divide among individual serving plates, top with a dollop of yogurt, and serve.

Calories Per Serving: 176

Fat: 0 g

Cholesterol: 0 mg

Protein: 3 g

Carbohydrates: 45 g

Dietary Fiber: 7 g

Sodium: 16 mg

❧ *Pear-Ricotta Pita* ❧

Pita rounds are spread with ricotta cheese and topped with pear chunks. This easy snack works well with nectarines, peaches, and blueberries, too.

PREPARATION TIME: 15 minutes ▪ *COOKING TIME: 10 minutes* ▪
YIELD: 8 servings

1½ *cups nonfat ricotta cheese*
4 *small pita breads, split*

2 *medium pears, peeled, cored, and diced*
2½ *tablespoons brown sugar*

1. Preheat oven to 450 degrees.
2. Blend cheese in blender or food processor until smooth.
3. Toast pita halves in oven until just crisp, about 5 minutes.
4. Divide cheese among the pita halves and top each with a mound of pear. Sprinkle a teaspoon of sugar over each pita and bake for 5 minutes. Serve at once.

Calories Per Serving: 134

Fat: 0 g

Cholesterol: 4 mg

Protein: 7 g

Carbohydrates: 26 g

Dietary Fiber: 0 g

Sodium: 182 mg

❧ *Pineapple Pudding* ❧

This satisfying pudding is a combination of pineapple, bananas, bread, spices, and maple syrup.

PREPARATION TIME: 15 minutes ▪ *COOKING TIME: 60 minutes* ▪
YIELD: 6 servings

6 slices nonfat bread
1½ cups evaporated skim milk
4 egg whites, beaten lightly
½ cup frozen apple juice concentrate,
   thawed
2 cups water-packed canned crushed
   pineapple, drained

2 medium bananas, peeled and sliced
1 teaspoon lemon juice
1¼ teaspoons ground cinnamon
¼ cup maple syrup
1 teaspoon vanilla extract

1. Preheat oven to 325 degrees.
2. Dice the bread and combine with all other ingredients in a large bowl. Mix well.
3. Transfer to an 8 × 11 × 2-inch nonstick baking dish and bake until set, about 1 hour. Allow to cool slightly before serving.

Calories Per Serving: 284
Fat: 1 g
Cholesterol: 2 mg
Protein: 11 g

Carbohydrates: 59 g
Dietary Fiber: 3 g
Sodium: 277 mg

❧ *Strawberry Kabobs* ❧

Strawberries, apples, bananas, and pineapple are marinated in honey and pineapple juice before broiling.

PREPARATION TIME: 15 minutes plus 30 minutes marinating time ▪
COOKING TIME: 3 minutes ▪ *YIELD: 8 servings*

¼ cup lemon juice
2 medium apples, cored and cut into
   1-inch chunks

2 medium bananas, cut into 1-inch
   chunks
¼ cup honey

¼ teaspoon cinnamon

2 cups juice-packed canned pineapple
  chunks, drained, juice reserved

2 cups hulled fresh strawberries

1. Sprinkle lemon juice over the apple and banana chunks.
2. Combine honey, cinnamon, and reserved pineapple juice in a separate bowl.
3. Add all the fruit and marinate for 30 minutes.
4. Thread fruit on 8 skewers and broil or grill for 3 to 4 minutes, turning frequently.
5. Serve on skewers.

Calories Per Serving: 106
Fat: 0 g
Cholesterol: 0 mg
Protein: 1 g

Carbohydrates: 28 g
Dietary Fiber: 2 g
Sodium: 2 mg

❧ *Spiced Rhubarb* ❧

Buy crisp bright red rhubarb. Here it is combined with oranges and cloves.

PREPARATION TIME: *20 minutes plus 1 hour chilling time*   ▪
COOKING TIME: *15 minutes*   ▪   YIELD: *6 servings*

3 cups water

2 cups sugar

½ teaspoon ground cloves

3 cups 1-inch rhubarb pieces

4 medium navel oranges, peeled and
  sectioned

1. Bring the water, sugar, and cloves to a boil in a large pot.
2. Add the rhubarb, reduce heat, and simmer for 10 minutes, or until rhubarb is just tender.
3. Remove from heat, drain, and stir in the orange sections. Chill for 1 hour before serving.

Calories Per Serving: 436
Fat: 0 g
Cholesterol: 0 mg
Protein: 3 g

Carbohydrates: 112 g
Dietary Fiber: 5 g
Sodium: 11 mg

❧ *Rhubarb Dessert* ❧

The stems are the only edible part of the rhubarb plant, which peaks between April and June.

PREPARATION TIME: 15 minutes plus 2 hours chilling time •
COOKING TIME: 8 minutes • *YIELD: 9 servings*

6 cups diced rhubarb stems	1 cup evaporated skim milk
¾ cup brown sugar	1 teaspoon vanilla extract
½ cup water	2 tablespoons cornstarch
1 teaspoon minced orange peel	2 tablespoons nonfat graham cracker
1 teaspoon ground cinnamon	crumbs

1. Combine rhubarb, brown sugar, water, orange peel, and cinnamon in a saucepan. Bring to a boil, stirring constantly. Reduce heat, cover, and cook until rhubarb is just tender, about 5 minutes.
2. Mix evaporated milk and vanilla extract in a saucepan. Gradually stir in cornstarch and mix until it is dissolved.
3. Stir the rhubarb mixture into the milk. Bring to a boil, reduce heat, and cook, stirring constantly, for 3 minutes.
4. Sprinkle with graham cracker crumbs and chill for 2 hours before serving.

Calories Per Serving: 133	Carbohydrates: 30 g
Fat: 1 g	Dietary Fiber: 1 g
Cholesterol: 0 mg	Sodium: 65 mg
Protein: 2 g	

❧ *Strawberry Soufflés* ❧

This soufflé should be baked in individual 3½-ounce nonstick soufflé dishes.

PREPARATION TIME: 15 minutes plus 30 minutes standing time •
COOKING TIME: 12 minutes • *YIELD: 6 servings*

*1 cup strawberries, hulled and
    chopped*
2½ tablespoons sugar

1 teaspoon all-purpose flour
4 egg whites, at room temperature

1. Mix strawberries and 1½ tablespoons sugar in a small bowl.
2. Preheat oven to 350 degrees.
3. Dust 6 small soufflé dishes with flour.
4. Beat egg whites until stiff peaks form. Sprinkle remaining 1 tablespoon sugar on egg whites and beat until well mixed. Drain any excess liquid from the strawberries and fold them into the egg whites.
5. Spoon the mixture into the soufflé dishes and place them on a baking sheet and bake until the soufflés rise and the tops begin to brown, about 12 minutes. Serve at once.

Calories Per Serving: 98
Fat: 0 g
Cholesterol: 0 mg
Protein: 4 g

Carbohydrates: 17 g
Dietary Fiber: 1 g
Sodium: 56 mg

❧ *Honey-Baked Dried Fruit* ❧

This mixture of dried fruit, nuts, and cocoa powder is baked with honey.

*PREPARATION TIME: 20 minutes • COOKING TIME: 28 minutes •
YIELD: 12 servings*

1 tablespoon chopped toasted almonds
¼ cup seeded raisins
¼ cup chopped dried apricots
¼ cup chopped pitted prunes
¼ cup chopped dates

½ cup all-purpose flour
¼ cup unsweetened cocoa powder
1 teaspoon ground cinnamon
½ cup brown sugar
½ cup honey

1. Line the bottom of a shallow 9-inch nonstick baking pan with wax paper. Preheat oven to 300 degrees.
2. Combine almonds, raisins, apricots, prunes, and dates in a large bowl.
3. Mix flour, cocoa powder, and cinnamon. Add to the fruit mixture and mix well.

4. Combine brown sugar and honey in a small saucepan. Bring to a boil.

5. Remove from heat and quickly pour over the fruit mixture. Mix until all ingredients are moist. Spread the mixture evenly in the baking dish and bake until set, about 25 minutes.

6. Allow to cool 5 minutes. Transfer to individual plates and serve.

Calories Per Serving: 172

Fat: 1 g

Cholesterol: 0 mg

Protein: 2 g

Carbohydrates: 42 g

Dietary Fiber: 1 g

Sodium: 8 mg

VEGETABLE DISHES

꧁

Artichokes with Carrot and Potatoes · Asparagus with Tomatoes
· Roasted Beets, Carrots, and Turnips · Marinated Beets ·
Lemon-Dijon Broccoli · Broccoli with Tomato Sauce · Spicy
Broccoli and Chickpeas · Broccoli, Cauliflower, and Lentils ·
Ginger-Steamed Broccoli, Carrots, and Zucchini · Green Beans
with Mushrooms · Jalapeño-Ginger Green Beans with Potatoes
· Ginger-Cumin Green Beans with Cauliflower · Hungarian
Green Beans and Cabbage · Sweet and Sour Cabbage ·
Jalapeño-Garlic Cabbage · Dijon Carrots · Pureed Carrots,
Corn, and Cauliflower · Honey-Lemon Carrots and Turnips ·
Roasted Carrots, Potatoes, and Turnips · Simmered Carrot-
Pineapple Curry · Dijon Squash and Carrots · Succotash ·
Microwaved Curried Cauliflower and Peas · Ginger-Cumin
Cauliflower · Baked Corn · Grilled Corn with Lime ·
Eggplant Pizza · Gingered Eggplant and Potatoes · Lemon-
Garlic Kale · Shiitake Mushrooms with Radicchio · Jalapeño-
Okra-Corn Stew · Baked Onion Rings · Parsley Mashed
Potatoes · Potato-Turnip Bake · Potatoes and Eggplant ·
Jalapeño Potatoes with Peas · Potato Pancakes · Parmesan

Potato Strips • Baked Sweet Potatoes • Sweet Potatoes and
Lentils • Pear–Apple–Sweet Potato Bake • Gingered Pumpkin
and Beans • Braised Spinach with Garlic • Spicy Spinach-and-
Potato Sauté • Spinach and Red Pepper • Gingered Sugar
Snaps • Butternut Curry • Couscous-Stuffed Acorn Squash •
Pattypan Squash, Spinach, and Kidney Beans • Squash Curry •
Butternut Squash Stuffed with Vegetables • Stuffed Acorn
Squash • Couscous-and-Vegetable-Stuffed Peppers • Veggie-
Stuffed Potatoes • Cabbage-Stuffed Tomatoes • Sun-Dried
Tomatoes with Beans • Red Peppers with Corn Stuffing •
Chili-Vegetable Tacos • Shiitake-Tomatillo Tacos • Red
Pepper–Corn Tortillas • Roasted Vegetable Medley • Thyme-
Roasted Vegetables • Grilled Vegetables • Green Bean Stew •
Eggplant Stew • Spiced Eggplant Ratatouille • Parsnip-Squash
Stew • Pumpkin Stew • Early Spring Vegetable Stew •
Apple–Green Bean Curry • Potato-Tomato Casserole •
Vegetables with Fennel • Mixed Curried Vegetables •
Summer Squash Paella • Ethiopian Stew

❧ *Artichokes with Carrot and Potatoes* ❧

In this vegetable stew, carrot, potatoes, and artichoke hearts are flavored with tarragon, thyme, and black pepper.

PREPARATION TIME: 5 minutes • *COOKING TIME: 25 minutes* •
YIELD: 8 servings

2¼ cups low-sodium nonfat chicken broth
2 medium onions, chopped
1 medium clove garlic, minced
2 cups water
1 medium carrot, scraped and chopped

6 cups chopped potatoes
3 cups fresh cooked or frozen artichoke hearts
1 teaspoon dried tarragon
1 teaspoon dried thyme
¼ teaspoon ground black pepper

1. Heat ¼ cup broth in a large saucepan. Add onions, and sauté for 4 minutes. Add garlic and continue to sauté for 1 minute.
2. Add the remaining broth, water, and remaining ingredients. Bring to a boil. Reduce heat, cover, and simmer until potatoes are tender, about 20 minutes.
3. Transfer to individual bowls and serve.

Calories Per Serving: 220
Fat: 1 g
Cholesterol: 0 mg
Protein: 8 g

Carbohydrates: 49 g
Dietary Fiber: 7 g
Sodium: 180 mg

❧ *Asparagus with Tomatoes* ❧

Asparagus, mushrooms, tomatoes, and scallions are cooked in a sherry-ginger sauce. The peak season for fresh asparagus is February through June. Look for firm, bright green (or pale ivory) stalks with tight tips.

PREPARATION TIME: 15 minutes • *COOKING TIME: 12 minutes* •
YIELD: 4 servings

1 tablespoon sherry
1 tablespoon reduced-sodium soy sauce
1 teaspoon water
2 tablespoons low-sodium tomato juice
1 teaspoon minced fresh gingerroot

4 cups fresh asparagus (cut diagonally into 1½-inch lengths)
4 scallions, cut into 1-inch lengths
1½ cups sliced mushrooms
2 large tomatoes, each cut into 8 vertical wedges

1. Whisk together the sherry, soy sauce, and water.
2. Heat tomato juice in a large saucepan. Add gingerroot and sauté for 30 seconds. Add asparagus and scallions and sauté until asparagus is just tender crisp, about 3 minutes. Add mushrooms and continue to sauté for 1 additional minute.
3. Stir in sherry sauce and tomatoes. Simmer, stirring constantly, until heated through, about 1 minute. Serve at once.

Calories Per Serving: 59
Fat: 1 g
Cholesterol: 0 mg
Protein: 5 g

Carbohydrates: 12 g
Dietary Fiber: 1 g
Sodium: 162 mg

❧ Roasted Beets, Carrots, and Turnips ❧

Carrots, turnips, and beets are roasted and seasoned with black pepper. Choose turnips that are small but heavy for their size with firm roots and bright-colored leaves.

PREPARATION TIME: 15 minutes ▪ *COOKING TIME: 30 minutes* ▪
YIELD: 8 servings

8 medium turnips, cut into 3-inch strips
8 medium carrots, cut into 3-inch strips

8 small beets, cut into 3-inch strips
¼ teaspoon ground black pepper

1. Preheat oven to 350 degrees.
2. Arrange turnips in a nonstick baking dish lightly sprayed with olive oil spray and roast for 15 minutes.
3. Add carrots and beets and roast, turning several times, until vegetables are just tender, about 15 additional minutes.
4. Transfer to individual plates, sprinkle with pepper and serve.

Calories Per Serving: 162   Carbohydrates: 39 g
Fat: 0 g   Dietary Fiber: 7 g
Cholesterol: 0 mg   Sodium: 75 mg
Protein: 3 g

◔ *Marinated Beets* ◔

In this refreshing dish, beets are served with a yogurt dressing. Fresh beets can be stored in a plastic bag in the refrigerator for up to 3 weeks.

*PREPARATION TIME: 10 minutes plus 2 hours marinating time •
COOKING TIME: 35 minutes • YIELD: 4 servings*

4 cups small whole beets   *2 tablespoons minced fresh parsley*
2 cups nonfat plain yogurt   *¼ teaspoon ground white pepper*
4 scallions, minced   *¼ teaspoon ground black pepper*

1. Place the beets in a saucepan, cover with water, and bring to a boil. Reduce heat and simmer until beets are just tender, about 35 minutes.
2. Mix the yogurt, scallions, parsley, white pepper, and black pepper in a bowl. Add the beets to the yogurt mixture, stir to coat, cover and refrigerate for 2 hours before serving.

Calories Per Serving: 172   Carbohydrates: 34 g
Fat: 0 g   Dietary Fiber: 8 g
Cholesterol: 3 mg   Sodium: 264 mg
Protein: 10 g

❧ *Lemon-Dijon Broccoli* ❧

Steamed broccoli is topped with a seasoned yogurt sauce. Yogurt is a good source of B vitamins, protein, and calcium.

PREPARATION TIME: 20 minutes • COOKING TIME: 4 minutes •
YIELD: 6 servings

6 cups chopped broccoli
½ cup nonfat plain yogurt
1 tablespoon Dijon mustard
1 tablespoon lemon juice

2 teaspoons minced lemon peel
2 cloves garlic, minced
1 scallion, minced
¼ teaspoon ground black pepper

1. Place the broccoli in a steamer basket over boiling water, cover, and steam until it is tender crisp, about 4 minutes.
2. Whisk together the yogurt, mustard, lemon juice, lemon peel, and garlic.
3. Transfer broccoli to a large serving bowl. Top with the sauce, minced scallion, and black pepper, and serve.

Calories Per Serving: 42
Fat: 0 g
Cholesterol: 0 mg
Protein: 4 g

Carbohydrates: 8 g
Dietary Fiber: 3 g
Sodium: 93 mg

❧ *Broccoli with Tomato Sauce* ❧

Steamed broccoli is served with a garlic-and-lemon-flavored tomato sauce.

PREPARATION TIME: 15 minutes • COOKING TIME: 7 minutes •
YIELD: 4 servings

5 cups chopped broccoli
2 tablespoons low-sodium tomato juice
2 cloves garlic, minced
1 tablespoon fresh minced lemon peel

½ teaspoon dried rosemary
2 tablespoons low-sodium nonfat chicken broth
1 tablespoon lemon juice

1. Place broccoli in a steamer basket over boiling water and steam until tender-crisp, about 4 minutes.
2. Heat tomato juice in a skillet. Add garlic and sauté for 30 seconds. Stir in lemon peel and rosemary, and sauté for 1 additional minute. Add broth and lemon juice, and simmer until liquid is reduced to about 1 tablespoon, about 1 minute.
3. Transfer broccoli to serving bowl and top with sauce.

Calories Per Serving: 38	Carbohydrates: 7 g
Fat: 0 g	Dietary Fiber: 4 g
Cholesterol: 0 mg	Sodium: 44 mg
Protein: 4 g	

❧ *Spicy Broccoli and Chickpeas* ❧

This Indian dish contains chickpeas, broccoli, onion, tomato, garlic, and gingerroot.

PREPARATION TIME: 15 minutes • *COOKING TIME: 30 minutes* • *YIELD: 4 servings*

¼ cup low-sodium nonfat chicken broth	½ teaspoon ground turmeric
1 medium onion, diced	½ teaspoon ground cumin
1 medium tomato, chopped	¼ teaspoon dried coriander
2 cloves garlic, minced	2 cups low-sodium canned chickpeas, rinsed and drained
½ tablespoon minced fresh gingerroot	2 cups broccoli florets
1 jalapeño pepper, seeded and minced	1 cup water

1. Heat broth in a large saucepan. Add onion, tomato, garlic, gingerroot, and jalapeño pepper. Sauté until onion begins to soften, about 4 minutes. Add turmeric, cumin, and coriander, and sauté for 1 additional minute.
2. Stir in the chickpeas, broccoli, and water, and simmer, stirring frequently, for 25 minutes.
3. Serve at once.

Calories Per Serving: 153

Carbohydrates: 29 g

Fat: 0 g

Dietary Fiber: 1 g

Cholesterol: 0 mg

Sodium: 536 mg

Protein: 9 g

✤ ❧ *Broccoli, Cauliflower, and Lentils* ☙

This dish is made with cauliflower, lentils, broccoli, and potatoes. Lentils are a good source of iron and phosphorus.

PREPARATION TIME: 20 minutes • *COOKING TIME: 1 hour, 6 minutes* •
YIELD: 8 servings

1 cup dried lentils

2 medium tomatoes, chopped

5 cups water

2 teaspoons ground cumin

½ cup low-sodium nonfat chicken
*   broth*

¼ teaspoon cayenne pepper

3 medium potatoes, chopped

1 medium onion, chopped

2 cups chopped broccoli

4 cloves garlic, minced

2 cups chopped cauliflower

1. Place lentils and water in a saucepan. Bring to a boil, reduce heat, and simmer for 40 minutes. Remove from heat and set aside.
2. Heat broth in a large saucepan. Add onion and garlic and sauté for 2 minutes. Add tomatoes and sauté for 3 more minutes. Add cumin and cayenne pepper and sauté for 1 additional minute.
3. Combine the lentils, their cooking liquid, potatoes, broccoli, and cauliflower with the onion mixture. Cook, stirring several times, over medium heat until potatoes and cauliflower are just tender, about 15 minutes. Serve at once.

Calories Per Serving: 159

Carbohydrates: 30 g

Fat: 1 g

Dietary Fiber: 10 g

Cholesterol: 0 mg

Sodium: 61 mg

Protein: 10 g

ও *Ginger-Steamed Broccoli, Carrots, ও and Zucchini*

Broccoli, carrots, and squash are flavored with gingerroot. Fresh unpeeled gingerroot can be stored tightly wrapped in the refrigerator for up to 3 weeks.

PREPARATION TIME: 10 minutes • COOKING TIME: 8 minutes •
YIELD: 6 servings

¾ cup apple juice
4 cups chopped broccoli
2 medium carrots, scraped and
   chopped

2 cups chopped zucchini
2 teaspoon minced fresh gingerroot

1. Bring apple juice to a boil in the bottom of a steamer.
2. Place broccoli, carrots, zucchini, and gingerroot in the steamer basket and steam until vegetables are just tender-crisp, about 4 minutes. Serve at once.

Calories Per Serving: 48
Fat: 0 g
Cholesterol: 0 mg
Protein: 3 g

Carbohydrates: 11 g
Dietary Fiber: 3 g
Sodium: 27 mg

ও *Green Beans with Mushrooms* ও

Yellow squash, tomatoes, green beans, and mushrooms are seasoned with dry mustard, oregano, and red wine vinegar.

PREPARATION TIME: 15 minutes • COOKING TIME: 10 minutes •
YIELD: 4 servings

¼ cup low-sodium nonfat chicken
   broth

1 tablespoon red wine vinegar
½ teaspoon dried oregano

¼ teaspoon dry mustard
2 cups fresh green beans, cut into
   2-inch lengths
1 cup sliced mushrooms

2 cups chopped yellow summer
   squash
2 medium tomatoes, cut in wedges

1. Combine broth, vinegar, oregano, and mustard in a saucepan and bring to a boil. Add beans. Return to a boil, reduce heat, cover, and simmer 5 minutes.
2. Add mushrooms and squash, and simmer for 3 additional minutes. Add tomatoes and continue to simmer until all ingredients are heated through, about 2 more minutes. Serve at once.

Calories Per Serving: 56
Fat: 0 g
Cholesterol: 0 mg
Protein: 3 g

Carbohydrates: 12 g
Dietary Fiber: 3 g
Sodium: 57 mg

❧ *Jalapeño-Ginger Green Beans with Potatoes* ❧

Green beans and potatoes are prepared with carrots, onions, and ginger-root.

PREPARATION TIME: 15 minutes ▪ *COOKING TIME: 15 minutes* ▪
YIELD: 6 servings

4 cups water
3 cups cubed potatoes
3 cups fresh green beans, cut into
   2-inch lengths
3 medium carrots, chopped
½ cup low-sodium nonfat chicken
   broth

2 medium onions, sliced
1 jalapeño pepper, seeded and minced
2 cloves garlic, minced
1 teaspoon minced fresh gingerroot
¼ teaspoon ground black pepper

1. Bring water to a boil in a saucepan. Add potatoes, green beans, and carrots. Return to a boil, reduce heat, cover, and simmer for 5 minutes.
2. Heat ¼ cup broth in another saucepan. Add onions and jalapeño, and

sauté until onions begin to soften, about 3 minutes. Stir in garlic, gingerroot, and black pepper, and sauté for 2 additional minutes.

3. Stir in potato mixture and remaining broth and simmer until potatoes are just tender, about 5 minutes. Serve at once.

Calories Per Serving: 158	Carbohydrates: 36 g
Fat: 0 g	Dietary Fiber: 5 g
Cholesterol: 0 mg	Sodium: 61 mg
Protein: 5 g	

❧ *Ginger-Cumin Green Beans* ❧ *with Cauliflower*

In this recipe, potatoes, cabbage, cauliflower, green beans, and peas are served over rice. Cabbage can be stored tightly wrapped in the refrigerator for about a week.

PREPARATIOİN TIME: 20 minutes • COOKING TIME: 23 minutes •
YIELD: 8 servings

¾ cup low-sodium nonfat chicken broth	2 cups green beans, cut into 1-inch pieces
1 medium onion, chopped	2 teaspoons ground cumin
3 cloves garlic, minced	1 teaspoon ground ginger
2 medium potatoes, diced	¼ teaspoon cayenne pepper
3 cups chopped cabbage	1 cup fresh or frozen green peas
3 cups chopped cauliflower	4 cups cooked white rice

1. Heat ¼ cup broth in a large saucepan. Add onion and garlic, and sauté until onion is just tender, about 3 minutes.
2. Add remaining broth, potatoes, cabbage, cauliflower, beans, cumin, ginger, and cayenne. Bring to a boil, reduce heat, and simmer until cauliflower is just tender, about 15 minutes. Stir in peas and heat through, about 5 minutes.
3. Serve on beds of rice.

Calories Per Serving: 229

Carbohydrates: 50 g

Fat: 1 g

Dietary Fiber: 3 g

Cholesterol: 0 mg

Sodium: 42 mg

Protein: 7 g

❧ *Hungarian Green Beans and Cabbage* ❧

This is a variation on a traditional Hungarian dish, paprikash.

PREPARATION TIME: 15 minutes   •   COOKING TIME: 12 minutes   •
YIELD: 4 servings

1¼ cups low-sodium nonfat chicken
   broth
1 medium onion, chopped
2 cups green beans, cut into 1-inch
   lengths
2 cloves garlic, minced

1½ teaspoons paprika
½ cup low-sodium tomato sauce
3 cups shredded cabbage
1 tablespoon lemon juice
¼ teaspoon ground black pepper

1. Heat ¼ cup broth in a large saucepan. Add onion and sauté until it begins to soften, about 2 minutes. Add beans and garlic, and sauté for 1 additional minute.
2. Stir in the remaining broth, paprika, and tomato sauce. Bring to a boil,
   reduce heat, and simmer for 5 minutes. Add cabbage and continue to
   simmer for 4 more minutes.
3. Stir in lemon juice and black pepper, and serve.

Calories Per Serving: 98

Carbohydrates: 20 g

Fat: 1 g

Dietary Fiber: 5 g

Cholesterol: 0 mg

Sodium: 133 mg

Protein: 6 g

✥ *Sweet and Sour Cabbage* ✥

In this recipe, cabbage and raisins are simmered in apple juice and vinegar.

PREPARATION TIME: 10 minutes • *COOKING TIME: 20 minutes* •
YIELD: 8 servings

8 cups shredded red cabbage
1 cup apple juice
½ cup seedless raisins

3 tablespoons vinegar
¼ teaspoon ground black pepper

1. Place cabbage and apple juice in a large saucepan. Bring to a boil, reduce heat, cover, and simmer for 10 minutes.
2. Add raisins and vinegar. Return to a boil. Reduce heat, cover, and simmer until cabbage is just tender, about 10 additional minutes. Sprinkle with black pepper and serve.

Calories Per Serving: 97
Fat: 1 g
Cholesterol: 0 mg
Protein: 2 g

Carbohydrates: 24 g
Dietary Fiber: 2 g
Sodium: 40 mg

✥ *Jalapeño-Garlic Cabbage* ✥

Cabbage is cooked with onion, garlic, cheese, and jalapeño pepper. Choose cabbage with tightly packed, crisp leaves.

PREPARATION TIME: 15 minutes plus 5 minutes standing time •
COOKING TIME: 27 minutes • *YIELD: 8 servings*

¼ cup low-sodium nonfat chicken
    broth
1 medium onion, thinly sliced
5 cloves garlic, minced
6 cups shredded cabbage

1 cup water
2 cups skim milk
3 tablespoons cornstarch
½ cup shredded nonfat Swiss cheese
1 jalapeño pepper, seeded and minced

1. Heat broth in a large saucepan. Add onion and garlic, and sauté until onion begins to soften, about 3 minutes.

2. Add cabbage and water. Bring to a boil. Reduce heat, cover, and simmer, stirring several times, until cabbage is tender, about 20 minutes.
3. Combine milk and cornstarch. Stir until cornstarch is dissolved. Stir into the cabbage mixture. Bring to a boil, stirring constantly. Continue to cook and stir for 2 minutes.
4. Remove from heat. Stir in cheese and jalapeño pepper before serving.

Calories Per Serving: 71	Carbohydrates: 12 g
Fat: 0 g	Dietary Fiber: 2 g
Cholesterol: 2 mg	Sodium: 172 mg
Protein: 6 g	

❧ *Dijon Carrots* ❧

Carrots are roasted in a honey-mustard sauce. Carrots are high in vitamin A and available all year round.

PREPARATION TIME: 10 minutes • *COOKING TIME: 20 minutes* •
YIELD: 6 servings

6 large carrots, cut into 3-inch sticks	*1 tablespoon vinegar*
2 tablespoons honey	*1 tablespoon Dijon mustard*
2 tablespoons water	*¼ teaspoon ground black pepper*

1. Preheat oven to 400 degrees.
2. Spread carrot sticks in a nonstick pan and roast for 10 minutes.
3. Whisk together the honey, water, vinegar, mustard, and black pepper.
4. Pour sauce over the carrots, stir to coat them well, and continue roasting until the carrots are tender-crisp, about 10 minutes.

Calories Per Serving: 56	Carbohydrates: 13 g
Fat: 0 g	Dietary Fiber: 2 g
Cholesterol: 0 mg	Sodium: 88 mg
Protein: 1 g	

❧ *Pureed Carrots, Corn, and Cauliflower* ❧

This puree blends carrots, corn, and cauliflower with buttermilk.

PREPARATION TIME: 10 minutes • *COOKING TIME: 11 minutes* •
YIELD: 4 servings

¾ cup water	*¼ cup nonfat buttermilk*
1 cup chopped carrots	*⅛ teaspoon ground black pepper*
½ cup fresh or frozen corn kernels	*½ teaspoon ground nutmeg*
½ cup chopped cauliflower	*1 tablespoon minced scallion*

1. Bring water, carrots, corn, and cauliflower to a boil in a saucepan. Reduce heat, cover, and simmer until carrots are tender, about 10 minutes.
2. Drain water and transfer vegetables to a food processor or blender, and puree.
3. Return puree to the saucepan. Stir in buttermilk, pepper, and nutmeg. Warm through, about 1 minute, sprinkle with scallions, and serve.

Calories Per Serving: 35	Carbohydrates: 8 g
Fat: 0 g	Dietary Fiber: 1 g
Cholesterol: 0 mg	Sodium: 20 mg
Protein: 1 g	

❧ *Honey-Lemon Carrots and Turnips* ❧

Steamed carrots, parsnips, turnips, and onion are combined with a lemon-dill sauce. Dried dill should be stored in a dark and cool place.

PREPARATION TIME: 20 minutes • *COOKING TIME: 9 minutes* •
YIELD: 6 servings

3 cups carrots, cut into ½-inch slices	*2 tablespoons honey*
1 cup chopped parsnips	*1½ tablespoons cornstarch*
3 cups chopped turnips	*1 teaspoon minced fresh lemon peel*
1 onion, cut into 6 vertical wedges	*1 teaspoon dried dill weed*
⅓ cup water	*¼ teaspoon ground black pepper*

1. Place the carrots, parsnips, turnips, and onion in a steamer basket over boiling water. Cover and steam until vegetables are tender-crisp, about 8 minutes.
2. Combine water, honey, cornstarch, lemon peel, dill weed, and black pepper in a small bowl.
3. Transfer the steamed vegetables to a saucepan, pour the sauce over the vegetables, and heat through.

Calories Per Serving: 117
Fat: 0 g
Cholesterol: 0 mg
Protein: 2 g

Carbohydrates: 29 g
Dietary Fiber: 6 g
Sodium: 58 mg

❧ *Roasted Carrots, Potatoes, and Turnips* ❧

Root vegetables (onions, carrots, potatoes, and turnips) are cooked with marjoram, rosemary, and black pepper. Fresh turnips are available year round, but at their peak from October through February.

PREPARATION TIME: 10 minutes · *COOKING TIME: 50 minutes* ·
YIELD: 6 servings

2 medium onions, coarsely chopped
4 medium carrots, coarsely chopped
2 cups coarsely chopped potatoes
4 cloves garlic, minced

2 cups coarsely chopped turnips
1 teaspoon dried marjoram
½ teaspoon dried rosemary
¼ teaspoon ground black pepper

1. Preheat oven to 400 degrees.
2. Place onions, carrots, potatoes, garlic, and turnips on a large sheet of aluminum foil and sprinkle with marjoram, rosemary, and black pepper. Fold foil tightly around the vegetables and place in the oven for 40 minutes.
3. Open the foil, and return vegetables to the oven for an additional 10 minutes.

Calories Per Serving: 133
Fat: 0 g
Cholesterol: 0 mg
Protein: 3 g

Carbohydrates: 31 g
Dietary Fiber: 5 g
Sodium: 49 mg

❧ *Simmered Carrot-Pineapple Curry* ❧

In this sweet dish carrots and pineapple are flavored with brown sugar and curry powder. Carrots are high in vitamin A.

PREPARATION TIME: 10 minutes • *COOKING TIME: 16 minutes* •
YIELD: 6 servings

2 cups juice-packed crushed canned
   pineapple, ½ cup juice reserved
1½ tablespoons brown sugar

½ teaspoon curry powder
3 cups shredded carrots

1. Combine pineapple juice, brown sugar, and curry powder in a nonstick skillet. Place over medium heat and stir until sugar is dissolved, about 1 minute.
2. Stir in pineapple and carrots. Reduce heat, cover, and simmer, stirring occasionally, for 15 minutes. Serve at once.

Calories Per Serving: 84
Fat: 0 g
Cholesterol: 0 mg
Protein: 1 g

Carbohydrates: 21 g
Dietary Fiber: 3 g
Sodium: 23 mg

❧ *Dijon Squash and Carrots* ❧

Carrots and zucchini are cooked in a honey-mustard sauce.

PREPARATION TIME: 10 minutes • *COOKING TIME: 20 minutes* •
YIELD: 4 servings

¼ cup low-sodium nonfat chicken
   broth
1½ cups thin strips carrots
1½ cups thin strips zucchini

1 teaspoon red wine vinegar
1 teaspoon honey
2 teaspoons Dijon mustard

1. Heat broth in a saucepan. Add carrots, cover, and simmer for 10 minutes. Add zucchini and continue to simmer until vegetables are almost tender, about 5 additional minutes.
2. Combine vinegar, honey, and mustard and stir into the vegetables. Simmer until liquid evaporates, about 5 minutes. Serve at once.

Calories Per Serving: 37
Fat: 0 g
Cholesterol: 0 mg
Protein: 1 g

Carbohydrates: 7 g
Dietary Fiber: 2 g
Sodium: 152 mg

❧ Succotash ❧

Red bell pepper, cumin, and hot pepper sauce add zest to this old standard.

PREPARATION TIME: 15 minutes • COOKING TIME: 16 minutes •
YIELD: 6 servings

¾ cup low-sodium nonfat chicken
   broth
1 medium red bell pepper, cored and
   diced
1 small onion, chopped
2 cloves garlic, minced
1 teaspoon ground cumin
1 cup chopped zucchini

¼ cup chopped fresh parsley
¼ teaspoon ground black pepper
⅛ teaspoon hot pepper sauce
1½ cups fresh or thawed frozen corn
   kernels
1 cup fresh or thawed frozen lima
   beans

1. Heat ¼ cup broth in a saucepan. Add bell pepper, onion, and garlic, and sauté until pepper begins to soften, about 4 minutes.

2. Add cumin, zucchini, remaining broth, parsley, black pepper, hot pepper sauce, corn, and lima beans. Bring to a boil, reduce heat, and simmer until lima beans and corn are tender, about 10 minutes. Serve immediately.

Calories Per Serving: 170
Fat: 1 g
Cholesterol: 0 mg
Protein: 10 g

Carbohydrates: 34 g
Dietary Fiber: 2 g
Sodium: 53 mg

❧ *Microwaved Curried Cauliflower and Peas* ❧

Cauliflower, tomato, onion, and green peas are baked with curry powder. Cauliflower is high in vitamin C and has some iron.

PREPARATION TIME: 10 minutes • *COOKING TIME: 6 minutes* • *YIELD: 4 servings*

4 cups chopped cauliflower
1 small tomato, coarsely chopped
½ medium onion, sliced
2 cloves garlic, minced

½ cup low-sodium nonfat chicken broth
1 teaspoon curry powder
1 cup fresh or frozen green peas

1. Place cauliflower, tomato, onion, garlic, and broth in a microwaveable dish. Sprinkle with curry powder. Toss gently, cover, and microwave on HIGH for 3 minutes.
2. Stir in green peas, cover, and microwave on HIGH until peas are just tender, about 3 additional minutes. Serve at once.

Calories Per Serving: 76
Fat: 0 g
Cholesterol: 0 mg
Protein: 5 g

Carbohydrates: 14 g
Dietary Fiber: 2 g
Sodium: 89 mg

❧ *Ginger-Cumin Cauliflower* ❧

Cauliflower is flavored with garlic, ginger, cumin, and turmeric.

PREPARATION TIME: 5 minutes • *COOKING TIME: 8 minutes* •
YIELD: 4 servings

¼ cup low-sodium nonfat chicken
  broth
1 clove garlic, minced
1 teaspoon ground ginger
1 teaspoon ground cumin

½ teaspoon ground turmeric
5 cups chopped cauliflower
½ cup water
⅛ teaspoon black pepper

1. Heat broth in a large skillet. Add garlic, ginger, cumin, and turmeric. Sauté for 1 minute.
2. Add cauliflower and water. Bring to a boil, reduce heat, cover, and simmer until cauliflower is just tender-crisp, about 7 minutes. Sprinkle with pepper and serve.

Calories Per Serving: 40
Fat: 0 g
Cholesterol: 0 mg
Protein: 3 g

Carbohydrates: 7 g
Dietary Fiber: 0
Sodium: 60 mg

❧ *Baked Corn* ❧

Corn is baked with yogurt, dill, and black pepper.

PREPARATION TIME: 15 minutes • *COOKING TIME: 25 minutes* •
YIELD: 4 servings

½ cup plain nonfat yogurt
1½ teaspoons cornstarch
1 teaspoon dried dill weed
¼ teaspoon ground black pepper

1½ cups fresh or thawed frozen corn
  kernels
1½ slices nonfat cheddar

1. Preheat oven to 375 degrees.
2. Whisk together the yogurt, cornstarch, dill, and black pepper. Stir in corn and mix well.
3. Pour into a baking dish and bake, uncovered, for 20 minutes.
4. Remove from oven and stir well. Place the cheese on top of the corn, and return dish to the oven until the cheese is melted, about 5 minutes. Serve at once.

Calories Per Serving: 101
Fat: 0 g
Cholesterol: 3 mg
Protein: 8 g

Carbohydrates: 20 g
Dietary Fiber: 2 g
Sodium: 100 mg

❧ *Grilled Corn with Lime* ❧

Corn on the cob is great at summertime barbecues. Fresh corn can be refrigerated for 1 day but is best when used the day it is purchased.

PREPARATION TIME: 10 minutes plus 30 minutes soaking time •
COOKING TIME: 20 minutes • *YIELD: 6 servings*

6 ears of corn, unshucked
2 limes, quartered

ground black pepper

1. Place the unshucked ears in a large pot and cover with cold water. Allow to soak for 30 minutes.
2. Place the unshucked, soaked corn on a hot grill. Cook, turning every 5 minutes, until corn is tender, about 20 minutes.
3. Remove from grill and allow to cool sufficiently to handle. Remove husks from corn, rub ears with lime quarters, sprinkle with black pepper, and serve at once.

Calories Per Serving: 124
Fat: 1 g
Cholesterol: 0 mg
Protein: 4 g

Carbohydrates: 31 g
Dietary Fiber: 3 g
Sodium: 6 mg

❧ Eggplant Pizza ❧

This pizza has an eggplant crust. Eggplant is available year round, but is at its peak season during August and September.

PREPARATION TIME: 10 minutes • COOKING TIME: 11 minutes •
YIELD: 6 servings

*2 medium eggplants, peeled and cut
    into ½-inch rounds
2 cloves garlic, minced
1 teaspoon dried basil*

*½ teaspoon dried oregano
1 cup low-sodium tomato sauce
1 cup nonfat cottage cheese
¾ cup grated nonfat mozzarella*

1. Preheat broiler.
2. Arrange eggplant slices on a nonstick baking dish and broil until tender, about 4 minutes per side. Remove from oven and set aside. Reduce heat to 450 degrees.
3. Mix together garlic, basil, oregano, and tomato sauce.
4. Spread tomato sauce mixture on each slice, place cottage cheese on sauce, top with grated mozzarella, and bake until cheese melts, about 3 minutes. Serve at once.

Calories Per Serving: 95
Fat: 0 g
Cholesterol: 7 mg
Protein: 13 g

Carbohydrates: 10 g
Dietary Fiber: 1 g
Sodium: 223 mg

❧ Gingered Eggplant and Potatoes ❧

This tasty stew contains eggplant, potatoes, onion, bell pepper, gingerroot, and beans flavored with parsley and cayenne.

PREPARATION TIME: 15 minutes • COOKING TIME: 45 minutes •
YIELD: 8 servings

*¼ cup low-sodium nonfat chicken
    broth
1 medium onion, chopped*

*1 medium red bell pepper, cored and
    chopped
1 tablespoon minced fresh gingerroot*

*2 medium tomatoes, chopped, with
   juice*
2 cups chopped eggplant
¼ cup minced fresh parsley
¼ teaspoon cayenne pepper

3 medium potatoes, chopped
2 cups water
*2 cups low-sodium canned Great
   Northern beans, rinsed and
   drained*

1. Heat broth in a large saucepan. Add onion, bell pepper, and gingerroot, and sauté until pepper begins to soften, about 5 minutes.
2. Add tomatoes, with their juice, and eggplant and continue to cook, stirring frequently, for 4 more minutes. Add parsley and cayenne, and cook for 1 additional minute.
3. Stir in potatoes and water, and bring to a boil. Reduce heat and simmer, stirring several times, until potatoes are tender, about 30 minutes. Add beans and simmer until heated through, about 5 minutes. Serve at once.

Calories Per Serving: 101
Fat: 0
Cholesterol: 0 mg
Protein: 6 g

Carbohydrates: 22 g
Dietary Fiber: 3 g
Sodium: 19 mg

✤ *Lemon-Garlic Kale* ✤

Kale and onion are cooked in lemon juice and garlic. Look for small bunches of rich green kale without any yellowing leaves.

*PREPARATION TIME: 15 minutes • COOKING TIME: 10 minutes •
YIELD: 4 servings*

*2 tablespoons low-sodium nonfat
   chicken broth*
1 medium onion, chopped
2 cloves garlic, minced

*6 cups chopped kale (stems removed
   and discarded)*
3 tablespoons lemon juice
½ teaspoon ground black pepper

1. Heat the broth in a large skillet. Add onion and garlic, and sauté for 2 minutes.
2. Add kale and lemon juice, reduce heat to low, and cook until kale is tender, about 8 minutes.

3. Drain excess liquid, transfer to a serving dish, sprinkle with black pepper, and serve.

Calories Per Serving: 41   Carbohydrates: 8 g
Fat: 0 g   Dietary Fiber: 3 g
Cholesterol: 0 mg   Sodium: 78 mg
Protein: 3 g

❧ *Shiitake Mushrooms with Radicchio* ❧

Shiitake mushrooms and radicchio are cooked with sun-dried tomatoes and balsamic vinegar.

PREPARATION TIME: 10 minutes plus 30 minutes soaking time ▪
COOKING TIME: 15 minutes ▪ YIELD: 4 servings

4 sun-dried tomatoes
1 cup water
¼ cup low-sodium tomato juice
2 cloves garlic, minced
½ medium onion, chopped

1 cup coarsely chopped shiitake
    mushrooms
4 cups shredded radicchio
3 tablespoons balsamic vinegar
¼ teaspoon ground black pepper

1. Soak tomatoes in water for 30 minutes. Drain and chop.
2. Heat tomato juice in a large skillet. Add garlic, onion, and sun-dried tomatoes, and sauté until onion begins to soften, about 4 minutes.
3. Add mushrooms, radicchio, and vinegar, and sauté for 8 minutes more. Remove from heat, sprinkle with black pepper, and serve.

Calories Per Serving: 124   Carbohydrates: 30 g
Fat: 0 g   Dietary Fiber: 3 g
Cholesterol: 0 mg   Sodium: 46 mg
Protein: 5 g

❧ *Jalapeño-Okra-Corn Stew* ❧

In this spicy stew, okra and corn are seasoned with onion, jalapeño pepper, tomatoes, black pepper, and cayenne pepper. Fresh okra can be refrigerated in a plastic bag for up to 3 days.

PREPARATION TIME: *15 minutes* • COOKING TIME: *24 minutes* • YIELD: *4 servings*

¼ cup low-sodium nonfat chicken broth
1 medium onion, chopped
2 cloves garlic, minced
1 jalapeño pepper, seeded and minced
2 cups low-sodium canned tomatoes, chopped, with juice reserved

1 cup okra, cut into ½-inch slices
2 cups fresh, canned (drained), or thawed frozen corn kernels
¼ teaspoon ground black pepper
⅛ teaspoon cayenne pepper

1. Heat the broth in a saucepan. Add onion and sauté until it begins to soften, about 2 minutes. Add garlic and jalapeño pepper, and sauté for another 2 minutes.
2. Stir in the tomatoes, okra, and 2 tablespoons reserved tomato juice. Cover and simmer for 15 minutes. Add corn, black pepper, and cayenne pepper. Cover and simmer for an additional 5 minutes before serving.

Calories Per Serving: 140
Fat: 1 g
Cholesterol: 0 mg
Protein: 6 g

Carbohydrates: 32 g
Dietary Fiber: 5 g
Sodium: 243 mg

❧ *Baked Onion Rings* ❧

Crunchy cornflakes and egg whites are used as a batter for these fat-free onion rings.

PREPARATION TIME: *15 minutes* • COOKING TIME: *10 minutes* • YIELD: *4 servings*

3¾ cups cornflakes

¼ teaspoon ground black pepper

3 egg whites

¼ cup skim milk

¼ cup all-purpose flour

2 medium sweet onions, cut into

½-inch-thick slices

1. Preheat oven to 400 degrees.
2. Combine cornflakes and black pepper in a blender or food processor, and blend to make fine crumbs. Transfer to a small plate.
3. Whisk together the egg whites, milk, and flour.
4. Dip the onion slices into the egg white mixture, then in the corn flake crumbs, and place on a nonstick baking sheet. Bake until browned, about 10 minutes. Serve at once.

Calories Per Serving: 170

Fat: 0 g

Cholesterol: 2 mg

Protein: 9 g

Carbohydrates: 37 g

Dietary Fiber: 3 g

Sodium: 374 mg

❧ *Parsley Mashed Potatoes* ❧

These mashed potatoes are made with buttermilk and seasoned with parsley and cayenne pepper. Store potatoes in a cool, dark, well ventilated place for up to 2 weeks. If you refrigerate them, they will become sweet and turn dark when you cook them.

PREPARATION TIME: 18 minutes • *COOKING TIME: 20 minutes* •

YIELD: 5 servings

4 cups water

4 cups diced peeled potatoes

1 cup nonfat buttermilk

¼ cup skim milk

½ cup minced fresh parsley

¼ teaspoon cayenne pepper

2 scallions, minced

1. Bring water and potatoes to a boil in a large saucepan and cook until potatoes are tender, about 20 minutes.
2. Combine the buttermilk and the skim milk in a small saucepan and warm over low heat.

3. Drain the boiled potatoes and place with the warmed milk in a blender or food processor. Add the parsley and cayenne, and blend until the desired consistency is achieved. Transfer to a serving bowl, sprinkle with scallions, and serve.

Calories Per Serving: 185
Fat: 0 g
Cholesterol: 1 mg
Protein: 6 g

Carbohydrates: 41 g
Dietary Fiber: 2 g
Sodium: 44 mg

❧ *Potato-Turnip Bake* ❧

Potatoes, sweet potatoes, and turnips are layered in a casserole, topped with buttermilk, and baked.

PREPARATION TIME: 15 minutes • *COOKING TIME: 30 minutes* •
YIELD: 6 servings

2 medium potatoes, peeled and thinly
  sliced
¼ teaspoon ground black pepper
2 medium sweet potatoes, peeled and
  thinly sliced

2 medium turnips, peeled and thinly
  sliced
½ cup nonfat buttermilk

1. Preheat oven to 375 degrees.
2. Place half the potatoes in a layer on the bottom of a casserole dish. Sprinkle with pepper. Repeat with half the sweet potatoes, then half the turnips.
3. Continue layers with the remaining potatoes and turnips.
4. Pour the buttermilk over the dish and bake until the top begins to brown, about 30 minutes. Allow to cool 5 minutes before serving.

Calories Per Serving: 104
Fat: 0 g
Cholesterol: 0 mg
Protein: 3 g

Carbohydrates: 24 g
Dietary Fiber: 3 g
Sodium: 43 mg

❧ Potatoes and Eggplant ❧

Potatoes and eggplant are cooked in a sauce made of garlic, gingerroot, cumin, coriander, and onion.

PREPARATION TIME: 15 minutes • COOKING TIME: 19 minutes •
YIELD: 8 servings

*¼ cup low-sodium nonfat chicken
    broth*
4 cloves garlic, minced
1 tablespoon minced fresh gingerroot
2 teaspoons ground cumin
1 teaspoon ground coriander

1 medium onion, sliced
4 cups coarsely chopped potatoes
*3 cups eggplant, peeled and cut into
    1-inch cubes*
½ teaspoon ground black pepper

1. Heat broth in a large saucepan. Add garlic, gingerroot, cumin, coriander, and onion. Sauté until onion just begins to soften, about 4 minutes.
2. Add potatoes and eggplant. Reduce heat, cover, and cook until potatoes and eggplant are done, about 15 minutes. Sprinkle with black pepper and serve at once.

Calories Per Serving: 146
Fat: 0 g
Cholesterol: 1 mg
Protein: 5 g

Carbohydrates: 32 g
Dietary Fiber: 2 g
Sodium: 40 mg

❧ Jalapeño Potatoes with Peas ❧

Potatoes and peas are flavored with a rich mixture of onion, jalapeño, gingerroot, cumin powder, and parsley. March through May and August through November are the peak months for fresh green peas.

PREPARATION TIME: 15 minutes • COOKING TIME: 25 minutes •
YIELD: 8 servings

6 cups water
2 pounds small red potatoes

*¼ cup low-sodium nonfat chicken
    broth*

1 medium onion, chopped
1 teaspoon minced gingerroot
1 jalapeño pepper, seeded and minced
½ teaspoon ground cumin
¼ cup chopped fresh parsley

3 medium tomatoes, chopped, with
    their juice
1 cup fresh or thawed frozen green
    peas

1. Combine water and potatoes in a large saucepan. Boil until potatoes are just tender, about 12 minutes. Remove from heat, allow to cool sufficiently to handle, and cut into bite-sized pieces.

2. Heat broth in a large skillet. Add onion, gingerroot, jalapeño, cumin, and 2 tablespoons parsley, and sauté until onion begins to soften, about 4 minutes.

3. Add tomatoes with their juice and 2 tablespoons parsley, and simmer for 5 minutes.

4. Stir in potatoes and peas, and heat through, about 4 additional minutes. Garnish with remaining parsley and serve.

Calories Per Serving: 131
Fat: 0 g
Cholesterol: 0 mg
Protein: 4 g

Carbohydrates: 30 g
Dietary Fiber: 3 g
Sodium: 80 mg

❧ *Potato Pancakes* ❧

Potato pancakes are topped with cinnamon and applesauce.

PREPARATION TIME: 15 minutes, plus 10 minutes standing time ▪
COOKING TIME: 6 minutes ▪ *YIELD: 4 servings*

4 medium baking potatoes, peeled
2 quarts boiling water
6 egg whites
2 scallions, minced

1 tablespoon chopped fresh parsley
¼ teaspoon ground black pepper
1 cup unsweetened applesauce
½ teaspoon ground cinnamon

1. Plunge potatoes into water and blanch for 2 minutes. Drain and allow to stand for 10 minutes. When cool enough to handle, grate the potatoes.

2. Mix together the grated potatoes, egg whites, scallions, parsley, and black pepper.
3. For each pancake, place ¼ cup batter onto a nonstick skillet and cook until brown, about 4 minutes on each side.
4. Combine the applesauce and cinnamon. Place a dollop on each pancake and serve.

Calories Per Serving: 314	Carbohydrates: 68 g
Fat: 0 g	Dietary Fiber: 7 g
Cholesterol: 0 mg	Sodium: 104 mg
Protein: 11 g	

❧ *Parmesan Potato Strips* ❧

These oven-baked "french fries" are tossed with Parmesan cheese.

PREPARATION TIME: 5 minutes • COOKING TIME: 25 minutes •
YIELD: 4 servings

4 medium baking potatoes, peeled   *2 tablespoons nonfat Parmesan*
¼ teaspoon ground black pepper

1. Preheat oven to 475 degrees.
2. Slice potatoes into "french fried" sticks.
3. Arrange in a single layer on a nonstick baking sheet and bake until golden, about 25 minutes.
4. Sprinkle with black pepper and Parmesan and serve.

Calories Per Serving: 123	Carbohydrates: 28 g
Fat: 0 g	Dietary Fiber: 3 g
Cholesterol: 3 mg	Sodium: 13 mg
Protein: 4 g	

Baked Sweet Potatoes

In this recipe, sweet potatoes are baked with thyme and black pepper.

PREPARATION TIME: 15 minutes • *COOKING TIME: 30 minutes* •
YIELD: 4 servings

½ cup low-sodium nonfat chicken
   broth
¼ teaspoon dried thyme

½ teaspoon ground black pepper
4 large sweet potatoes, peeled and
   diced

1. Preheat oven to 375 degrees.
2. Mix the broth, thyme, and black pepper. Place sweet potato cubes in a
   shallow casserole and cover with the broth mixture.
3. Bake the potatoes, covered, until just tender, about 30 minutes. Serve
   immediately.

Calories Per Serving: 121
Fat: 0 g
Cholesterol: 0 mg
Protein: 3 g

Carbohydrates: 28 g
Dietary Fiber: 3 g
Sodium: 53 mg

Sweet Potatoes and Lentils

The classic pairing of turmeric and cumin flavor this combination of sweet
potatoes and lentils.

PREPARATION TIME: 15 minutes • *COOKING TIME: 50 minutes* •
YIELD: 6 servings

¼ cup low-sodium nonfat chicken
   broth
1 medium onion, minced
3 cloves garlic, minced
½ teaspoon ground turmeric

½ teaspoon ground cumin
¼ teaspoon ground black pepper
1 cup dried lentils
4 cups water
2 cups diced sweet potatoes

1. Heat the broth in a saucepan. Add onion and garlic, and sauté until onion begins to soften, about 4 minutes. Stir in the turmeric, cumin, and black pepper, and continue to sauté for 1 additional minute.
2. Stir in the lentils and water. Bring to a boil, reduce heat, and simmer, stirring several times, for 15 minutes.
3. Add the sweet potatoes and continue to simmer, stirring occasionally, until lentils are tender, about 30 minutes.
4. Transfer to individual bowls and serve at once.

Calories Per Serving: 174   Carbohydrates: 38 g
Fat: 0 g   Dietary Fiber: 5 g
Cholesterol: 0 mg   Sodium: 31 mg
Protein: 5 g

🗼 ❧ *Pear–Apple–Sweet Potato Bake* ❧

Baked apples, pears, and sweet potatoes are flavored with brown sugar and cinnamon, then served with yogurt. Store sweet potatoes in a cool, dark, and dry place for up to 2 weeks.

PREPARATION TIME: 10 minutes • COOKING TIME: 1 hour, 15 minutes •
YIELD: 6 servings

4 medium apples, peeled, cored, and sliced

4 medium pears, peeled, cored, and sliced

4 medium sweet potatoes, peeled and sliced

6 tablespoons apple cider

1 tablespoon lemon juice

1 teaspoon ground cinnamon

2 tablespoons brown sugar

½ cup nonfat plain yogurt

1. Preheat oven to 350 degrees.
2. Alternate slices of apple, pear, and sweet potato in a shallow nonstick baking dish.
3. Mix the cider, lemon juice, and cinnamon. Pour the mixture over the baking dish, cover, and bake for 1 hour.
4. Sprinkle the top with brown sugar and return to the oven for 15 minutes.

5. Transfer to individual bowls, top with a tablespoon of yogurt and serve at once.

Calories Per Serving: 215
Fat: 1 g
Cholesterol: 0 mg
Protein: 2 g

Carbohydrates: 54 g
Dietary Fiber: 7 g
Sodium: 9 mg

❧ *Gingered Pumpkin and Beans* ❧

Pumpkin and kidney beans are flavored with parsley, black pepper, garlic, and gingerroot.

PREPARATION TIME: 15 minutes • COOKING TIME: 38 minutes • YIELD: 8 servings

¼ cup low-sodium nonfat chicken broth
5 cups peeled and diced pumpkin
2 medium onions, diced
3 medium tomatoes, chopped
4 cloves garlic, minced

1 tablespoon minced fresh gingerroot
2 tablespoons minced fresh parsley
½ teaspoon ground black pepper
2 cups water
3 cups low-sodium canned kidney beans, rinsed and drained

1. Heat broth in a large saucepan. Add pumpkin and onions, and sauté for 4 minutes. Add tomatoes, garlic, and gingerroot, and sauté for an additional 3 minutes.
2. Stir in parsley, black pepper, and water. Bring to a boil, reduce heat, and simmer until pumpkin is tender, about 25 minutes.
3. Add beans and simmer until beans are heated through, about 6 minutes. Serve immediately.

Calories Per Serving: 140
Fat: 1 g
Cholesterol: 0 mg
Protein: 8 g

Carbohydrates: 28 g
Dietary Fiber: 8 g
Sodium: 18 mg

❧ *Braised Spinach with Garlic* ❧

In this very simple side dish, fresh spinach is boiled with garlic. Fresh spinach is available year round.

PREPARATION TIME: 10 minutes ▪ *COOKING TIME: 3 minutes* ▪
YIELD: 4 servings

1½ cups water
6 cloves garlic, thinly sliced
8 cups chopped fresh spinach

1 tablespoon reduced-sodium soy
sauce

1. Bring water to a boil in a large saucepan. Add garlic and simmer for 1 minute.
2. Add spinach and soy sauce. Reduce heat, cover, and simmer until spinach is tender, about 2 minutes. Serve at once.

Calories Per Serving: 34
Fat: 0 g
Cholesterol: 0 mg
Protein: 4 g

Carbohydrates: 6 g
Dietary Fiber: 3 g
Sodium: 239 mg

❧ *Spicy Spinach-and-Potato Sauté* ❧

Here is a tasty stew of spinach and potatoes cooked with scallions, paprika, cayenne pepper, and hot pepper sauce.

PREPARATION TIME: 15 minutes ▪ *COOKING TIME: 20 minutes* ▪
YIELD: 6 servings

3 cups water
4 medium potatoes, diced
¼ cup low-sodium nonfat chicken
broth
1 medium onion, chopped
2 cloves garlic, minced

2 cups chopped spinach
2 scallions, chopped
1 teaspoon paprika
¼ teaspoon cayenne pepper
2 teaspoons hot pepper sauce

1. Bring water and potatoes to a boil in a saucepan. Cook until potatoes are just tender, about 12 minutes.
2. Heat broth in a large skillet. Add onion and garlic, and sauté until onion is tender, about 4 minutes. Add potatoes, spinach, scallions, paprika, cayenne pepper, and hot pepper sauce. Cook until spinach wilts, about 4 minutes. Serve hot.

Calories Per Serving: 95 Carbohydrates: 22 g
Fat: 0 g Dietary Fiber: 2 g
Cholesterol: 0 mg Sodium: 42 mg
Protein: 3 g

☙ *Spinach and Red Pepper* ❧

Spinach, red bell pepper, and onion are cooked in reduced-sodium soy sauce. Bell peppers can be stored in the refrigerator in a plastic bag for up to a week.

PREPARATION TIME: 10 minutes • *COOKING TIME: 9 minutes* •
YIELD: 6 servings

2 tablespoons low-sodium nonfat chicken broth
1 medium onion, thinly sliced
1 medium red bell pepper, cored and chopped

1 jalapeño pepper, seeded and minced
¼ cup water
1 tablespoon reduced-sodium soy sauce
5 cups chopped spinach

1. Heat broth in a large skillet. Add onion and sauté for 2 minutes. Add bell pepper and jalapeño, and sauté for 2 additional minutes.
2. Combine water and soy sauce and add to the onion-pepper mixture. Add spinach and toss to coat, cover the skillet, and cook until spinach has wilted, about 5 minutes. Serve hot.

Calories Per Serving: 40 Carbohydrates: 8 g
Fat: 0 g Dietary Fiber: 3 g
Cholesterol: 0 mg Sodium: 253 mg
Protein: 3 g

❧ *Gingered Sugar Snaps* ❧

Radishes, sugar snap peas, bell pepper, and gingerroot are served with an orange-honey sauce. Look for radishes that feel firm.

PREPARATION TIME: 15 minutes • *COOKING TIME: 7 minutes* •
YIELD: 4 servings

2 tablespoons low-sodium nonfat chicken broth
2 cups halved radishes
2 cups sugar snap peas, ends trimmed
1 medium green bell pepper, cored and cut into thin strips

1 tablespoon minced fresh gingerroot
¼ cup orange juice
1 teaspoon honey
¼ teaspoon ground black pepper

1. Heat broth in a saucepan. Add radishes and sauté for 4 minutes.
2. Add peas, bell pepper, and gingerroot. Continue to sauté until vegetables are just tender-crisp, about 3 minutes.
3. Mix orange juice, honey, and black pepper in a mixing bowl. Stir into the vegetables. Toss to coat with the sauce, transfer to individual bowls, and serve.

Calories Per Serving: 80
Fat: 0 g
Cholesterol: 0 mg
Protein: 4 g

Carbohydrates: 16 g
Dietary Fiber: 3 g
Sodium: 8 mg

❧ *Butternut Curry* ❧

Butternut squash is cooked in a tomato-curry sauce. This winter squash is available all year round but is best from early fall through the winter.

PREPARATION TIME: 15 minutes • *COOKING TIME: 38 minutes* •
YIELD: 6 servings

¼ cup low-sodium nonfat chicken broth

1 medium onion, chopped
2 cloves garlic, minced

1 jalapeño pepper, seeded and minced

3 medium tomatoes, chopped

¼ cup chopped fresh parsley

1 tablespoon curry powder

1½ teaspoons ground cumin

½ teaspoon ground black pepper

¼ teaspoon ground turmeric

2 cups water

4 cups peeled, chopped butternut
   squash

1. Heat broth in a large saucepan. Add onion, garlic, and jalapeño, and sauté until onion begins to soften, about 3 minutes. Add tomatoes, parsley, curry powder, cumin, black pepper, and turmeric. Sauté for 3 additional minutes.
2. Stir in water and squash, bring to a boil, and reduce heat. Simmer, stirring several times, until squash is tender, about 30 minutes. Serve hot.

Calories Per Serving: 83

Fat: 1 g

Cholesterol: 0 mg

Protein: 2 g

Carbohydrates: 20 g

Dietary Fiber: 4 g

Sodium: 98 mg

❧ *Couscous-Stuffed Acorn Squash* ❧

Acorn squash is stuffed with sun-dried tomatoes and couscous. Sun-dried tomatoes are rich in flavor and sold either packed in oil or dry, packed in cellophane.

PREPARATION TIME: *20 minutes plus 30 minutes tomato soaking time and 10 minutes standing time* • COOKING TIME: *40 minutes* • YIELD: *6 servings*

3 medium acorn squash

2 tablespoons low-sodium nonfat
   chicken broth

1 medium onion, chopped

4 scallions, sliced

1 cup sun-dried tomatoes, soaked in
   warm water for 30 minutes, then
   drained

2 cloves garlic, minced

1½ cups water

2 tablespoons minced fresh parsley

½ teaspoon ground black pepper

1 cup uncooked couscous

1. Preheat oven to 375 degrees.
2. Cut squash in half and remove seeds. Arrange halves cut side down in a shallow baking dish. Surround squash with water ¼ inch deep and bake for 30 minutes.
3. Remove squash from oven and allow to cool.
4. Heat broth in a saucepan. Add onion, scallions, tomatoes, and garlic and sauté until onion softens, about 5 minutes. Add water, parsley, and black pepper, and bring to a boil. Remove from heat, stir in couscous, and allow to stand, covered, for 5 minutes.
5. Scoop the flesh from the squash halves, chop coarsely, and mix into the couscous. Fill the squash halves with the couscous mixture, arrange on a serving platter, and serve.

Calories Per Serving: 347

Carbohydrates: 82 g

Fat: 1 g

Dietary Fiber: 12 g

Cholesterol: 0 mg

Sodium: 68 mg

Protein: 11 g

❧ *Pattypan Squash, Spinach, and Kidney Beans* ❧

Pattypan squash is a summer squash with pale-green skin.

PREPARATION TIME: 15 minutes · *COOKING TIME: 8 minutes* ·
YIELD: 4 servings

2 tablespoons low-sodium nonfat chicken broth
2 cups chopped pattypan squash
1 medium green bell pepper, cored and cut into strips
1 scallion, minced

2 cups chopped fresh spinach
1 cup low-sodium canned kidney beans, rinsed and drained
2 teaspoons dried basil
¼ teaspoon ground black pepper

1. Heat broth in a large saucepan. Add squash, bell pepper, and scallion, and sauté until pepper begins to soften, about 4 minutes.
2. Add spinach and beans and cook, stirring several times, for 3 additional minutes. Stir in basil and black pepper, and continue to cook for 1 more minute. Remove from heat and serve immediately.

Calories Per Serving: 88

Fat: 1 g

Cholesterol: 0 mg

Protein: 5 g

Carbohydrates: 17 g

Dietary Fiber: 5 g

Sodium: 42 g

❧ *Squash Curry* ❧

This dish contains squash, chickpeas, onions, garlic, jalapeño pepper, and gingerroot.

PREPARATION TIME: 20 minutes • *COOKING TIME: 42 minutes* •
YIELD: 10 servings

¼ cup low-sodium nonfat chicken
   broth

4 cups peeled and chopped acorn
   squash

2 medium onions, diced

2 medium tomatoes, diced, with juice

4 cloves garlic, minced

1 jalapeño pepper, seeded and minced

1 tablespoon fresh minced gingerroot

1½ tablespoons curry powder

½ teaspoon ground black pepper

3 cups water

2 cups low-sodium canned chickpeas,
   rinsed and drained

1. Heat broth in a large saucepan. Add squash and onions, and sauté for 4 minutes. Add tomatoes with their juice, garlic, jalapeño pepper, and gingerroot, and continue to sauté for 3 additional minutes. Add curry powder and black pepper. Sauté for 1 more minute.

2. Stir in water. Bring to a boil, reduce heat, and simmer for 20 minutes. Stir in chickpeas and simmer for 10 additional minutes. Serve at once.

Calories Per Serving: 83

Fat: 0 g

Cholesterol: 0 mg

Protein: 2 g

Carbohydrates: 17 g

Dietary Fiber: 3 g

Sodium: 162 mg

❧ *Butternut Squash Stuffed with Vegetables* ❧

Butternut squash is stuffed with onion, bell peppers, lima beans, corn, oregano, thyme, black pepper, and nutmeg. Squash contains vitamins A and C.

PREPARATION TIME: 20 minutes • COOKING TIME: 60 minutes •
YIELD: 8 servings

2 medium butternut squash
2 cups water
2 cups fresh or frozen lima beans
¼ cup low-sodium nonfat chicken
    broth
1 medium onion, chopped
1 medium red bell pepper, cored and
    chopped

1 medium green bell pepper, cored
    and chopped
1 jalapeño pepper, seeded and minced
4 cloves garlic, minced
2 cups fresh or frozen corn kernels
1½ teaspoons dried oregano
½ teaspoon dried thyme
½ teaspoon ground black pepper
¼ teaspoon nutmeg

1. Preheat oven to 350 degrees.
2. Halve the squash lengthwise and remove the seeds. Place ¼ inch of water in a shallow baking dish. Add the squash, cut side down, and bake until tender, about 35 minutes. Remove from oven, drain remaining water, and turn squash cut side up. Allow to cool sufficiently to handle.
3. Bring 2 cups water to boil in a saucepan. Add lima beans and cook for 10 minutes.
4. Heat broth in another saucepan. Add onion, bell peppers, jalapeño, and garlic, and sauté until peppers begin to soften, about 5 minutes. Add lima beans, corn, oregano, thyme, and black pepper. Reduce heat to low and cook, stirring several times, for 5 additional minutes.
5. Scoop out the flesh from the squash, chop, and combine with the lima bean mixture. Divide the mixture among the squash shells and place under the broiler until lightly brown, about 5 minutes. Sprinkle with nutmeg and serve.

Calories Per Serving: 156
Fat: 0 g
Cholesterol: 3 mg
Protein: 7 g

Carbohydrates: 34 g
Dietary Fiber: 7 g
Sodium: 108 mg

❧ *Stuffed Acorn Squash* ❧

Acorn squash is cooked in the microwave.

PREPARATION TIME: 10 minutes • *COOKING TIME: 7 minutes* •
YIELD: 4 servings

2 medium acorn squash
2 cups unsweetened applesauce
¼ cup raisins

¼ teaspoon ground allspice
¼ teaspoon ground cinnamon

1. Place the acorn squash in a microwave-safe dish and microwave them on HIGH for 2 minutes. Cut the squash in half and remove the seeds.
2. Mix together the applesauce, raisins, allspice, and cinnamon, and fill the squash halves with the mixture.
3. Return to the microwave and microwave on HIGH until squash is tender, about 5 minutes. Serve at once.

Calories Per Serving: 267
Fat: 1 g
Cholesterol: 0 mg
Protein: 3 g

Carbohydrates: 70 g
Dietary Fiber: 7 g
Sodium: 15 mg

❧ *Couscous-and-Vegetable-Stuffed Peppers* ❧

These super peppers are stuffed with carrot, mushrooms, onion, tomatoes, and couscous.

PREPARATION TIME: 20 minutes • *COOKING TIME: 20 minutes* •
YIELD: 4 servings

¼ cup low-sodium nonfat chicken
　broth
1 medium carrot, finely chopped
1 cup chopped mushrooms
½ cup chopped onion
2 medium tomatoes, chopped
2 cloves garlic, minced
1½ cups water

½ cup uncooked couscous
1 tablespoon balsamic vinegar
½ teaspoon dried oregano
½ teaspoon ground cumin
¼ teaspoon ground black pepper
4 medium green bell peppers, stems
　and cores removed

1. Preheat oven to 375 degrees.
2. Heat broth in a large skillet. Add carrot, mushrooms, onion, tomatoes, and garlic. Sauté until onion begins to soften, about 3 minutes.
3. Bring water to a boil. Stir in couscous, remove from heat, and allow to stand, covered, for 5 minutes.
4. Combine couscous, sautéed vegetables, vinegar, oregano, cumin, and black pepper. Mix well.
5. Stuff bell peppers with the couscous-vegetable mixture, arrange in a nonstick baking dish, and bake until peppers are tender and all ingredients are heated through, about 20 minutes. Serve hot.

Calories Per Serving: 173
Fat: 1 g
Cholesterol: 0 mg
Protein: 9 g

Carbohydrates: 34 g
Dietary Fiber: 4 g
Sodium: 101 mg

❧ *Veggie-Stuffed Potatoes* ❧

Baked potatoes are stuffed with broccoli, mushrooms, scallions, bell pepper, and yogurt. Potatoes are low in sodium and high in potassium, complex carbohydrates, and vitamins C and B_6.

PREPARATION TIME: *5 minutes* • COOKING TIME: *15 minutes* •
YIELD: *6 servings*

6 large baking potatoes
1½ cups chopped broccoli
½ cup sliced mushrooms
2 scallions, sliced
¼ cup minced green bell pepper

2 teaspoons water
½ cup nonfat plain yogurt
½ cup skim milk
1 teaspoon Dijon mustard
⅛ teaspoon ground nutmeg

1. Cook potatoes in microwave on HIGH for 5 minutes. Turn and cook for 5 more minutes. Remove potatoes from microwave.
2. Combine broccoli, mushrooms, scallions, bell pepper, and water in a microwave-safe casserole. Cover and cook on HIGH until broccoli is just tender-crisp, about 2 minutes. Drain.
3. Whisk together the yogurt, milk, mustard, and nutmeg. Pour over the broccoli mixture, cover, and cook on HIGH power, stirring every 30 seconds, until mixture thickens, about 3 minutes.
4. Split potatoes open, top with broccoli mixture, and serve at once.

Calories Per Serving: 252
Fat: 0 g
Cholesterol: 1 mg
Protein: 7 g

Carbohydrates: 56 g
Dietary Fiber: 6 g
Sodium: 68 mg

❧ Cabbage-Stuffed Tomatoes ❧

Tomatoes are stuffed with a delicious combination of cabbage, tart apples, corn kernels, bell pepper, and onion.

PREPARATION TIME: 25 minutes • YIELD: 8 servings

3 cups shredded cabbage
1 medium Granny Smith apple, peeled, cored, and finely chopped
½ cup low-sodium canned corn kernels, drained
1 medium green bell pepper, cored and finely chopped
½ cup finely chopped onion

6 tablespoons dry white wine
2 tablespoons sugar
¼ cup nonfat plain yogurt
½ teaspoon celery seeds
½ teaspoon dry mustard
¼ teaspoon ground white pepper
8 large fresh tomatoes, cored
¼ cup chopped fresh parsley

1. Combine cabbage, apple, corn, bell pepper, and onion. Toss gently.
2. Mix together wine, sugar, yogurt, celery seeds, mustard, and white pepper. Add dressing to the cabbage mixture and toss to coat all ingredients.
3. Stuff the tomatoes with the cabbage mixture. Sprinkle with parsley and serve.

Calories Per Serving: 80

Carbohydrates: 18 g

Fat: 1 g

Dietary Fiber: 3 g

Cholesterol: 0 mg

Sodium: 23 mg

Protein: 3 g

ꙮ *Sun-Dried Tomatoes with Beans* ꙮ

Green beans are sautéed with sun-dried tomatoes and garlic.

PREPARATION TIME: 15 minutes plus 30 minutes soaking time •
COOKING TIME: 6 minutes • *YIELD: 6 servings*

6 sun-dried tomatoes

4 cloves garlic, minced

2 cups water

2 tablespoons nonfat bread crumbs

1½ pounds green beans, ends removed

2 tablespoons nonfat Parmesan

¼ teaspoon ground black pepper

¼ cup low-sodium tomato juice

1. Cover tomatoes with water and soak for 30 minutes. Drain and chop.
2. Place beans in the steamer basket over 3 cups boiling water, cover, and steam for 3 minutes.
3. Heat tomato juice in a large skillet. Add garlic and chopped tomatoes, and sauté for 3 minutes.
4. Add beans, bread crumbs, Parmesan, and black pepper. Toss well and serve.

Calories Per Serving: 149

Carbohydrates: 33 g

Fat: 1 g

Dietary Fiber: 4 g

Cholesterol: 1 mg

Sodium: 175 mg

Protein: 8 g

❧ *Red Peppers with Corn Stuffing* ❧

These peppers are stuffed with corn and tomatoes and topped with nonfat mozzarella cheese.

PREPARATION TIME: *20 minutes* • COOKING TIME: *36 minutes* •
YIELD: *6 servings*

¼ cup low-sodium nonfat chicken broth
¼ cup minced onion
¼ cup minced celery
1 cup fresh or thawed frozen corn kernels
1 cup fresh or thawed frozen green peas

2 medium tomatoes, chopped
¼ teaspoon ground black pepper
1 cup nonfat bread crumbs
4 egg whites
6 medium red bell peppers, cored and stems and tops removed
¼ cup nonfat mozzarella
½ teaspoon paprika

1. Preheat oven to 350 degrees.
2. Heat broth in a saucepan. Add onion and celery, and sauté until onion begins to soften, about 3 minutes. Stir in corn, green peas, tomatoes, black pepper, and bread crumbs, and remove from heat.
3. Stir egg whites into the vegetable mixture and mix well. Stuff the peppers with the vegetables. Place in a shallow baking dish with ½ inch of water and bake for 30 minutes. Top each pepper with mozzarella cheese and continue to bake until cheese is melted, about 3 minutes.
4. Remove from oven, sprinkle with paprika, and serve at once.

Calories Per Serving: 118
Fat: 1 g
Cholesterol: 1 mg
Protein: 7 g

Carbohydrates: 23 g
Dietary Fiber: 3 g
Sodium: 150 mg

❧ *Chili-Vegetable Tacos* ❧

These tacos contain gingerroot, carrot, potato, and peas cooked with chili powder.

PREPARATION TIME: 15 minutes • COOKING TIME: 16 minutes •
YIELD: 4 servings

2 tablespoons low-sodium nonfat
　chicken broth
2 cloves garlic, minced
2 teaspoons minced fresh gingerroot
2 teaspoons chili powder
¾ cup water
1 small potato, sliced

1 medium carrot, scraped and sliced
　diagonally into ½-inch slices
1 cup chopped cauliflower
1 medium red bell pepper, cored and
　diced
¼ cup frozen green peas
4 medium or large corn tortillas,
　warmed

1. Heat broth in a saucepan. Add garlic and gingerroot, and sauté for 1 minute. Add chili powder, water, potato, and carrot. Bring to a boil, reduce heat, cover, and simmer for 5 minutes.
2. Stir in cauliflower, bell pepper, and peas, and continue to simmer until peas and potatoes are tender, about 5 minutes.
3. Divide the vegetables among the tortillas and fold over and serve.

Calories Per Serving: 140
Fat: 1 g
Cholesterol: 0 mg
Protein: 4 g

Carbohydrates: 30 g
Dietary Fiber: 2 g
Sodium: 68 mg

❧ *Shiitake-Tomatillo Tacos* ❧

Tomatillos are widely used in Mexico and the Southwest. They are available in many supermarkets.

PREPARATION TIME: 20 minutes • COOKING TIME: 11 minutes •
YIELD: 4 servings

¾ *cup low-sodium nonfat chicken broth*
½ *pound shiitake mushrooms, minced*
2 *medium onions, minced*
2 *cloves garlic, minced*
2 *jalapeño peppers, seeded and minced*

1 *teaspoon dried cilantro*
¼ *teaspoon ground cumin*
12 *fresh tomatillos, husked and finely chopped*
4 *medium or large corn tortillas, warmed to soften*
¼ *teaspoon ground black pepper*

1. Heat ¼ cup broth in a large skillet. Add shiitakes and sauté for 3 minutes. Add onions, garlic, and jalapeño peppers, and continue to sauté until onions begin to soften, about 2 minutes.
2. Stir in remaining broth, cilantro, cumin, and tomatillos. Bring to a boil, reduce heat, cover, and simmer until tomatillos are just soft, about 6 minutes.
3. Place tortillas on individual plates. Top with the tomatillos, sprinkle with black pepper, fold, and serve.

Calories Per Serving: 110
Fat: 1 g
Cholesterol: 0 mg
Protein: 4 g

Carbohydrates: 22 g
Dietary Fiber: 8 g
Sodium: 287 mg

❧ *Red Pepper–Corn Tortillas* ❧

An onion–red pepper–corn filling is topped with prepared salsa.

PREPARATION TIME: 15 minutes • *COOKING TIME: 10 minutes* •
YIELD: 4 servings

¼ *cup chopped onion*
½ *cup chopped red bell pepper*
¼ *cup fresh or thawed frozen corn kernels*

¼ *teaspoon ground black pepper*
2 *tablespoons nonfat prepared salsa*
4 *medium or large corn tortillas, warmed to soften*

1. Preheat oven to 400 degrees.
2. Combine onion, bell pepper, corn, and black pepper. Toss together.

3. Place ¼ cup vegetables and 1 teaspoon salsa on each tortilla and roll up.

4. Arrange the tortillas on a nonstick baking sheet and bake until heated through, about 10 minutes. Serve warm.

Calories Per Serving: 78   Carbohydrates: 17 g
Fat: 1 g   Dietary Fiber: 3 g
Cholesterol: 0 mg   Sodium: 81 mg
Protein: 3 g

❧ *Roasted Vegetable Medley* ❧

Zucchini, bell peppers, mushrooms, onion, and celery are roasted with Worcestershire sauce, vinegar, tarragon, and lemon peel. Serve as an entree, side dish, or as a filling for pitas.

PREPARATION TIME: 10 minutes • *COOKING TIME: 15 minutes* •
YIELD: 4 servings

2 cups chopped zucchini   *1 medium onion, chopped*
1 medium red bell pepper, cored and *2 stalks celery, sliced*
  chopped   *1 tablespoon Worcestershire sauce*
1 medium green bell pepper, cored   *1 tablespoon rice wine vinegar*
  and chopped   *¾ teaspoon dried tarragon*
3 cups quartered mushrooms   *1 tablespoon minced lemon peel*

1. Preheat oven to 400 degrees.

2. Place zucchini, bell peppers, mushrooms, onion, and celery on a sheet of aluminum foil and sprinkle with Worcestershire sauce, vinegar, tarragon, and lemon peel. Fold the foil tightly around the vegetables and bake for 15 minutes. Serve hot.

Calories Per Serving: 56   Carbohydrates: 12 g
Fat: 0 g   Dietary Fiber: 3 g
Cholesterol: 0 mg   Sodium: 114 mg
Protein: 4 g

❧ *Thyme-Roasted Vegetables* ❧

Sweet potatoes, turnips, parsnips, and potato are baked with thyme. Thyme is a member of the mint family, and in its dried form is available year round.

PREPARATION TIME: 20 minutes • *COOKING TIME: 1 hour* •
YIELD: 6 servings

2 cups chopped sweet potato
2 cups chopped turnip
2 cups chopped parsnip
2 cups chopped potato

8 garlic cloves, peeled and left whole
1 tablespoon dried thyme
½ teaspoon ground black pepper
¼ cup fresh chopped parsley

1. Preheat oven to 375 degrees.
2. Combine all the ingredients except the parsley in a large heatproof casserole.
3. Bake, stirring occasionally, until vegetables are tender-crisp, about 1 hour.
4. Remove from oven and allow to cool slightly. Transfer to a serving platter, garnish with parsley, and serve.

Calories Per Serving: 212
Fat: 1 g
Cholesterol: 0 mg
Protein: 4 g

Carbohydrates: 49 g
Dietary Fiber: 6 g
Sodium: 47 mg

❧ *Grilled Vegetables* ❧

Zucchini, tomatoes, bell pepper, mushrooms, and cauliflower are marinated with herbs and soy sauce and grilled in this tasty summertime snack.

PREPARATION TIME: 20 minutes plus 3 hours marinating time •
COOKING TIME: 8 minutes • *YIELD: 4 servings*

1 medium zucchini, thickly sliced

2 tomatoes, quartered

1 red bell pepper, cored and coarsely
   chopped

2 cups halved mushrooms

2 cups cauliflower florets

6 scallions, thinly sliced

1 medium onion, finely chopped

1 jalapeño pepper, seeded and minced

¼ cup reduced-sodium soy sauce

½ cup vinegar

¼ cup brown sugar

½ cup water

½ teaspoon ground cloves

1. Alternate the pieces of zucchini, tomatoes, bell pepper, mushrooms, and cauliflower on 4 skewers. Arrange the skewers in a single layer in a large shallow dish.
2. Place the scallions, onion, jalapeño, soy sauce, vinegar, brown sugar, water, and cloves in a food processor or blender. Process for 15 seconds.
3. Pour the marinade over the skewered vegetables, cover, and place in the refrigerator for 3 hours.
4. Cook the vegetables over a barbecue grill or under a broiler until the vegetables are tender-crisp, about 4 minutes on each side. Serve at once.

Calories Per Serving: 131
Fat: 1 g
Cholesterol: 0 mg
Protein: 5 g

Carbohydrates: 31 g
Dietary Fiber: 4 g
Sodium: 661 mg

❧ Green Bean Stew ❧

Potatoes and green beans are cooked with onion, garlic, jalapeño, tomatoes, and lemon juice.

PREPARATION TIME: 15 minutes · COOKING TIME: 25 minutes ·
YIELD: 6 servings

2 cups water

3 potatoes, diced

2 cups green beans, cut into 1-inch
   lengths

3 tablespoons low-sodium nonfat
   chicken broth

1 medium onion, chopped

2 cloves garlic, minced

1 jalapeño pepper, seeded and minced
½ teaspoon ground turmeric
½ teaspoon ground cumin

2 cups low-sodium canned tomatoes, drained
1 teaspoon lemon juice

1. Bring water and potatoes to a boil in a saucepan and cook until potatoes are just tender, about 12 minutes. Add beans and continue to cook for 3 additional minutes.
2. Heat broth in a large skillet. Add onion, garlic, and jalapeño, and sauté for 3 minutes. Add turmeric and cumin, and sauté for 1 additional minute.
3. Add potatoes and beans, tomatoes, and lemon juice, and simmer, stirring several times, for 6 minutes.
4. Transfer to individual bowls and serve.

Calories Per Serving: 102
Fat: 0 g
Cholesterol: 0 mg
Protein: 4 g

Carbohydrates: 24 g
Dietary Fiber: 3 g
Sodium: 110 mg

❧ *Eggplant Stew* ❧

In this spicy, hearty dish, eggplant is cooked with cayenne, gingerroot, tomatoes, rice, chickpeas, raisins, and lemon juice. Look for a firm eggplant that is heavy for its size and has smooth skin and no soft or brown spots.

PREPARATION TIME: 15 minutes ▪ *COOKING TIME: 20 minutes* ▪
YIELD: 8 servings

2 medium eggplants, halved lengthwise
1 cup low-sodium nonfat chicken broth
1 medium onion, chopped
2 cloves garlic, minced
¼ teaspoon cayenne pepper
½ teaspoon fresh minced gingerroot

3 tomatoes, chopped
1 cup cooked white rice
2 cups low-sodium canned chickpeas, rinsed and drained
½ cup raisins
¼ cup lemon juice
¼ cup fresh chopped parsley
½ teaspoon ground black pepper

1. Preheat broiler.
2. Place the eggplant halves cut side down in a nonstick baking dish and broil until tender, about 8 minutes. Remove from heat and set aside.
3. Heat ¼ cup broth in a large saucepan. Add onion and garlic, and sauté for 3 minutes. Add cayenne, gingerroot, and tomatoes, and sauté until liquid is absorbed, about 4 minutes.
4. Chop eggplant and add to the vegetable mixture. Add remaining broth, rice, chickpeas, raisins, and lemon juice, and simmer, stirring several times, until all ingredients are heated through, about 5 minutes.
5. Transfer to a large serving bowl. Garnish with parsley, sprinkle with black pepper, and serve.

Calories Per Serving: 179

Fat: 0 g

Cholesterol: 0 mg

Protein: 7 g

Carbohydrates: 38 g

Dietary Fiber: 1 g

Sodium: 230 mg

❧ *Spiced Eggplant Ratatouille* ❧

In this version of ratatouille, summer squash and spinach join the classic eggplant and tomatoes. Ratatouille can be served as a side dish, appetizer, or entree.

PREPARATION TIME: 20 minutes • COOKING TIME: 20 minutes •
YIELD: 10 servings

¼ cup low-sodium nonfat chicken
 broth

1 medium onion, thinly sliced

2 cloves garlic, minced

1 medium red bell pepper, cored and
 diced

2 cups diced eggplant

2 cups chopped yellow summer
 squash

4 medium tomatoes, diced, with juice

1 tablespoon dried basil

1 tablespoon dried oregano

¼ teaspoon cayenne pepper

2 cups chopped fresh spinach

1. Heat broth in a large saucepan. Add onion and garlic, and sauté until onion softens, about 4 minutes.

2. Add bell pepper, eggplant, squash, tomatoes with their juice, basil, oregano, and cayenne pepper. Simmer, stirring frequently, for 12 minutes.

3. Stir in spinach and continue to cook until all ingredients are heated through, about 4 minutes. Serve at once.

Calories Per Serving: 25   Carbohydrates: 5 g
Fat: 0 g   Dietary Fiber: 1 g
Cholesterol: 1 mg   Sodium: 16 mg
Protein: 1 g

❦ *Parsnip-Squash Stew* ❦

A parsnip is a creamy-white root with a sweet flavor and is available year round, but at its peak period in the fall and winter.

PREPARATION TIME: 20 minutes plus 10 minutes standing time ▪
COOKING TIME: 38 minutes ▪ *YIELD: 6 servings*

¼ cup low-sodium tomato juice   *1 tablespoon paprika*
1 medium onion, chopped   *1 tablespoon dried oregano*
1 medium red bell pepper, cored and   *½ teaspoon ground black pepper*
  chopped   *2 cups water*
2 cloves garlic, minced   *2 cups chopped parsnips*
1 medium tomato, chopped, with   *2 cups peeled, chopped Hubbard*
  juice   *squash*

1. Heat ¼ cup tomato juice in a large saucepan. Add onion, bell pepper, and garlic, and sauté until onion begins to soften, about 4 minutes.

2. Add tomato with juice, paprika, oregano, and black pepper, and sauté for an additional 4 minutes.

3. Add water, parsnips, and squash. Bring to a boil, reduce heat, and simmer, stirring several times, until parsnips and squash are just tender, about 30 minutes. Serve hot.

Calories Per Serving: 58
Fat: 0 g
Cholesterol: 0 mg
Protein: 3 g

Carbohydrates: 12 g
Dietary Fiber: 2 g
Sodium: 36 mg

❧ *Pumpkin Stew* ❧

This spicy rice stew is flavored with garlic, jalapeño, and paprika. Pumpkin is a good source of vitamin A.

PREPARATION TIME: 20 minutes • *COOKING TIME: 34 minutes* •
YIELD: 10 servings

¼ cup low-sodium nonfat chicken
   broth
1 medium onion, chopped
3 cloves garlic, minced
1 jalapeño pepper, seeded and minced
3 medium tomatoes, chopped
¼ cup fresh minced parsley
1 tablespoon paprika

1 tablespoon dried oregano
½ teaspoon ground black pepper
4 cups chopped fresh pumpkin
3 cups water
2 cups fresh or thawed frozen corn
   kernels
4 cups cooked white rice

1. Heat broth in a large saucepan. Add onion, garlic, and jalapeño, and sauté until onion begins to soften, about 4 minutes.
2. Add tomatoes, parsley, paprika, oregano, and black pepper, and simmer, stirring occasionally, until mixture begins to thicken, about 5 minutes.
3. Stir in pumpkin, water, and corn. Bring to a boil, reduce heat, and simmer, stirring several times, until pumpkin is tender, about 25 minutes.
4. To achieve a thicker stew, mash the pumpkin against the side of the pan. Stir well and serve over rice.

Calories Per Serving: 156
Fat: 1 g
Cholesterol: 0 mg
Protein: 4 g

Carbohydrates: 35 g
Dietary Fiber: 2 g
Sodium: 46 mg

❧ *Early Spring Vegetable Stew* ❧

PREPARATION TIME: *15 minutes* • COOKING TIME: *10 minutes* •
YIELD: *4 servings*

½ *cup low-sodium nonfat chicken
 broth*
2 *cups diced potatoes*
4 *scallions, chopped*
3 *medium carrots, scraped and cut
 into ¼-inch slices*

1 *cup sugar snap peas*
1 *cup sliced mushrooms*
1 *cup fresh green peas*
1 *teaspoon dried mint*
1 *teaspoon lemon juice*

1. Combine broth, potatoes, scallions, and carrots in a saucepan. Bring to
   a boil. Reduce heat, cover, and simmer for 5 minutes.
2. Add snap peas, mushrooms, green peas, mint, and lemon juice. Return
   to a boil, reduce heat, cover, and simmer until vegetables are just tender,
   about 5 minutes. Serve at once.

Calories Per Serving: 202
Fat: 1 g
Cholesterol: 0 mg
Protein: 7 g

Carbohydrates: 44 g
Dietary Fiber: 6 g
Sodium: 105 mg

❧ *Apple–Green Bean Curry* ❧

Ten spices are combined in this multiflavored curry.

PREPARATION TIME: *25 minutes* • COOKING TIME: *48 minutes* •
YIELD: *10 servings*

¼ cup low-sodium nonfat chicken
  broth
3 cups coarsely chopped onions
2 cloves garlic, minced
1 teaspoon minced fresh gingerroot
1½ tablespoons ground cumin
1½ tablespoons ground coriander
1½ teaspoons ground cinnamon
1 teaspoon turmeric
½ teaspoon cayenne pepper
½ teaspoon ground fennel seeds
¼ teaspoon ground cardamom
¼ teaspoon ground cloves
4 cups chopped zucchini

5½ cups water
1 cup green beans
2 medium tart apples, cored and
  chopped
1 medium yellow bell pepper, cored
  and chopped
1 medium red bell pepper, cored and
  chopped
1 cup chopped dried apricots
2 cups uncooked couscous
½ cup raisins
½ cup sugarless all-fruit strawberry
  jam
3 tablespoons lemon juice

1. Heat the broth in a large saucepan. Add the onions and garlic, and sauté until onions begin to soften, about 3 minutes. Stir in the gingerroot, cumin, coriander, cinnamon, turmeric, cayenne, fennel, cardamom, and cloves. Continue to sauté for 3 additional minutes.

2. Add the zucchini and 1½ cups water. Stir well, cover, and simmer for 10 minutes. Stir in the green beans, apples, bell peppers, and apricots. Continue to simmer, stirring frequently, until vegetables are just tender, about 25 minutes. Add water as necessary.

3. Bring remaining 4 cups of water to a boil in a saucepan. Stir in couscous, remove from heat, and allow to stand for 5 minutes.

4. Stir raisins, jam, and lemon juice into the vegetable mixture and continue to simmer until all ingredients are heated through, about 2 minutes.

5. Serve the vegetables over the couscous.

Calories Per Serving: 316
Fat: 1 g
Cholesterol: 0 mg
Protein: 9 g

Carbohydrates: 70 g
Dietary Fiber: 6 g
Sodium: 24 mg

❧ *Potato-Tomato Casserole* ❧

Potatoes and tomatoes are combined with parsley, basil, garlic, and onion.

PREPARATION TIME: 20 minutes • *COOKING TIME: 40 minutes* •
YIELD: 6 servings

3 tablespoons minced fresh parsley
¼ teaspoon dried basil
1 clove garlic, minced
3 medium potatoes, cut into ¼-inch slices

1 medium onion, thinly sliced
3 medium tomatoes, peeled and sliced
¼ cup shredded nonfat cheddar

1. Preheat oven to 375 degrees.
2. Combine the parsley, basil, and garlic, and mix well.
3. Place half the potatoes in the bottom of the casserole. Sprinkle with half the parsley mixture. Add half the onion, then half the tomatoes. Repeat the layers.
4. Loosely cover the casserole with foil and bake for 35 minutes. Sprinkle cheese on top of the casserole, re-cover, and continue to bake until the cheese is melted, about 5 minutes. Serve hot.

Calories Per Serving: 102
Fat: 0 g
Cholesterol: 0 mg
Protein: 4 g

Carbohydrates: 22 g
Dietary Fiber: 3 g
Sodium: 47 mg

❧ *Vegetables with Fennel* ❧

Zucchini, yellow squash, pinto beans, corn, green and red bell peppers, and onion are seasoned with fennel seeds and cayenne. Fennel has a sweet, aniselike flavor.

PREPARATION TIME: 20 minutes • *COOKING TIME: 19 minutes* •
YIELD: 12 servings

1½ cups low-sodium nonfat chicken broth

1 medium onion, chopped

1 medium green bell pepper, cored and cut into thin strips

1 medium red bell pepper, cored and cut into thin strips

2 cloves garlic, minced

½ teaspoon fennel seeds

⅛ teaspoon cayenne pepper

2 medium potatoes, chopped

1 medium sweet potato, chopped

2 cups green beans, cut into 1-inch lengths

1 cup water

1 medium zucchini, chopped

1 medium yellow squash, chopped

1 cup low-sodium canned pinto beans, rinsed and drained

1 cup fresh or thawed frozen corn kernels

2 tablespoons lime juice

½ cup chopped fresh parsley

1. Heat ¼ cup broth in a large saucepan. Add onion, bell peppers, and garlic, and sauté for 3 minutes.
2. Stir in remaining broth, fennel seeds, cayenne pepper, potatoes, and sweet potato. Cover and simmer for 7 minutes. Add green beans and simmer for 5 additional minutes.
3. Add water, zucchini, yellow squash, pinto beans, corn, and lime juice. Bring to a boil, reduce heat, and simmer until squash is just tender, about 4 minutes.
4. Transfer to a serving bowl, garnish with parsley, and serve.

Calories Per Serving: 124

Fat: 0 g

Cholesterol: 0 mg

Protein: 5 g

Carbohydrates: 27 g

Dietary Fiber: 3 g

Sodium: 97 mg

❧ Mixed Curried Vegetables ❧

This version of vegetable curry includes chickpeas, raisins, and yogurt, and is served with rice.

PREPARATION TIME: 20 minutes • *COOKING TIME: 32 minutes* •
YIELD: 12 servings

1 cup low-sodium nonfat chicken
   broth
1 medium onion, chopped
2 stalks celery, chopped
1 medium red bell pepper, cored and
   chopped
2 teaspoons turmeric
1 tablespoon curry powder
2 cups canned low-sodium tomatoes,
   chopped, with their juice
2 medium carrots, chopped

1 medium potato, diced
2 cups chopped cauliflower
2 cups chopped broccoli
1 cup chopped yellow summer squash
1 cup sliced mushrooms
One 16-ounce can low-sodium chickpeas
½ cup raisins
1 cup nonfat plain yogurt
6 cups cooked white rice

1. Heat ¼ cup broth in a large saucepan. Add onion, celery, and red bell pepper, and sauté until pepper begins to soften, about 7 minutes.
2. Add remaining broth, turmeric, curry powder, tomatoes with their juice, carrots, and potato. Bring to a boil, reduce heat, and simmer until carrots are just tender-crisp, about 15 minutes.
3. Stir in cauliflower and broccoli and simmer for an additional 5 minutes. Add squash, mushrooms, chickpeas, and raisins, and simmer for 5 minutes more.
4. Stir in yogurt. Divide rice among individual plates, top with vegetables, and serve at once.

Calories Per Serving: 216
Fat: 1 g
Cholesterol: 0 mg
Protein: 7 g

Carbohydrates: 46 g
Dietary Fiber: 2 g
Sodium: 120 mg

❧ *Summer Squash Paella* ❧

This Spanish-inspired rice dish contains carrots, peas, corn, leeks, squash, and asparagus. Asparagus can be stored tightly wrapped in a plastic bag for 3 days in the refrigerator.

PREPARATION TIME: 20 minutes plus 10 minutes standing time ▪
COOKING TIME: 55 minutes ▪ *YIELD: 8 servings*

¼ cup low-sodium nonfat chicken
  broth
2 cups sliced leeks
2 cups chopped yellow summer
  squash
4 cloves garlic, minced
4 cups water
1½ cups uncooked white rice
½ cup uncooked wild rice

2 medium carrots, scraped and
  chopped
1 cup fresh or frozen green peas
2 cups fresh or frozen corn kernels
¼ cup minced fresh parsley
2 teaspoons dried thyme
½ teaspoon turmeric
½ teaspoon ground black pepper
16 asparagus spears

1. Preheat oven to 375 degrees.
2. Heat broth in a large Dutch oven. Add leeks, squash, and garlic, and sauté for 5 minutes.
3. Stir in water, white rice, wild rice, carrots, peas, corn, parsley, thyme, turmeric, and black pepper. Cover and bake for 45 minutes.
4. Remove from oven. Toss rice, arrange the asparagus in a circle on the rice, and cover. Bake for an additional 5 minutes. Serve at once.

Calories Per Serving: 251
Fat: 1 g
Cholesterol: 0 mg
Protein: 8 g

Carbohydrates: 55 g
Dietary Fiber: 4 g
Sodium: 27 mg

✑ *Ethiopian Stew* ✑

A hearty, nonfat "meal in a bowl," which includes onions, carrots, potatoes, and cabbage.

PREPARATION TIME: *20 minutes* ▪ COOKING TIME: *34 minutes* ▪
YIELD: *8 servings*

¼ cup low-sodium nonfat chicken
  broth
3 medium onions, chopped
4 cloves garlic, minced

½ teaspoon ground ginger
½ teaspoon turmeric
½ teaspoon ground black pepper
4 cups water

3 medium carrots, scraped and chopped
1 turnip, peeled and diced

3 medium potatoes, peeled and chopped
3 cups shredded cabbage

1. Heat broth in a large saucepan. Add onions and garlic, and sauté until onions begin to soften, about 3 minutes. Add ginger, turmeric, and black pepper, and sauté for 1 additional minute.
2. Add water, carrots, turnip, potatoes, and cabbage and bring to a boil. Reduce heat and simmer until carrots are just tender, about 30 minutes.
3. Transfer to individual bowls and serve at once.

Calories Per Serving: 85
Fat: 0 g
Cholesterol: 0 mg
Protein: 2 g

Carbohydrates: 19 g
Dietary Fiber: 3 g
Sodium: 30 mg

SOUPS

❧

Asparagus-Spinach Soup ▪ Sherried Broccoli Bisque ▪
Broccoli-Potato Soup ▪ Broccoli–Sweet Potato Soup ▪
Cabbage-Rice Soup ▪ Cabbage-Squash Soup ▪ Tarragon-
Celery-Broccoli Soup ▪ Carrot-Cauliflower Soup with
Dill ▪ Carrot-Turnip Soup ▪ Cream of Carrot Soup ▪
Sherried Corn-Vegetable Soup ▪ Curried Corn-Potato Soup ▪
Dijon-Corn Soup ▪ Corn and Zucchini Soup ▪ Eggplant
Soup ▪ Tarragon-Pea Soup ▪ Lima Bean–Corn–Potato Soup ▪
Mushroom-Barley Soup ▪ Mushroom-Spinach Soup ▪ Orange
Juice Soup ▪ Gingered Potato Soup ▪ Potato-Leek Soup ▪
Portuguese Potato-Kale Soup ▪ Sweet Potato Soup ▪ Curried
Pumpkin Soup ▪ Pumpkin-Corn Soup ▪ Acorn Squash Soup
with Spinach ▪ Jalapeño-Butternut Soup ▪ Butternut-Garlic
Soup ▪ Hubbard Squash Soup ▪ Winter Squash Soup ▪
Apple-Squash Soup ▪ Squash-Pepper Soup ▪ Yellow Summer
Squash Soup ▪ Basic Tomato Soup ▪ Sun-Dried Tomato–Leek
Soup ▪ Fresh Tomato–Couscous Soup ▪ Tomato-Corn-Chile
Soup ▪ Tomato-Squash Soup ▪ Turnip-Parsnip Soup ▪ Turnip
Soup with Roasted Garlic ▪ Creamy Dijon-Zucchini Soup ▪

Zucchini Soup with White Wine • Barley Soup • Chilled
Borscht • Hot Vegetable Borscht • November Soup • Winter
Vegetable Soup • Garlic-Veggie Soup • Spiced Vegetable–
Chickpea Soup • Garden Variety Soup • Mulligatawny Soup •
Tomato-Vegetable Soup • Vegetable-Rice Soup • Mango-
Papaya Soup • Melon-Berry Gazpacho • Two-Melon Soup •
Cold Carrot Soup with Thyme • Chilled Carrot-Leek Soup
• Chilled Cucumber Soup • Chilled Red Pepper Soup •
Chilled Vegetable-Couscous Soup • Chilled Black Bean Soup •
Chilled Black Bean–Corn Soup • Gazpacho with White Beans
• Split Pea Soup with Brown Rice • Yellow Split Pea Soup •
Artichoke-Bean Soup • Butternut-Bean Soup • White Bean
and Spinach Soup • Sweet Potato–Bean Soup • Okra–
Spinach–Pinto Bean Gumbo • Pinto Bean–Winter Vegetable
Soup • Great Northern Bean–Vegetable Soup • Pinto
Bean and Zucchini Soup • Lentil Soup with Acorn Squash •
Succotash–Black-eyed Pea Soup • Lentil-Barley Soup with
Turnips • Shiitake-Lentil Soup • Lentil-Rice Soup • Spinach-
Lentil Soup • Harira • Black-eyed Pea Soup • Black-eyed
Pea–Cabbage Soup • Bean-Barley Soup • Three-Bean Gumbo
• Spiced Vegetable Gumbo

❧ *Asparagus-Spinach Soup* ❧

Although this soup can be served anytime, it's especially delicious when fresh asparagus and spinach leaves are first available in the early spring.

PREPARATION TIME: *25 minutes* • COOKING TIME: *36 minutes* •
YIELD: *6 servings*

4½ cups low-sodium nonfat chicken
  broth
⅔ cup chopped onion
⅓ cup chopped scallion

3½ cups chopped asparagus
1 cup chopped spinach leaves
½ teaspoon dried tarragon
¼ teaspoon ground black pepper

1. Heat ¼ cup broth in a heavy pot over medium heat. Add onion and scallion, and sauté for 5 minutes.
2. Stir in the asparagus and sauté for 1 additional minute.
3. Add the remaining broth and bring to a boil. Reduce heat, cover, and simmer for 25 minutes.
4. Place asparagus mixture, spinach, tarragon, and black pepper in a blender or food processor. Blend until smooth. Return to the pot and reheat over low heat for 5 minutes.
5. Transfer to individual bowls and serve.

Calories Per Serving: 55
Fat: 0 g
Cholesterol: 0 mg
Protein: 7 g

Carbohydrates: 8 g
Dietary Fiber: 1 g
Sodium: 125 mg

❧ *Sherried Broccoli Bisque* ❧

This thick, rich soup is flavored with onion, garlic, sherry, parsley, and nutmeg. Medium-size round white potatoes are best suited for boiling.

PREPARATION TIME: *20 minutes* • COOKING TIME: *40 minutes* •
YIELD: *12 servings*

2 tablespoons low-sodium nonfat
 chicken broth
2 small onions, diced
1 cup sliced celery
3 cloves garlic, crushed
6 cups peeled and chopped broccoli
 stems

8 cups water
3 cups diced white potatoes
½ cup sherry
¼ cup fresh parsley, chopped
1 teaspoon dried thyme
½ teaspoon ground black pepper
2 cups skim milk

1. Heat broth in a large saucepan. Add onions, celery, garlic, and 1 cup chopped broccoli stems. Sauté for 5 minutes. Add water, potatoes, sherry, parsley, thyme, and black pepper. Bring to a boil, reduce heat, and simmer, stirring several times, for 25 minutes.
2. Add remaining broccoli. Stir in milk and simmer for an additional 10 minutes.
3. Place mixture in a food processor or a blender and process for 10 seconds.
4. Transfer to individual bowls and serve.

Calories Per Serving: 102
Fat: 0 g
Cholesterol: 1 mg
Protein: 5 g

Carbohydrates: 19 g
Dietary Fiber: 3 g
Sodium: 61 mg

NH ☑ ✓

❧ *Broccoli-Potato Soup* ❧

This broccoli–potato soup is flavored with garlic and curry powder. Look for deep green broccoli tinged with purple.

PREPARATION TIME: 15 minutes ▪ *COOKING TIME: 25 minutes* ▪
YIELD: 6 servings

6 cups low-sodium nonfat chicken
 broth
4 cups chopped broccoli, florets and
 stems

2 large potatoes, chopped
2 cloves garlic, minced
1 teaspoon curry powder

1. Bring broth to a boil in a large saucepan. Add broccoli, potatoes, and garlic. Reduce heat and simmer until vegetables are just tender, about 15 minutes.
2. Stir in the curry powder and simmer for 5 more minutes.
3. Transfer to a blender or food processor and puree.
4. Divide among individual soup bowls and serve.

Calories Per Serving: 134
Fat: 0 g
Cholesterol: 0 mg
Protein: 11 g

Carbohydrates: 24 g
Dietary Fiber: 4 g
Sodium: 190 mg

❧ Broccoli–Sweet Potato Soup ❧

Broccoli, a rich source of vitamins A and C, calcium, and iron, is paired with sweet potatoes and squash.

PREPARATION TIME: 20 minutes • COOKING TIME: 25 minutes •
YIELD: 12 servings

8¼ cups low-sodium nonfat chicken broth
1 medium onion, chopped
4 cups chopped sweet potatoes
2 cups chopped yellow summer squash
2 cups chopped zucchini

2 cups chopped broccoli
2 cups chopped potatoes
2 stalks celery, chopped
2 teaspoons ground cumin
1 teaspoon ground black pepper
2 cups skim milk

1. Heat ¼ cup broth in a large soup pot. Add onion and sauté until onion begins to soften, about 3 minutes. Add sweet potatoes, yellow squash, zucchini, broccoli, potatoes, and celery, and sauté for 5 additional minutes.
2. Stir in remaining broth. Bring to a boil, reduce heat, and simmer until vegetables are just tender, about 15 minutes. Add cumin, black pepper, and milk, and continue to simmer until all ingredients are heated through, about 2 additional minutes.
3. Transfer to individual bowls and serve at once.

Calories Per Serving: 121
Fat: 1 g
Cholesterol: 1 mg
Protein: 7 g

Carbohydrates: 24 g
Dietary Fiber: 4 g
Sodium: 218 mg

❧ *Cabbage-Rice Soup* ❧

A perfect winter soup full of cabbage, turnip, and sweet potato.

PREPARATION TIME: *15 minutes* • COOKING TIME: *23 minutes* •
YIELD: *8 servings*

6¼ cups low-sodium nonfat vegetable
broth
1 medium onion, chopped
4 cloves garlic, minced
½ cup uncooked white rice
2 medium carrots, scraped and
chopped

1 medium potato, chopped
1 turnip, peeled and chopped
1 sweet potato, chopped
2 cups shredded cabbage
1 teaspoon dried oregano
¼ teaspoon ground black pepper

1. Heat ¼ cup broth in a large saucepan. Add onion and garlic, and sauté until onion begins to soften, about 3 minutes.
2. Add remaining broth and all other ingredients. Bring to a boil, reduce heat, and simmer until rice is tender, about 20 minutes.
3. Transfer to individual bowls and serve at once.

Calories Per Serving: 140
Fat: 0 g
Cholesterol: 0 mg
Protein: 3 g

Carbohydrates: 32 g
Dietary Fiber: 3 g
Sodium: 90 mg

❧ *Cabbage-Squash Soup* ❧

A nonfat variation of a traditional Italian favorite.

PREPARATION TIME: *20 minutes* • COOKING TIME: *50 minutes* •
YIELD: *12 servings*

¼ cup low-sodium nonfat chicken
  broth
1 medium onion, diced
2 cloves garlic, minced
2 cups diced yellow summer squash
1 cup shredded cabbage
2 carrots, scraped and sliced

6 cups water
3 cups low-sodium canned tomatoes,
  with juice
2 cups diced potatoes
1 tablespoon dried basil
2 cups green beans, cut into 1-inch
  lengths

1. Heat broth in a large saucepan. Add onion and garlic, and sauté until onion is soft, about 3 minutes. Add squash, cabbage, and carrots, and continue to sauté for 5 additional minutes.
2. Add water, tomatoes with their juice, potatoes, and basil. Bring to a boil, reduce heat, and simmer, stirring several times, for 30 minutes. Add green beans and return to a simmer for 5 more minutes.
3. Transfer to individual bowls and serve.

Calories Per Serving: 88
Fat: 0 g
Cholesterol: 0 mg
Protein: 3 g

Carbohydrates: 20 g
Dietary Fiber: 3 g
Sodium: 59 mg

❧ *Tarragon-Celery-Broccoli Soup* ❧

This soup of broccoli and red potatoes works as either a great first course or a meal.

PREPARATION TIME: *15 minutes* • COOKING TIME: *48 minutes* •
YIELD: *6 servings*

*4 cups low-sodium nonfat chicken
  broth*
6 cups chopped broccoli
1 cup chopped celery
1 cup chopped onion

2 cups chopped red potatoes
2 cloves garlic, chopped
½ teaspoon dried tarragon
2 tablespoons chopped fresh parsley

1. Bring broth to a boil in a large saucepan. Add broccoli, celery, onion, red potatoes, garlic, and tarragon. Return to a boil, reduce heat, and simmer for 45 minutes.
2. Remove from heat, transfer soup to a blender or food processor, and puree. Return puree to the saucepan and heat through.
3. Sprinkle with parsley and serve.

Calories Per Serving: 151
Fat: 1 g
Cholesterol: 0 mg
Protein: 10 g

Carbohydrates: 29 g
Dietary Fiber: 6 g
Sodium: 174 mg

❧ *Carrot-Cauliflower Soup with Dill* ❧

This colorful soup contains carrots, onion, cauliflower, white potatoes, dill, and black pepper. Shop for a firm cauliflower with compact florets and crisp, green leaves. The size of a head of cauliflower does not affect its quality.

PREPARATION TIME: 15 minutes ▪ *COOKING TIME: 20 minutes* ▪
YIELD: 4 servings

*2½ cups low-sodium nonfat chicken
  broth*
1 medium onion, chopped
*6 medium carrots, scraped and cut
  into ½-inch slices*

1½ cups chopped white potatoes
2 cups water
2 cups chopped cauliflower
½ teaspoon dried dill
¼ teaspoon ground black pepper

1. Heat ¼ cup of broth in a large saucepan. Add onion and sauté until onion just begins to soften, about 3 minutes.

2. Add carrots, potatoes, remaining broth, and water. Bring to a boil, reduce heat, cover, and simmer for 5 minutes.
3. Add cauliflower and continue to simmer until vegetables are just tender, about 12 minutes. Add dill and stir well. Sprinkle with black pepper and serve.

Calories Per Serving: 163
Fat: 1 g
Cholesterol: 0 mg
Protein: 5 g

Carbohydrates: 36 g
Dietary Fiber: 5 g
Sodium: 486 mg

❧ Carrot-Turnip Soup ❧

Carrots, turnips, onion, and celery come together in this warming soup flavored with lemon and nutmeg.

PREPARATION TIME: 15 minutes ▪ COOKING TIME: 45 minutes ▪
YIELD: 8 servings

3 cups low-sodium nonfat chicken
  broth
4 medium carrots, scrubbed and
  chopped
2 medium turnips, chopped

1 medium onion, chopped
2 cups chopped celery
3 cups skim milk
½ teaspoon ground nutmeg
1 tablespoon lemon juice

1. Bring broth to a boil in a large saucepan. Add carrots, turnips, onion, and celery. Return to a boil, reduce heat, and simmer for 45 minutes.
2. Add the milk, nutmeg, and lemon juice, heat through and serve.

Calories Per Serving: 121
Fat: 1 g
Cholesterol: 2 mg
Protein: 7 g

Carbohydrates: 23 g
Dietary Fiber: 4 g
Sodium: 152 mg

❧ *Cream of Carrot Soup* ❧

Diced carrots and dill are paired in this soup rich in beta carotene.

PREPARATION TIME: 15 minutes ▪ *COOKING TIME: 24 minutes* ▪
YIELD: 6 servings

4 cups low-sodium nonfat chicken
   broth
4 cups diced carrots
1 medium onion, chopped
2 cups diced potato

½ teaspoon dried marjoram
⅛ teaspoon ground black pepper
1½ cups evaporated skim milk
1 tablespoon dried dill

1. Bring broth to a boil in a large saucepan. Add carrots, onion, diced potato, marjoram, and black pepper. Return to a boil, reduce heat, cover, and simmer until carrots are just tender, about 20 minutes.
2. Transfer vegetable mixture to a blender or food processor and process until smooth.
3. Return the puree to the soup pot. Add evaporated milk and simmer, stirring constantly, until heated through, about 4 minutes.
4. Transfer the soup to individual bowls, sprinkle with the dill, and serve at once.

Calories Per Serving: 151
Fat: 0 g
Cholesterol: 2 mg
Protein: 11 g

Carbohydrates: 26 g
Dietary Fiber: 4 g
Sodium: 216 mg

❧ *Sherried Corn-Vegetable Soup* ❧

This spicy soup is made with sherry, onion, celery, turnips, and corn.

PREPARATION TIME: 15 minutes ▪ *COOKING TIME: 45 minutes* ▪
YIELD: 8 servings

2 tablespoons low-sodium nonfat
　chicken broth
2 cups chopped onions
2 stalks celery, chopped
1 medium green bell pepper, cored
　and diced
3 cloves garlic, minced
6 cups water

2 cups peeled and diced turnips
2 cups diced acorn squash
¼ cup dry sherry
2 tablespoons dried parsley
2 teaspoons paprika
½ teaspoon ground black pepper
1 cup fresh, canned (drained), or
　thawed frozen corn kernels

1. Heat broth in a large saucepan. Add onions, celery, green bell pepper, and garlic, and sauté until vegetables are just tender, about 5 minutes.
2. Add water, turnips, squash, sherry, parsley, paprika, and black pepper. Bring to a boil, reduce heat, and simmer, stirring occasionally, until turnips are just tender, about 35 minutes.
3. Add corn kernels and continue to simmer for 5 additional minutes.
4. Transfer to individual bowls and serve at once.

Calories Per Serving: 102
Fat: 0 g
Cholesterol: 0 mg
Protein: 3 g

Carbohydrates: 22 g
Dietary Fiber: 4 g
Sodium: 45 mg

❧ Curried Corn-Potato Soup ❧

This curried soup takes only 25 minutes to cook. Curry powder is a blend of more than 20 spices, herbs, and seeds, and can be stored in an airtight container for up to 2 months.

PREPARATION TIME: 15 minutes • COOKING TIME: 25 minutes •
YIELD: 4 servings

2 cups low-sodium nonfat chicken
　broth
1 medium onion, finely chopped
1 teaspoon curry powder
4 cups peeled and diced potatoes
1 stalk celery, sliced

½ teaspoon ground black pepper
¼ teaspoon cayenne pepper
2 cups fresh, canned (drained), or
　thawed frozen corn kernels
2 cups skim milk

1. Heat ¼ cup broth in a large saucepan. Add onion and curry powder, and sauté until onion is just tender, about 5 minutes.
2. Add remaining broth, potatoes, and celery. Stir in black pepper and cayenne pepper. Bring to a boil, reduce heat, and simmer until potatoes are tender, about 15 minutes.
3. Add corn and milk and simmer for an additional 5 minutes. Serve at once.

Calories Per Serving: 358
Fat: 1 g
Cholesterol: 2 mg
Protein: 16 g

Carbohydrates: 76 g
Dietary Fiber: 7 g
Sodium: 185 mg

❥ *Dijon-Corn Soup* ❧

This corn-and-potato soup is brightened with the clean, sharp flavor of Dijon mustard.

PREPARATION TIME: *10 minutes* • COOKING TIME: *35 minutes* •
YIELD: *8 servings*

2 cups water
1 cup peeled and diced potatoes
1½ cups evaporated skim milk
3 cups fresh, canned (drained), or
   thawed frozen corn kernels
½ cup diced onion

½ cup diced celery
1 tablespoon Dijon mustard
2 cloves garlic, crushed
2 teaspoons honey
⅛ teaspoon cayenne pepper
2 cups skim milk

1. Bring water to a boil in a saucepan. Add potatoes and boil until just tender, about 15 minutes. Remove from heat, drain, and set aside.
2. Bring evaporated milk to a boil in a saucepan. Add corn, onion, celery, mustard, garlic, honey, and cayenne pepper. Return to a boil, reduce heat, and simmer until corn is tender, about 15 minutes.
3. Place half the potatoes and half the corn mixture in a blender or food processor and puree.
4. Combine the puree, the remaining potatoes, and skim milk. Gently heat through and serve.

Calories Per Serving: 150

Carbohydrates: 30 g

Fat: 0 g

Dietary Fiber: 2 g

Cholesterol: 3 mg

Sodium: 151 mg

Protein: 8 g

❧ *Corn and Zucchini Soup* ❧

Zucchini, corn, and yogurt are the basis of this soup.

PREPARATION TIME: 15 minutes • *COOKING TIME: 4 minutes* •
YIELD: 12 servings

*6 cups low-sodium nonfat chicken
broth*

2 cups diced zucchini

1 small onion, chopped

*6 cups fresh, canned (drained), or
thawed frozen corn kernels*

¼ teaspoon ground black pepper

¾ cup nonfat plain yogurt

¼ cup minced fresh parsley

1. Bring broth to a boil in a saucepan. Add zucchini and onion. Return to a boil, reduce heat, cover, and simmer for 2 minutes.
2. Stir in corn and black pepper, cover, and simmer for 2 additional minutes.
3. Transfer mixture to a blender or food processor and process until smooth. Place soup in individual bowls, top with a tablespoon of yogurt, garnish with parsley, and serve.

Calories Per Serving: 92

Carbohydrates: 20 g

Fat: 1 g

Dietary Fiber: 2 g

Cholesterol: 0 mg

Sodium: 183 mg

Protein: 6 g

❧ *Eggplant Soup* ❧

This tasty soup includes carrot, potatoes, and parsley. Eggplant should be stored in a cool, dry place and used within 2 days of purchase.

PREPARATION TIME: 15 minutes plus 10 minutes cooling time •
COOKING TIME: 38 minutes • *YIELD: 10 servings*

5¼ cups low-sodium nonfat chicken broth
1½ cups chopped onion
3 cloves garlic, minced
1½ teaspoons curry powder
1 cup scraped and grated carrot
4 cups peeled and diced eggplant
2 cups peeled and chopped red potatoes
5 cups skim milk
¼ cup chopped fresh parsley
½ teaspoon ground black pepper

1. Heat ¼ cup broth in a large saucepan. Add onion and sauté until softened, about 7 minutes. Add garlic and curry powder, and sauté 1 additional minute.
2. Stir in the remaining broth, carrot, eggplant, and potatoes. Bring to a boil, reduce heat, and simmer until potatoes are soft, about 30 minutes. Remove from heat and allow to cool for 10 minutes.
3. Puree the soup in a blender or food processor. Return the soup to the saucepan, add milk, and heat through. Garnish with parsley, sprinkle with black pepper, and serve.

Calories Per Serving: 114
Fat: 0 g
Cholesterol: 2 mg
Protein: 6 g
Carbohydrates: 21 g
Dietary Fiber: 2 g
Sodium: 450 mg

❧ *Tarragon-Pea Soup* ❧

Tarragon, scallions, sherry, and white pepper accent this green pea soup.

PREPARATION TIME: 20 minutes • *COOKING TIME: 18 minutes* •
YIELD: 4 servings

2 tablespoons low-sodium nonfat
   chicken broth

2 scallions, chopped

3 cups fresh or frozen, thawed green
   peas

2 cups water

2 tablespoons sherry

1½ cups skim milk

¼ teaspoon ground white pepper

½ teaspoon dried tarragon

1. Heat broth in a large saucepan. Add scallions and sauté until they begin to soften, about 2 minutes.
2. Add peas, water, and sherry. Bring to a boil, reduce heat, and simmer until peas are tender, about 15 minutes.
3. Transfer peas to a blender or food processor. Add milk and white pepper, and puree.
4. Return pureed peas to pan and heat through, about 1 minute. Sprinkle with tarragon and serve.

Calories Per Serving: 128

Fat: 1 g

Cholesterol: 2 mg

Protein: 9 g

Carbohydrates: 21 g

Dietary Fiber: 4 g

Sodium: 67 mg

❧ *Lima Bean–Corn–Potato Soup* ❧

This thick and hearty chowder is full of vegetables and seasoned with garlic and jalapeños.

PREPARATION TIME: 20 minutes ▪ COOKING TIME: 35 minutes ▪
YIELD: 8 servings

4¼ cups low-sodium nonfat chicken
   broth

1 medium onion, diced

1 medium green bell pepper, cored
   and diced

1 cup diced celery

3 cloves garlic, minced

1 jalapeño pepper, seeded and minced

2 cups diced potatoes

1 tablespoon paprika

1 tablespoon dried oregano

¼ teaspoon ground black pepper

2 cups fresh or frozen, thawed lima
   beans

2 cups fresh or frozen, thawed corn
   kernels

3 cups skim milk

1. Heat ½ cup broth in a large saucepan. Add onion, green bell pepper, celery, garlic, and jalapeño, and sauté until pepper begins to soften, about 5 minutes.
2. Add remaining broth, potatoes, paprika, oregano, and black pepper. Bring to a boil, reduce heat, and simmer until potatoes are just tender, about 20 minutes.
3. Stir in lima beans, corn, and milk. Continue to simmer, stirring several times, until limas are just tender, about 10 additional minutes.
4. Transfer to individual bowls and serve.

Calories Per Serving: 309
Fat: 1 g
Cholesterol: 2 mg
Protein: 14 g

Carbohydrates: 61 g
Dietary Fiber: 3 g
Sodium: 169 mg

❧ *Mushroom-Barley Soup* ❧

This soup contains white and shiitake mushrooms as well as onion, celery, carrots, and sherry.

PREPARATION TIME: 20 minutes ▪ *COOKING TIME: 45 minutes* ▪
YIELD: 8 servings

6¼ cups low-sodium nonfat chicken broth
¾ cup diced onion
½ cup diced celery
½ cup diced carrot
4 cloves garlic, minced
1 cup sliced white mushrooms

1 cup sliced shiitake mushrooms
¼ cup barley
2 tablespoons sherry
2 tablespoons rice wine vinegar
¼ cup skim milk
2 tablespoons chopped fresh scallions
½ teaspoon ground black pepper

1. Heat ¼ cup broth in a large saucepan. Add onion, celery, and carrot, and sauté until carrots begin to soften, about 4 minutes. Add the garlic and sauté for an additional 4 minutes.
2. Add the white mushrooms and the shiitake mushrooms, and continue to sauté for 4 more minutes. Stir in the barley and sauté for 2 additional minutes.

3. Add the remaining broth and bring to a boil. Reduce heat and simmer for 30 minutes.

4. Stir in the sherry, rice vinegar, milk, scallions, and black pepper. Heat through, transfer to individual bowls, and serve.

Calories Per Serving: 68   Carbohydrates: 14 g
Fat: 0 g   Dietary Fiber: 2 g
Cholesterol: 1 mg   Sodium: 614 mg
Protein: 2 g

❧ *Mushroom-Spinach Soup* ❧

This mushroom-and-spinach soup is made with carrots, onion, celery, and barley.

PREPARATION TIME: 15 minutes ▪ *COOKING TIME: 45 minutes* ▪
YIELD: 10 servings

6 cups sliced mushrooms   ⅛ teaspoon cayenne pepper
4 carrots cut into ¼-inch-thick medal-   8 cups low-sodium nonfat chicken
   lions   broth
1 medium onion, chopped   2 cups water
3 cups sliced celery   4 cups chopped spinach
½ cup barley   ½ teaspoon ground black pepper

1. Combine mushrooms, carrots, onion, celery, barley, cayenne, broth, and water in a large saucepan. Bring to a boil, reduce heat, and simmer for 35 minutes.

2. Add spinach and continue to cook for 10 minutes.

3. Sprinkle with black pepper and serve.

Calories Per Serving: 107   Carbohydrates: 17 g
Fat: 1 g   Dietary Fiber: 5 g
Cholesterol: 0 mg   Sodium: 211 mg
Protein: 10 g

❧ *Orange Juice Soup* ❧

This sweet, warm soup is made with orange juice, orange sections, and vanilla.

PREPARATION TIME: *15 minutes* • COOKING TIME: *2 minutes* •
YIELD: *4 servings*

2 cups orange juice
¼ cup sugar
2 tablespoons cornstarch

2 navel oranges, peeled and sectioned,
    each section quartered
⅛ teaspoon vanilla extract

1. Mix orange juice, sugar, and cornstarch in a small saucepan until cornstarch is thoroughly dissolved.
2. Bring mixture to a boil, and cook, stirring constantly, for 1½ minutes. Remove from heat. Stir in vanilla.
3. Divide orange pieces among 4 individual bowls, pour sauce over the oranges, and serve at once.

Calories Per Serving: 154
Fat: 0 g
Cholesterol: 0 mg
Protein: 2 g

Carbohydrates: 37 g
Dietary Fiber: 6 g
Sodium: 3 mg

❧ *Gingered Potato Soup* ❧

This soup contains both sweet and white potatoes.

PREPARATION TIME: *10 minutes* • COOKING TIME: *25 minutes* •
YIELD: *4 servings*

3 cups water
2 cups peeled and diced sweet potatoes
1 cup peeled and diced white potato

½ cup chopped onion
¼ cup chopped celery
1 teaspoon ground ginger
½ teaspoon ground black pepper

1. Place water in a large saucepan. Bring to a boil. Add sweet potatoes, white potato, onion, and celery. Return to a boil, reduce heat, and simmer, covered, until potatoes are tender, about 25 minutes. Remove from heat.
2. Stir in ginger and black pepper, transfer to a blender or food processor, and puree.
3. Place in individual bowls and serve.

Calories Per Serving: 236	Carbohydrates: 55 g
Fat: 1 g	Dietary Fiber: 6 g
Cholesterol: 0 mg	Sodium: 37 mg
Protein: 4 g	

❧ *Potato-Leek Soup* ❧

In this recipe, potatoes are combined with skim milk, parsley, and leeks for a rich, creamy soup. Look for leeks with crisp, brightly colored tops and an unblemished white portion.

PREPARATION TIME: 15 minutes • *COOKING TIME: 1 hour, 5 minutes* •
YIELD: 6 servings

3 cups low-sodium nonfat chicken broth	*2½ cups peeled and diced potatoes*
5 cups sliced leeks	*1 cup skim milk*
	3 tablespoons chopped fresh parsley

1. Bring broth to a boil in a saucepan. Add leeks and potatoes. Return to a boil, reduce heat, cover, and simmer for 1 hour.
2. Pour into a blender or food processor and blend until smooth.
3. Return to the saucepan, stir in milk, and heat through, about 5 minutes. Garnish with parsley and serve.

Calories Per Serving: 147	Carbohydrates: 31 g
Fat: 1 g	Dietary Fiber: 3 g
Cholesterol: 1 mg	Sodium: 206 mg
Protein: 6 g	

❧ *Portuguese Potato-Kale Soup* ❧

This recipe combines kale with potatoes, white beans, onion, and garlic.

PREPARATION TIME: 15 minutes • *COOKING TIME: 35 minutes* •
YIELD: 8 servings

2 tablespoons low-sodium nonfat
   chicken broth
1 medium onion, chopped
3 cloves garlic, crushed
6 cups water
3 cups diced white potatoes

½ teaspoon ground black pepper
3 cups chopped fresh kale
1 cup low-sodium canned Great
   Northern beans, rinsed and
   drained
¼ cup fresh parsley, chopped

1. Heat the broth in a large saucepan. Add the onion and garlic, and sauté until the onion just begins to soften, about 3 minutes.
2. Add water, potatoes, and black pepper. Bring to a boil, reduce heat, and simmer for 20 minutes.
3. Stir in the kale and simmer for another 10 minutes.
4. Add the beans and parsley, and heat through before serving.

Calories Per Serving: 123
Fat: 0 g
Cholesterol: 0 mg
Protein: 5 g

Carbohydrates: 26 g
Dietary Fiber: 5 g
Sodium: 31 mg

❧ *Sweet Potato Soup* ❧

This quick and easy sweet potato soup is flavored with bell peppers, jalapeños, and garlic. Store sweet potatoes in a cool, dark place, but do not refrigerate.

PREPARATION TIME: 15 minutes • *COOKING TIME: 15 minutes* •
YIELD: 6 servings

3 cups low-sodium nonfat chicken broth

4 medium sweet potatoes, diced

2 green bell peppers, cored and chopped

1 jalapeño pepper, seeded and chopped

2 garlic cloves, minced

1. Bring broth to a boil in a large saucepan. Add sweet potatoes, return to a boil, reduce heat, and simmer for 10 minutes. Add bell peppers, jalapeño, and garlic, and continue to simmer until potatoes are tender, about 5 minutes more.
2. Remove from heat, place in a blender or food processor and blend until smooth. If soup is too thick, stir in additional water or broth.
3. Transfer to individual bowls and serve.

Calories Per Serving: 36

Fat: 0 g

Cholesterol: 0 mg

Protein: 3 g

Carbohydrates: 6 g

Dietary Fiber: 1 g

Sodium: 128 mg

❧ *Curried Pumpkin Soup* ❧

This creamy soup is spiced with gingerroot, curry powder, and black pepper.

PREPARATION TIME: *10 minutes* ▪ COOKING TIME: *20 minutes* ▪
YIELD: *4 servings*

3 tablespoons water

1 medium onion, chopped

½ teaspoon fresh grated gingerroot

¼ teaspoon curry powder

¼ teaspoon ground black pepper

1 cup pumpkin puree

1 cup low-sodium nonfat chicken broth

½ cup skim milk

½ cup evaporated skim milk

2 tablespoons chopped fresh scallions

1. Heat water in a large saucepan. Add onion and sauté until water is evaporated, about 6 minutes. Remove from heat.
2. Stir in gingerroot, curry powder, and black pepper. Add pumpkin puree and mix well. Stir in the broth and skim milk. Return to heat and bring

to a boil. Reduce heat and simmer for 10 minutes. Stir in the evaporated milk and continue to simmer for 4 more minutes.

3. Sprinkle with scallions and serve.

Calories Per Serving: 71
Fat: 0 g
Cholesterol: 2 mg
Protein: 6 g

Carbohydrates: 12 g
Dietary Fiber: 2 g
Sodium: 97 mg

❧ *Pumpkin-Corn Soup* ❧

Pumpkin and corn are simmered with red bell pepper and celery, then spiced with cumin.

PREPARATION TIME: *15 minutes* • COOKING TIME: *50 minutes* •
YIELD: *10 servings*

*2 tablespoons low-sodium nonfat
chicken broth*
1 medium onion, diced
*1 medium red bell pepper, cored and
diced*
1 cup sliced celery
2 cloves garlic, minced

7 cups water
4 cups peeled and diced pumpkin
2 tablespoons dried parsley
2 teaspoons ground cumin
½ teaspoon ground black pepper
*2 cups fresh, canned (drained), or
thawed frozen corn kernels*

1. Heat broth in a large saucepan. Add onion, red bell pepper, celery, and garlic, and sauté for 5 minutes.
2. Add water, pumpkin, parsley, cumin, and black pepper. Bring to a boil, reduce heat, and simmer, stirring occasionally, until pumpkin is tender, about 35 minutes.
3. Stir in corn and continue to simmer for an additional 10 minutes.
4. Transfer to individual bowls and serve.

Calories Per Serving: 55
Fat: 0 g
Cholesterol: 0 mg
Protein: 2 g

Carbohydrates: 13 g
Dietary Fiber: 2 g
Sodium: 32 g

❧ *Acorn Squash Soup with Spinach* ❧

Spinach and acorn squash are simmered with yellow bell pepper, onion, garlic, and rice.

PREPARATION TIME: 10 minutes • COOKING TIME: 35 minutes •
YIELD: 10 servings

¼ cup low-sodium nonfat chicken
  broth
1 medium onion, chopped
1 medium yellow bell pepper, cored
  and diced
2 cloves garlic, minced

5 cups water
4 cups peeled and chopped acorn
  squash
¾ cup uncooked white rice
½ teaspoon ground white pepper
1 cup chopped spinach leaves

1. Heat broth in a large saucepan. Add onion, bell pepper, and garlic, and sauté for 5 minutes.
2. Add water, squash, rice, and white pepper. Bring to a boil, reduce heat, and simmer for 20 minutes.
3. Stir in spinach and continue to simmer for 10 additional minutes.
4. Transfer to individual bowls and serve.

Calories Per Serving: 92
Fat: 0 g
Cholesterol: 2 mg
Protein: 4 g

Carbohydrates: 20 g
Dietary Fiber: 1 g
Sodium: 46 mg

❧ *Jalapeño-Butternut Soup* ❧

Onion, garlic, ginger, jalapeño pepper, curry and cumin flavor this soup. Butternut squash is a large, cylindrical winter squash that ranges in color from yellow to camel.

PREPARATION TIME: 15 minutes plus 15 minutes cooling time •
COOKING TIME: 40 minutes • YIELD: 10 servings

¼ cup low-sodium nonfat chicken
  broth

1 large onion, diced
1 cup sliced celery

3 cloves garlic, minced

1 tablespoon fresh grated gingerroot

1 jalapeño pepper, seeded and minced

2 tomatoes, chopped

1 tablespoon curry powder

2 teaspoons ground cumin

½ teaspoon ground black pepper

4 cups peeled and diced butternut
   squash

5 cups water

1. Heat broth in a large saucepan. Add onion, celery, garlic, gingerroot, and jalapeño pepper, and sauté for 5 minutes.
2. Add tomatoes, curry powder, cumin, and black pepper, and sauté for additional 3 minutes. Add squash and water. Bring to a boil, reduce heat, and simmer, stirring several times, for 30 minutes.
3. Remove from heat and allow to cool for 15 minutes. Place in a food processor or blender and process until smooth.
4. Return soup to heat and bring to a gentle simmer before serving.

Calories Per Serving: 40

Fat: 0 g

Cholesterol: 0 mg

Protein: 2 g

Carbohydrates: 9 g

Dietary Fiber: 1 g

Sodium: 74 g

❧ *Butternut-Garlic Soup* ❧

Roasted garlic makes this hearty soup memorable. Fresh garlic is available year round and should be stored in a dark, cool place away from other foods.

PREPARATION TIME: *20 minutes* • COOKING TIME: *1 hour, 20 minutes* •
YIELD: *6 servings*

1 butternut squash (about 2 pounds),
   cut into quarters

1 garlic bulb

3½ cups low-sodium nonfat chicken
   broth

⅛ teaspoon ground nutmeg

1½ teaspoons lemon juice

½ teaspoon ground black pepper

1. Preheat oven to 375 degrees.
2. Arrange the squash pieces in a shallow baking pan. Add ½ inch of water and bake until the squash is tender, about 30 minutes.

3. Cut off the top of the garlic bulb to reveal just the tips of the cloves inside. Place the whole garlic bulb in a garlic roaster or wrap it tightly in aluminum foil. Place it in the oven and bake with the squash for 30 more minutes.
4. Remove the garlic cloves from the bulb, peel, and transfer them along with the squash to a blender.
5. Add ½ cup broth and blend until smooth.
6. Transfer the squash-garlic mixture to a large saucepan. Add remaining broth, nutmeg, lemon juice, and black pepper. Bring to a boil, reduce heat, cover, and simmer for 20 minutes. Serve in individual bowls.

Calories Per Serving: 72	Carbohydrates: 17 g
Fat: 0 g	Dietary Fiber: 3 g
Cholesterol: 0 mg	Sodium: 401 mg
Protein: 2 g	

❧ *Hubbard Squash Soup* ❧

Hubbard squash, carrots, brown sugar, gingerroot, cinnamon, and mace make up this savory soup. Mace is a sweet spice that comes from the membrane covering a nutmeg seed.

PREPARATION TIME: 15 minutes   ▪   COOKING TIME: 30 minutes   ▪
YIELD: 6 servings

3 cups peeled and diced Hubbard squash	*2 tablespoons brown sugar*
4 medium carrots, sliced	*2 tablespoons fresh grated gingerroot*
1 medium onion, chopped	*½ teaspoon ground cinnamon*
6 cups low-sodium nonfat chicken broth	*½ teaspoon ground mace*
	¼ cup lemon juice

1. Place squash, carrots, onion, broth, brown sugar, gingerroot, cinnamon, and mace in a large pot. Bring to a boil, reduce heat, and simmer until squash is tender, about 30 minutes.

2. Remove from heat and stir in lemon juice.
3. Transfer soup to a blender or food processor and puree. Return puree to the pot, heat through, and serve.

Calories Per Serving: 117

Fat: 1 g

Cholesterol: 0 mg

Protein: 6 g

Carbohydrates: 25 g

Dietary Fiber: 3 g

Sodium: 359 mg

❧ *Winter Squash Soup* ❧

This soup contains turnips, Hubbard squash, carrots, and potato. Hubbard squash is a large winter squash with a thick, bumpy, hard shell ranging in color from dark green to bright orange. It is available from September to March.

PREPARATION TIME: 15 minutes plus 10 minutes standing time •
COOKING TIME: 45 minutes • *YIELD: 10 servings*

2 tablespoons low-sodium nonfat chicken broth

1 medium onion, chopped

4 cloves garlic, minced

1 teaspoon minced jalapeño pepper

7 cups water

3 cups peeled and diced Hubbard squash

2 medium turnips, chopped

2 medium carrots, chopped

1 medium potato, chopped

8 whole cloves

2 tablespoons dried parsley

1. Heat broth in a large saucepan. Add onion, garlic, and jalapeño pepper. Sauté for 5 minutes.
2. Add water and all other ingredients. Bring to a boil, reduce heat, and simmer, stirring occasionally, until vegetables are tender, about 40 minutes.
3. Remove from heat, allow to stand for 10 minutes, and serve.

Calories Per Serving: 69

Carbohydrates: 16 g

Fat: 0 mg

Dietary Fiber: 3 g

Cholesterol: 0 mg

Sodium: 37 mg

Protein: 3 g

❧ *Apple-Squash Soup* ❧

The main ingredients in this sweet, thick soup are apples, butternut squash, onions, and curry powder.

PREPARATION TIME: 15 minutes ▪ *COOKING TIME: 35 minutes* ▪
YIELD: 6 servings

3¼ cups low-sodium nonfat chicken broth

2 cups chopped onions

4 teaspoons curry powder

8 cups peeled and chopped butternut squash

2 medium apples, peeled, cored, and chopped

1 cup apple juice

¼ teaspoon ground black pepper

1. Heat ¼ cup broth in a large pot. Add onions and curry powder. Bring to a boil, reduce heat, cover, and simmer until onions are tender, about 10 minutes.
2. Add remaining broth, squash, and apples. Bring to a boil. Reduce heat and simmer until squash and apples are tender, about 20 minutes.
3. Transfer onions, squash, and apples to a food processor or blender. Add 1 cup of the cooking liquid and process until smooth.
4. Return the blended soup to the pot, add the apple juice and 2 cups of the remaining cooking liquid, and heat through. Sprinkle with black pepper and serve.

Calories Per Serving: 148

Carbohydrates: 35 g

Fat: 1 g

Dietary Fiber: 3 g

Cholesterol: 0 mg

Sodium: 421 mg

Protein: 3 g

❧ *Squash-Pepper Soup* ❧

Yellow squash, zucchini, and green pepper are the main ingredients in this soup. Be sure to pick squash that are heavy and have a hard, deep-colored rind free of blemishes or moldy spots.

PREPARATION TIME: 15 minutes plus 10 minutes cooling time •
COOKING TIME: 30 minutes • *YIELD: 4 servings*

2 cups low-sodium nonfat chicken broth	1 medium green bell pepper, cored and diced
3 leeks, white parts only, thinly sliced	2 cups chopped yellow squash
2 cloves garlic, crushed	3 cups chopped zucchini
2 cups peeled and diced red potatoes	1 scallion, chopped
2 cups water	2 tablespoons lemon juice
	¼ teaspoon ground black pepper

1. Heat ¼ cup broth in a large saucepan. Add leeks and garlic, and sauté until leeks soften, about 4 minutes.
2. Add potatoes, remaining broth, and water. Bring to a boil, reduce heat, and simmer for 12 minutes. Stir in green bell pepper, yellow squash, and zucchini, and continue to simmer until squash is tender, about 8 minutes. Remove from heat and allow to cool for 10 minutes.
3. Transfer mixture to a blender or food processor and blend until smooth. Return to saucepan. Stir in scallion, lemon juice, and black pepper, and heat through before serving.

Calories Per Serving: 263
Fat: 1 g
Cholesterol: 2 mg
Protein: 11 g

Carbohydrates: 56 g
Dietary Fiber: 7 g
Sodium: 477 mg

❧ *Yellow Summer Squash Soup* ❧

Summer squash, basil, garlic, and oregano bring flavor to this soup. Fresh squash is available year round in most supermarkets with a peak period during late spring.

PREPARATION TIME: 15 minutes plus 10 minutes cooling time •
COOKING TIME: 25 minutes • *YIELD: 6 servings*

1¼ cups low-sodium nonfat chicken broth	*2 cloves garlic, minced*
½ cup chopped onion	*1 teaspoon dried basil*
1 medium tomato, chopped	*¾ teaspoon dried oregano*
2 cups water	*¼ teaspoon ground black pepper*
2 cups yellow summer squash, cut into ¼-inch-thick round slices	*½ cup nonfat buttermilk*
	1 tablespoon honey
	½ teaspoon lemon juice

1. Heat 2 tablespoons broth in a large soup pot. Add onion and tomato, and sauté until onion is just tender, about 5 minutes.
2. Add remaining broth, water, squash, garlic, basil, oregano, and black pepper. Bring to a boil, reduce heat, cover, and simmer until squash is tender, about 15 minutes.
3. Remove from heat and allow to cool for 10 minutes.
4. Stir buttermilk into soup. Transfer to a blender or food processor and puree.
5. Return soup to pot and stir in honey and lemon juice. Place over low heat and warm to serving temperature.

Calories Per Serving: 50	Carbohydrates: 10 g
Fat: 0 g	Dietary Fiber: 1 g
Cholesterol: 1 mg	Sodium: 39 mg
Protein: 3 g	

❧ *Basic Tomato Soup* ❧

This quick and easy tomato soup is seasoned with garlic.

PREPARATION TIME: 10 minutes • *COOKING TIME: 8 minutes* •
YIELD: 2 servings

¼ cup low-sodium nonfat chicken broth	*3 cups low-sodium canned tomatoes, with juice*
3 cloves garlic, minced	*¼ teaspoon ground black pepper*

1. Heat broth in a medium saucepan. Add garlic and sauté for 2 minutes.
2. Stir in tomatoes and their juice and transfer mixture to a blender. Blend until smooth.
3. Return soup to the saucepan, sprinkle with black pepper, and heat through before serving.

Calories Per Serving: 83	Carbohydrates: 17 g
Fat: 1 g	Dietary Fiber: 3 g
Cholesterol: 0 mg	Sodium: 139 mg
Protein: 5 g	

❧ *Sun-Dried Tomato–Leek Soup* ❧

Leeks and sun-dried tomatoes are paired in this creamy soup.

PREPARATION TIME: 20 minutes • *COOKING TIME: 30 minutes* •
YIELD: 8 servings

2¾ cups low-sodium nonfat chicken broth	*1 leek, chopped*
½ medium onion, chopped	*5 cups water*
½ cup sun-dried tomatoes, soaked in water for 30 minutes and chopped	*3 tablespoons nonfat Parmesan*
	½ cup skim milk
	¼ teaspoon ground black pepper

1. Heat ¼ cup broth in a large saucepan. Add onion and sun-dried tomatoes, and sauté until onion begins to soften, about 4 minutes. Add leek and sauté for 4 more minutes.

2. Stir in remaining broth and water. Bring to a boil, reduce heat, cover, and simmer for 20 minutes. Remove from heat.

3. Remove vegetables and place them in a blender or food processor. Puree until smooth. Return puree to the saucepan with the broth. Stir in Parmesan cheese, milk, and black pepper.

4. Transfer to individual bowls and serve at once.

Calories Per Serving: 90	Carbohydrates: 19 g
Fat: 0 g	Dietary Fiber: 2 g
Cholesterol: 1 mg	Sodium: 209 mg
Protein: 6 g	

❧ Fresh Tomato–Couscous Soup ❧

Couscous makes this tomato soup unique and savory. Packaged precooked couscous is available in most supermarkets.

PREPARATION TIME: 10 minutes plus 10 minutes standing time　•
COOKING TIME: 20 minutes　•　YIELD: 4 servings

3 cups low-sodium nonfat chicken broth
1 medium onion, chopped
3 tomatoes, chopped, with juice

½ teaspoon dried oregano
⅛ teaspoon cayenne pepper
½ cup uncooked couscous

1. Place 2 cups broth in a large saucepan. Add onion, tomatoes, oregano, and cayenne. Bring to a boil, reduce heat, and simmer for 20 minutes.

2. In a separate saucepan bring remaining broth to a boil. Stir in the couscous. Remove from heat, cover, and allow to stand until liquid is absorbed, about 10 minutes.

3. Stir couscous into the soup.

4. Transfer to individual bowls and serve.

Calories Per Serving: 144	Carbohydrates: 26 g
Fat: 1 g	Dietary Fiber: 5 g
Cholesterol: 0 mg	Sodium: 139 mg
Protein: 9 g	

❧ *Tomato-Corn-Chile Soup* ❧

Green chiles, cumin, tomatoes, onion, and bell pepper create this South-western–style soup.

PREPARATION TIME: 20 minutes • *COOKING TIME: 25 minutes* •
YIELD: 8 servings

*4¼ cups low-sodium nonfat chicken
 broth*
1 medium onion, chopped
*1 medium red bell pepper, cored and
 chopped*
3 cloves garlic, minced
½ tablespoon chili powder
½ tablespoon ground cumin

½ teaspoon ground black pepper
4 cups water
*3 cups low-sodium canned tomatoes,
 crushed*
*1½ cups canned mild green chiles,
 chopped*
*2 cups fresh or thawed frozen corn
 kernels*

1. Heat ¼ cup broth in a large saucepan. Add onion, red bell pepper, garlic, chili powder, cumin, and black pepper, and sauté until bell pepper begins to soften, about 5 minutes.
2. Add remaining broth, water, tomatoes, and green chiles. Bring to a boil, reduce heat, and simmer for 15 minutes. Stir in corn and simmer for 5 more minutes. Serve hot.

Calories Per Serving: 83
Fat: 1 g
Cholesterol: 0 mg
Protein: 5 g

Carbohydrates: 17 g
Dietary Fiber: 4 g
Sodium: 354 mg

❧ *Tomato-Squash Soup* ❧

Carrot, onion, celery, and yellow summer squash are the main ingredients in this creamy soup.

PREPARATION TIME: 20 minutes • *COOKING TIME: 45 minutes* •
YIELD: 12 servings

8½ cups low-sodium nonfat chicken
   broth
1 medium carrot, minced
1 medium onion, minced
1 stalk celery, minced
4 cups minced yellow summer squash
4 cloves garlic, minced

1 tablespoon dried basil
½ cup all-purpose flour
2 cups low-sodium canned tomatoes,
   chopped, with juice
½ teaspoon ground black pepper
1 cup skim milk

1. Heat ½ cup broth in a large pot over medium heat. Add carrot, onion, celery, and squash. Simmer gently for 5 minutes.
2. Add garlic and basil. Gradually stir in flour and cook for 5 minutes.
3. Add the remaining broth and the tomatoes, bring to a boil, then reduce heat and simmer for 30 minutes.
4. Add black pepper and milk, and heat through. Serve hot.

Calories Per Serving: 71
Fat: 0 g
Cholesterol: 2 mg
Protein: 3 g

Carbohydrates: 12 g
Dietary Fiber: 2 g
Sodium: 580 mg

❧ Turnip-Parsnip Soup ❧

Turnips and parsnips are the featured ingredients in this hearty, chilled wintertime soup.

PREPARATION TIME: 15 minutes plus 2 hours chilling time •
COOKING TIME: 50 minutes • YIELD: 8 servings

¼ cup low-sodium nonfat chicken
   broth
1 medium onion, diced
5 cups water
2 cups diced turnips
1 cup diced potatoes

1 cup chopped parsnips
½ cup chopped fresh parsley
½ teaspoon ground black pepper
2 cups skim milk
2 scallions, chopped

1. Heat broth in a large saucepan. Add onion and sauté until onion begins to soften, about 5 minutes.

2. Add water, turnips, potatoes, parsnips, parsley, and black pepper. Bring to a boil, reduce heat, and simmer, stirring several times, for 45 minutes. Remove from heat and stir in milk.
3. Transfer the soup to a blender or food processor and process until smooth. Chill for 2 hours.
4. Garnish with scallions and serve.

Calories Per Serving: 97   Carbohydrates: 20 g
Fat: 0 g   Dietary Fiber: 2 g
Cholesterol: 1 mg   Sodium: 65 mg
Protein: 5 g

❧ *Turnip Soup with Roasted Garlic* ❧

Roasted garlic, onions, and turnips bring flavor to this unique soup. Unbroken bulbs of garlic can be stored for up to 8 weeks. Once broken from the bulb, individual cloves will keep 3 to 10 days.

PREPARATION TIME: 20 minutes plus 45 minutes cooling time •
COOKING TIME: 1 hour, 35 minutes • *YIELD: 6 servings*

2 onions, quartered   2½ cups low-sodium nonfat chicken
1 whole garlic bulb, with top cut off   broth
4 cups chopped turnips   1 cup evaporated skim milk

1. Preheat oven to 300 degrees.
2. Place onions, garlic, and turnips in a large glass baking dish. Add 1 cup broth and bake for 1½ hours.
3. Remove from oven and allow to cool for 45 minutes.
4. Transfer the onions and turnips to a blender or food processor. Squeeze out the roasted cloves from the garlic bulb and add to the blender or processor. Add the cooking liquid from the baking dish. Process until smooth.
5. Pour the puree into a large saucepan. Stir in the remaining broth and the evaporated milk, stir well, and heat through. Serve at once.

Calories Per Serving: 97
Fat: 1 g
Cholesterol: 2 mg
Protein: 7 g

Carbohydrates: 18 g
Dietary Fiber: 3 g
Sodium: 244 mg

❧ *Creamy Dijon-Zucchini Soup* ❧

Zucchini, onion, garlic, curry powder, mustard, and broth are used in this warming country soup. Look for small, firm zucchini with skins that are a vibrant color and free of blemishes. Zucchini's color can vary from dark to light green.

PREPARATION TIME: 10 minutes • COOKING TIME: 15 minutes •
YIELD: 6 servings

4 cups chopped zucchini
1 medium onion, chopped
2 cloves garlic, crushed
2 teaspoons curry powder
2 tablespoons Dijon mustard

4 cups low-sodium nonfat chicken
 broth
1 cup nonfat plain yogurt
1 cup cooked white rice

1. Place the zucchini, onion, garlic, curry powder, mustard, and broth in a large saucepan. Bring to a boil, reduce heat, and simmer for 10 minutes.
2. Transfer to a blender or food processor and puree.
3. Return the soup to the saucepan, stir in the yogurt and rice, and heat through. Serve in individual bowls.

Calories Per Serving: 106
Fat: 1 g
Cholesterol: 1 mg
Protein: 8 g

Carbohydrates: 17 g
Dietary Fiber: 2 g
Sodium: 264 mg

❧ *Zucchini Soup with White Wine* ❧

This zucchini soup is seasoned with garlic, parsley, and onion.

PREPARATION TIME: 10 minutes plus 10 minutes cooling time •
COOKING TIME: 15 minutes • *YIELD: 6 servings*

2¼ cups low-sodium nonfat chicken
   broth
1 medium onion, chopped
¼ cup white wine

4 cups diced zucchini
½ teaspoon ground black pepper
2 cloves garlic, minced
¼ cup coarsely chopped fresh parsley

1. Heat ¼ cup broth in a large saucepan. Add onion and sauté until tender, about 3 minutes.
2. Add remaining broth, wine, zucchini, black pepper, and garlic. Bring to a boil, reduce heat, and simmer until zucchini is tender, about 12 minutes. Remove from heat and allow to cool for 10 minutes.
3. Place the mixture in a blender or food processor and blend until smooth. Return the soup to the saucepan, stir in the parsley, and heat through. Serve in individual bowls.

Calories Per Serving: 43
Fat: 1 g
Cholesterol: 0 mg
Protein: 4 g

Carbohydrates: 6 g
Dietary Fiber: 1 g
Sodium: 131 mg

❧ *Barley Soup* ❧

Barley is often used in cereals, breads, and soups. Here it is combined with onion, celery, parsley, carrots, and red wine.

PREPARATION TIME: 15 minutes • *COOKING TIME: 1 hour, 40 minutes* •
YIELD: 10 servings

7 cups low-sodium nonfat chicken
   broth
3 cups water
1 cup barley
2 cups chopped onion
2 cups chopped celery
4 cloves garlic, crushed

4 medium carrots, grated
1 teaspoon dried oregano
½ teaspoon ground black pepper
½ cup red wine
½ cup chopped fresh parsley
2 medium tomatoes, chopped
¾ cup low-sodium tomato paste

1. Combine broth, water, barley, onion, celery, garlic, and carrots in a large
   saucepan. Bring to a boil. Add oregano, black pepper, and wine. Return
   to a boil, reduce heat, and simmer for 1 hour.
2. Stir in the parsley, tomatoes, and tomato paste and simmer for another
   half hour before serving.

Calories Per Serving: 144
Fat: 1 g
Cholesterol: 0 mg
Protein: 7 g

Carbohydrates: 28 g
Dietary Fiber: 6 g
Sodium: 311 mg

❧ Chilled Borscht ❧

This unusual borscht includes turnips and apple in addition to beets. Serve
it topped with nonfat yogurt or sour cream.

PREPARATION TIME: 30 minutes plus 2 hours chilling time ▪
COOKING TIME: 60 minutes ▪ YIELD: 8 servings

2 tablespoons low-sodium nonfat
   chicken broth
1 medium onion, diced
1 cup sliced celery
2 cloves garlic, minced
6 cups water

2 cups peeled and diced beets
2 cups peeled and diced turnips
2 tablespoons minced parsley
½ teaspoon ground black pepper
1 large apple, peeled, cored, and
   diced

1. Heat broth in a large saucepan. Add onion, celery, and garlic, and sauté
   for 5 minutes.

2. Add water, beets, turnips, parsley, and black pepper. Bring to a boil, reduce heat, and simmer for 45 minutes.
3. Stir in the apple and continue to simmer for 10 additional minutes.
4. Transfer soup to a blender or food processor and blend until smooth.
5. Chill for 2 hours before serving.

Calories Per Serving: 83	Carbohydrates: 19 g
Fat: 0 g	Dietary Fiber: 5 g
Cholesterol: 0 mg	Sodium: 81 mg
Protein: 2 g	

❧ *Hot Vegetable Borscht* ❧

In this tangy borscht, tomato juice, onion, carrot, beets, potatoes, and cabbage are accented with honey and lemon juice.

PREPARATION TIME: 30 minutes ▪ *COOKING TIME: 35 minutes* ▪
YIELD: 6 servings

3 cups water	*1 cup peeled and diced potatoes*
1 cup low-sodium tomato juice	*2 cups shredded cabbage*
¾ cup chopped onion	*1½ tablespoons honey*
1 medium carrot, diced	*1½ tablespoons lemon juice*
1 cup peeled and shredded beets	

1. Place water and tomato juice in a heavy soup pot and bring to a boil.
2. Add onion, carrot, beets, potatoes, and cabbage. Return to a boil, reduce heat, cover, and simmer for 30 minutes.
3. Remove 2 cups soup from pot and puree in a blender or food processor.
4. Return pureed soup to pot. Stir in honey and lemon juice, cover, and simmer for 5 minutes.
5. Transfer to individual bowls and serve.

Calories Per Serving: 109	Carbohydrates: 25 g
Fat: 0 g	Dietary Fiber: 3 g
Cholesterol: 0 mg	Sodium: 63 mg
Protein: 4 g	

❧ November Soup ❧

This full-bodied soup evokes many rich, inviting sensations of fall.

PREPARATION TIME: 20 minutes　•　COOKING TIME: 20 minutes　•
YIELD: 8 servings

6 cups low-sodium nonfat chicken broth	2 cups chopped turnips
2 cups diced sweet potatoes	1 teaspoon ground cinnamon
2 cups diced butternut squash	1 teaspoon ground ginger
2 cups diced apples	1 teaspoon ground nutmeg
1 small onion, chopped	¼ cup maple syrup
2 medium carrots, chopped	1 cup skim milk
	¼ teaspoon ground black pepper

1. Bring broth to a boil in a large pot. Add sweet potatoes, squash, apples, onion, carrots, and turnips. Return to a boil and reduce heat. Stir in cinnamon, ginger, nutmeg, and maple syrup, and simmer until vegetables begin to soften, about 15 minutes.
2. Transfer the mixture to a blender or food processor and puree until smooth. Return the puree to the soup pot, stir in the milk and black pepper, and heat through. Serve at once.

Calories Per Serving: 120	Carbohydrates: 26 g
Fat: 1 g	Dietary Fiber: 3 g
Cholesterol: 1 mg	Sodium: 244 mg
Protein: 5 g	

❧ Winter Vegetable Soup ❧

This hearty stew is filled with vegetables. Be sure to add the broccoli last, so it will not be overcooked.

PREPARATION TIME: 20 minutes　•　COOKING TIME: 30 minutes　•
YIELD: 8 servings

2 cups low-sodium nonfat chicken
  broth
1 medium turnip, diced
1 medium carrot, scraped and sliced
1 medium onion, chopped
1 leek, chopped
1 stalk celery, chopped
3 cloves garlic, minced

3 cups water
2 cups peeled, diced acorn squash
2 cups shredded cabbage
1 jalapeño pepper, seeded and minced
3 cups peeled and chopped broccoli
  stems
½ teaspoon ground black pepper

1. Bring 1 cup broth to a boil in a large saucepan. Add turnip, carrot, onion, leek, celery, and garlic. Simmer over medium heat for 5 minutes.
2. Add remaining broth, water, squash, cabbage, and jalapeño pepper. Bring to a boil, reduce heat, and simmer until turnips and carrot are not quite tender, about 20 minutes.
3. Add broccoli and black pepper, and continue to simmer until broccoli is just tender, about 5 minutes. Serve in individual bowls.

Calories Per Serving: 64
Fat: 1 g
Cholesterol: 0 mg
Protein: 4 g

Carbohydrates: 14 g
Dietary Fiber: 4 g
Sodium: 180 mg

❧ *Garlic-Veggie Soup* ❧

Carrots, turnip, potatoes, tomatoes, and kidney beans are the featured ingredients in this soup.

PREPARATION TIME: *20 minutes* • COOKING TIME: *35 minutes* •
YIELD: *10 servings*

7 cups low-sodium nonfat chicken
  broth
3 cups water
1 medium onion, chopped
2 cups sliced carrots
4 cloves garlic, minced
1 bay leaf
¼ teaspoon cayenne pepper

3 cups diced turnip
1 cup unpeeled, diced potatoes
2 medium tomatoes, chopped
2 cups low-sodium canned kidney
  beans, rinsed and drained
¼ cup minced fresh parsley
½ teaspoon ground black pepper

1. Place broth, water, onion, carrots, garlic, bay leaf, and cayenne pepper in a large saucepan. Bring to a boil, reduce heat, and simmer for 10 minutes.
2. Add turnip and potatoes, and simmer until the turnip is done, about 20 minutes.
3. Stir in the tomatoes, kidney beans, parsley, and black pepper, and simmer to heat through, about 5 minutes. Remove bay leaf before serving.

Calories Per Serving: 69

Carbohydrates: 13 g

Fat: 1 g

Dietary Fiber: 3 g

Cholesterol: 0 mg

Sodium: 269 mg

Protein: 5 g

✿ *Spiced Vegetable–Chickpea Soup* ✿

This soup contains apricots, raisins, chickpeas, and spinach.

PREPARATION TIME: 20 minutes   •   COOKING TIME: 56 minutes   •
YIELD: 8 servings

¼ cup low-sodium nonfat chicken broth

1 medium onion, chopped

1 medium green bell pepper, cored and diced

2 cups chopped zucchini

2 stalks celery, chopped

3 cloves garlic, minced

1 tablespoon minced fresh gingerroot

1 jalapeño pepper, seeded and minced

2 tablespoons curry powder

1 tablespoon ground cumin

2 teaspoons ground coriander

¼ teaspoon turmeric

¼ teaspoon ground cloves

¼ teaspoon ground black pepper

5 cups water

2 cups cooked or low-sodium canned chickpeas, rinsed and drained

½ cup raisins

4 juice-packed canned apricots, drained and chopped

2 cups chopped spinach

1. Heat broth in a large saucepan. Add onion, green bell pepper, zucchini, and celery. Sauté until pepper begins to soften, about 5 minutes. Add the garlic, gingerroot, jalapeño, curry powder, cumin, coriander, turmeric, cloves, and black pepper.

2. Stir in the water, chickpeas, and raisins. Bring to a boil, reduce heat, and simmer, stirring several times, for 40 minutes. Add apricots and spinach, and continue to simmer for an additional 10 minutes.
3. Transfer to individual bowls and serve.

Calories Per Serving: 123
Fat: 0 g
Cholesterol: 0 mg
Protein: 6 g

Carbohydrates: 27 g
Dietary Fiber: 3 g
Sodium: 290 mg

❧ *Garden Variety Soup* ❧

Seven vegetables are featured in this soup with pearl barley and parsley.

PREPARATION TIME: 15 minutes ▪ *COOKING TIME: 45 minutes* ▪
YIELD: 10 servings

6¼ cups low-sodium vegetable broth
2 medium onions, chopped
4 cloves garlic, minced
1 medium red bell pepper, cored and
*   chopped*
2 cups low-sodium tomato juice
1 cup pearl barley
2 medium tomatoes, chopped
3 cups chopped spinach leaves

1 cup chopped fresh parsley
1 tablespoon dried basil
1 cup fresh or frozen, thawed lima
*   beans*
1 cup chopped yellow summer squash
1 cup fresh or frozen, thawed green
*   peas*
¼ teaspoon ground black pepper

1. Heat ¼ cup broth in a large saucepan. Add onions, garlic, and red bell pepper, and sauté until pepper begins to soften, about 5 minutes.
2. Add the remaining broth, tomato juice, barley, and tomatoes. Bring to a boil, reduce heat, and simmer for 30 minutes. Add spinach, parsley, basil, limas, squash, and peas, and continue to simmer until vegetables are just tender, about 10 additional minutes.
3. Transfer soup to individual bowls, sprinkle with black pepper, and serve.

Calories Per Serving: 210
Fat: 1 g
Cholesterol: 0 mg
Protein: 9 g

Carbohydrates: 44 g
Dietary Fiber: 6 g
Sodium: 70 mg

❧ *Mulligatawny Soup* ❧

This is a delicious nonfat variation of the traditional spicy Indian soup.

PREPARATION TIME: 20 minutes ▪ *COOKING TIME: 30 minutes* ▪
YIELD: 8 servings

6¼ cups low-sodium nonfat chicken
 broth
2 medium onions, chopped
2 stalks celery, chopped
1 medium green bell pepper, cored
 and chopped
2 cups water
½ teaspoon turmeric

½ teaspoon ground coriander
2 medium carrots, diced
2 cups peeled chopped potatoes
2 medium tomatoes, chopped
3 tablespoons lemon juice
1 teaspoon dried cilantro
½ teaspoon ground black pepper

1. Heat ¼ cup broth in a large saucepan. Add onions, celery, and green bell pepper, and sauté until pepper begins to soften, about 5 minutes.
2. Add remaining broth, water, turmeric, coriander, carrots, and potatoes. Bring to a boil, reduce heat, and simmer until potatoes are just tender, about 20 minutes.
3. Stir in tomatoes, lemon juice, cilantro, and black pepper, and continue to simmer until all ingredients are heated through, about 5 additional minutes.
4. Transfer to individual bowls and serve.

Calories Per Serving: 108
Fat: 0 g
Cholesterol: 0 mg
Protein: 8 g

Carbohydrates: 19 g
Dietary Fiber: 3 g
Sodium: 155 mg

❧ *Tomato-Vegetable Soup* ❧

Tomato soup is enhanced with zucchini, green pepper, mushrooms, and celery.

PREPARATION TIME: 25 minutes plus 2 hours standing time •
COOKING TIME: 12 minutes • *YIELD: 4 servings*

6 medium tomatoes
½ cup low-sodium nonfat chicken
   broth
1 medium red bell pepper, cored and
   diced
2 garlic cloves, minced
2 tablespoons low-sodium tomato
   paste

¼ teaspoon ground thyme
1 cup diced zucchini
1 medium green bell pepper, cored
   and diced
1 cup sliced mushrooms
1 celery stalk, diced
1 teaspoon dried basil
¼ teaspoon ground black pepper

1. Blanch tomatoes in large pot of boiling water for 1 minute. Plunge into cold water to cool. Remove the skins and quarter tomatoes. Place them in a blender or food processor and puree.
2. Heat ¼ cup broth in a large saucepan. Add red bell pepper and sauté until it just begins to soften, about 3 minutes. Add garlic and tomato paste, and continue to sauté for 2 additional minutes. Stir in thyme. Remove from heat and allow to stand at room temperature for 2 hours.
3. Heat remaining broth in a large skillet over medium heat. Add zucchini, green bell pepper, mushrooms, celery, and basil, and sauté until tender-crisp, about 6 minutes.
4. Combine tomato puree, vegetable mixture, and black pepper. Bring to a simmer and heat through.
5. Transfer to individual bowls and serve.

Calories Per Serving: 76
Fat: 1 g
Cholesterol: 0 mg
Protein: 4 g

Carbohydrates: 16 g
Dietary Fiber: 4 g
Sodium: 125 mg

❧ *Vegetable-Rice Soup* ❧

This thick soup contains onion, garlic, celery, bell peppers, tomatoes, brown rice, and paprika.

PREPARATION TIME: 15 minutes　•　COOKING TIME: 45 minutes　•
YIELD: 8 servings

6 cups low-sodium nonfat chicken
　broth
1 medium onion, chopped
4 cloves garlic, crushed
2 stalks celery, sliced
2 medium green bell peppers, cored
　and coarsely chopped

3 medium tomatoes, chopped, with
　juice
½ cup uncooked brown rice
1 tablespoon paprika
⅛ teaspoon cayenne pepper
½ teaspoon ground black pepper
½ cup finely chopped fresh parsley

1. Place broth in a large saucepan. Add onion, garlic, celery, green bell peppers, tomatoes, rice, paprika, and cayenne pepper.
2. Bring to a boil, reduce heat, and simmer until rice is just tender, about 45 minutes.
3. Transfer to individual bowls, sprinkle with black pepper, and garnish with parsley before serving.

Calories Per Serving: 97
Fat: 0 g
Cholesterol: 0 mg
Protein: 7 g

Carbohydrates: 17 g
Dietary Fiber: 2 g
Sodium: 146 mg

❧ *Mango-Papaya Soup* ❧

This is a cool and delicate fruit soup.

PREPARATION TIME: 15 minutes plus 2 hours chilling time　•　YIELD: 4 servings

1 cup peeled, chopped mango
1 cup peeled, chopped papaya

1 cup fresh or juice-packed, canned,
　pineapple chunks

1 medium orange, peeled and
 chopped
¼ cup orange juice

1 tablespoon brown sugar
1 cup nonfat vanilla yogurt

1. Combine the fruit chunks, orange juice, and brown sugar in a blender or food processor, and process until smooth.
2. Transfer to a bowl and stir in yogurt. Mix thoroughly and chill for 2 hours.

Calories Per Serving: 134
Fat: 0 g
Cholesterol: 1 mg
Protein: 4 g

Carbohydrates: 31 g
Dietary Fiber: 4 g
Sodium: 39 mg

❧ *Melon-Berry Gazpacho* ❧

This cooling, sweet treat is a blend of 5 fruits, tomatoes, and orange juice.

PREPARATION TIME: 15 minutes plus 1 hour chilling time • YIELD: 8 servings

1 cup chopped, seeded watermelon
1 cup chopped cantaloupe
1 cup chopped honeydew melon
1 cup seedless grape halves
2 kiwifruits, peeled and chopped
1 cup quartered strawberries
5 medium tomatoes, chopped, with
 juice

2 tablespoons rice wine vinegar
1 tablespoon brown sugar
1 tablespoon grated lemon peel
½ teaspoon ground cardamom
⅛ teaspoon hot pepper sauce
2½ cups orange juice

1. Combine watermelon, cantaloupe, honeydew, grapes, kiwi, and strawberries in a large bowl.
2. Place tomatoes and their juice in a blender or food processor and puree.
3. Whisk together the vinegar, brown sugar, lemon peel, cardamom, and hot pepper sauce. Stir in orange juice and tomato puree. Pour over the fruit and mix well.
4. Chill for 1 hour before serving.

Calories Per Serving: 99   Carbohydrates: 24 g
Fat: 1 g   Dietary Fiber: 3 g
Cholesterol: 0 mg   Sodium: 15 mg
Protein: 2 g

❧ *Two-Melon Soup* ❧

Honeydew and cantaloupe are sweetened with brown sugar and sprinkled
with cinnamon.

PREPARATION TIME: 15 minutes plus 2 hours chilling time • YIELD: 4 servings

2 cups chopped honeydew melon   *1 tablespoon brown sugar*
2 cups chopped cantaloupe   *1 cup nonfat vanilla yogurt*
1 tablespoon lemon juice   *¼ teaspoon ground cinnamon*

1. Combine honeydew, cantaloupe, lemon juice, and brown sugar in a
   blender or food processor and process until smooth.
2. Transfer to a bowl and stir in yogurt. Mix thoroughly and refrigerate for
   2 hours.
3. Sprinkle with cinnamon and serve.

Calories Per Serving: 124   Carbohydrates: 30 g
Fat: 0 g   Dietary Fiber: 2 g
Cholesterol: 1 mg   Sodium: 54 mg
Protein: 4 g

❧ *Cold Carrot Soup with Thyme* ❧

This carrot soup with yogurt is served cold. Carrots should be stored in a
plastic bag in the refrigerator and away from apples, which emit ethylene
gas that can give carrots a bitter taste.

PREPARATION TIME: 20 minutes plus 1 hour chilling time •
COOKING TIME: 20 minutes • YIELD: 6 servings

4 cups water
6 medium carrots, shredded
1 medium potato, diced
1 medium onion, minced

½ teaspoon ground thyme
2 cloves garlic, crushed
½ cup nonfat plain yogurt
½ cup nonfat buttermilk

1. Bring water to a boil in a large saucepan. Add carrots, potato, onion, thyme, and garlic. Return to a boil, reduce heat, and simmer until vegetables begin to soften, about 20 minutes.
2. Transfer the soup to a blender or food processor and puree. Pour puree into a large bowl. Whisk in yogurt and buttermilk.
3. Cover and refrigerate until chilled through, about 1 hour, before serving.

Calories Per Serving: 95
Fat: 0 g
Cholesterol: 1 mg
Protein: 4 g

Carbohydrates: 21 g
Dietary Fiber: 2 g
Sodium: 70 mg

❧ *Chilled Carrot-Leek Soup* ❧

Carrots are added to the classic vichyssoise recipe.

PREPARATION TIME: *15 minutes plus 1 hour, 10 minutes chilling time* •
COOKING TIME: *35 minutes* • YIELD: *8 servings*

2 tablespoons low-sodium nonfat
    chicken broth
1 medium onion, diced
1 leek, chopped
3 medium carrots, scraped and diced
4 cups water

2 cups peeled and chopped potatoes
2 tablespoons dried parsley
1 teaspoon ground white pepper
2 cups skim milk
2 scallions, chopped

1. Heat broth in a large saucepan. Add onion, leek, and carrots, and sauté over medium heat until carrots begin to soften, about 5 minutes.
2. Add water, potatoes, parsley, and white pepper. Bring to a boil, reduce heat, and simmer, stirring occasionally, for 30 minutes. Add milk and return to a simmer.

3. Remove soup from heat and allow to cool for 10 minutes. Transfer to a food processor or blender and puree.
4. Pour into a large bowl, cover, and refrigerate for 1 hour.
5. Garnish with scallions and serve.

Calories Per Serving: 98   Carbohydrates: 20 g
Fat: 0 g   Dietary Fiber: 3 g
Cholesterol: 1 mg   Sodium: 59 mg
Protein: 5 g

✎ *Chilled Cucumber Soup* ✎

Whole cucumbers can be stored in a plastic bag in the refrigerator for up to 10 days.

PREPARATION TIME: 10 minutes plus 2 hours chilling time • YIELD: 6 servings

4 small cucumbers, peeled and   2½ cups skim milk
  chopped   ¼ teaspoon ground black pepper
1 small onion   2 tablespoons chopped fresh parsley or
2 cloves garlic, minced   dill
2½ cups low-sodium nonfat chicken
  broth

1. Place cucumbers, onion, and garlic in a blender or food processor and puree until smooth.
2. Combine blended vegetables, broth, milk, and black pepper in a large bowl. Chill for 2 hours.
3. Garnish with fresh parsley or dill and serve.

Calories Per Serving: 76   Carbohydrates: 13 g
Fat: 0 g   Dietary Fiber: 0 g
Cholesterol: 2 mg   Sodium: 374 mg
Protein: 5 g

❧ *Chilled Red Pepper Soup* ❧

This cold soup has the robust flavor of roasted red bell peppers, leeks, and buttermilk.

PREPARATION TIME: 15 minutes plus 15 minutes cooling time and 30 minutes chilling time ▪ *COOKING TIME: 45 minutes* ▪ *YIELD: 4 servings*

3 large red bell peppers
4 leeks (white parts only), sliced
2 cups low-sodium nonfat chicken broth

2 cups nonfat buttermilk
¼ teaspoon ground black pepper

1. Preheat broiler.
2. Arrange the peppers on a baking sheet and place under the broiler until their skin begins to char. Remove from the broiler, place in a paper bag, and allow to cool for 15 minutes.
3. Combine the leeks and broth in a large saucepan and bring to a boil. Reduce heat and simmer for 20 minutes.
4. Peel the bell peppers. Core and chop the peppers. Add to the broth and leeks, and simmer for an additional 20 minutes.
5. Allow the mixture to cool. Transfer to a blender and puree. Pour into a bowl and add the buttermilk. Sprinkle with black pepper and chill for 30 minutes before serving.

Calories Per Serving: 149
Fat: 1 g
Cholesterol: 2 mg
Protein: 10 g

Carbohydrates: 27 g
Dietary Fiber: 3 g
Sodium: 174 mg

❧ *Chilled Vegetable-Couscous Soup* ❧

This variation of gazpacho includes couscous.

PREPARATION TIME: 20 minutes plus 1 hour chilling time ▪
COOKING TIME: 5 minutes ▪ *YIELD: 6 servings*

1 cup water

¼ cup uncooked couscous

2 medium tomatoes, diced

1 small onion, diced

1 yellow bell pepper, cored and chopped

1 red bell pepper, cored and chopped

1 small cucumber, diced

1 jalapeño pepper, seeded and minced

2 cloves garlic, minced

½ cup chopped fresh parsley

2 teaspoons dried basil

¼ teaspoon ground black pepper

2 cups low-sodium tomato juice

6 basil leaves

1. Bring water to a boil in a saucepan. Stir in couscous, remove from heat, and allow to stand for 5 minutes.
2. Combine remaining ingredients in a blender or food processor. Blend briefly.
3. Transfer to a large bowl, stir in couscous, cover, and chill for 1 hour.
4. Divide soup among individual bowls, garnish each with a basil leaf, and serve.

Calories Per Serving: 58

Fat: 0 g

Cholesterol: 0 mg

Protein: 2 g

Carbohydrates: 13 g

Dietary Fiber: 3 g

Sodium: 50 mg

❧ *Chilled Black Bean Soup* ❧

This cold and refreshing black bean gazpacho is perfect for summer main dishes.

PREPARATION TIME: 15 minutes plus 1 hour chilling time • YIELD: 4 servings

2 tomatoes, chopped, with juice

1 medium onion, diced

1 medium green bell pepper, cored and diced

1 small cucumber, peeled and chopped

1 jalapeño pepper, seeded and minced

2 cloves garlic, minced

1 teaspoon dried cilantro

1 teaspoon ground cumin

¼ teaspoon ground black pepper

2 cups low-sodium tomato juice

1¼ cups cooked or low-sodium canned black beans, rinsed and drained

¼ cup minced fresh parsley

1. Combine tomatoes, their juice, onion, green bell pepper, cucumber, jalapeño, garlic, cilantro, cumin, and black pepper in a food processor or blender. Blend very briefly.
2. Stir in tomato juice and beans and chill for 1 hour. Transfer to individual bowls, top each with minced parsley, and serve.

Calories Per Serving: 127
Fat: 1 g
Cholesterol: 0 mg
Protein: 7 g

Carbohydrates: 26 g
Dietary Fiber: 6 g
Sodium: 394 mg

❧ *Chilled Black Bean–Corn Soup* ❧

Canned beans are combined with tomato juice, cucumbers, red onions, yellow bell peppers, and jalapeño.

PREPARATION TIME: *20 minutes plus 4 hours chilling time* •
COOKING TIME: *3 minutes* • YIELD: *8 servings*

6 cups low-sodium tomato juice
1 medium red onion, finely chopped
3 cloves garlic, minced
½ cup fresh or frozen, thawed corn kernels
2 cups cooked or low-sodium canned black beans, drained
1 medium cucumber, finely chopped
1 medium yellow bell pepper, cored and finely chopped

1 cup finely chopped zucchini
1 stalk celery, finely chopped
4 scallions, thinly sliced
1 jalapeño pepper, seeded and minced
½ cup minced fresh parsley
2 tablespoons red wine vinegar
2 tablespoons lemon juice
½ teaspoon ground black pepper

1. Heat ¼ cup tomato juice in a saucepan. Add onion and garlic, and sauté until onion begins to soften, about 3 minutes.
2. Combine remaining ingredients in a large bowl. Pour remaining tomato juice over vegetables and chill in the refrigerator for 4 hours.
3. Transfer to individual bowls and serve.

Calories Per Serving: 104

Fat: 0 g

Cholesterol: 0 mg

Protein: 6 g

Carbohydrates: 22 g

Dietary Fiber: 5 g

Sodium: 59 mg

❧ *Gazpacho with White Beans* ❧

In this flavorful gazpacho, white beans join the classic ingredients.

PREPARATION TIME: 15 minutes plus 2 hours chilling time • *YIELD: 6 servings*

5 cups low-sodium tomato juice

2 cups low-sodium canned Great Northern beans, drained and rinsed

2 medium tomatoes, chopped, with juice

1 small cucumber, peeled and diced

1 medium red bell pepper, cored and diced

4 scallions, chopped

½ cup diced celery

1 teaspoon dried basil

¼ cup minced fresh parsley

1 teaspoon dried oregano

1 tablespoon red wine vinegar

2 cloves garlic, crushed

¼ teaspoon ground cumin

¼ teaspoon ground black pepper

1. Combine all ingredients.
2. Mix well and refrigerate for 2 hours before serving.

Calories Per Serving: 161

Fat: 1 g

Cholesterol: 0 mg

Protein: 9 g

Carbohydrates: 32 g

Dietary Fiber: 4 g

Sodium: 49 mg

❧ *Split Pea Soup with Brown Rice* ❧

This split pea soup is made with cumin, cinnamon, and cayenne. Split peas are yellow or green and, when dried, usually split along a natural seam.

PREPARATION TIME: 15 minutes • *COOKING TIME: 50 minutes* •
YIELD: 6 servings

1 cup split peas
½ cup uncooked brown rice
6 cups low-sodium nonfat chicken broth
3 medium onions, chopped
4 cloves garlic, crushed
1 teaspoon ground cumin
½ teaspoon ground cinnamon
⅛ teaspoon cayenne pepper
1 tablespoon lemon juice
½ cup chopped fresh parsley
½ teaspoon ground black pepper

1. Combine peas, rice, and 5 cups broth in a large saucepan. Bring to a boil, reduce heat, cover, and simmer until peas and rice are tender, about 35 minutes.
2. Combine remaining broth in another saucepan with onions, garlic, cumin, cinnamon, and cayenne pepper. Bring to a boil, reduce heat, and simmer until onions are tender, about 15 minutes.
3. Combine onion mixture with the peas and rice. Stir in lemon juice, parsley, and black pepper.
4. Transfer to individual bowls and serve.

Calories Per Serving: 239
Fat: 1 g
Cholesterol: 0 mg
Protein: 17 g
Carbohydrates: 41 g
Dietary Fiber: 3 g
Sodium: 182 mg

Yellow Split Pea Soup

Curry powder adds special flavor to this split pea soup.

PREPARATION TIME: *10 minutes* ▪ COOKING TIME: *45 minutes* ▪ YIELD: *8 servings*

2 cups yellow split peas
6 cups low-sodium nonfat chicken broth
2 cups water
2 medium onions, chopped
4 medium carrots, scraped and chopped
2 cups chopped celery
1 bay leaf
1 tablespoon curry powder
½ teaspoon ground black pepper

1. Place split peas, broth, and water in a large soup pot. Bring to a boil, reduce heat, and simmer for 20 minutes.
2. Stir in remaining ingredients. Return to a boil, reduce heat, and simmer for another 25 minutes. Remove bay leaf.
3. Transfer in batches to a blender or food processor and blend briefly to achieve desired consistency. Serve at once.

Calories Per Serving: 234   Carbohydrates: 38 g
Fat: 1 g   Dietary Fiber: 4 g
Cholesterol: 0 mg   Sodium: 205 mg
Protein: 20

❧ *Artichoke-Bean Soup* ❧

Carrots and potatoes are combined with artichoke hearts, white beans, and tomatoes in this savory soup.

PREPARATION TIME: 10 minutes • COOKING TIME: 28 minutes •
YIELD: 8 servings

2 medium onions, chopped
4 cloves garlic, crushed
6 cups low-sodium nonfat chicken broth
⅛ teaspoon cayenne pepper
3 medium carrots, scraped and chopped
2 cups chopped potatoes

2 medium tomatoes, chopped, with juice
1 cup artichoke hearts, chopped
2 cups low-sodium canned Great Northern beans, drained
½ cup chopped fresh parsley
¼ teaspoon ground black pepper

1. Place onions, garlic, and ½ cup broth in a large saucepan. Bring to a boil, reduce heat, and simmer until onions are soft, about 5 minutes.
2. Stir in remaining broth, cayenne pepper, carrots, and potatoes. Bring to a boil, reduce heat, and simmer until potatoes are tender, about 20 minutes.
3. Add tomatoes with their juice and remaining ingredients. Continue to simmer until heated through, about 3 minutes. Serve at once.

Calories Per Serving: 171
Fat: 0 g
Cholesterol: 0 mg
Protein: 12 g

Carbohydrates: 32 g
Dietary Fiber: 4 g
Sodium: 368 mg

❧ *Butternut-Bean Soup* ❧

Squash and white beans are flavored with curry and gingerroot.

PREPARATION TIME: 20 minutes • *COOKING TIME: 40 minutes* •
YIELD: 10 servings

*¼ cup low-sodium nonfat chicken
  broth*
1 medium onion, diced
1 cup diced celery
2 cloves garlic, crushed
1 jalapeño pepper, seeded and minced
1 tablespoon fresh grated gingerroot
*4 cups peeled, chopped butternut
  squash*

¼ cup minced fresh parsley
1 teaspoon dried thyme
1 tablespoon curry powder
1 teaspoon ground cumin
6 cups water
1 cup chopped spinach
*1½ cups low-sodium canned Great
  Northern beans, drained and
  rinsed*

1. Heat broth in a large saucepan. Add onion, celery, garlic, jalapeño pepper, and gingerroot. Sauté over medium heat for 6 minutes.
2. Add squash, and sauté for additional 3 minutes. Stir in parsley, thyme, curry powder, and cumin, and sauté for 1 more minute.
3. Add water. Bring to a boil, reduce heat, and simmer, stirring occasionally, for 20 minutes.
4. Stir in spinach and beans, and simmer for 10 more minutes. Transfer to individual bowls and serve.

Calories Per Serving: 78
Fat: 0 g
Cholesterol: 0 mg
Protein: 4 g

Carbohydrates: 15 g
Dietary Fiber: 1 g
Sodium: 70 mg

❧ *White Bean and Spinach Soup* ❧

Almost like a minestrone, this soup is enriched with leeks, mushrooms, tomato paste, and basil.

PREPARATION TIME: 20 minutes • *COOKING TIME: 26 minutes* •
YIELD: 8 servings

¼ cup low-sodium nonfat chicken broth
2 cups chopped leeks
1 cup diced celery
2 cups sliced mushrooms
4 cloves garlic, minced
6 cups water
2 cups low-sodium canned Great
    Northern beans, rinsed and
    drained

2 medium carrots, scraped and diced
1 medium potato, peeled and diced
3 cups rinsed and chopped spinach
3 tablespoons low-sodium tomato
    paste
1 tablespoon dried basil
1 tablespoon dried oregano

1. Heat broth in a large soup pot. Add leeks, celery, mushrooms, and garlic. Sauté until leeks begin to soften, about 6 minutes.
2. Add all remaining ingredients. Bring to a boil, reduce heat, and simmer, stirring occasionally, for 20 minutes.
3. Transfer to individual bowls and serve.

Calories Per Serving: 159
Fat: 1 g
Cholesterol: 0 mg
Protein: 8 g

Carbohydrates: 32 g
Dietary Fiber: 3 g
Sodium: 75 mg

❧ *Sweet Potato–Bean Soup* ❧

This rich soup is made with corn, white beans, carrots, leeks, and celery.

PREPARATION TIME: 15 minutes • *COOKING TIME: 32 minutes* •
YIELD: 6 servings

¼ cup low-sodium nonfat chicken
    broth

2 cups chopped leeks
2 medium carrots, chopped

1 cup diced celery

3 cloves garlic, minced

4 cups water

2 cups low-sodium canned Great Northern beans, rinsed and drained

2 cups diced sweet potatoes

1 teaspoon dried thyme

1 teaspoon ground black pepper

2 cups skim milk

1½ cups fresh or thawed frozen corn kernels

1 teaspoon dried dill

1. Heat broth in a large soup pot. Add leeks, carrots, celery, and garlic. Sauté over medium heat until carrots are just tender, about 7 minutes.
2. Add water, beans, sweet potatoes, thyme, and pepper. Bring to a boil, reduce heat, and simmer until potatoes are tender, about 20 minutes.
3. Stir in milk, corn, and dill. Simmer, stirring occasionally, until heated through, about 5 minutes. Serve at once.

Calories Per Serving: 163

Fat: 1 g

Cholesterol: 1 mg

Protein: 0 g

Carbohydrates: 34 g

Dietary Fiber: 5 g

Sodium: 96 mg

❧ Okra–Spinach–Pinto Bean Gumbo ❧

Okra is teamed with pinto beans and spinach in this thick, robust soup.

PREPARATION TIME: 20 minutes • COOKING TIME: 36 minutes •
YIELD: 10 servings

¼ cup low-sodium nonfat chicken broth

1 medium onion, diced

1 medium green bell pepper, cored and diced

1 cup diced celery

4 cloves garlic, minced

6 cups water

1 cup cooked or low-sodium canned pinto beans, rinsed and drained

2 cups low-sodium canned tomatoes, crushed, with juice

2 medium carrots, thinly sliced

¼ cup minced fresh parsley

1 tablespoon dried oregano

1 teaspoon dried thyme

½ teaspoon ground black pepper

¼ teaspoon cayenne pepper

1 cup chopped fresh or thawed frozen okra

3 cups chopped fresh spinach

4 cups cooked white rice

3 scallions, minced

1. Heat broth in a large soup pot. Add onion, green bell pepper, celery, and garlic. Sauté until pepper begins to soften, about 6 minutes.
2. Add water, beans, tomatoes with juice, carrots, parsley, oregano, thyme, black pepper, and cayenne pepper. Bring to a boil, reduce heat, and simmer, stirring occasionally, for 15 minutes.
3. Add okra and spinach. Return to a boil, reduce heat, and simmer for an additional 15 minutes.
4. Stir rice into soup and heat through.
5. Serve over beds of rice in individual bowls topped with minced scallions.

Calories Per Serving: 160	Carbohydrates: 34 g
Fat: 1 g	Dietary Fiber: 3 g
Cholesterol: 0 mg	Sodium: 56 mg
Protein: 5 g	

✬ *Pinto Bean–Winter Vegetable Soup* ✬

This vegetable soup, filled with herbs and beans, is perfect for cold winter nights.

PREPARATION TIME: 20 minutes • COOKING TIME: 1 hour, 15 minutes •
YIELD: 10 servings

2½ cups low-sodium nonfat chicken broth	¼ cup chopped fresh parsley
1 leek, white part only, sliced	2 teaspoons dried basil
1½ medium onions, thinly sliced	5 cups water
3 cloves garlic, minced	1 bay leaf
2 stalks celery, sliced	2 cups cooked or low-sodium canned pinto beans, rinsed and drained
2 medium carrots, scraped and sliced	2 cups shredded cabbage
2 parsnips, peeled and chopped	2 medium tomatoes, chopped
1 small potato, peeled and diced	

1. Bring ½ cup broth to a boil in a large saucepan. Add leek, onions, garlic, celery, and carrots. Reduce heat and simmer for 20 minutes.
2. Add parsnips, potato, parsley, basil, remaining broth, and 4½ cups water. Return to a boil, reduce heat, add bay leaf, and simmer for 40 minutes.

3. Place remaining water and beans in a blender or food processor and blend until smooth.

4. Stir cabbage and pureed beans into the soup. Cook for 10 minutes. Add tomatoes and cook for an additional 5 minutes. Remove bay leaf and serve.

Calories Per Serving: 149   Carbohydrates: 30 g
Fat: 1 g   Dietary Fiber: 4 g
Cholesterol: 0 mg   Sodium: 46 mg
Protein: 6 g

❧ *Great Northern Bean–Vegetable Soup* ❧

This bean soup is rich in protein.

PREPARATION TIME: 10 minutes • COOKING TIME: 28 minutes •
YIELD: 6 servings

¼ cup low-sodium nonfat chicken broth
1 stalk celery, chopped
1 medium carrot, scraped and chopped
1 medium onion, chopped
½ cup chopped fresh parsley

4 cups low-sodium canned Great Northern beans, rinsed and drained
4 cups water
½ cup low-sodium tomato paste
⅛ teaspoon cayenne pepper
¼ teaspoon ground black pepper

1. Heat broth in a large saucepan over medium heat. Add celery, carrot, and onion, and sauté until soft, about 8 minutes.

2. Add parsley, beans, water, tomato paste, cayenne pepper, and black pepper. Bring to a boil, reduce heat, and simmer for 20 minutes. Transfer to individual bowls and serve.

Calories Per Serving: 238   Carbohydrates: 45 g
Fat: 1 g   Dietary Fiber: 2 g
Cholesterol: 0 mg   Sodium: 48 mg
Protein: 15 g

❧ *Pinto Bean and Zucchini Soup* ❧

Pinto beans, macaroni, and tomatoes make this a quick and simple soup.

PREPARATION TIME: 15 minutes • *COOKING TIME: 18 minutes* •
YIELD: 6 servings

¼ cup low-sodium nonfat chicken
   broth
1 medium onion, diced
3 cloves garlic, minced
1 teaspoon dried thyme
2 cups chopped low-sodium canned
   tomatoes, with juice

2 cups cooked or low-sodium canned
   pinto beans, rinsed and drained
1 teaspoon chili powder
½ teaspoon ground black pepper
4 cups chopped zucchini
2 ounces uncooked macaroni
6 cups water

1. Heat broth in a large saucepan. Add onion, garlic, and thyme, and sauté until onion begins to soften, about 3 minutes.
2. Add tomatoes with their juice, pinto beans, chili powder, black pepper, zucchini, macaroni, and water. Bring to a boil, reduce heat, and simmer until macaroni is just tender, about 15 minutes.
3. Transfer to individual bowls and serve.

Calories Per Serving: 156
Fat: 1 g
Cholesterol: 0 mg
Protein: 9 g

Carbohydrates: 30 g
Dietary Fiber: 6 g
Sodium: 39 mg

❧ *Lentil Soup with Acorn Squash* ❧

A savory soup of lentils, curry, and squash. If lentils are stored airtight at room temperature, they will remain usable for up to a year.

PREPARATION TIME: 20 minutes • *COOKING TIME: 57 minutes* •
YIELD: 8 servings

6 cups water
1 cup dried lentils

¼ cup low-sodium nonfat chicken
   broth

1 medium onion, diced
1 cup diced celery
3 cloves garlic, minced
1 jalapeño pepper, seeded and minced
2 cups peeled and chopped acorn
   squash

2 medium carrots, scraped and thinly
   sliced
1 tablespoon curry powder
1 teaspoon ground cumin
½ teaspoon ground black pepper
¼ teaspoon ground cloves

1. Bring water to a boil in a large saucepan. Stir in lentils. Return to a boil, reduce heat, and simmer until lentils are tender, about 30 minutes. Remove from heat and set aside.
2. Heat broth in a large soup pot. Add onion, celery, garlic, and jalapeño, and sauté for 6 minutes. Add squash, carrots, curry powder, cumin, black pepper, and cloves, and sauté for 1 additional minute.
3. Stir in lentils with their cooking liquid. Bring to a boil, reduce heat, and simmer, stirring occasionally, for 20 minutes. Serve at once.

Calories Per Serving: 72
Fat: 0 g
Cholesterol: 0 mg
Protein: 4 g

Carbohydrates: 15 g
Dietary Fiber: 2 g
Sodium: 98 mg

৶ *Succotash—Black-eyed Pea Soup* ৶

Black-eyed peas, black beans, and pasta are ingredients in this hearty, healthy soup.

PREPARATION TIME: 15 minutes • *COOKING TIME: 40 minutes* •
YIELD: 6 servings

½ cup fresh or frozen corn kernels
½ cup fresh or frozen lima beans
1 medium carrot, chopped
2 cloves garlic, minced
¼ cup minced fresh parsley
1 teaspoon dried basil
¾ cup low-sodium tomato juice

¼ teaspoon ground black pepper
½ cup bowtie pasta
4 cups water
1 cup cooked or low-sodium canned
   black beans, rinsed and drained
1 cup cooked or low-sodium canned
   black-eyed peas, rinsed and drained

1. Combine corn, lima beans, carrot, garlic, parsley, basil, tomato juice, black pepper, pasta, and water in a large soup pot. Bring to a boil, reduce heat, and simmer for 20 minutes.
2. Stir in black beans and black-eyed peas and continue to simmer for another 20 minutes. Transfer to individual bowls and serve at once.

Calories Per Serving: 147
Fat: 1 g
Cholesterol: 0 mg
Protein: 8 g

Carbohydrates: 29 g
Dietary Fiber: 6 g
Sodium: 21 mg

❧ *Lentil-Barley Soup with Turnips* ❧

Turnips bring a unique flavor to this lentil and barley soup. Turnips can be refrigerated, tightly wrapped, for 2 weeks and should be washed, trimmed, and peeled before using.

PREPARATION TIME: *15 minutes* • COOKING TIME: *46 minutes* •
YIELD: *8 servings*

¼ cup low-sodium nonfat chicken broth
1 medium onion, diced
1 medium red bell pepper, cored and diced
1 cup diced celery
3 cloves garlic, minced
6 cups water
2 cups peeled and diced turnips

1 cup dried lentils
½ cup pearl barley
2 medium carrots, scraped and thinly sliced
¼ cup minced fresh parsley
1 tablespoon dried oregano
½ teaspoon ground black pepper
2 cups crushed low-sodium canned tomatoes, with juice

1. Heat broth in a large soup pot. Add onion, red bell pepper, celery, and garlic. Sauté until pepper begins to soften, about 6 minutes.
2. Add water, turnips, lentils, barley, carrots, parsley, oregano, and black pepper. Bring to a boil, reduce heat, and simmer, stirring occasionally, for 20 minutes.
3. Stir in tomatoes with their juice, and continue to simmer until lentils and barley are just tender, about 20 minutes. Serve hot.

Calories Per Serving: 100
Fat: 1 g
Cholesterol: 0 mg
Protein: 4 g

Carbohydrates: 22 g
Dietary Fiber: 5 g
Sodium: 62 mg

❧ *Shiitake-Lentil Soup* ❧

This is a simple, low-fat Ethiopian soup.

PREPARATION TIME: 25 minutes • *COOKING TIME: 35 minutes* •
YIELD: 6 servings

5 cups water
1½ cups dried lentils
2 cups minced shiitake mushrooms
2 egg whites, lightly beaten
⅓ cup chopped fresh parsley
¼ teaspoon ground black pepper

¼ cup low-sodium nonfat chicken
   broth
1 medium onion, sliced
4 ounces uncooked vermicelli, broken
   into short pieces
¼ cup lemon juice

1. Bring water to a boil in a large heavy saucepan. Stir in lentils. Return to a boil, reduce heat, and simmer for 20 minutes.
2. Combine minced shiitakes, egg whites, parsley, and black pepper. Form the mixture into small "meat" balls (about 24) and place in the refrigerator until ready to cook.
3. Heat broth in a skillet. Add half of the onion slices, and sauté until onion begins to soften, about 3 minutes. Remove from heat, drain, and set aside.
4. When the lentils are tender, mash them to thicken the soup and stir in the vermicelli.
5. Add the "meat" balls, and simmer until they are heated through and vermicelli is just tender, about 12 minutes. Remove from heat and stir in lemon juice.
6. Divide the remaining onion slices among individual serving bowls, add the soup, and serve.

Calories Per Serving: 223
Fat: 1 g
Cholesterol: 0 mg
Protein: 15 g

Carbohydrates: 41 g
Dietary Fiber: 16 g
Sodium: 14 mg

❧ *Lentil-Rice Soup* ❧

Lentils, rice, carrots, and turnips are featured in this traditional, easily assembled soup.

PREPARATION TIME: 15 minutes • *COOKING TIME: 40 minutes* •
YIELD: 6 servings

7 cups water	*4 cloves garlic, minced*
½ cup dried lentils	*1 teaspoon dried basil*
2 medium carrots, chopped	*1 teaspoon dried thyme*
1 cup chopped turnips	*¼ teaspoon ground black pepper*
2 small onions, chopped	*3½ cups crushed low-sodium canned*
1 green bell pepper, cored and	*tomatoes*
chopped	*1 cup uncooked white rice*

1. Bring water to a boil in a large saucepan. Stir in lentils, carrots, turnips, onions, green bell pepper, garlic, basil, thyme, and black pepper. Return to a boil, reduce heat, and simmer for 20 minutes.
2. Stir in tomatoes and rice. Return to a boil, reduce heat, and simmer until rice is just tender, about 20 minutes. Serve at once.

Calories Per Serving: 150	Carbohydrates: 31 g
Fat: 1 g	Dietary Fiber: 6 g
Cholesterol: 0 mg	Sodium: 37 mg
Protein: 6 g	

❧ *Spinach-Lentil Soup* ❧

This spicy soup is full of garlic and tomatoes. Spinach can be refrigerated in a plastic bag for up to 3 days.

PREPARATION TIME: 15 minutes • *COOKING TIME: 42 minutes* •
YIELD: 8 servings

1 cup dried lentils	*2 medium onions, chopped*
6 cups low-sodium nonfat chicken	*4 cloves garlic, crushed*
broth	*⅛ teaspoon cayenne pepper*

½ cup bulgur

¼ cup fresh chopped parsley

3½ cups chopped low-sodium canned
    tomatoes, with juice

4 cups chopped spinach leaves

½ teaspoon ground black pepper

1. Place lentils and broth in a large saucepan. Bring to a boil, reduce heat, and simmer for 20 minutes.
2. Add onions, garlic, cayenne pepper, bulgur, parsley, and tomatoes with their juice. Simmer until bulgur is just tender, about 20 minutes.
3. Add spinach and simmer until the spinach wilts, about 2 minutes.
4. Sprinkle with black pepper before serving.

Calories Per Serving: 109
Fat: 1 g
Cholesterol: 0 mg
Protein: 10 g

Carbohydrates: 19 g
Dietary Fiber: 5 g
Sodium: 168 mg

❧ *Harira* ❧

This tasty soup is a favorite in the Middle East.

PREPARATION TIME: *20 minutes* ▪ COOKING TIME: *35 minutes* ▪
YIELD: *10 servings*

2 medium onions, chopped

2 cups chopped celery

1 medium yellow bell pepper, cored
    and chopped

6 cups low-sodium nonfat chicken
    broth

1 teaspoon turmeric

½ teaspoon ground cinnamon

¼ teaspoon cayenne pepper

1 medium potato, chopped

2 medium carrots, scraped and
    chopped

3 medium tomatoes, chopped

1 cup chopped zucchini

1 cup cooked macaroni

1 cup cooked or low-sodium canned
    chickpeas, rinsed and drained

½ teaspoon ground black pepper

¼ cup lemon juice

¼ cup chopped fresh parsley

1. Combine onions, celery, yellow bell pepper, and ½ cup broth in a large saucepan. Bring to a boil, reduce heat, and simmer until celery begins to soften, about 10 minutes.
2. Stir in remaining broth, turmeric, cinnamon, cayenne pepper, potato, carrots, and tomatoes. Return to a boil, reduce heat, and simmer until potatoes are tender, about 20 minutes.
3. Add zucchini, macaroni, chickpeas, black pepper, and lemon juice. Heat through.
4. Transfer to individual bowls, garnish with parsley, and serve.

Calories Per Serving: 118	Carbohydrates: 21 g
Fat: 0 g	Dietary Fiber: 2 g
Cholesterol: 0 mg	Sodium: 205 mg
Protein: 8 g	

❧ *Black-eyed Pea Soup* ❧

This hearty soup is seasoned with onions, gingerroot, cayenne pepper, cinnamon, and cumin.

PREPARATION TIME: 15 minutes • COOKING TIME: 30 minutes •
YIELD: 6 servings

2 medium onions, chopped
3 cloves garlic, crushed
1 teaspoon fresh grated gingerroot
¼ teaspoon cayenne pepper
1 teaspoon ground cumin
¼ teaspoon ground cinnamon
5 cups low-sodium nonfat chicken broth

1 cup diced sweet potato
2 medium tomatoes, coarsely chopped
2 cups fresh or frozen green peas
1 cup low-sodium canned black-eyed peas, rinsed and drained
¼ teaspoon ground black pepper

1. Combine onions, garlic, gingerroot, cayenne pepper, cumin, cinnamon, and 1 cup broth in a large saucepan. Bring to a boil, reduce heat, and simmer until vegetables just begin to soften, about 5 minutes.

2. Add remaining broth, sweet potato, and tomatoes, and continue to simmer for 15 minutes. Stir in green peas and simmer for 5 more minutes.
3. Transfer soup to a blender and puree. Return to saucepan.
4. Add black-eyed peas and simmer until heated through.
5. Sprinkle with black pepper and serve.

Calories Per Serving: 174	Carbohydrates: 35 g
Fat: 1 g	Dietary Fiber: 7 g
Cholesterol: 0 mg	Sodium: 383 mg
Protein: 7 g	

❧ *Black-eyed Pea–Cabbage Soup* ❧

Here is a hearty soup inspired by the cuisine of the American South.

PREPARATION TIME: *15 minutes* • COOKING TIME: *30 minutes* •
YIELD: *8 servings*

*6 cups low-sodium nonfat chicken
  broth*
1 medium onion, chopped
2 cloves garlic, minced
3 stalks celery, sliced thin
*2 medium carrots, scraped and
  chopped*
*1 medium yellow bell pepper, cored
  and chopped*

½ teaspoon cayenne pepper
3 medium tomatoes, chopped
4 cups chopped cabbage
*1 cup low-sodium canned black-eyed
  peas, rinsed and drained*
1 teaspoon dried basil
½ teaspoon ground black pepper

1. Place ½ cup broth in a large saucepan. Add onion, garlic, and celery. Bring to a boil, reduce heat, and simmer until celery begins to soften, about 10 minutes.
2. Stir in the remaining broth, carrots, yellow bell pepper, cayenne, tomatoes, and cabbage. Bring to a boil, reduce heat, and simmer until carrots are just tender, about 20 minutes.
3. Add black-eyed peas, basil, and black pepper, and heat through.
4. Transfer to individual bowls and serve.

Calories Per Serving: 88

Fat: 0 g

Cholesterol: 0 mg

Protein: 8 g

Carbohydrates: 14 g

Dietary Fiber: 3 g

Sodium: 269 mg

❦ *Bean-Barley Soup* ❧

This bean soup has three kinds of beans, vegetables, and spices. It makes a filling and complete meal.

PREPARATION TIME: 20 minutes • COOKING TIME: 1 hour, 10 minutes •
YIELD: 10 servings

¼ cup low-sodium nonfat chicken broth

1 medium red onion, chopped

1 medium red bell pepper, cored and diced

2 stalks celery, diced

5 cloves garlic, minced

1 jalapeño pepper, seeded and minced

6 cups water

1 cup low-sodium canned kidney beans, rinsed and drained

2 cups cooked or low-sodium canned black beans, rinsed and drained

1 cup low-sodium canned Great Northern beans, rinsed and drained

2 medium carrots, scraped and sliced

2 cups peeled and chopped potatoes

½ cup pearl barley

¼ cup minced fresh parsley

1½ tablespoons dried oregano

1 tablespoon chili powder

1 teaspoon ground black pepper

2 cups chopped spinach leaves

1. Heat broth in a large pot. Add onion, red bell pepper, and celery. Sauté until pepper begins to soften, about 5 minutes. Add garlic and jalapeño pepper, and sauté for 5 more minutes.
2. Add water, kidney beans, black beans, Great Northern beans, carrots, potatoes, barley, parsley, oregano, chili powder, and black pepper. Bring to a boil, reduce heat, and simmer, stirring occasionally, for 50 minutes. Stir in spinach and simmer for 10 additional minutes.
3. Transfer to individual bowls and serve.

Calories Per Serving: 165

Fat: 1 g

Cholesterol: 0 mg

Protein: 8 g

Carbohydrates: 32 g

Dietary Fiber: 6 g

Sodium: 254 mg

❧ *Three-Bean Gumbo* ❧

Okra is a key ingredient for any gumbo. In this recipe, black-eyed peas, corn, lima beans, and green beans are joined with the okra.

PREPARATION TIME: 20 minutes • *COOKING TIME: 45 minutes* •
YIELD: 10 servings

3¼ cups low-sodium nonfat chicken
  broth
2 tablespoons all-purpose flour
1 cup chopped onion
1 cup chopped celery
1 jalapeño pepper, seeded and minced
2 cups chopped green bell peppers
2 cups thinly sliced okra
1 teaspoon dried oregano
1 teaspoon paprika
½ teaspoon dried thyme

3 cups water
2 medium tomatoes, seeded and
  crushed
1½ cups low-sodium canned black-
  eyed peas, rinsed and drained
1½ cups fresh or frozen, thawed lima
  beans
1½ cups fresh or frozen corn kernels
1 cup green beans, cut into 2-inch
  pieces

1. Heat ¼ cup broth in a large saucepan. Stir in flour. Add onion, celery, jalapeño pepper, green bell peppers, okra, oregano, paprika, and thyme. Sauté for 5 minutes.

2. Add remaining broth, water, and tomatoes. Bring to a boil, reduce heat, and simmer for 15 minutes. Add black-eyed peas and lima beans. Simmer for 15 additional minutes.

3. Stir in corn and green beans and continue to cook for 10 minutes more. Serve at once.

Calories Per Serving: 137

Fat: 1 g

Cholesterol: 0 mg

Protein: 8 g

Carbohydrates: 27 g

Dietary Fiber: 6 g

Sodium: 180 mg

❧ *Spiced Vegetable Gumbo* ❧

This thick gumbo is made with black-eyed peas, carrots, onion, and five herbs and spices.

PREPARATION TIME: 20 minutes • *COOKING TIME: 45 minutes* •
YIELD: 8 servings

½ cup low-sodium nonfat chicken
   broth
1 medium onion, diced
1 cup sliced okra
1 cup diced celery
4 cloves garlic, minced
2 medium tomatoes, diced, with juice
¼ cup minced fresh parsley
2 teaspoons dried oregano
2 teaspoons paprika
1 teaspoon dried thyme

½ teaspoon ground black pepper
¼ teaspoon cayenne pepper
½ cup low-sodium tomato puree
2 medium carrots, scraped and
   chopped
1½ cups fresh or frozen green peas
1½ cups white rice
2 cups low-sodium canned black-eyed
   peas, rinsed and drained
6 cups water

1. Heat ¼ cup broth in a large pot. Add onion, okra, celery, and garlic. Sauté until onion begins to soften, about 8 minutes.
2. Stir in remaining broth, tomatoes and their juice, parsley, oregano, paprika, thyme, black pepper, and cayenne pepper. Simmer for 7 minutes.
3. Add tomato puree, carrots, green peas, rice, black-eyed peas, and water. Bring to a boil, reduce heat, and simmer, stirring occasionally, for 30 minutes. Transfer to individual serving bowls and serve at once.

Calories Per Serving: 139
Fat: 0 g
Cholesterol: 0 mg
Protein: 6 g

Carbohydrates: 29 g
Dietary Fiber: 4 g
Sodium: 249 mg

SALADS

❦

Easy Sweet-and-Sour Beets ▪ Broccoli-Cauliflower Salad ▪
Broccoli–Red Onion Salad ▪ Cauliflower–Green Bell
Pepper Salad ▪ Carrot-Raisin Salad ▪ Fresh Corn Salad ▪
Corn, Bell Pepper, and Carrot Salad ▪ Cucumber-Tomato
Salad ▪ Jalapeño-Lime-Cucumber Salad ▪ Pickled Cucumbers
▪ Dilled Cucumber Salad ▪ Cucumbers with Horseradish ▪
Green Beans and Tomatoes with Honey-Garlic Dressing ▪ Green
Bean–Zucchini Salad ▪ Jicama Salad ▪ Red Pepper–Artichoke
Salad ▪ Red Onion Salad ▪ Marinated Onions ▪ Spinach-
Mushroom-Citrus Salad ▪ Spinach Salad with Tomato Dressing ▪
Spinach Salad with Jicama and Oranges ▪ Spinach-Beet Salad ▪
Sugar Snap Pea Salad ▪ Spicy Tomato and Red Onion Salad
▪ Zucchini-Stuffed Tomatoes ▪ Gingered Vegetables ▪ Simple
Salad ▪ Mixed Green Salad with Balsamic Vinegar ▪ Romaine–
Red Leaf Lettuce Salad with Poppy-Seed Dressing ▪ Fruit Salad
with Greens and Balsamic Dressing ▪ Carrot, Beet, and Cabbage
Coleslaw ▪ Ginger Slaw ▪ Fruit Slaw ▪ Pineapple Slaw ▪
Rainbow Coleslaw ▪ Yellow Bell Pepper Slaw ▪ Poppy-Seed
Coleslaw ▪ Tropical Slaw ▪ Dilled Potato Salad ▪

▪ ▪ ▪   179

Red Pepper–Potato Salad • Caraway-Potato Salad • Chickpea-
Potato Salad • Red Potato and Green Bean Salad • Potato Salad
with Pickle Relish • Dijon Potato Salad • Vegetable-Potato
Salad • Grapefruit-Spinach Salad • Sweet and Tangy Fruit
Salad • Kiwi-Rice Salad • Wild Rice–Red Grape Salad •
Bean-Artichoke Salad • Mango and Corn Salad with Black
Beans • Pinto Bean–Corn Salad

❧ *Easy Sweet-and-Sour Beets* ❧

Canned beets are marinated in vinegar and sugar.

PREPARATION TIME: 10 minutes plus 10 minutes cooling time and 2 hours chilling time ▪ *COOKING TIME: 2 minutes* ▪ *YIELD: 8 servings*

6 cups low-sodium canned sliced beets, drained, ⅔ cup liquid reserved

1½ tablespoons cornstarch
⅓ cup vinegar
⅓ cup sugar

1. Place reserved beet liquid in a saucepan. Gradually add the cornstarch and stir until dissolved.
2. Stir in vinegar and sugar. Add beets and bring mixture to a boil, stirring often. Continue to cook and stir for 2 minutes.
3. Remove from heat and allow to cool for 10 minutes. Transfer to a bowl and place in the refrigerator for 2 hours before serving.

Calories Per Serving: 95
Fat: 0 g
Cholesterol: 0 mg
Protein: 2 g

Carbohydrates: 23 g
Dietary Fiber: 3 g
Sodium: 96 mg

❧ *Broccoli-Cauliflower Salad* ❧

A medley of vegetables is topped with a garlic-and-vinegar dressing.

PREPARATION TIME: 30 minutes plus overnight chilling time ▪
YIELD: 12 servings

2 cups cauliflower florets
2 cups broccoli florets
2 medium carrots, sliced diagonally
2 stalks celery, sliced diagonally
1 medium green bell pepper, cored and chopped

4 scallions, sliced
4 cloves garlic, minced
1 cup red wine vinegar
1 cup water
⅛ teaspoon cayenne pepper
¼ teaspoon ground black pepper

1. Combine cauliflower, broccoli, carrots, celery, green bell pepper, and scallions in a large bowl.
2. Mix garlic, vinegar, water, cayenne pepper, and black pepper. Pour over the vegetables and toss to coat.
3. Transfer to a large glass container, cover, and refrigerate overnight before serving.

Calories Per Serving: 21
Fat: 0 g
Cholesterol: 0 mg
Protein: 1 g

Carbohydrates: 5 g
Dietary Fiber: 1 g
Sodium: 21 mg

❧ Broccoli—Red Onion Salad ❧

This tart, warm salad is served with a vinegar-and-yogurt dressing.

PREPARATION TIME: 15 minutes ▪ COOKING TIME: 3 minutes ▪
YIELD: 6 servings

3 cups water
6 cups broccoli florets
⅓ cup nonfat plain yogurt

2 tablespoons vinegar
½ cup raisins
½ medium red onion, thinly sliced

1. Bring water to a rapid boil in the bottom of a steamer. Steam broccoli over water until it is just tender-crisp, about 3 minutes. Remove from heat and drain well.
2. Whisk together the yogurt and vinegar. Pour over the warm broccoli. Toss with raisins and onion slices, and serve.

Calories Per Serving: 67
Fat: 0 g
Cholesterol: 0 mg
Protein: 3 g

Carbohydrates: 16 g
Dietary Fiber: 4 g
Sodium: 30 mg

❧ Cauliflower—Green Bell Pepper Salad ❧

In this salad, cauliflower is combined with carrot, celery, scallions, and parsley. Tightly wrapped raw cauliflower can be refrigerated for 3 to 5 days.

PREPARATION TIME: 15 minutes • YIELD: 6 servings

6 cups cauliflower florets
¾ cup shredded carrot
½ cup chopped celery
1 medium green bell pepper, cored
  and chopped

3 scallions, sliced
½ cup chopped fresh parsley
½ cup nonfat Italian dressing

1. Combine all vegetables in a large bowl.
2. Pour the dressing over the salad and toss to coat ingredients. Serve at once or refrigerate for later use.

Calories Per Serving: 41
Fat: 0 g
Cholesterol: 0 mg
Protein: 2 g

Carbohydrates: 8 g
Dietary Fiber: 1 g
Sodium: 54 mg

❧ Carrot-Raisin Salad ❧ ✓

Carrots and raisins are topped with a nonfat yogurt-honey-lemon dressing. Raisins can be stored tightly wrapped at room temperature for several months.

PREPARATION TIME: 10 minutes plus 1 hour chilling time • YIELD: 6 servings

3 cups shredded carrots
1 cup raisins
⅓ cup nonfat plain yogurt
¼ cup skim milk

1 tablespoon honey
1 tablespoon lemon juice
¼ teaspoon ground black pepper

1. Combine carrots and raisins in a large bowl.
2. Mix together the yogurt, milk, honey, lemon juice, and black pepper. Stir the dressing into the carrot mixture and mix well. Refrigerate for 1 hour before serving.

Calories Per Serving: 118
Fat: 0 g
Cholesterol: 0 mg
Protein: 2 g

Carbohydrates: 29 g
Dietary Fiber: 3 g
Sodium: 37 mg

❧ *Fresh Corn Salad* ❧

Corn, beans, celery, onion, and green and red bell peppers are topped with an herb-and-lemon sauce.

PREPARATION TIME: 10 minutes • *COOKING TIME: 2 minutes* • *YIELD: 4 servings*

1 cup water
1 cup fresh corn kernels
1 cup low-sodium canned navy beans, drained and rinsed
1 cup chopped celery
1 small onion, chopped

1 green bell pepper, cored and chopped
2 tablespoons chopped red bell pepper
1 clove garlic, minced
¼ teaspoon ground black pepper
1 teaspoon dried basil
3 tablespoons lemon juice

1. Bring water to a boil. Add corn kernels and cook for 2 minutes. Remove from heat, drain, and allow to cool to room temperature.
2. Combine corn, beans, celery, onion, green bell pepper, and red bell pepper in a large bowl.
3. Whisk together the garlic, black pepper, basil, and lemon juice. Pour over the salad and toss to coat all ingredients.
4. Serve in individual bowls.

Calories Per Serving: 111
Fat: 0 g
Cholesterol: 0 mg
Protein: 6 g

Carbohydrates: 24 g
Dietary Fiber: 2 g
Sodium: 230 mg

❧ *Corn, Bell Pepper, and Carrot Salad* ❦

This colorful salad is topped with a tasty tomato-and-mustard sauce. Dry mustard can be stored in a dark, dry place for up to 6 months.

PREPARATION TIME: 15 minutes • *YIELD: 6 servings*

1 cup low-sodium tomato sauce
¼ cup sugar
¼ cup vinegar
1 teaspoon Worcestershire sauce
2 cloves garlic, minced
½ teaspoon dry mustard

2 cups low-sodium canned corn kernels, drained
1 medium green bell pepper, cored and chopped
2 cups sliced carrots

1. Combine tomato sauce, sugar, vinegar, Worcestershire sauce, garlic, and dry mustard in a large bowl.
2. Stir in corn, green bell pepper, and carrots. Mix well and serve.

Calories Per Serving: 115
Fat: 0 g
Cholesterol: 0 mg
Protein: 3 g

Carbohydrates: 28 g
Dietary Fiber: 3 g
Sodium: 40 mg

❧ *Cucumber-Tomato Salad* ❦

Tomatoes, cucumbers, and onion are topped with garlic, yogurt, and lemon juice in this simple, summery salad.

PREPARATION TIME: 10 minutes plus 1 hour chilling time • *YIELD: 4 servings*

4 medium tomatoes, diced
2 medium cucumbers, diced
1 medium red onion, chopped
3 cloves garlic, minced

½ cup nonfat plain yogurt
1 tablespoon lemon juice
1 tablespoon dried basil

1. Mix tomatoes, cucumbers, and onion in a large serving bowl.
2. Whisk together the garlic, yogurt, and lemon juice. Add basil. Pour over vegetables and toss.
3. Serve on individual plates.

Calories Per Serving: 79
Fat: 1 g
Cholesterol: 1 mg
Protein: 4 g

Carbohydrates: 16 g
Dietary Fiber: 2 g
Sodium: 37 mg

❧ *Jalapeño-Lime-Cucumber Salad* ❧

A tangy dressing made of jalapeño, garlic, soy sauce, lime juice, basil, and brown sugar is tossed with sliced cucumbers.

PREPARATION TIME: 10 minutes plus 1 hour chilling time   ▪   YIELD: 4 servings

1 jalapeño pepper, seeded and minced
1 clove garlic, minced
1 tablespoon reduced-sodium soy
   sauce

2 tablespoons lime juice
1 teaspoon dried basil
1 teaspoon brown sugar
2 medium cucumbers, sliced

1. Combine the jalapeño, garlic, soy sauce, lime juice, basil, and brown sugar.
2. Pour dressing over the cucumber in a serving bowl and mix thoroughly. Chill in the refrigerator for 1 hour before serving.

Calories Per Serving: 32
Fat: 0 g
Cholesterol: 0 mg
Protein: 2 g

Carbohydrates: 7 g
Dietary Fiber: 0 g
Sodium: 240 mg

❧ *Pickled Cucumbers* ❧

These cucumber pickles are quick and easy to make. Cut cucumbers can be stored in the refrigerator for up to 5 days.

PREPARATION TIME: 15 minutes • YIELD: 8 servings

4 teaspoons rice wine vinegar
⅛ teaspoon cayenne pepper
2 teaspoons sugar

1 teaspoon sesame oil
2 large cucumbers, sliced diagonally crosswise

1. Whisk together the vinegar, cayenne pepper, sugar, and oil.
2. Combine cucumbers and vinegar mixture and mix well. Allow to stand for 10 minutes, mix again, and serve.

Calories Per Serving: 21
Fat: 1 g
Cholesterol: 0 mg
Protein: 1 g

Carbohydrates: 4 g
Dietary Fiber: 0 g
Sodium: 150 mg

❧ *Dilled Cucumber Salad* ❧

Cucumbers are marinated in a lemon-garlic-yogurt dressing.

PREPARATION TIME: 10 minutes plus 2 hours chilling time • YIELD: 6 servings

3 tablespoons lemon juice
½ teaspoon sugar
2 cups nonfat plain yogurt

2 cloves garlic, minced
3 medium cucumbers, thinly sliced
¼ teaspoon dried dill

1. Whisk together the lemon juice, sugar, yogurt, and garlic.
2. Place the cucumber slices in a shallow bowl and spoon the dressing over them. Cover and chill for 2 hours before sprinkling with dill and serving.

Calories Per Serving: 66

Carbohydrates: 11 g

Fat: 0 g

Dietary Fiber: 0 g

Cholesterol: 1 mg

Sodium: 62 mg

Protein: 5 g

❧ *Cucumbers with Horseradish* ❧

Cucumbers, scallions, and radishes are marinated in horseradish and vinegar.

PREPARATION TIME: 10 minutes plus 1 hour chilling time ▪ *YIELD: 8 servings*

3 tablespoons vinegar

1 tablespoon prepared horseradish

4 medium cucumbers, thinly sliced

3 scallions, minced

2 radishes, thinly sliced

1 teaspoon dried dill

¼ teaspoon ground black pepper

1. Whisk together the vinegar and horseradish.
2. Combine cucumbers, scallions, radishes, and dill in a large bowl. Pour dressing over salad and chill for 1 hour. Sprinkle with black pepper and serve.

Calories Per Serving: 22

Carbohydrates: 5 g

Fat: 0 g

Dietary Fiber: 0 g

Cholesterol: 0 mg

Sodium: 45 mg

Protein: 1 g

❧ *Green Beans and Tomatoes with* ❧ *Honey-Garlic Dressing*

Green beans, tomatoes, and onion are tossed in a dressing made of vinegar, honey, garlic, and black pepper. Green beans are available year round but are at their peak from May to October.

PREPARATION TIME: 15 minutes plus 2 hours chilling time ▪
COOKING TIME: 3 minutes ▪ *YIELD: 6 servings*

2 cups water

2 cups trimmed green beans

2 tomatoes, cut into wedges

½ cup very thin wedges red onion

2 tablespoons red wine vinegar

2 tablespoons honey

3 cloves garlic, minced

¼ teaspoon ground black pepper

1. Bring water to a boil in a steamer. Add beans and steam until just tender-crisp, about 3 minutes. Remove from heat, plunge into cold water, and drain.
2. Combine beans, tomatoes, and onion in a large serving bowl. Toss well.
3. Whisk together the vinegar, honey, garlic, and black pepper. Pour over the beans and toss to coat all ingredients. Chill for 2 hours before serving.

Calories Per Serving: 55

Fat: 0 g

Cholesterol: 0 mg

Protein: 1 g

Carbohydrates: 13 g

Dietary Fiber: 2 g

Sodium: 6 mg

❧ *Green Bean–Zucchini Salad* ❧

Thin strips of zucchini and green beans are whisked together with sour cream, dill, lemon juice, and black pepper.

PREPARATION TIME: *10 minutes* • COOKING TIME: *5 minutes* •
YIELD: *6 servings*

2 cups water

4 cups green bean halves

4 cups thinly sliced zucchini

¼ cup nonfat sour cream

2 teaspoons dried dill

2 teaspoons lemon juice

¼ teaspoon ground black pepper

1. Bring water to a boil in a saucepan. Add beans and return to a boil. Reduce heat and simmer for 3 minutes. Add zucchini and continue to simmer until beans are just tender, about 2 additional minutes. Remove from heat and drain.
2. Whisk together the sour cream, dill, lemon juice, and black pepper. Add to green beans and zucchini, toss to coat all ingredients, and serve at once.

Calories Per Serving: 48

Carbohydrates: 10 g

Fat: 0 g

Dietary Fiber: 2 g

Cholesterol: 0 mg

Sodium: 11 mg

Protein: 4 g

❧ *Jicama Salad* ❧

Jicamas are large root vegetables with a thin brown skin and white, crunchy flesh. They have a sweet, nutty flavor. Here they are combined with oranges.

PREPARATION TIME: 20 minutes plus 3 hours chilling time • *YIELD: 8 servings*

3 cups julienned jicama

1 cup orange juice

*4 navel oranges, peeled and divided
    into sections*

¼ cup lime juice

1 tablespoon sugar

1 cup very thin wedges red onion

1. Combine jicama strips, orange sections, and onion in a large bowl.
2. Whisk together the orange juice, lime juice, and sugar. Pour over salad and toss to coat all ingredients. Cover and chill for 3 hours before serving.

Calories Per Serving: 69

Carbohydrates: 17 g

Fat: 0 g

Dietary Fiber: 7 g

Cholesterol: 0 mg

Sodium: 29 mg

Protein: 2 g

❧ *Red Pepper–Artichoke Salad* ❧

Artichoke hearts, red bell peppers, celery, olives, and basil are tossed with yogurt and black pepper in this cool salad. Artichoke hearts are available frozen or canned.

PREPARATION TIME: 15 minutes • *YIELD: 6 servings*

1½ cups chopped water-packed 2 teaspoons dried basil
 canned artichoke hearts ¼ cup nonfat plain yogurt
½ cup chopped red bell pepper 1 tablespoon vinegar
½ cup sliced celery 1 teaspoon dried oregano
6 ripe olives, sliced ¼ teaspoon ground black pepper

1. Combine artichoke hearts, red bell pepper, celery, olives, and basil in a large bowl.
2. Whisk together the yogurt, vinegar, oregano, and black pepper.
3. Pour the yogurt dressing over the salad and toss to coat.
4. Serve on individual plates.

Calories Per Serving: 53 Carbohydrates: 11 g
Fat: 1 g Dietary Fiber: 3 g
Cholesterol: 0 mg Sodium: 273 mg
Protein: 3 g

❧ *Red Onion Salad* ❧

Red onion is mixed with bell peppers and vinegar in this tangy salad. Red onions, also called Italian onions, are available year round.

PREPARATION TIME: 15 minutes plus 20 minutes standing time and 2 hours chilling time ▪ *COOKING TIME: 5 minutes* ▪ *YIELD: 6 servings*

½ cup balsamic vinegar 1 medium green bell pepper, cored
½ cup sugar and thinly sliced
1 medium red onion, thinly sliced 1 medium yellow bell pepper, cored
  and thinly sliced

1. Combine vinegar and sugar in a saucepan. Bring to a boil, reduce heat, and simmer for 5 minutes. Remove pan from heat and allow to cool for 10 minutes.
2. Combine onion and bell pepper slices in a large bowl. Pour vinegar mixture over vegetables and allow to stand at room temperature for 20

minutes. Transfer to refrigerator and chill for 2 hours. Drain excess liquid before serving.

Calories Per Serving: 11
Fat: 0 g
Cholesterol: 0 mg
Protein: 1 g

Carbohydrates: 2 g
Dietary Fiber: 0 g
Sodium: 12 mg

❧ *Marinated Onions* ❧

This onion salad is made with lime juice and cayenne pepper. Once cut, an onion should be tightly wrapped, refrigerated, and used within 5 days or frozen in an airtight container for up to 3 months.

PREPARATION TIME: 5 minutes plus 1 hour chilling time ▪ *YIELD: 8 servings*

1 large onion, minced
2 tablespoons lime juice

¼ teaspoon cayenne pepper
¼ teaspoon ground black pepper

1. Mix onion and lime juice in a bowl. Sprinkle with cayenne pepper and black pepper.
2. Allow to chill in the refrigerator for 1 hour before serving.

Calories Per Serving: 9
Fat: 0 g
Cholesterol: 0 mg
Protein: 0 g

Carbohydrates: 2 g
Dietary Fiber: 0 g
Sodium: 1 mg

❧ *Spinach-Mushroom-Citrus Salad* ❧

Spinach is combined with onion, mushrooms, and orange pieces and topped with a celery seed–lemon dressing. Do not wash and cut spinach until you are ready to serve it.

PREPARATION TIME: 20 minutes ▪ *YIELD: 4 servings*

4 cups torn fresh spinach pieces
1 medium onion, sliced
1 cup sliced mushrooms
1 medium navel orange, peeled and
    chopped

¼ cup lemon juice
½ teaspoon celery seed
¼ teaspoon ground black pepper

1. Place spinach, onion, mushrooms, and orange pieces in a large serving bowl.
2. Whisk together the lemon juice, celery seed, and black pepper. Pour over the salad, toss well, and serve.

Calories Per Serving: 54
Fat: 0 g
Cholesterol: 0 mg
Protein: 3 g

Carbohydrates: 12 g
Dietary Fiber: 5 g
Sodium: 47 mg

❧ *Spinach Salad with Tomato Dressing* ❧

A dressing of tomato juice, vinegar, a dash of olive oil, Worcestershire sauce, and Parmesan tops this simple spinach salad.

PREPARATION TIME: *10 minutes* • YIELD: *4 servings*

3 cups torn fresh spinach pieces
1 medium cucumber, peeled and sliced
½ medium red onion, thinly sliced
¼ cup low-sodium tomato juice
1 tablespoon red wine vinegar

½ teaspoon olive oil
1 teaspoon Worcestershire sauce
¼ teaspoon ground black pepper
1 teaspoon nonfat Parmesan

1. Combine spinach, cucumber, and onion in a large bowl.
2. Whisk together tomato juice, vinegar, olive oil, Worcestershire sauce, black pepper, and Parmesan. Pour over the salad. Toss to coat all ingredients and serve.

Calories Per Serving: 36

Fat: 1 g

Cholesterol: 0 mg

Protein: 2 g

Carbohydrates: 6 g

Dietary Fiber: 2 g

Sodium: 84 mg

❧ *Spinach Salad with Jicama and Oranges* ❧

Orange slices, spinach leaves, and jicama are tossed with an orange-vinegar dressing.

PREPARATION TIME: 15 minutes   •   YIELD: 4 servings

*2 navel oranges, peeled and thinly
    sliced crosswise
4 cups torn fresh spinach pieces
1 cup shredded jicama*

*2 tablespoons orange juice
2 tablespoons rice wine vinegar
½ teaspoon dried basil
¼ teaspoon ground black pepper*

1. Combine the orange slices, spinach leaves, and jicama in a large serving bowl.
2. Whisk together the orange juice, rice wine vinegar, basil, and black pepper. Pour over the salad, toss well, and serve.

Calories Per Serving: 63

Fat: 0 g

Cholesterol: 0 mg

Protein: 3 g

Carbohydrates: 14 g

Dietary Fiber: 8 g

Sodium: 106 mg

❧ *Spinach-Beet Salad* ❧

This simple composed salad is topped with balsamic vinegar.

PREPARATION TIME: 15 minutes   •   YIELD: 6 servings

*12 fresh spinach leaves
4 cups low-sodium canned sliced beets
1 medium cucumber, thinly sliced*

*1 medium onion, thinly sliced
1 tablespoon balsamic vinegar
1 tablespoon fresh chopped parsley*

1. Divide spinach leaves among 4 individual serving plates. Top each with beet, cucumber, and onion slices. Drizzle salad with balsamic vinegar, garnish with parsley, and serve.

Calories Per Serving: 148
Fat: 1 g
Cholesterol: 0 mg
Protein: 7 g

Carbohydrates: 32 g
Dietary Fiber: 10 g
Sodium: 225 mg

❧ *Sugar Snap Pea Salad* ❧

Sugar snap peas, jicama, and onion are tossed with a honey-mustard sauce in this salad. Sugar snap peas have plump, crisp, bright green pods and can be stored in the refrigerator for up to 3 days.

PREPARATION TIME: 15 minutes ・ *COOKING TIME: 1 minute* ・
YIELD: 4 servings

4 cups water
1 cup trimmed sugar snap peas
1 teaspoon Dijon mustard
1 tablespoon honey

¼ cup apple juice
4 cups torn romaine lettuce pieces
¾ cup julienned jicama
¼ cup very thin wedges red onion

1. Bring water to a boil in a saucepan. Drop in peas and immediately remove saucepan from heat. Plunge the peas into cold water, drain, and set aside.
2. Mix the mustard, honey, and apple juice.
3. Combine snap peas, lettuce, jicama, and onion. Pour dressing over the salad, toss well, and serve.

Calories Per Serving: 61
Fat: 0 g
Cholesterol: 0 mg
Protein: 3 g

Carbohydrates: 13 g
Dietary Fiber: 3 g
Sodium: 54 mg

❧ *Spicy Tomato and Red Onion Salad* ❧

This tomato and onion salad is topped with a dressing made with Worcestershire sauce.

PREPARATION TIME: 10 minutes • *YIELD: 4 servings*

4 medium tomatoes, cut into wedges
1 medium red onion, thinly sliced
1 tablespoon Worcestershire sauce

1 tablespoon red wine vinegar
½ teaspoon olive oil

1. Combine tomato wedges and onion slices in a large bowl.
2. Mix together the Worcestershire sauce, vinegar, and olive oil. Pour over the salad and serve.

Calories Per Serving: 49
Fat: 1 g
Cholesterol: 0 mg
Protein: 2 g

Carbohydrates: 10 g
Dietary Fiber: 2 g
Sodium: 49 mg

❧ *Zucchini-Stuffed Tomatoes* ❧

These tomatoes are stuffed with zucchini, onion, jalapeño, corn, garlic, and bulgur. Bulgur, a steamed, dried, and crushed wheat, is a staple of Middle Eastern cooking.

PREPARATION TIME: 20 minutes • *COOKING TIME: 35 minutes* •
YIELD: 4 servings

4 tomatoes
¼ teaspoon ground black pepper
1 cup low-sodium tomato juice
½ teaspoon ground cumin
⅛ teaspoon cayenne pepper
1 cup diced zucchini

¼ cup chopped onion
1 jalapeño pepper, seeded and minced
2 cloves garlic, minced
½ cup bulgur
¾ cup fresh, canned, or thawed
  frozen corn kernels

1. Remove a ½-inch slice from the stem end of each tomato. Set stem ends aside.
2. Remove the seeds and pulp from the tomatoes. Sprinkle the inside of each tomato with black pepper and allow them to stand for 10 minutes.
3. Preheat oven to 350 degrees. Line a shallow baking dish with aluminum foil.
4. Mix the tomato juice, cumin, and cayenne pepper in a saucepan and bring to a boil. Stir in zucchini, onion, jalapeño, garlic, and bulgur. Return to a boil, reduce heat, cover, and simmer until bulgur is tender, about 15 minutes. Remove from heat and stir in corn kernels.
5. Arrange tomatoes on the baking dish and divide the bulgur mixture among the tomatoes. Replace the reserved tomato tops, and bake until tomatoes are heated through, about 20 minutes. Serve hot.

Calories Per Serving: 136　　Carbohydrates: 31 g
Fat: 1 g　　Dietary Fiber: 8 g
Cholesterol: 0 mg　　Sodium: 128 mg
Protein: 5 g

❧ *Gingered Vegetables* ❧

Cucumbers, carrots, and onion are covered with a vinegar dressing flavored with fresh gingerroot.

PREPARATION TIME: 10 minutes plus 12 hours chilling time • *YIELD: 6 servings*

½ cup rice wine vinegar　　*2 medium cucumbers, sliced diago-*
2 tablespoons brown sugar　　*nally*
1 tablespoon grated fresh gingerroot　　*3 medium carrots, sliced diagonally*
　　1 medium onion, thinly sliced

1. Whisk together the vinegar, brown sugar, and gingerroot.
2. Combine the cucumbers, carrots, and onion. Pour the dressing over the vegetables and toss well. Cover and refrigerate for 12 hours before serving.

Calories Per Serving: 48   Carbohydrates: 12 g
Fat: 0 g   Dietary Fiber: 1 g
Cholesterol: 0 mg   Sodium: 16 mg
Protein: 1 g

❧ *Simple Salad* ❧

This basic salad is made with red leaf lettuce, tomatoes, onion, cucumber, and olives.

PREPARATION TIME: 15 minutes ▪ *YIELD: 8 servings*

4 medium tomatoes, cut into wedges   *6 pitted ripe olives, sliced*
1 medium red onion, cut into very   *1 head red leaf lettuce, torn into*
  thin wedges   *pieces*
1 medium cucumber, peeled and sliced *½ cup nonfat Italian dressing*
  crosswise

1. Combine tomatoes, onion, cucumber, olives, and lettuce.
2. Pour dressing over salad, toss well, and serve.

Calories Per Serving: 39   Carbohydrates: 7 g
Fat: 1 g   Dietary Fiber: 2 g
Cholesterol: 0 mg   Sodium: 33
Protein: 2 g

❧ *Mixed Green Salad with Balsamic Vinegar* ❧

This garden salad is accented with red onion, shredded carrot, and cucumber.

PREPARATION TIME: 10 minutes ▪ *YIELD: 6 servings*

2 cups torn fresh spinach pieces   *2 cups torn radicchio pieces*
2 cups torn arugula pieces   *2 cups torn red leaf lettuce pieces*

2 medium tomatoes, cut into thin
  wedges
1 small red onion, thinly sliced
2 cups shredded carrots

1 medium cucumber, thinly sliced
1 cup bean sprouts
¼ cup balsamic vinegar
¼ teaspoon ground black pepper

1. Combine spinach, arugula, radicchio, lettuce, tomatoes, onion, carrots, cucumber, and bean sprouts. Transfer to a serving bowl.
2. Pour vinegar over salad, sprinkle with black pepper, and toss to coat all ingredients and serve.

Calories Per Serving: 90
Fat: 1 g
Cholesterol: 0 mg
Protein: 5 g

Carbohydrates: 19 g
Dietary Fiber: 5 g
Sodium: 90 mg

❧ Romaine–Red Leaf Lettuce Salad ❧ with Poppy-Seed Dressing

Lettuce is topped with a poppy seed and yogurt dressing. It takes 900,000 poppy seeds to equal a pound.

PREPARATION TIME: 15 minutes • *YIELD: 4 servings*

6 cups torn romaine lettuce
2 cups torn red leaf lettuce
2 medium tomatoes, chopped
½ cup nonfat plain yogurt
1 tablespoon honey

¼ cup orange juice
1½ teaspoons poppy seeds
½ teaspoon red wine vinegar
⅛ teaspoon ground white pepper

1. Combine romaine, red leaf lettuce, and tomatoes in a large bowl.
2. Whisk together the yogurt, honey, orange juice, poppy seeds, vinegar, and white pepper.
3. Pour dressing over salad and toss to coat ingredients before serving.

Calories Per Serving: 66   Carbohydrates: 12 g
Fat: 1 g   Dietary Fiber: 2 g
Cholesterol: 1 mg   Sodium: 40 mg
Protein: 4 g

❧ Fruit Salad with Greens and ❧ Balsamic Dressing

This salad, which combines crisp greens and fresh fruit, is a good source of dietary fiber.

PREPARATION TIME: 15 minutes • YIELD: 6 servings

4 cups torn spinach   1 tablespoon honey
5 cups torn romaine lettuce   1 tablespoon balsamic vinegar
2½ cups cantaloupe balls   1 tablespoon water
1½ cups hulled and sliced strawberries   1 teaspoon lemon juice

1. Combine spinach, lettuce, cantaloupe, and strawberries in a large bowl.
2. Whisk together the honey, vinegar, water, and lemon juice, and pour over the salad. Toss well to coat all ingredients and serve at once.

Calories Per Serving: 61   Carbohydrates: 13 g
Fat: 0 g   Dietary Fiber: 3 g
Cholesterol: 0 mg   Sodium: 39 mg
Protein: 3 g

❧ Carrot, Beet, and Cabbage Coleslaw ❧

This is a colorful coleslaw with a yogurt dressing.

PREPARATION TIME: 15 minutes plus 2 hours chilling time • YIELD: 6 servings

3 cups shredded cabbage   1 medium carrot, shredded
2 beets, shredded   ¼ cup nonfat mayonnaise

½ cup nonfat plain yogurt

2 garlic cloves, minced

½ teaspoon ground black pepper

1. Combine cabbage, beets, and carrot.
2. Whisk together the mayonnaise, yogurt, garlic, and black pepper. Add to the cabbage mixture and toss to blend all ingredients.
3. Chill in the refrigerator for 2 hours before serving.

Calories Per Serving: 113
Fat: 0 g
Cholesterol: 1 mg
Protein: 4 g

Carbohydrates: 26 g
Dietary Fiber: 4 g
Sodium: 220 mg

❧ *Ginger Slaw* ❧ √   N# ☑

Cabbage, radishes, scallions, cucumber, green bell pepper, and carrot are tossed with a sweet and sour ginger sauce.

PREPARATION TIME: *15 minutes plus 10 minutes standing time and 2 hours chilling time* ▪ YIELD: *12 servings*

4 cups water

5 cups shredded cabbage

1 cup sliced radishes

4 scallions, sliced

1 medium cucumber, sliced

1 medium green bell pepper, cored
  and julienned

1 cup shredded carrot

1 cup vinegar

1 teaspoon fresh grated gingerroot

⅓ cup sugar

½ teaspoon ground black pepper

1. Bring water to a boil in a saucepan.
2. Place cabbage in another saucepan and add enough boiling water to cover the cabbage. Allow to stand for 10 minutes, then drain. Rinse with cold water and drain well.
3. Combine cabbage, radishes, scallions, cucumber, green bell pepper, and carrot in a large bowl.
4. Whisk together the vinegar, gingerroot, sugar, and black pepper. Pour over the salad, mix well, and chill for 2 hours before serving.

Calories Per Serving: 45

Carbohydrates: 11 g

Fat: 0 g

Dietary Fiber: 2 g

Cholesterol: 0 mg

Sodium: 18 mg

Protein: 1 g

❧ *Fruit Slaw* ❧

In this coleslaw the cabbage is balanced with orange and pineapple.

PREPARATION TIME: 15 minutes ▪ YIELD: 6 servings

1 cup crushed water-packed canned
  pineapple, undrained

1 navel orange, peeled and chopped

2 cups shredded red cabbage

¾ cup nonfat plain yogurt

3 cups shredded green cabbage

¼ cup orange juice

3 tablespoons vinegar

1. Combine pineapple and red and green cabbage in a large serving bowl. Stir in orange pieces and toss.
2. Whisk together the yogurt, orange juice, and vinegar. Pour over the slaw, toss well, and serve.

Calories Per Serving: 69

Carbohydrates: 15 g

Fat: 0 g

Dietary Fiber: 2 g

Cholesterol: 1 mg

Sodium: 41 mg

Protein: 4 g

❧ *Pineapple Slaw* ❧

Pineapple and cabbage are seasoned with a tangy yogurt dressing.

PREPARATION TIME: 15 minutes plus 1 hour chilling time ▪
COOKING TIME: 2 minutes ▪ YIELD: 6 servings

4 cups shredded cabbage
½ cup finely chopped onion
¼ cup vinegar
1 tablespoon sugar

½ teaspoon ground black pepper
½ cup nonfat plain yogurt
1 cup crushed juice-packed canned
    pineapple, drained

1. Mix cabbage and onion in a large bowl.
2. Combine vinegar, sugar, and black pepper in a small saucepan. Bring to a boil, reduce heat, and cook, stirring, until sugar is dissolved, about 2 minutes.
3. Pour vinegar mixture over cabbage and onion. Stir in yogurt and pineapple, cover, and refrigerate for 1 hour before serving.

Calories Per Serving: 51
Fat: 0 g
Cholesterol: 0 mg
Protein: 2 g

Carbohydrates: 12 g
Dietary Fiber: 2 g
Sodium: 25 mg

ও *Rainbow Coleslaw* ৩

A colorful, zesty, nonfat alternative to the traditional favorite.

PREPARATION TIME: *20 minutes plus 20 minutes chilling time* ▪
YIELD: *6 servings*

3 tablespoons nonfat plain yogurt
3 tablespoons nonfat mayonnaise
3 tablespoons red wine vinegar
¼ cup minced scallion
¼ teaspoon ground black pepper
3 cups shredded green cabbage

2 cups shredded red cabbage
1 medium red bell pepper, cored and
    julienned
1 medium yellow bell pepper, cored
    and julienned
½ cup shredded carrot

1. Combine yogurt, mayonnaise, vinegar, scallion, and black pepper in a large bowl. Mix thoroughly.
2. Add green cabbage, red cabbage, red bell pepper, yellow bell pepper, and carrot, and toss to coat all ingredients. Cover and chill for 20 minutes before serving.

Calories Per Serving: 54

Fat: 0 g

Cholesterol: 0 mg

Protein: 2 g

Carbohydrates: 13 g

Dietary Fiber: 2 g

Sodium: 116 mg

❧ *Yellow Bell Pepper Slaw* ❧

This coleslaw is a mix of yellow bell pepper, two kinds of cabbage, Dijon mustard, and caraway seeds.

PREPARATION TIME: 15 minutes　•　YIELD: 4 servings

1 cup shredded red cabbage

1 cup shredded white cabbage

½ cup minced onion

1 medium yellow bell pepper, cored
　and chopped

1½ teaspoons caraway seeds

1 tablespoon Dijon mustard

2 tablespoons lemon juice

½ cup nonfat plain yogurt

½ teaspoon sugar

¼ teaspoon ground black pepper

1. Combine the red and white cabbage, onion, yellow bell pepper, and caraway seeds in a large bowl.
2. Whisk together the mustard, lemon juice, yogurt, sugar, and black pepper. Pour over the salad, toss well, and serve.

Calories Per Serving: 54

Fat: 1 g

Cholesterol: 0 mg

Protein: 3 g

Carbohydrates: 11 g

Dietary Fiber: 2 g

Sodium: 130 mg

❧ *Poppy-Seed Coleslaw* ❧

This coleslaw has a yogurt and poppy-seed dressing. Be sure to choose heads of cabbage that are heavy for their size and with crisp-looking leaves that are tightly packed.

PREPARATION TIME: 10 minutes　•　YIELD: 6 servings

5 cups shredded cabbage
2 cups grated carrots
¼ cup vinegar

¼ cup nonfat plain yogurt
2 teaspoons poppy seeds

1. Combine cabbage and carrots.
2. Whisk together the vinegar and yogurt. Stir the dressing into the slaw and add the poppy seeds. Toss to coat all ingredients, and serve.

Calories Per Serving: 46
Fat: 0 g
Cholesterol: 0 mg
Protein: 3 g

Carbohydrates: 11 g
Dietary Fiber: 2 g
Sodium: 40 mg

✌ *Tropical Slaw* ✌

Cabbage is combined with bell pepper, onion, and pineapple, and topped with a honey-mustard sauce. Savoy cabbage has a loose, full head of crinkled leaves varying from dark to pale green.

PREPARATION TIME: *20 minutes plus 2 hours chilling time* • YIELD: *6 servings*

4 cups shredded Savoy cabbage
1 medium red bell pepper, cored and
   finely chopped
1 medium onion, finely chopped
½ cup crushed juice-packed canned
   pineapple, drained
¼ teaspoon ground black pepper

1 tablespoon honey
2 tablespoons lemon juice
2 teaspoons Dijon mustard
1 tablespoon rice wine vinegar
⅔ cup nonfat buttermilk
½ cup nonfat sour cream

1. Combine cabbage, red bell pepper, onion, and pineapple in a large bowl. Sprinkle with black pepper and toss.
2. Whisk together the honey, lemon juice, mustard, and vinegar. Pour over salad and toss to coat.
3. Mix the buttermilk and sour cream, and stir into the salad.
4. Cover and refrigerate for 2 hours. Drain any excess liquid before serving.

Calories Per Serving: 65 Carbohydrates: 13 g
Fat: 0 g Dietary Fiber: 2 g
Cholesterol: 0 mg Sodium: 86 mg
Protein: 4 g

❧ *Dilled Potato Salad* ❧

Dill is the perfect accompaniment to potatoes and is used in many cuisines.

PREPARATION TIME: 15 minutes plus 10 minutes cooling time ▪
COOKING TIME: 12 minutes ▪ *YIELD: 6 servings*

4 cups water *2 teaspoons dried dill*
2 pounds new potatoes *3 scallions, finely chopped*
⅓ cup nonfat plain yogurt *¼ teaspoon ground black pepper*
2 tablespoons red wine vinegar

1. Bring water to a boil in a saucepan. Add potatoes and cook until just tender, about 12 minutes. Remove from heat and allow to cool.
2. Cut potatoes into chunks.
3. Mix the yogurt, vinegar, and dill. Combine the dressing and the potatoes. Stir in the scallions, sprinkle with black pepper, and serve.

Calories Per Serving: 143 Carbohydrates: 33 g
Fat: 0 g Dietary Fiber: 3 g
Cholesterol: 0 mg Sodium: 9 mg
Protein: 3 g

❧ *Red Pepper–Potato Salad* ❧

Potatoes, red bell pepper, onion, scallions, and celery are given a honey-and-mustard dressing.

PREPARATION TIME: 10 minutes plus 1 hour chilling time ▪
COOKING TIME: 15 minutes ▪ *YIELD: 6 servings*

2 cups water

4 medium potatoes, diced

½ cup chopped red onion

2 scallions, chopped

1 medium red bell pepper, cored and
    chopped

1 stalk celery, chopped

1 tablespoon lemon juice

1 tablespoon honey

2 tablespoons Dijon mustard

½ cup nonfat plain yogurt

¼ teaspoon ground black pepper

1. Bring water to a boil in a saucepan. Add potatoes and cook until just tender, about 15 minutes. Drain well.
2. Combine potatoes, onion, scallions, red bell pepper, and celery. Toss well.
3. Whisk together the lemon juice, honey, mustard, yogurt, and black pepper.
4. Stir dressing into the vegetable mixture and chill for 1 hour before serving.

Calories Per Serving: 178

Fat: 1 g

Cholesterol: 0 mg

Protein: 5 g

Carbohydrates: 40 g

Dietary Fiber: 3 g

Sodium: 160 mg

❧ *Caraway-Potato Salad* ❧

Here a classic potato salad is spiced with caraway seeds and dressed with yogurt.

PREPARATION TIME: *15 minutes plus 1 hour chilling time* •
COOKING TIME: *15 minutes* • YIELD: *6 servings*

2 cups water

4 large potatoes, cut into ¾-inch cubes

½ cup chopped red onion

2 scallions, chopped

½ cup fresh chopped parsley

2 teaspoons caraway seeds

¼ teaspoon cayenne pepper

1 tablespoon lime juice

1 cup nonfat plain yogurt

1. Bring water to a boil in a saucepan. Add potatoes and cook until just tender, about 15 minutes. Drain well.
2. Combine potatoes, red onion, scallions, and parsley in a large serving bowl.
3. Whisk together the caraway seeds, cayenne pepper, lime juice, and yogurt.
4. Stir the dressing into the potato mix and toss to coat all ingredients. Chill for 1 hour before serving.

Calories Per Serving: 172	Carbohydrates: 38 g
Fat: 0 g	Dietary Fiber: 3 g
Cholesterol: 1 g	Sodium: 39 mg
Protein: 6 g	

❧ *Chickpea-Potato Salad* ❧

This potato salad includes carrot, chickpeas, onion, black pepper, and dill.

PREPARATION TIME: 15 minutes plus 1 hour chilling time ▪
COOKING TIME: 17 minutes ▪ *YIELD: 6 servings*

½ cup low-sodium nonfat chicken broth
½ cup water
3 large potatoes, cut into ¾-inch cubes
1 medium carrot, thinly sliced
1 cup chopped onion
2 cloves garlic, minced

2 cups cooked or low-sodium canned chickpeas, rinsed and drained
2 teaspoons dried dill
½ teaspoon ground black pepper
2 tablespoons lemon juice
¼ cup nonfat plain yogurt

1. Bring broth and water to a boil in a saucepan. Add potatoes, carrot, onion, and garlic, and cook until potatoes are just tender, about 15 minutes. Remove from heat.
2. Add chickpeas, dill, and black pepper, and toss gently.
3. Whisk together the lemon juice and yogurt and stir into the potato mixture. Chill in the refrigerator for 1 hour and serve.

Calories Per Serving: 213
Fat: 1 g
Cholesterol: 1 mg
Protein: 10 g

Carbohydrates: 44 g
Dietary Fiber: 4 g
Sodium: 74 mg

❧ *Red Potato and Green Bean Salad* ❧

There is a taste of southern France in this salad made of potatoes, celery, scallions, and green beans.

PREPARATION TIME: 20 minutes plus 1 hour chilling time •
COOKING TIME: 15 minutes • *YIELD: 6 servings*

5 cups water
4 cups unpeeled red potatoes, cut into
   ¾-inch cubes
2 cups green beans, cut into 1-inch
   lengths
⅓ cup nonfat plain yogurt
2 teaspoons Dijon mustard

1 teaspoon red wine vinegar
1 teaspoon dried basil
½ teaspoon dried rosemary
½ teaspoon ground black pepper
1 cup finely chopped celery
4 scallions, chopped

1. Bring 4 cups water to a boil in a saucepan. Add potatoes and simmer until just tender, about 12 minutes. Remove from heat, drain, and set aside.
2. Bring remaining water to a boil. Add beans and simmer until just tender-crisp, about 3 minutes. Remove from heat, drain, and rinse immediately under cold water.
3. Whisk together the yogurt, mustard, vinegar, basil, rosemary, and black pepper.
4. Combine the potatoes, green beans, celery, scallions, and dressing in a large serving bowl. Toss to coat all ingredients and refrigerate for 1 hour before serving.

Calories Per Serving: 153

Fat: 0 g

Cholesterol: 0 mg

Protein: 6 g

Carbohydrates: 33 g

Dietary Fiber: 4 g

Sodium: 97 mg

☙ *Potato Salad with Pickle Relish* ❧

Pickle relish and egg whites are combined with potatoes, celery, and a yogurt dressing.

PREPARATION TIME: 20 minutes   •   COOKING TIME: 15 minutes   •
YIELD: 8 servings

2 quarts water

6 medium potatoes

2 celery stalks, sliced

1 medium red onion, chopped

¼ cup vinegar

¼ teaspoon ground black pepper

3 tablespoons sweet pickle relish

3 hard-boiled egg whites, chopped

¼ cup nonfat mayonnaise

½ cup nonfat plain yogurt

2 tablespoons fresh minced parsley

1. Bring water to a boil in a large saucepan. Add potatoes and boil until just tender, about 15 minutes. Remove from heat and allow to cool, then dice.
2. Combine potatoes, celery, onion, vinegar, and black pepper. Mix pickle relish, egg whites, mayonnaise, and yogurt. Stir relish mixture into the potatoes and toss to coat all ingredients. Sprinkle with parsley and serve.

Calories Per Serving: 127

Fat: 0 g

Cholesterol: 0 mg

Protein: 4 g

Carbohydrates: 28 g

Dietary Fiber: 2 g

Sodium: 202 mg

❦ *Dijon Potato Salad* ❧

Here is a low-fat potato salad incorporating the taste and color of carrot and green beans.

PREPARATION TIME: 15 minutes · COOKING TIME: 15 minutes ·
YIELD: 6 servings

4 cups water	½ teaspoon ground thyme
4 cups potato chunks	1 medium red bell pepper, cored and
1 medium carrot, chopped	chopped
2 cups green beans, cut into 1-inch	1 medium yellow bell pepper, cored
lengths	and diced
2 cups nonfat plain yogurt	½ cup chopped onion
2 tablespoons Dijon mustard	1 teaspoon dried dill
2 tablespoons rice wine vinegar	¼ teaspoon black pepper

1. Bring water to a boil in a saucepan. Add potatoes and simmer for 10 minutes. Add carrot and green beans, and continue to simmer until potatoes are just tender, about 5 additional minutes. Remove from heat, drain, and allow to cool.
2. Combine yogurt, mustard, rice wine vinegar, and thyme. Mix thoroughly.
3. Transfer potatoes, carrot, and beans to a large serving bowl. Add red and yellow bell peppers and onion. Stir dressing into the vegetables, sprinkle with dill and black pepper, and serve.

Calories Per Serving: 216	Carbohydrates: 46 g
Fat: 1 g	Dietary Fiber: 4 g
Cholesterol: 2 mg	Sodium: 199 mg
Protein: 9 g	

❦ *Vegetable-Potato Salad* ❧

This variation of traditional potato salad includes broccoli and cauliflower.

PREPARATION TIME: 15 minutes · COOKING TIME: 2 minutes ·
YIELD: 8 servings

1½ cups chopped broccoli
1½ cups chopped cauliflower
6 hard-boiled egg whites, chopped
3 stalks celery, finely chopped
3 scallions, finely chopped

½ cup nonfat plain yogurt
3 tablespoons nonfat sour cream
3 tablespoons nonfat mayonnaise
1 tablespoon lemon juice
1 tablespoon dried dill

1. Place broccoli and cauliflower in the steamer basket over boiling water, cover, and steam until just tender-crisp, about 2 minutes. Plunge into cold water and drain thoroughly.
2. Combine broccoli, cauliflower, egg whites, celery, and scallions in a large serving bowl.
3. Whisk together the yogurt, sour cream, mayonnaise, lemon juice, and dill. Combine dressing with vegetable mixture and toss to coat all ingredients and serve.

Calories Per Serving: 45
Fat: 0 g
Cholesterol: 0 mg
Protein: 5 g

Carbohydrates: 6 g
Dietary Fiber: 1 g
Sodium: 121 mg

❧ *Grapefruit-Spinach Salad* ❧

Spinach, grapefruit, red bell peppers, and red onion are dressed with a trio of fruit juices.

PREPARATION TIME: 10 minutes ▪ *YIELD: 6 servings*

3 medium grapefruits, peeled and sectioned, each section halved
2 medium red bell peppers, cored and cut into ¼-inch strips
1 small red onion, thinly sliced

8 cups torn bite-sized pieces fresh spinach
2 tablespoons lemon juice
1 tablespoon lime juice
3 tablespoons grapefruit juice

1. Combine grapefruit pieces, bell peppers, onion, and spinach in a large serving bowl. Toss gently.
2. Mix lemon juice, lime juice, and grapefruit juice. Pour dressing over the salad and toss to coat all ingredients and serve.

Calories Per Serving: 63
Fat: 0 g
Cholesterol: 0 mg
Protein: 3 g

Carbohydrates: 14 g
Dietary Fiber: 4 g
Sodium: 60 mg

❧ *Sweet and Tangy Fruit Salad* ❧

Pineapple, mango, papaya, and blueberries are featured in this refreshing salad.

PREPARATION TIME: 15 minutes • YIELD: 4 servings

2 cups juice-packed canned pineapple chunks
1 cup chopped mango
1 cup chopped papaya
1 cup fresh blueberries

1½ cups nonfat plain yogurt
2 tablespoons brown sugar
1 teaspoon lemon juice
1 teaspoon dried mint

1. Combine pineapple, mango, papaya, and blueberries.
2. Stir together the yogurt, brown sugar, and lemon juice. Add the dressing to the fruit and toss gently.
3. Divide among individual plates, top with mint, and serve.

Calories Per Serving: 215
Fat: 0 g
Cholesterol: 0 mg
Protein: 6 g

Carbohydrates: 50 g
Dietary Fiber: 3 g
Sodium: 80 mg

❧ *Kiwi-Rice Salad* ❧

Kiwi, apple, celery, red bell pepper, and scallions are mixed with rice. Ripe kiwifruits are soft but not spongy (just like a ripe peach) and can be stored in the refrigerator for up to a week.

PREPARATION TIME: 15 minutes plus 2 hours chilling time • YIELD: 8 servings

2 kiwifruits, peeled, halved vertically,
and sliced into half round pieces
1 medium apple, cored and cut into
¾-inch cubes
3 cups cooked white rice
1 stalk celery, sliced

1 medium red bell pepper, cored and
cut into thin strips
3 scallions, thinly sliced
2 tablespoons chopped fresh parsley
¼ cup rice wine vinegar

1. Combine the kiwi, apple, rice, celery, bell pepper, scallions, and parsley in a large bowl.
2. Pour the vinegar over the salad and toss well. Cover and refrigerate for 2 hours before serving.

Calories Per Serving: 127
Fat: 1 g
Cholesterol: 0 mg
Protein: 2 g

Carbohydrates: 28 g
Dietary Fiber: 2 g
Sodium: 14 mg

❧ *Wild Rice–Red Grape Salad* ❧

Wild rice and red grapes are topped with a lemon-curry-yogurt dressing. In order to clean wild rice thoroughly before cooking, place it in a medium bowl, fill it with cold water, set aside for a few minutes, then pour out the water with any debris that floats to the surface.

PREPARATION TIME: 15 minutes plus 1 hour cooling time •
COOKING TIME: 50 minutes • *YIELD: 6 servings*

1½ cups water
1½ cups low-sodium nonfat chicken
broth
1 cup uncooked wild rice
1 medium green bell pepper, cored
and chopped

1 cup halved seedless red grapes
3 scallions, chopped
¼ cup chopped fresh parsley
2 tablespoons lemon juice
1 teaspoon curry powder
½ cup nonfat plain yogurt

1. Bring water and broth to a boil in a saucepan. Stir in rice, return to a boil, reduce heat, and simmer until rice is just tender, about 50 minutes. Remove from heat and allow to cool to room temperature.

2. Combine cooled rice, green bell pepper, grapes, scallions, and parsley in a large serving bowl.
3. Whisk together the lemon juice, curry powder, and yogurt. Add dressing to the salad, toss to coat all ingredients, and serve.

Calories Per Serving: 174	Carbohydrates: 37 g
Fat: 1 g	Dietary Fiber: 2 g
Cholesterol: 1 mg	Sodium: 118 mg
Protein: 8 g	

❧ *Bean-Artichoke Salad* ❧

This salad of green beans, chickpeas, and pinto beans is tossed with a balsamic dressing.

PREPARATION TIME: 25 minutes　•　COOKING TIME: 2 minutes　•
YIELD: 8 servings

2½ cups green beans, cut into 2-inch pieces	½ cup thinly sliced onion
⅓ cup balsamic vinegar	2 cups cooked or low-sodium canned chickpeas, rinsed and drained
¼ cup chopped fresh parsley	2 cups cooked or low-sodium canned pinto beans, rinsed and drained
1 tablespoon dried basil	
3 cloves garlic, minced	2 cups water-packed canned artichoke hearts, chopped
¼ teaspoon ground black pepper	
1 large carrot, sliced	1 medium tomato, cut into thin wedges

1. Place green beans in a steamer basket over boiling water, cover, and steam until tender-crisp, about 2 minutes. Plunge into cold water, then drain thoroughly.
2. Mix vinegar, parsley, basil, garlic, and black pepper.
3. Combine green beans, carrot, onion, chickpeas, pinto beans, and artichoke hearts in a large bowl. Pour dressing over the salad, toss gently, top with tomato slices, and serve.

Calories Per Serving: 190

Carbohydrates: 37 g

Fat: 1 g

Dietary Fiber: 8 g

Cholesterol: 1 mg

Sodium: 349 mg

Protein: 10 g

❧ *Mango and Corn Salad with Black Beans* ❧

Fruit, vegetables, and beans are combined in this cumin-accented salad.

PREPARATION TIME: 15 minutes • YIELD: 3 servings

¼ cup low-sodium nonfat chicken broth

2 tablespoons lime juice

2 tablespoons water

1 teaspoon ground cumin

¼ teaspoon ground black pepper

2 cloves garlic, minced

1½ cups peeled, cubed fresh mango

½ cup fresh or thawed frozen corn kernels

½ cup diced red onion

2 cups cooked or low-sodium canned black beans, rinsed and drained

1 medium green bell pepper, cored and cut into thin strips

1. Whisk together the broth, lime juice, water, cumin, black pepper, and garlic in a medium bowl.
2. Add mango, corn, onion, beans, and green bell pepper to the dressing, and toss to coat all ingredients and serve.

Calories Per Serving: 164

Carbohydrates: 34 g

Fat: 1 g

Dietary Fiber: 7 g

Cholesterol: 0 mg

Sodium: 64 mg

Protein: 7 g

❧ *Pinto Bean–Corn Salad* ❧

This quick and easy salad is made with corn and beans and flavored with chili powder and cumin.

PREPARATION TIME: 15 minutes • YIELD: 4 servings

1 cup cooked or low-sodium canned
   pinto beans, rinsed and drained
1 cup canned or thawed frozen corn
   kernels
1 medium green bell pepper, cored
   and chopped
1 stalk celery, chopped

3 scallions, sliced
¼ cup lemon juice
1 teaspoon chili powder
2 cloves garlic, minced
1 tablespoon Dijon mustard
1 teaspoon ground cumin

1. Combine beans, corn, green bell pepper, celery, and scallions in a large bowl.
2. Whisk together lemon juice, chili powder, garlic, mustard, and cumin. Pour over the salad, toss to coat, and serve.

Calories Per Serving: 116
Fat: 1 g
Cholesterol: 0 mg
Protein: 6 g

Carbohydrates: 24 g
Dietary Fiber: 5 g
Sodium: 101 mg

RICE, GRAIN, AND PASTA DISHES

❧

Cilantro-Jalapeño Rice with Spinach ▪ Thai Rice ▪ Jalapeño-Pumpkin Pilaf ▪ Rice with Shiitake Mushrooms ▪ Lemon-Mushroom Rice with Peas ▪ Rice with Oranges and Celery ▪ Tomato-Onion Rice ▪ Basmati Rice with Spicy Kale ▪ Gingered Rice with Spinach ▪ Parmesan-Spinach Rice ▪ Green and Red Rice ▪ Mushroom-Pumpkin Rice ▪ Creamy Tomato-Bean Risotto ▪ Basmati Rice with Mushrooms ▪ Rice with Carrots, Cumin, and Black Beans ▪ Vegetable Biryani ▪ Rice with Succotash ▪ Curried Brown Rice–Vegetable Stew ▪ Baked Black-eyed Pea–Rice Casserole ▪ Wild Rice Toss ▪ Nonfat Wild Rice Quiche ▪ Curried Rice Salad ▪ White and Wild Rice Salad ▪ Wild Rice–Radish Salad ▪ Black Bean–Couscous Salad ▪ Couscous-Romaine Salad ▪ Yellow Squash Couscous ▪ Couscous with Black-eyed Peas ▪ Garden Couscous with White Wine Sauce ▪ Couscous with Chickpeas, Artichokes, and Spinach ▪ Mixed Vegetable Couscous ▪ Couscous-Apricot Toss ▪ Orange Couscous ▪ Kiwi-Raspberry Couscous ▪ Apricot-Yam Bulgur ▪ Bulgur with Zucchini and Bell Peppers ▪ Lentils and Bulgur ▪ Lentils, Onion, and Red Pepper with

Bulgur ▪ Barley-Vegetable-Bean Stew ▪ Mushroom-Kale Barley ▪ Hominy–Pinto Bean Stew ▪ Chili Orecchiette Pasta ▪ Capellini with Broccoli Sauce ▪ Bowtie Pasta with Spinach ▪ Penne-Broccoflower Toss ▪ Fusilli–Broccoli Salad ▪ Pasta Shells Primavera ▪ Linguine with Yellow Squash–Tomato Sauce ▪ Pasta with Vegetables and Cannellini Beans ▪ Leftover Pasta and Vegetables ▪ Pasta Shells with Chiles and Beans ▪ Baked Ziti ▪ Balsamic Pasta Salad

❧ *Cilantro-Jalapeño Rice with Spinach* ❧

Rice is cooked with spinach, red bell pepper, onion, black pepper, and chili powder. Tossing cooked rice with a fork before serving allows the steam to escape and the grains to separate.

PREPARATION TIME: 15 minutes • *COOKING TIME: 25 minutes* •
YIELD: 4 servings

¼ cup low-sodium nonfat chicken broth	2 cups water
1 medium onion, chopped	1 cup uncooked white rice
2 cloves garlic, minced	¼ cup chopped fresh parsley
1 medium red bell pepper, cored and chopped	1 teaspoon chili powder
1 jalapeño pepper, seeded and minced	¼ teaspoon ground black pepper
	2 cups chopped fresh spinach
	1 teaspoon dried cilantro

1. Heat broth in a saucepan. Add onion, garlic, red bell pepper, and jalapeño pepper, and sauté until peppers begin to soften, about 5 minutes.
2. Add water, rice, parsley, chili powder, and black pepper. Bring to a boil, reduce heat, cover, and simmer until rice is just tender, about 15 minutes.
3. Add spinach and cilantro, and continue to simmer until spinach is wilted, about 5 minutes. Serve at once.

Calories Per Serving: 211
Fat: 1 g
Cholesterol: 0 mg
Protein: 5 g

Carbohydrates: 46 g
Dietary Fiber: 2 g
Sodium: 155 mg

❧ *Thai Rice* ❧ ✓ NH ☑

In this festive Thai dish, rice is mixed with onion, gingerroot, lemongrass, and jalapeño pepper. Lemongrass is available fresh or dried in Asian markets and often is sold in supermarkets.

PREPARATION TIME: 15 minutes • *COOKING TIME: 18 minutes* •
YIELD: 4 servings

2 tablespoons low-sodium nonfat
   chicken broth
2 tablespoons minced red onion
1 tablespoon minced fresh gingerroot
2 teaspoons minced lemongrass
   (optional)

1 jalapeño pepper, seeded and minced *check for heat first*
1 teaspoon ground coriander
½ teaspoon turmeric *need for color*
1 cup uncooked white rice
2 cups water

1. Heat broth in a saucepan. Add onion, gingerroot, lemongrass, and jalapeño pepper. Sauté for 2 minutes. Add coriander and turmeric, and sauté for 1 additional minute.
2. Add rice and water. Bring to a boil, reduce heat, cover, and simmer for 15 minutes or until rice is tender. Serve at once.

Calories Per Serving: 234
Fat: 1 g
Cholesterol: 0 mg
Protein: 4 g

Carbohydrates: 53 g
Dietary Fiber: 1 g
Sodium: 134 mg

See notes in keep finder.

❧ *Jalapeño-Pumpkin Pilaf* ❧

In this variation on a Near Eastern dish, baked pumpkin is combined with rice, onion, bell pepper, jalapeño, zucchini, yellow summer squash, and scallions.

PREPARATION TIME: 20 minutes • *COOKING TIME: 1 hour* •
YIELD: 8 servings

3 cups chopped pumpkin	*1 cup chopped zucchini*
¼ cup low-sodium nonfat chicken broth	*1 cup chopped yellow summer squash*
1 medium onion, diced	*3 scallions, minced*
1 medium red bell pepper, cored and chopped	*½ teaspoon ground black pepper*
1 jalapeño pepper, seeded and minced	*1½ cups uncooked white rice*
	3 cups water
	½ cup chopped fresh parsley

1. Preheat oven to 350 degrees.
2. Place pumpkin in a casserole and bake until just tender, about 30 minutes.
3. Heat broth in a large saucepan. Add onion, red bell pepper, jalapeño, zucchini, yellow squash, and scallions, and sauté until vegetables are just tender, about 5 minutes. Stir in black pepper and rice, and continue to sauté for 1 additional minute.
4. Add water, bring to a boil, reduce heat, and simmer until rice is tender, about 20 minutes.
5. Combine the pumpkin and rice mixture in a large bowl. Toss gently, sprinkle with parsley, and serve.

Calories Per Serving: 148	Carbohydrates: 34 g
Fat: 0 g	Dietary Fiber: 3 g
Cholesterol: 0 mg	Sodium: 49 mg
Protein: 3 g	

❧ *Rice with Shiitake Mushrooms* ❧

This rice dish is richly flavored with shiitake mushrooms, onion, garlic, and cayenne. Shiitake mushrooms are available year round, but have peak seasons in spring and autumn.

PREPARATION TIME: 15 minutes　•　COOKING TIME: 25 minutes　•
YIELD: 6 servings

4 cups low-sodium nonfat chicken
  broth
1 medium onion, chopped
2 cloves garlic, minced
2 cups uncooked white rice

½ cup sliced shiitake mushrooms
⅛ teaspoon cayenne pepper
½ cup chopped fresh parsley
¼ teaspoon ground black pepper

1. Bring broth to a boil in a saucepan. Add onion, garlic, and rice. Return to a boil, reduce heat, cover, and simmer for 15 minutes.
2. Add mushrooms and cayenne pepper, cover, and continue to simmer for 10 additional minutes, until the liquid is absorbed and the rice is tender.
3. Transfer to a large bowl, stir in parsley, sprinkle with black pepper, and serve.

Calories Per Serving: 185
Fat: 0 g
Cholesterol: 0 mg
Protein: 8 g

Carbohydrates: 37 g
Dietary Fiber: 1 g
Sodium: 120 mg

❧ *Lemon-Mushroom Rice with Peas* ❧

This rice dish contains onion, bell peppers, celery, tomatoes, mushrooms, oregano, and cayenne pepper. Cooked rice should be firm but tender.

PREPARATION TIME: 15 minutes • *COOKING TIME: 35 minutes* •
YIELD: 8 servings

3 cups low-sodium nonfat chicken
  broth
1 medium onion, chopped
1 medium yellow bell pepper, cored
  and chopped
1 medium red bell pepper, cored and
  chopped
2 stalks celery, sliced
1 cup uncooked white rice

3 medium tomatoes, chopped
1 teaspoon dried oregano
⅛ teaspoon cayenne pepper
1 cup sliced mushrooms
1 cup fresh or frozen peas
½ cup chopped fresh parsley
2 tablespoons lemon juice
¼ teaspoon ground black pepper

1. Bring broth to a boil in a saucepan. Add onion, yellow and red bell peppers, celery, rice, tomatoes, oregano, and cayenne pepper. Return to a boil, reduce heat, cover, and simmer for 25 minutes.
2. Add mushrooms and continue to simmer for 5 minutes. Add peas and continue to simmer until rice is just tender, about 5 additional minutes.
3. Remove from heat and drain excess liquid. Stir in parsley and lemon juice, sprinkle with black pepper, and serve.

Calories Per Serving: 137	Carbohydrates: 28 g
Fat: 0 g	Dietary Fiber: 2 g
Cholesterol: 0 mg	Sodium: 79 mg
Protein: 6 g	

❧ *Rice with Oranges and Celery* ❧

Rice is sweetened with orange juice and oranges in this colorful summer dish.

Preparation Time: 10 minutes • Cooking Time: 28 minutes •
Yield: 4 servings

1 cup water	*1 cup uncooked white rice*
1½ cups orange juice	*3 navel oranges, sectioned and each*
4 scallions, thinly sliced	*section quartered*
¾ cup thinly sliced celery	

1. Bring water and juice to a boil in a saucepan. Add scallions and celery, return to a boil, reduce heat, and simmer for 5 minutes.
2. Stir in rice. Return to a boil, reduce heat, cover, and simmer until rice is just tender, about 20 minutes. Drain.
3. Stir in orange pieces and serve.

Calories Per Serving: 179	Carbohydrates: 41 g
Fat: 0 g	Dietary Fiber: 3 g
Cholesterol: 0 mg	Sodium: 15 mg
Protein: 3 g	

❧ *Tomato-Onion Rice* ❧

This rice dish is made with onion, garlic, tomatoes, bay leaf, and oregano. Be sure to remove the bay leaf before serving.

PREPARATION TIME: 10 minutes • *COOKING TIME: 25 minutes* •
YIELD: 4 servings

2½ cups low-sodium nonfat chicken broth	1 cup uncooked white rice
1 medium onion, chopped	3 medium tomatoes, chopped
3 cloves garlic, minced	1 bay leaf
	1 teaspoon dried oregano

1. Bring broth to a boil in a saucepan. Add onion, garlic, rice, tomatoes, bay leaf, and oregano.
2. Return to a boil, reduce heat, cover, and simmer until rice is just tender, about 25 minutes. Drain. Remove bay leaf before serving.

Calories Per Serving: 220
Fat: 1 g
Cholesterol: 0 mg
Protein: 9 g

Carbohydrates: 24 g
Dietary Fiber: 1 g
Sodium: 116 mg

❧ *Basmati Rice with Spicy Kale* ❧

Basmati rice is combined with onion, jalapeño pepper, garlic, and kale. When cooked, its long grains become light and dry and separate easily.

PREPARATION: 10 minutes • *COOKING TIME: 24 minutes* •
YIELD: 4 servings

2¼ cups low-sodium nonfat chicken broth	1 cup uncooked basmati rice
1 medium onion, chopped	½ teaspoon ground cumin
1 jalapeño pepper, seeded and minced	½ teaspoon ground black pepper
2 cloves garlic, minced	2 cups finely chopped fresh kale
	¼ cup chopped fresh parsley

1. Heat ¼ cup broth in a large saucepan. Add onion, jalapeño, and garlic, and sauté until onion begins to soften, about 4 minutes.
2. Add remaining broth, rice, cumin, and black pepper. Bring to a boil, reduce heat, cover, and simmer until rice is just tender, about 15 minutes.
3. Stir in kale and continue to simmer for 5 minutes. Drain any remaining liquid. Transfer to a large bowl, sprinkle with parsley, and serve.

Calories Per Serving: 213
Fat: 0 g
Cholesterol: 0 mg
Protein: 6 g

Carbohydrates: 44 g
Dietary Fiber: 3 g
Sodium: 131 mg

✆ *Gingered Rice with Spinach* ✇

Rice is cooked with gingerroot and served with steamed spinach. Look for mature fresh gingerroot with a smooth skin and a fresh, spicy fragrance.

PREPARATION TIME: 10 minutes • *COOKING TIME: 24 minutes* •
YIELD: 6 servings

2½ cups low-sodium nonfat chicken broth
2 cloves garlic, minced
2 tablespoons grated fresh gingerroot

1 cup uncooked white rice
4 cups chopped fresh spinach leaves
¼ teaspoon ground black pepper

1. Bring broth to a boil in a saucepan. Add garlic, gingerroot, and rice. Return to a boil, reduce heat, and simmer until rice is just tender, about 20 minutes.
2. Place spinach in a steamer basket over 2 cups of water, cover, and steam until just tender, about 2 minutes.
3. Transfer rice to a serving bowl and mix in spinach. Sprinkle with black pepper and serve.

Calories Per Serving: 139
Fat: 0 g
Cholesterol: 0 mg
Protein: 6 g

Carbohydrates: 28 g
Dietary Fiber: 1 g
Sodium: 101 mg

❧ *Parmesan-Spinach Rice* ❧

Nutmeg brings a delicately sweet flavor to this creamy dish.

PREPARATION: 10 minutes • COOKING TIME: 18 minutes •
YIELD: 4 servings

2½ cups low-sodium nonfat chicken
  broth
½ cup minced onion
¼ cup sliced mushrooms
2 cloves garlic, minced

1 cup uncooked white rice
⅛ teaspoon ground nutmeg
1 cup chopped fresh spinach
¼ cup skim milk
1 tablespoon nonfat Parmesan

1. Heat ¼ cup broth in a large saucepan. Add onion, mushrooms, and garlic, and sauté until onion begins to soften, about 3 minutes.
2. Stir in remaining broth, rice, and nutmeg. Bring to a boil, reduce heat, cover, and simmer until rice is just tender, about 15 minutes. Remove from heat, drain any remaining liquid, stir in spinach, milk, and Parmesan.

Calories Per Serving: 218
Fat: 0 g
Cholesterol: 1 mg
Protein: 9 g

Carbohydrates: 43 g
Dietary Fiber: 1 g
Sodium: 140 mg

❧ *Green and Red Rice* ❧

Rice, tomatoes, and peas are seasoned with garlic and oregano.

PREPARATION TIME: 10 minutes • COOKING TIME: 30 minutes •
YIELD: 6 servings

1¾ cups low-sodium nonfat chicken
  broth
1 cup uncooked white rice
2 medium tomatoes, chopped, ¼ cup
  juice reserved

3 cloves garlic, minced
1 cup fresh or frozen green peas
1 teaspoon dried oregano
⅛ teaspoon ground white pepper
2 scallions, minced

1. Bring broth to a boil in a saucepan. Stir in rice. Return to a boil, reduce heat, cover, and simmer until liquid is absorbed and rice is just tender, about 20 minutes.
2. Heat reserved tomato juice in a skillet. Add tomatoes, garlic, peas, oregano, and white pepper. Sauté until peas are just tender, about 5 minutes.
3. Combine rice and tomatoes. Toss gently, sprinkle with minced scallions, and serve.

Calories Per Serving: 154   Carbohydrates: 33 g
Fat: 0 g   Dietary Fiber: 2 g
Cholesterol: 0 mg   Sodium: 23 mg
Protein: 5 g

❧ *Mushroom-Pumpkin Rice* ❧

In this pumpkin-and-spinach variation on a classic Italian recipe, rice is cooked with pumpkin, mushrooms, carrot, and spinach.

PREPARATION TIME: 15 minutes plus 5 minutes standing time •
COOKING TIME: 24 minutes • *YIELD: 10 servings*

¼ cup low-sodium nonfat chicken broth
1 medium onion, chopped
1½ cups sliced mushrooms
2 cloves garlic, minced
2 cups diced pumpkin

2 cups uncooked white rice
1 medium carrot, scraped and diced
1½ cups chopped fresh spinach
½ teaspoon ground black pepper
5 cups water
3 tablespoons nonfat Parmesan

1. Heat broth in a large saucepan. Add onion, mushrooms, and garlic, and sauté until onion begins to soften, about 4 minutes.
2. Add pumpkin, rice, carrot, spinach, black pepper, and 2½ cups water. Bring to a boil. Reduce heat, cover, and simmer, stirring frequently, for 10 minutes.
3. Stir in remaining water. Return to a boil, reduce heat, cover, and simmer, stirring frequently, for an additional 10 minutes.

4. Remove from heat, allow to stand for 5 minutes, and stir in Parmesan before serving.

Calories Per Serving: 172
Fat: 0 g
Cholesterol: 2 mg
Protein: 5 g

Carbohydrates: 37 g
Dietary Fiber: 1 g
Sodium: 36 mg

❧ *Creamy Tomato-Bean Risotto* ❧

This risotto recipe contains Great Northern beans, sun-dried tomatoes, and arborio rice, which has short, fat grains. Risotto has to be stirred constantly.

PREPARATION TIME: 15 minutes plus 1 hour tomato soaking time •
COOKING TIME: 28 minutes • *YIELD: 6 servings*

¾ cup sun-dried tomatoes
1½ cups water
¼ cup low-sodium nonfat chicken broth
1 medium onion, minced
2 cloves garlic, minced
4 cups water

2 cups arborio rice
¼ teaspoon ground black pepper
1½ cups low-sodium canned Great Northern beans, rinsed and drained
1 cup chopped fresh spinach leaves
3 tablespoons nonfat Parmesan

1. Cover the tomatoes with water and allow to soak for 1 hour. Drain liquid and chop the tomatoes.
2. Heat the broth in a large saucepan. Add the onion and garlic, and sauté until onion begins to soften, about 3 minutes. Add tomatoes and sauté for 2 more minutes.
3. Stir in 2 cups of water, rice, and black pepper. Bring to a boil. Reduce heat, and simmer, stirring often, for 10 minutes. Add remaining water, beans, and spinach. Return to a boil, reduce heat, and simmer, stirring, until rice becomes creamy, about 8 minutes.
4. Remove from heat, stir in Parmesan, and serve at once.

Calories Per Serving: 417
Fat: 1 g
Cholesterol: 3 mg
Protein: 15 g

Carbohydrates: 90 g
Dietary Fiber: 2 g
Sodium: 88 mg

❧ *Basmati Rice with Mushrooms* ❧

Basmati rice is a long-grained rice with a fine texture. It has a nutlike flavor and can be found in Indian and Middle Eastern markets and at some supermarkets.

PREPARATION: 10 minutes plus 5 minutes standing time •
COOKING TIME: 28 minutes • *YIELD: 4 servings*

2¼ cups low-sodium nonfat chicken broth
1 stalk celery, chopped
½ cup chopped onion
2 cloves garlic, minced

½ teaspoon dried thyme
¼ teaspoon ground black pepper
1 cup mushrooms, sliced
1 cup uncooked basmati rice

1. Heat ¼ cup broth in a saucepan. Add celery, onion, and garlic, and sauté until onion begins to soften, about 3 minutes.
2. Add thyme, black pepper, mushrooms, and rice, and stir to mix thoroughly. Add remaining broth. Bring to a boil, reduce heat, cover, and simmer until rice is just tender, about 25 minutes.
3. Remove from heat, drain any remaining liquid, and allow to stand for 5 minutes before serving.

Calories Per Serving: 210
Fat: 0 g
Cholesterol: 0 mg
Protein: 5 g

Carbohydrates: 45 g
Dietary Fiber: 2 g
Sodium: 45 mg

❧ *Rice with Carrots, Cumin, and Black Beans* ❧

Rice, carrot, onion, and black beans are spiced with cumin and garlic.

PREPARATION: 10 minutes • *COOKING TIME: 18 minutes* •
YIELD: 4 servings

1¾ *cups low-sodium nonfat chicken*
   broth
1 *medium carrot, chopped*
1 *small onion, finely chopped*
2 *cloves garlic, minced*
1 *teaspoon ground cumin*

1 *cup uncooked white rice*
1 *cup cooked or low-sodium canned*
   black beans, rinsed and drained
¼ *cup chopped fresh parsley*
1 *tablespoon lime juice*

1. Heat ¼ cup broth in a saucepan. Add carrot, onion, and garlic, and sauté until onion begins to soften, about 3 minutes.
2. Stir in cumin, rice, beans, and remaining broth. Bring to a boil, reduce heat, cover, and simmer until rice is just tender, about 15 minutes.
3. Remove from heat and drain any remaining liquid. Stir in the parsley and lime juice, and serve.

Calories Per Serving: 209
Fat: 0 g
Cholesterol: 0 mg
Protein: 5 g

Carbohydrates: 45 g
Dietary Fiber: 1 g
Sodium: 37 mg

❧ *Vegetable Biryani* ❧

Onion, potato, carrot, cauliflower, green bell pepper, raisins, chickpeas, green peas, and tomato are served with rice in this classic Indian recipe.

PREPARATION TIME: 20 minutes • *COOKING TIME: 55 minutes* •
YIELD: 8 servings

3 *cups low-sodium nonfat chicken*
   broth

1½ *cups uncooked white rice*
1 *teaspoon turmeric*

1 medium onion, chopped	*1 teaspoon ground cumin*
1 medium potato, diced	*1 teaspoon coriander*
1 medium carrot, scraped and diced	*¼ teaspoon cayenne pepper*
2 cups chopped cauliflower	*½ teaspoon ground cinnamon*
1 medium green bell pepper, cored	*1 cup cooked or low-sodium canned*
and chopped	*chickpeas, rinsed and drained*
½ cup raisins	*½ cup fresh or frozen green peas*
2 teaspoons fresh minced gingerroot	*1 medium tomato, chopped*

1. Place 2½ cups broth in a large saucepan. Bring to a boil and add rice and turmeric. Reduce heat, cover, and simmer for 30 minutes.
2. Heat remaining broth in another saucepan. Add onion, potato, carrot, cauliflower, green bell pepper, raisins, gingerroot, cumin, coriander, cayenne pepper, and cinnamon. Simmer until the vegetables are just tender, about 15 minutes.
3. Add the vegetables to the rice. Stir in the chickpeas, green peas, and tomato. Cover and simmer until the liquid is absorbed, about 10 minutes.
4. Transfer to individual plates and serve at once.

Calories Per Serving: 213	Carbohydrates: 58 g
Fat: 1 g	Dietary Fiber: 2 g
Cholesterol: 0 mg	Sodium: 195 mg
Protein: 9 g	

❧ *Rice with Succotash* ❧

This rice dish contains zucchini and Parmesan as well as lima beans and corn. Rice is cholesterol- and gluten-free.

PREPARATION TIME: 15 minutes ▪ *COOKING TIME: 25 minutes* ▪
YIELD: 8 servings

3 cups water	*2 cloves garlic, minced*
1½ cups uncooked white rice	*1 cup zucchini, cut into crosswise slices*
¼ cup low-sodium nonfat chicken	*1 cup fresh, canned, or frozen corn*
broth	*kernels*
1 medium onion, sliced	*1 teaspoon dried thyme*

4 cups frozen lima beans, cooked and
   drained

1 medium tomato, finely chopped
¼ cup nonfat Parmesan

1. Bring water to a boil in a large skillet. Add rice, stir, and return to a boil.
2. Reduce heat, cover, and simmer until water is absorbed and rice is just tender, about 15 minutes.
3. Heat broth in a saucepan. Add onion, garlic, zucchini, corn, and thyme. Sauté until onion and zucchini begin to soften, about 5 minutes.
4. Stir in lima beans and continue to simmer, adding water as needed, until heated through, about 5 minutes.
5. Transfer rice to individual serving bowls, top with zucchini–corn–lima bean mixture, sprinkle with tomato and Parmesan, and serve.

Calories Per Serving: 171
Fat: 1 g
Cholesterol: 0 mg
Protein: 8 g

Carbohydrates: 34 g
Dietary Fiber: 6 g
Sodium: 22 mg

❧ Curried Brown Rice–Vegetable Stew ❧

In this dish, brown rice is cooked with onion, bell pepper, gingerroot, jalapeño pepper, tomatoes, carrots, spinach, and black-eyed peas.

PREPARATION: 20 minutes plus 10 minutes standing time   •
COOKING TIME: 40 minutes   •   YIELD: 10 servings

3¼ cups low-sodium nonfat chicken
   broth
1 medium onion, chopped
1 medium red bell pepper, cored and
   chopped
1 tablespoon minced fresh gingerroot
1 jalapeño pepper, seeded and minced
3 medium tomatoes, chopped
2 teaspoons curry powder

½ teaspoon thyme
½ teaspoon ground black pepper
1½ cups uncooked brown rice
2 medium carrots, scraped and
   chopped
¼ cup low sodium tomato paste
3 cups chopped spinach
1 cup low-sodium canned low-fat
   black-eyed peas, rinsed and drained

1. Heat ¼ cup broth in a large saucepan. Add onion, red bell pepper, gingerroot, and jalapeño, and sauté until onion begins to soften, about 4 minutes.
2. Add tomatoes, curry powder, thyme, and black pepper, and continue to sauté for 1 additional minute.
3. Stir in remaining broth, rice, carrots, and tomato paste. Bring to a boil, reduce heat, cover, and simmer for 30 minutes. Add spinach and black-eyed peas and continue to simmer until rice is just tender, about 5 additional minutes.
4. Remove from heat, fluff the rice, and allow to stand for 10 minutes before serving.

Calories Per Serving: 160   Carbohydrates: 33 g
Fat: 1 g   Dietary Fiber: 3 g
Cholesterol: 0 mg   Sodium: 78 mg
Protein: 5 g

❧ *Baked Black-eyed Pea–Rice Casserole* ❧

Rice is baked with black-eyed peas, tomatoes, and onion. Black-eyed peas are available fresh, canned, or frozen.

PREPARATION TIME: 15 minutes • COOKING TIME: 40 minutes •
YIELD: 4 servings

1½ cups water
¾ cup uncooked white rice
2 tablespoons low-sodium nonfat chicken broth
1 medium onion, chopped
½ teaspoon ground black pepper

½ teaspoon cayenne pepper
2 cups chopped low-sodium canned tomatoes, with juice
2 cups low-sodium canned black-eyed peas, rinsed and drained

1. Preheat oven to 350 degrees.
2. Bring water to a boil in a saucepan. Add rice. Stir once, return to a boil, reduce heat, cover, and simmer until rice is just tender, about 15 minutes.

3. Heat broth in a skillet. Add onion and sauté until just tender. Add black pepper, cayenne pepper, tomatoes and their juice, and black-eyed peas. Return to a boil, reduce heat, and simmer 5 minutes.
4. Layer half the rice in a nonstick baking dish. Top with a layer of half the tomato–black-eyed pea mixture. Repeat layers.
5. Bake for 15 minutes and serve hot.

Calories Per Serving: 168	Carbohydrates: 36 g
Fat: 1 g	Dietary Fiber: 7 g
Cholesterol: 0 mg	Sodium: 34 mg
Protein: 5 g	

❧ *Wild Rice Toss* ❧

Wild rice and pearl barley are combined with mushrooms, peas, herbs, and spices. If wild rice is overcooked, it will become too starchy.

PREPARATION TIME: 15 minutes • COOKING TIME: 30 minutes •
YIELD: 4 servings

1 cup low-sodium nonfat chicken broth	*¼ teaspoon ground ginger*
1½ cups water	*½ cup chopped mushrooms*
½ cup uncooked wild rice	*1 teaspoon dried coriander*
¼ cup pearl barley	*3 tablespoons chopped fresh parsley*
½ teaspoon dried oregano	*½ cup frozen green peas*
1 teaspoon curry powder	*2 tablespoons nonfat Parmesan*

1. Bring broth and water to a boil in a saucepan. Stir in rice, barley, oregano, curry powder, and ginger. Return to a boil, reduce heat, cover, and simmer for 20 minutes.
2. Add mushrooms, coriander, 2 tablespoons parsley, and peas, and continue to simmer until rice and barley are just tender, about 10 additional minutes.
3. Remove from heat and drain. Sprinkle with remaining parsley and Parmesan, and serve.

Calories Per Serving: 166
Fat: 1 g
Cholesterol: 0 mg
Protein: 8 g

Carbohydrates: 33 g
Dietary Fiber: 6 g
Sodium: 75 mg

❧ *Nonfat Wild Rice Quiche* ❧

Quiche, which is traditionally made with eggs, butter, and cheese, can be one of the worst offenders in the high-fat category. This variation is made with a rice crust, egg whites, and nonfat cheeses.

PREPARATION TIME: *20 minutes plus 10 minutes standing time* •
COOKING TIME: *43 minutes* • YIELD: *6 servings*

7 egg whites
1½ cups cooked wild rice
2 tablespoons nonfat Parmesan
2 tablespoons low-sodium nonfat
  chicken broth
2 cups sliced zucchini
1 medium red bell pepper, cored and
  chopped

2 cloves garlic, minced
½ teaspoon dried basil
¼ teaspoon ground black pepper
¾ cup shredded nonfat mozzarella
1 cup evaporated skim milk
2 tablespoons all-purpose flour

1. Preheat oven to 350 degrees.
2. Combine 1 egg white, rice, and 1½ tablespoons Parmesan. Mix thoroughly. Form into a crust in a nonstick 9-inch pie pan.
3. Heat broth in a saucepan. Add zucchini, red bell pepper, garlic, basil, and black pepper. Sauté until zucchini begins to soften, about 3 minutes. Remove from heat and allow to cool slightly.
4. Stir mozzarella into the zucchini mixture and spread over the pie crust.
5. Whisk together the remaining egg whites, evaporated milk, and flour, and pour over the zucchini mixture. Bake until quiche is done through, about 40 minutes. Remove from oven and allow to stand for 10 minutes before cutting and serving.

Calories Per Serving: 144

Fat: 0 g

Cholesterol: 5 mg

Protein: 16 g

Carbohydrates: 19 g

Dietary Fiber: 1 g

Sodium: 255 mg

❧ *Curried Rice Salad* ❧

This chilled salad contains rice, red bell pepper, artichoke hearts, fat-free mayonnaise, curry powder, and onion.

PREPARATION TIME: 10 minutes plus 2 hours chilling time •
COOKING TIME: 25 minutes • *YIELD: 6 servings*

*2 cups low-sodium nonfat chicken
    broth*

1 cup water

1½ cups uncooked white rice

1 medium red bell pepper, chopped

*1 6-ounce jar water-packed artichoke
    hearts, chopped*

⅓ cup nonfat mayonnaise

¾ teaspoon curry powder

1 medium onion, chopped

1. Bring broth and water to a boil in a saucepan. Stir in rice. Return to a boil, reduce heat, cover, and simmer until just tender, about 25 minutes.
2. Combine rice, bell pepper, artichokes, mayonnaise, curry powder, and onion. Chill for 2 hours before serving.

Calories Per Serving: 214

Fat: 0 g

Cholesterol: 0 mg

Protein: 5 g

Carbohydrates: 46 g

Dietary Fiber: 1 g

Sodium: 258 mg

❧ *White and Wild Rice Salad* ❧

For this chilled salad, wild rice, white rice, and red and green bell peppers are combined and tossed with a mustard dressing.

PREPARATION TIME: 10 minutes plus 1 hour chilling time •
COOKING TIME: 25 minutes • *YIELD: 6 servings*

3 cups low-sodium nonfat chicken
   broth

¾ cup uncooked wild rice

¾ cup uncooked white rice

4 scallions, finely chopped

2 medium red bell peppers, cored and
   diced

2 medium green bell peppers, cored
   and diced

2 tablespoons lemon juice

½ teaspoon dry mustard

½ teaspoon dried basil

½ teaspoon dried oregano

2 cloves garlic, minced

¼ teaspoon ground black pepper

1. Bring broth to a boil in a saucepan. Add wild rice and white rice. Return to a boil, reduce heat, cover, and simmer until rices are just tender, about 25 minutes. Remove from heat and allow to cool to room temperature.
2. Combine the cooled rice, scallions, and red and green bell peppers. Toss well.
3. Whisk together the lemon juice, mustard, basil, oregano, garlic, and black pepper.
4. Pour the dressing over the rice and toss well. Refrigerate for 1 hour before serving.

Calories Per Serving: 194

Fat: 1 g

Cholesterol: 0 mg

Protein: 7 g

Carbohydrates: 41 g

Dietary Fiber: 1 g

Sodium: 171 mg

❧ Wild Rice–Radish Salad ❧

A mustard dressing coats this salad made with wild rice, bell pepper, and radishes. Radishes can be refrigerated in a plastic bag for up to five days.

PREPARATION TIME: 10 minutes · YIELD: 4 servings

1 cup cooked chilled wild rice

¼ cup finely chopped yellow bell
   pepper

¼ cup thinly sliced radishes

1 scallion, minced

½ tablespoon prepared horseradish

½ tablespoon Dijon mustard

2 tablespoons dry white wine

1. Combine the rice, yellow bell pepper, radishes, and scallion in a bowl. Toss well.
2. Mix the horseradish, mustard, and wine, and pour over the salad. Toss to coat all ingredients and serve.

Calories Per Serving: 54
Fat: 0 g
Cholesterol: 0 mg
Protein: 2 g

Carbohydrates: 10 g
Dietary Fiber: 1 g
Sodium: 86 mg

❧ *Black Bean–Couscous Salad* ❧

This chilled couscous dish with tomatoes, bell peppers, scallions, beans, and corn is a great main dish for a summer meal.

PREPARATION TIME: 15 minutes plus 5 minutes standing time and 1 hour chilling time • *YIELD: 8 servings*

1½ cups water
1 cup uncooked couscous
3 medium tomatoes, chopped
2 medium green bell peppers, cored and chopped
4 scallions, sliced

1 cup cooked or low-sodium canned black beans, rinsed and drained
1 cup fresh or thawed frozen corn kernels
2 tablespoons minced fresh parsley
½ teaspoon ground black pepper
2 tablespoons lime juice

1. Bring water to a boil in a saucepan. Stir in couscous. Remove from heat, cover, and allow to stand for 5 minutes.
2. Combine tomatoes, bell peppers, scallions, beans, corn, parsley, black pepper, and lime juice in a large serving bowl. Add couscous, toss well, and refrigerate for 1 hour before serving.

Calories Per Serving: 149
Fat: 0 g
Cholesterol: 0 mg
Protein: 6 g

Carbohydrates: 31 g
Dietary Fiber: 7 g
Sodium: 11 mg

❧ *Couscous-Romaine Salad* ❧

Here the very versatile couscous from North Africa is used to enhance a flavorful, distinctive salad.

PREPARATION TIME: 20 minutes plus 5 minutes standing time   •
YIELD: 6 servings

2 cups water	*4 cups torn romaine lettuce leaves*
¾ cup uncooked couscous	*⅓ cup lemon juice*
2 medium tomatoes, chopped	*1 clove garlic, minced*
4 scallions, chopped	*1 teaspoon ground cumin*
1 cup chopped fresh parsley	*¼ teaspoon cayenne pepper*
1 tablespoon dried cilantro	*½ teaspoon ground black pepper*
3 radishes, thinly sliced	

1. Bring 1⅔ cups water to a boil in a saucepan. Stir in couscous. Remove from heat, cover, and allow to stand for 5 minutes.
2. Combine tomatoes, scallions, parsley, cilantro, radishes, and lettuce in a large bowl.
3. Whisk together the lemon juice, remaining water, garlic, cumin, cayenne pepper, and black pepper.
4. Add couscous to the salad. Pour dressing over the salad and toss to coat all ingredients.
5. Transfer to individual plates and serve at once.

Calories Per Serving: 144	Carbohydrates: 30 g
Fat: 0 g	Dietary Fiber: 4 g
Cholesterol: 0 mg	Sodium: 21 mg
Protein: 5 g	

❧ *Yellow Squash Couscous* ❧

Squash, tomatoes, bell pepper, and scallions are spiced with ginger and cayenne.

PREPARATION TIME: 15 minutes plus 5 minutes standing time   •
COOKING TIME: 5 minutes   •   YIELD: 4 servings

¼ cup low-sodium nonfat chicken broth

2 scallions, chopped

1 medium green bell pepper, cored and chopped

2 cloves garlic, minced

2 medium tomatoes, chopped

1 cup chopped yellow summer squash

1 cup cooked or low-sodium canned chickpeas, rinsed and drained

1½ cups water

½ teaspoon curry powder

2 tablespoons chopped fresh parsley

½ teaspoon ground ginger

¼ teaspoon cayenne pepper

¾ cup uncooked couscous

1. Heat broth in a large skillet. Add scallions, green bell pepper, garlic, tomatoes, summer squash, and chickpeas, and sauté until pepper begins to soften, about 5 minutes.

2. Combine water, curry powder, parsley, ginger, and cayenne pepper in a saucepan. Bring to a boil, stir in couscous, and remove from heat. Cover and allow to stand for 5 minutes.

3. Transfer the couscous to individual plates, top with the vegetables, and serve at once.

Calories Per Serving: 170
Fat: 1 g
Cholesterol: 0 mg
Protein: 7 g

Carbohydrates: 35 g
Dietary Fiber: 7 g
Sodium: 127 mg

❧ *Couscous with Black-eyed Peas* ❧

Onion, bell pepper, zucchini, and black-eyed peas are combined with couscous.

PREPARATION TIME: *15 minutes plus 5 minutes standing time* •
COOKING TIME: *8 minutes* • YIELD: *4 servings*

¼ cup low-sodium nonfat chicken broth

1 medium onion, chopped

1 medium yellow bell pepper, cored and chopped

1 cup chopped zucchini

1 teaspoon paprika

½ teaspoon ground cumin

½ teaspoon ground black pepper

2 cups low-sodium canned black-eyed peas, rinsed and drained

1½ cups water

2 scallions, chopped

1 cup uncooked couscous

1. Heat broth in a saucepan. Add onion, yellow bell pepper, and zucchini, and sauté until pepper begins to soften, about 5 minutes.
2. Add paprika, cumin, black pepper, and black-eyed peas and simmer for 3 minutes.
3. Add water and scallions, and bring to a boil. Stir in couscous. Remove from heat, cover, and allow to stand for 5 minutes before serving.

Calories Per Serving: 260
Fat: 1 g
Cholesterol: 0 mg
Protein: 11 g

Carbohydrates: 52 g
Dietary Fiber: 12 g
Sodium: 33 mg

❧ *Garden Couscous with White Wine Sauce* ❧

This couscous dish is topped with chickpeas, onion, bell pepper, celery, and carrot.

PREPARATION TIME: 10 minutes plus 15 minutes standing time ▪
COOKING TIME: 10 minutes ▪ *YIELD: 6 servings*

1¾ cups low-sodium nonfat chicken broth
1 cup uncooked couscous
1 cup cooked or low-sodium canned chickpeas, rinsed and drained
2 cloves garlic, minced
½ cup minced onion

1 medium green bell pepper, cored and chopped
1 stalk celery, chopped
1 medium carrot, chopped
¼ cup white wine
¼ teaspoon ground black pepper
¼ teaspoon ground cinnamon

1. Bring 1½ cups of the broth to a boil in a saucepan. Stir in the couscous. Remove from heat and allow to stand for 5 minutes.
2. Heat remaining broth in a large skillet. Add chickpeas, garlic, onion, green bell pepper, celery, carrot, and wine. Cover and simmer for 10 minutes.
3. Stir in black pepper and cinnamon.
4. Transfer couscous to a large bowl, top with the vegetables, and serve at once.

Calories Per Serving: 177   Carbohydrates: 35 g
Fat: 0 g   Dietary Fiber: 8 g
Cholesterol: 0 mg   Sodium: 33 mg
Protein: 8 g

❧ *Couscous with Chickpeas, Artichokes,* ❧ *and Spinach*

In this North African recipe, couscous is mixed with onion, bell pepper, tomatoes, potatoes, artichoke hearts, chickpeas, and spinach.

PREPARATION TIME: 15 minutes plus 5 minutes standing time •
COOKING TIME: 25 minutes • *YIELD: 8 servings*

6 cups low-sodium nonfat chicken broth
1½ cups uncooked couscous
2 medium onions, chopped
3 cloves garlic, minced
1 medium green bell pepper, cored and chopped
1½ cups chopped potatoes
¼ teaspoon cayenne pepper

4 medium tomatoes, chopped
2 cups quartered artichoke hearts
1 cup cooked or low-sodium canned chickpeas, rinsed and drained
4 cups chopped fresh spinach
¼ cup chopped fresh parsley
¼ cup lemon juice
¼ teaspoon ground black pepper

1. Bring 3 cups broth to a boil in a saucepan. Add couscous. Remove from heat, cover, and allow to stand for 5 minutes.
2. Heat ¼ cup broth in another large saucepan. Add onions, garlic, and bell pepper, and sauté until pepper begins to soften, about 4 minutes.
3. Add remaining broth and potatoes. Bring to a boil, reduce heat, and simmer for 15 minutes. Add cayenne pepper, tomatoes, artichoke hearts, chickpeas, and spinach, and continue to simmer until spinach is wilted, about 4 additional minutes.
4. Stir in the parsley and lemon juice. Divide the couscous among individual serving bowls, top each with vegetables, sprinkle with black pepper, and serve at once.

Calories Per Serving: 281　　Carbohydrates: 55 g
Fat: 1 g　　Dietary Fiber: 12 g
Cholesterol: 0 mg　　Sodium: 271 mg
Protein: 14 g

❧ *Mixed Vegetable Couscous* ❧

In this recipe, couscous is topped with onions, carrots, parsnips, butternut squash, tomatoes, chickpeas, zucchini, and raisins. When buying parsnips, carrots, and other root vegetables, remove their leaves as soon as possible. The leaves wick moisture away from the vegetable.

PREPARATION TIME: 15 minutes plus 5 minutes standing time •
COOKING TIME: 37 minutes • *YIELD: 12 servings*

4 cups low-sodium nonfat chicken broth
2 medium onions, chopped
6 medium carrots, chopped
2 parsnips, chopped
2 cups chopped butternut squash
3 cups low-sodium canned tomatoes, chopped
¼ teaspoon cayenne pepper

¼ teaspoon ground cumin
2 cups cooked or low-sodium canned chickpeas, rinsed and drained
1 cup chopped zucchini
1 medium green bell pepper, cored and chopped
1 cup raisins
2 cups water
2 cups uncooked couscous

1. Place 2 cups broth, onions, carrots, parsnips, squash, tomatoes, cayenne pepper, and cumin in a large saucepan. Bring to a boil, reduce heat, and simmer until vegetables are tender, about 20 minutes.
2. Add chickpeas, zucchini, bell pepper, and raisins, and continue to simmer for 5 additional minutes.
3. Bring remaining broth and water to a boil in a saucepan. Stir in couscous. Remove from heat, cover, and allow to stand for 5 minutes.
4. Serve couscous topped with the vegetables.

Calories Per Serving: 229　　Carbohydrates: 48 g
Fat: 1 g　　Dietary Fiber: 9 g
Cholesterol: 0 mg　　Sodium: 163 mg
Protein: 9 g

❧ *Couscous-Apricot Toss* ❧

Couscous, apricots, and raisins are flavored with curry powder, cinnamon, and scallions.

PREPARATION TIME: 10 minutes plus 5 minutes standing time •
COOKING TIME: 2 minutes • *YIELD: 4 servings*

2 cups low-sodium nonfat chicken broth	½ teaspoon ground cinnamon
1 cup uncooked couscous	4 scallions, finely chopped
½ teaspoon curry powder	1 cup chopped dried apricots
	½ cup raisins

1. Bring broth to a boil in a saucepan. Stir in couscous, curry powder, and cinnamon. Remove from heat.
2. Mix in the scallions, apricots, and raisins, and allow to stand, covered, for 5 minutes.

Calories Per Serving: 352	Carbohydrates: 78 g
Fat: 1 g	Dietary Fiber: 8 g
Cholesterol: 0 mg	Sodium: 96 mg
Protein: 12 g	

❧ *Orange Couscous* ❧

Apricots, raisins, and orange juice are combined with couscous.

PREPARATION TIME: 10 minutes plus 5 minutes standing time •
COOKING TIME: 2 minutes • *YIELD: 3 servings*

1¾ cups orange juice	¼ cup raisins
1 cup uncooked couscous	1 teaspoon ground cinnamon
¼ cup chopped dried apricots	½ cup water

1. Bring 1½ cups orange juice to a boil in a small saucepan. Stir in couscous. Remove from heat, cover, and allow to stand for 5 minutes.

2. Heat remaining juice in another saucepan. Add apricots, raisins, and cinnamon, and sauté for 2 minutes.
3. Combine couscous and apricot mixture, and serve at once.

Calories Per Serving: 424
Fat: 0 g
Cholesterol: 0 mg
Protein: 11 g

Carbohydrates: 94 g
Dietary Fiber: 6 g
Sodium: 4 mg

❧ *Kiwi-Raspberry Couscous* ❧

This sweet variation of a traditional Middle Eastern favorite is made with kiwi, raspberries, and navel oranges.

PREPARATION TIME: *15 minutes plus 5 minutes standing time* •
YIELD: *6 servings*

2 cups water
1 cup couscous
1 medium navel orange, peeled, sectioned, and sections cut in half
1 kiwifruit, peeled and sliced
½ cup raspberries

½ cup orange juice
3 tablespoons honey
2 tablespoons vinegar
1 tablespoon minced lemon peel
¼ teaspoon ground white pepper

1. Bring water to a boil in a saucepan. Stir in couscous. Remove from heat, cover, and allow to stand for 5 minutes.
2. Combine oranges, kiwi, and raspberries in a large bowl.
3. Whisk together the orange juice, honey, vinegar, lemon peel, and white pepper.
4. Combine the fruit, dressing, and couscous, and toss to mix thoroughly. Serve at once.

Calories Per Serving: 207
Fat: 0 g
Cholesterol: 0 mg
Protein: 5 g

Carbohydrates: 48 g
Dietary Fiber: 8 g
Sodium: 9 mg

❧ *Apricot-Yam Bulgur* ❧

This sweet bulgur pilaf contains apricots and yams. Bulgur comes in coarse-, medium-, and fine-grain varieties.

PREPARATION TIME: 10 minutes • *COOKING TIME: 20 minutes* •
YIELD: 6 servings

¼ cup low-sodium nonfat chicken
   broth
1 medium onion, finely chopped
2 cups water
2 medium yams, peeled and cut into
   1-inch cubes

1 cup bulgur
¾ cup chopped dried apricots
1 tablespoon brown sugar
¼ teaspoon ground black pepper

1. Heat broth in a large saucepan. Add onion and sauté for 5 minutes.
2. Add water, yams, bulgur, apricots, brown sugar, and black pepper. Bring to a boil. Reduce heat, cover, and simmer, stirring frequently, until yams are just tender, about 15 minutes.
3. Serve at once.

Calories Per Serving: 208
Fat: 1 g
Cholesterol: 0 mg
Protein: 5 g

Carbohydrates: 49 g
Dietary Fiber: 8 g
Sodium: 23 mg

❧ *Bulgur with Zucchini and Bell Peppers* ❧

In this recipe, bulgur is topped with dilled zucchini and yellow bell peppers. Small zucchini are the tenderest. They should be firm and heavy for their size.

PREPARATION TIME: 10 minutes • *COOKING TIME: 9 minutes* •
YIELD: 5 servings

3 cups water

1½ cups uncooked bulgur

¼ cup low-sodium nonfat chicken
   broth

3 cups zucchini, cut into crosswise slices

3 cups chopped yellow bell peppers

1 cup chopped fresh parsley

1 teaspoon dried dill

¼ teaspoon cayenne pepper

3 teaspoons nonfat Parmesan

1. Bring water to a boil in a saucepan. Add bulgur. Return to a boil, reduce heat, cover, and simmer until bulgur begins to soften, about 5 minutes. Remove from heat and set aside.

2. Heat broth in another saucepan. Add zucchini and yellow bell peppers, and sauté for 2 minutes. Stir in parsley, dill, and cayenne pepper, and sauté for 2 additional minutes.

3. Divide bulgur among individual plates, top with zucchini and bell peppers, sprinkle with Parmesan, and serve.

Calories Per Serving: 190

Fat: 1 g

Cholesterol: 1 mg

Protein: 9 g

Carbohydrates: 40 g

Dietary Fiber: 12 g

Sodium: 124 mg

❧ Lentils and Bulgur ❧

In this Mediterranean dish, lentils are combined with bulgur and sautéed with onion. Dried lentils can be stored in an airtight container in a cool, dry place for up to a year.

PREPARATION TIME: 10 minutes ▪ COOKING TIME: 44 minutes ▪
YIELD: 3 servings

4½ cups water

1 cup dried lentils

½ cup uncooked bulgur

½ teaspoon ground black pepper

2 tablespoons low-sodium nonfat
   chicken broth

1 medium onion, chopped

1. Place water and lentils in a large saucepan. Bring to a boil, reduce heat, and simmer for 25 minutes. Stir in bulgur and black pepper, and continue to simmer until lentils are just tender, about 15 minutes.

2. Heat broth in a skillet, add onion, and sauté until onions become soft, about 4 minutes. Stir into the lentil mixture and serve at once.

Calories Per Serving: 238
Fat: 1 g
Cholesterol: 0 mg
Protein: 16 g

Carbohydrates: 44 g
Dietary Fiber: 19 g
Sodium: 27 mg

✌ *Lentils, Onion, and Red Pepper with Bulgur* ✌

Lentils and bulgur are combined with onion and red bell pepper. Leftover cooked lentils can be refrigerated for up to 5 days.

PREPARATION TIME: 10 minutes ▪ *COOKING TIME: 44 minutes* ▪
YIELD: 4 servings

4½ cups water
1 cup dried lentils
½ cup bulgur
½ teaspoon ground black pepper

¼ cup low-sodium nonfat chicken
*   broth*
1 medium onion, thinly sliced
1 medium red bell pepper, cored and
*   diced*

1. Bring water to a boil in a saucepan. Stir in the lentils and simmer for 25 minutes. Add bulgur and black pepper, and simmer until lentils are tender, about 15 more minutes.
2. Heat broth in a skillet. Add onion and red bell pepper. Sauté until just tender, about 4 minutes.
3. Combine the vegetables and the lentil mixture, and toss gently before serving.

Calories Per Serving: 187
Fat: 1 g
Cholesterol: 0 mg
Protein: 7 g

Carbohydrates: 41 g
Dietary Fiber: 12 g
Sodium: 29 mg

❧ *Barley-Vegetable-Bean Stew* ❧

This stew, seasoned with red pepper and cumin, contains eggplant, broccoli, tomatoes, and kidney beans. Fresh mushrooms are available year round but peak in fall and winter.

PREPARATION TIME: 20 minutes ▪ *COOKING TIME: 60 minutes* ▪
YIELD: 10 servings

3½ cups water
1 cup uncooked pearl barley
¼ cup low-sodium nonfat chicken
 broth
1 medium yellow bell pepper, cored
 and chopped
1 medium onion, diced
2 cups diced eggplant
2 cups sliced mushrooms
1 stalk celery, chopped
2 cloves garlic, minced

2 cups chopped low-sodium canned
 tomatoes, drained
½ cup water
2 teaspoons dried oregano
1 teaspoon cumin
½ teaspoon ground black pepper
¼ teaspoon cayenne pepper
2 cups chopped broccoli
1 cup low-sodium canned dark red
 kidney beans, rinsed and drained

1. Bring 3½ cups water to a boil in a saucepan. Stir in barley and cook, stirring several times, until barley is just tender, about 30 minutes. Set aside.
2. Heat broth in another saucepan. Add yellow bell pepper, onion, eggplant, mushrooms, celery, and garlic, and sauté until pepper begins to soften, about 5 minutes.
3. Add tomatoes, ½ cup water, oregano, cumin, black pepper, and cayenne pepper, and simmer for 15 minutes.
4. Stir in barley, broccoli, and kidney beans, and continue to simmer until broccoli is just tender, about 10 minutes.
5. Serve hot.

Calories Per Serving: 129
Fat: 1 g
Cholesterol: 0 mg
Protein: 6 g

Carbohydrates: 27 g
Dietary Fiber: 6 g
Sodium: 31 mg

❧ *Mushroom-Kale Barley* ❧

Fresh kale is sold throughout the winter months. Unwashed kale will keep in the refrigerator for 3 to 4 days in a perforated plastic bag.

PREPARATION TIME: 15 minutes • *COOKING TIME: 33 minutes* •
YIELD: 5 servings

2¼ cups low-sodium nonfat chicken broth
1 cup uncooked pearl barley
3 cloves garlic, minced

1½ cups sliced mushrooms
½ teaspoon dried thyme
¼ teaspoon ground black pepper
1½ cups chopped fresh kale

1. Bring 2 cups broth to a boil in a saucepan. Stir in barley. Return to a boil, reduce heat, and simmer until barley is tender, about 30 minutes.
2. Heat remaining broth in a nonstick skillet. Add garlic, mushrooms, thyme, and black pepper, and sauté until mushrooms are tender, about 2 minutes. Stir in kale and sauté for 1 additional minute.
3. Stir barley into kale mixture. Toss to mix well, and serve hot.

Calories Per Serving: 160
Fat: 1 g
Cholesterol: 0 mg
Protein: 6 g

Carbohydrates: 34 g
Dietary Fiber: 7 g
Sodium: 120 mg

❧ *Hominy–Pinto Bean Stew* ❧

This hearty dish is inspired by Native American and Mexican cooking. It contains onion, jalapeño, bell pepper, tomato, hominy, beans, paprika, oregano, and black pepper. Hominy is dried white or yellow corn kernels whose hull and germ have been removed.

PREPARATION TIME: 15 minutes • *COOKING TIME: 50 minutes* •
YIELD: 5 servings

3¼ cups low-sodium nonfat chicken
   broth
1 medium onion, chopped
1 jalapeño pepper, seeded and minced
1 medium green bell pepper, cored
   and chopped
1 cup chopped yellow summer squash
1 medium tomato, chopped
2 cloves garlic, minced

1 cup canned hominy
1 cup cooked or low-sodium canned
   pinto beans, rinsed and drained
2½ tablespoons low-sodium tomato
   paste
1 teaspoon paprika
1½ teaspoons dried oregano
½ teaspoon ground black pepper

1. Heat ¼ cup broth in a large saucepan. Add onion, jalapeño, green bell pepper, yellow squash, tomato, and garlic, and sauté until peppers begin to soften, about 5 minutes.
2. Add remaining broth, hominy, beans, tomato paste, paprika, oregano, and black pepper. Bring to a boil, reduce heat, and simmer, stirring occasionally, for 45 minutes.
3. Transfer to individual bowls and serve at once.

Calories Per Serving: 90
Fat: 1 g
Cholesterol: 0 mg
Protein: 4 g

Carbohydrates: 18 g
Dietary Fiber: 4 g
Sodium: 130 mg

❧ Chili Orecchiette Pasta ❧

Pasta shaped like little ears is served with a mixture of bell peppers, tomatoes, and corn.

PREPARATION TIME: 15 minutes • COOKING TIME: 15 minutes plus pasta
cooking time • YIELD: 6 servings

6 cups water
1 cup orecchiette pasta
¼ cup low-sodium nonfat chicken
   broth
1 medium onion, chopped

3 cloves garlic, minced
1 jalapleño pepper, seeded and
   minced
1 medium green bell pepper, cored
   and chopped

1 medium red bell pepper, cored and
   chopped
2 teaspoons chili powder
1 teaspoon cumin

1 teaspoon dried oregano
2 medium tomatoes, chopped
1 cup fresh, canned, or frozen,
   thawed corn kernels

1. Bring water to a rapid boil in a covered pot. Slowly add pasta. Stir occasionally to prevent pasta from sticking together. Cook until still firm to the bite. Drain.
2. While pasta cooks, heat broth in a saucepan. Add onion and garlic, and sauté until onion begins to soften, about 3 minutes. Add jalapeño and all bell peppers, and sauté until peppers begin to soften, about 3 additional minutes.
3. Stir in chili powder, cumin, oregano, tomatoes, and corn, and cook, stirring several times, for another 5 minutes.
4. Add pasta and continue to simmer until all ingredients are heated through, about 4 minutes. Serve at once.

Calories Per Serving: 108
Fat: 1 g
Cholesterol: 0 mg
Protein: 4 g

Carbohydrates: 24 g
Dietary Fiber: 3 g
Sodium: 82 mg

❧ *Capellini with Broccoli Sauce* ❧

Capellini is topped with a broccoli-tomato sauce.

PREPARATION TIME: 10 minutes • *COOKING TIME: 7 minutes plus pasta
cooking time* • *YIELD: 2 servings*

4 cups water
4 ounces capellini
1 cup chopped broccoli
2 cups low-sodium canned tomatoes
1 tablespoon lemon juice

2 cloves garlic, minced
½ teaspoon dried oregano
½ teaspoon dried basil
½ teaspoon dried thyme
¼ teaspoon ground black pepper

1. Bring water to a rapid boil in a large, covered pot. Add pasta by holding it in a bundle by one end and slowly bending it inside the pot as the pasta softens. Keep water boiling; stir pasta with a long-handled wooden fork to prevent it from sticking together. Pasta should be cooked through but still firm. Check for doneness by biting into a piece of pasta rinsed in cold water. Drain cooked pasta into a colander in the sink.

2. Place broccoli in a steamer basket over 2 cups boiling water and steam until just tender-crisp, about 3 minutes.

3. Combine broccoli, tomatoes, lemon juice, garlic, oregano, basil, thyme, and black pepper in a saucepan. Simmer until all ingredients are heated through, about 5 minutes.

4. Divide the pasta between individual plates, top with the broccoli sauce, and serve at once.

Calories Per Serving: 280　　　Carbohydrates: 57 g
Fat: 2 g　　　　　　　　　　　Dietary Fiber: 6 g
Cholesterol: 0 mg　　　　　　 Sodium: 62 mg
Protein: 11 g

❧ *Bowtie Pasta with Spinach* ❧

The sauce for this dish combines spinach with zucchini, bell pepper, mushrooms, and tomatoes. Be sure to rinse the spinach thoroughly before using.

PREPARATION TIME: 20 minutes　•　COOKING TIME: 10 minutes plus pasta cooking time　•　YIELD: 6 servings

2 quarts water
1 cup uncooked bowtie pasta
¼ cup low-sodium nonfat chicken
　broth
2 cloves garlic, minced
2 cups chopped zucchini
1 medium red bell pepper, cored and
　chopped

1 cup sliced mushrooms
2 medium tomatoes, chopped
2 cups chopped spinach
¼ cup chopped fresh parsley
1 teaspoon dried basil
1 teaspoon dried oregano
½ teaspoon ground black pepper
2 tablespoons nonfat Parmesan

1. Bring water to a rapid boil in a large, covered pot. Slowly stir in pasta. Return water to a boil. Stir pasta with a long handled wooden fork to prevent it from sticking together. Follow recommended cooking time on the package. Pasta should be cooked through but still firm. Check for doneness by biting into a piece of pasta rinsed in cold water. Drain cooked pasta into a colander in the sink.

2. Heat broth in a large skillet. Add garlic, zucchini, bell pepper, and mushrooms, and sauté until pepper begins to soften, about 5 minutes.

3. Add tomatoes, spinach, parsley, basil, and oregano. Reduce heat, cover, and simmer, stirring several times, for 5 minutes.

4. Combine pasta and vegetables in a large bowl. Sprinkle with black pepper and Parmesan, toss well, and serve.

Calories Per Serving: 89	Carbohydrates: 17 g
Fat: 1 g	Dietary Fiber: 3 g
Cholesterol: 0 mg	Sodium: 60 mg
Protein: 5 g	

৩ *Penne-Broccoflower Toss* ৩

Broccoflower is a cross between broccoli and cauliflower.

PREPARATION TIME: 10 minutes • COOKING TIME: 12 minutes plus pasta cooking time • YIELD: 6 servings

3 quarts water
6 ounces uncooked penne
¼ cup low-sodium nonfat chicken broth
4 cups chopped broccoflower

2 carrots, scraped and thinly sliced
2 cups chopped low-sodium canned tomatoes, with juice
½ teaspoon ground black pepper
2 tablespoons nonfat Parmesan

1. Bring water to a rapid boil in a large, covered pot. Slowly stir in pasta. Return water to a boil. Stir pasta with a long-handled wooden fork to prevent it from sticking together. Follow recommended cooking time on the package. Pasta should be cooked through but still firm. Check for doneness by biting into a piece of pasta rinsed in cold water. Drain cooked pasta into a colander in the sink.

2. Heat broth in a saucepan. Add broccoflower and carrots, and sauté for 4 minutes.
3. Add pasta to vegetables. Add tomatoes and black pepper, and heat through.
4. Transfer to a large bowl, sprinkle with Parmesan, and serve.

Calories Per Serving: 111	Carbohydrates: 22 g
Fat: 1 g	Dietary Fiber: 4 g
Cholesterol: 0 mg	Sodium: 53 mg
Protein: 5 g	

❧ *Fusilli-Broccoli Salad* ❧

Fusilli, broccoli, and bell peppers are tossed with a yogurt-vinegar dressing. Vinegar should be stored in a dark, cool place.

PREPARATION TIME: 10 minutes • *COOKING TIME: 3 minutes* •
YIELD: 4 servings

2 cups water	*¼ cup nonfat sour cream*
3 cups chopped broccoli	*2 tablespoons vinegar*
2 medium yellow bell peppers, cored and cut into thin strips	*4 scallions, chopped*
	1 teaspoon dried dill
¾ cup nonfat plain yogurt	*2 cups cooked fusilli*

1. Bring water to a boil in the bottom of a steamer. Place broccoli and yellow bell peppers in the steamer basket, cover, and steam until vegetables just begin to become tender, about 2 minutes.
2. Combine yogurt, sour cream, vinegar, scallions, and dill.
3. Place the pasta in a serving bowl. Add the dressing and vegetables, toss to coat all ingredients, and serve at once.

Calories Per Serving: 128	Carbohydrates: 25 g
Fat: 1 g	Dietary Fiber: 4 g
Cholesterol: 0 mg	Sodium: 134 mg
Protein: 6 g	

❧ *Pasta Shells Primavera* ❧

Pasta shells are tossed with onion, mushrooms, tomatoes, scallions, and garlic.

PREPARATION TIME: 10 minutes • *COOKING TIME: 6 minutes plus pasta cooking time* • *YIELD: 4 servings*

2 quarts water
1 cup medium pasta shells
¼ cup low-sodium nonfat chicken broth
1 medium onion, chopped

1 cup sliced mushrooms
2 medium tomatoes, chopped
2 scallions, chopped
2 cloves garlic, minced
¼ cup nonfat Italian dressing

1. Bring water to a rapid boil in a large, covered pot. Slowly stir in pasta. Return water to a boil. Stir pasta with a long-handled wooden fork to prevent it from sticking together. Follow recommended cooking time on the package. Pasta should be cooked through but still firm. Check for doneness by biting into a piece of pasta rinsed in cold water. Drain cooked pasta into a colander in the sink.
2. Heat broth in a large saucepan. Add onion and sauté until onion begins to soften, about 3 minutes.
3. Add mushrooms, tomatoes, scallions, and garlic. Sauté for 3 more minutes.
4. Combine pasta and vegetable mixture in a large bowl. Pour dressing over the pasta, toss to coat all ingredients, and serve at once.

Calories Per Serving: 142
Fat: 1 g
Cholesterol: 0 mg
Protein: 5 g

Carbohydrates: 29 g
Dietary Fiber: 3 g
Sodium: 229 mg

❧ *Linguine with Yellow Squash–Tomato Sauce* ❧

This hearty sauce for linguine is made of yellow squash, bell pepper, egg-plant, jalapeño pepper, tomato, parsley, basil, oregano, and hot pepper flakes.

PREPARATION TIME: 20 minutes ▪ *COOKING TIME: 35 minutes plus pasta cooking time* ▪ *YIELD: 8 servings*

¼ cup low-sodium nonfat chicken broth
1 cup diced yellow summer squash
1 medium green bell pepper, cored and chopped
1 cup chopped eggplant
2 cloves garlic, minced
1 jalapeño pepper, seeded and minced
3½ cups chopped low-sodium canned tomatoes, with juice

2 cups low-sodium tomato puree
¼ cup chopped fresh parsley
1 tablespoon dried basil
1 tablespoon dried oregano
½ teaspoon hot red pepper flakes
4 quarts water
1 pound uncooked linguine
2 scallions, minced

1. Heat broth in a large saucepan. Add yellow squash, green bell pepper, eggplant, and garlic, and sauté until pepper begins to soften, about 5 minutes.

2. Add jalapeño, tomatoes with their juice, tomato puree, parsley, basil, oregano, and hot pepper flakes. Bring to a boil, reduce heat, cover, and simmer, stirring several times, for 30 minutes.

3. Bring water to a rapid boil in a large, covered pot. Add pasta by holding it in a bundle by one end and slowly bending it inside the pot as the pasta softens. Keep water boiling; stir pasta with a long-handled wooden fork to prevent it from sticking together. Pasta should be cooked through but still firm. Check for doneness by biting into a piece of pasta rinsed in cold water. Drain cooked pasta into a colander in the sink.

4. Divide the pasta among individual plates. Top with the sauce, sprinkle with scallions, and serve.

Calories Per Serving: 105
Fat: 1 g
Cholesterol: 0 mg
Protein: 4 g

Carbohydrates: 22 g
Dietary Fiber: 5 g
Sodium: 66 mg

❧ *Pasta with Vegetables and Cannellini Beans* ❧

This pasta dish has a colorful mixture of onion, yellow summer squash, celery, mushrooms, beets, potato, white beans, and kale. Fresh beets are available year round. Look for ones with firm, smooth skins.

PREPARATION TIME: 20 minutes plus 10 minutes standing time •
COOKING TIME: 40 minutes • *YIELD: 12 servings*

¼ cup low-sodium nonfat chicken
   broth
1 medium onion, chopped
1 cup diced yellow summer squash
1 cup chopped green bell pepper
1 cup sliced mushrooms
2 stalks celery, chopped
4 cloves garlic, minced
8 cups water
4 cups diced beets

1 cup diced potato
1 tablespoon dried basil
1 tablespoon dried oregano
½ cup uncooked small pasta shells
¼ cup low-sodium tomato paste
1 cup low-sodium canned cannellini
   beans
2 cups chopped fresh kale
¼ cup nonfat Parmesan

1. Heat broth in a large saucepan. Add onion, yellow squash, green bell pepper, mushrooms, celery, and garlic, and sauté until onion begins to soften, about 5 minutes.
2. Add water, beets, potato, basil, and oregano. Bring to a boil, reduce heat, and simmer, stirring several times, for 20 minutes.
3. Stir in pasta, tomato paste, beans, and kale, and continue to simmer, stirring occasionally until pasta is just tender, about 15 minutes.
4. Remove from heat, allow to stand for 10 minutes, and serve.

Calories Per Serving: 115
Fat: 1 g
Cholesterol: 0 mg
Protein: 5 g

Carbohydrates: 24 g
Dietary Fiber: 5 g
Sodium: 101 mg

❧ *Leftover Pasta and Vegetables* ❧

Here is a delicious way to use up leftover pasta the night after. The topping is made with broccoli, cauliflower, and onion and cooks quickly in the microwave. Be sure to cut the vegetables into pieces that are the same size, so they will cook evenly.

PREPARATION TIME: 5 minutes • *COOKING TIME: 4 minutes* •
YIELD: 4 servings

*2 tablespoons low-sodium nonfat
 chicken broth
1 medium onion, chopped
1 cup chopped broccoli*

*1 cup chopped cauliflower
2 cups cooked pasta
3 tablespoons chopped fresh parsley
2 teaspoons lemon juice*

1. Combine broth, onion, broccoli, and cauliflower in a microwave-safe casserole. Cover and microwave on HIGH for 2 minutes.
2. Stir in pasta, parsley, and lemon juice, and microwave on HIGH until all ingredients are heated through, about 2 additional minutes. Serve hot.

Calories Per Serving: 130
Fat: 1 g
Cholesterol: 0 mg
Protein: 5 g

Carbohydrates: 26 g
Dietary Fiber: 3 g
Sodium: 19 mg

❧ *Pasta Shells with Chiles and Beans* ❧

This dish of kidney beans, chiles, corn, chili powder, parsley, and pasta can be made in less than a half hour.

PREPARATION TIME: 10 minutes • *COOKING TIME: 12 minutes* •
YIELD: 6 servings

*¼ cup low-sodium nonfat chicken broth
1 medium onion, chopped*

*1 medium red bell pepper, cored and
 chopped*

1 cup low-sodium canned kidney
   beans, rinsed and drained
½ cup chopped mild green chiles
1 cup fresh or frozen corn kernels

2 teaspoons chili powder
2 tablespoons chopped fresh parsley
3 cups cooked pasta shells

1. Heat broth in a large saucepan. Add onion and red bell pepper, and sauté until pepper begins to soften, about 5 minutes.
2. Stir in the beans, chiles, corn, chili powder, parsley, and pasta, and simmer until all ingredients are heated through, about 7 minutes. Serve at once.

Calories Per Serving: 156
Fat: 1 g
Cholesterol: 0 mg
Protein: 7 g

Carbohydrates: 31 g
Dietary Fiber: 4 g
Sodium: 90 mg

❧ *Baked Ziti* ❧

This baked pasta dish is made with ziti and vegetables topped with cheese.

PREPARATION TIME: 20 minutes • *COOKING TIME: 42 minutes plus pasta cooking time* • *YIELD: 8 servings*

½ cup low-sodium tomato juice
1 medium onion, chopped
4 cloves garlic, minced
2 cups diced eggplant
2 cups sliced mushrooms
3½ cups crushed low-sodium canned
   tomatoes, with juice

1 teaspoon dried oregano
1 teaspoon dried basil
½ teaspoon hot red pepper flakes
1½ cups canned roasted red peppers
6 quarts water
1½ cups uncooked ziti pasta
¾ cup nonfat mozzarella

1. Heat tomato juice in a large saucepan. Add onion, garlic, eggplant, and mushrooms, and sauté until onion begins to soften, about 4 minutes.
2. Stir in tomatoes with their juice, oregano, basil, and hot pepper flakes. Bring to a boil, reduce heat, cover, and simmer until vegetables are tender, about 15 minutes. Add roasted red peppers and continue to simmer for 5 more minutes.

3. Preheat oven to 350 degrees.

4. Bring water to a rapid boil in a large, covered pot. Slowly stir in pasta. Return water to a boil. Stir pasta with a long-handled wooden fork to prevent it from sticking together. Follow recommended cooking time on the package. Pasta should be cooked through but still firm. Check for doneness by biting into a piece of pasta rinsed in cold water. Drain cooked pasta into a colander in the sink.

5. Combine pasta with half the vegetable mixture and toss to mix. Spread pasta in the bottom of a nonstick baking dish, top with the remaining vegetable mixture, cover, and bake for 15 minutes. Remove lid from baking dish, top with mozzarella, and return to the oven until cheese melts, about 3 minutes. Serve at once.

Calories Per Serving: 146

Fat: 1 g

Cholesterol: 2 mg

Protein: 8 g

Carbohydrates: 28 g

Dietary Fiber: 3 g

Sodium: 214 mg

❧ *Balsamic Pasta Salad* ❧

Balsamic vinegar has long been prized in Italy for its unique, rich flavor. Here it enhances a hearty pasta salad.

PREPARATION TIME: 15 minutes • COOKING TIME: 2 minutes plus pasta cooking time • YIELD: 6 servings

2 quarts water

1½ cups uncooked medium pasta shells

¾ cup chopped broccoli

¾ cup chopped cauliflower

1 medium red bell pepper, cored and cut into ¼-inch strips

⅓ cup balsamic vinegar

3 tablespoons water

¼ teaspoon ground black pepper

2 cloves garlic, minced

2 teaspoons dried basil

2 tablespoons nonfat Parmesan

1. Bring water to a rapid boil in a large, covered pot. Slowly stir in pasta. Return water to a boil. Stir pasta with a long-handled wooden fork to prevent it from sticking together. Follow recommended cooking time

on the package. Pasta should be cooked through but still firm. Check for doneness by biting into a piece of pasta rinsed in cold water. Drain cooked pasta into a colander in the sink.

2. Place broccoli, cauliflower, and red bell pepper in a steamer basket over boiling water, cover, and steam for 2 minutes. Plunge into cold water and drain thoroughly.

3. Whisk together the vinegar, water, black pepper, and garlic.

4. Combine dressing, vegetables, and pasta in a large serving bowl. Toss to coat all ingredients, and sprinkle with basil and Parmesan. Serve at once.

Calories Per Serving: 108 Carbohydrates: 22 g

Fat: 1 g Dietary Fiber: 2 g

Cholesterol: 0 mg Sodium: 236 mg

Protein: 4 g

BEAN DISHES

❧

Cumin-Cilantro Black Beans • Black Beans and Carrots • Beans with Orzo • Black Beans with Pumpkin • Black Bean–Jalapeño Succotash • Black Beans with Summer Squash • Black Beans and Rice • Black Bean Burritos • Burritos with Black Bean–Corn–Raisin Stuffing • Black Bean Chili • Microwave Black Bean Chili with Cornbread Topping • Curried Chickpeas and Potatoes • Spicy Chickpeas • Curried Lentils and Rice • Lentils with Paprika • Tomato-Garlic Lentils • Lentil–Chickpea–Kidney Bean Chili • Lentil-Vegetable Stew • Pumpkin–Pinto Bean Stew • Pinto Beans and Potatoes • Hominy and Vegetables • Red Beans and Rice • Bean Pot • Kidney Bean Chili • Red Bean and Vegetable Stew • New Year's Black-eyed Peas • Spicy Black-eyed Peas • Black-eyed Peas and Spinach • Black-eyed Pea Stew • Carrot-Lentil Stew • Cannellini Beans, Tomatoes, and Rice • Cannellini Beans and Red Peppers • Cannellini Beans with Shells and Sage • Baked Wild Rice and Cannellini Beans • "Baked" Beans • Acorn Squash, Rice, and Tomatoes • Great Northern Bean–Vegetable

Curry ▪ Bean-Potato Scramble ▪ White Bean Pilaf ▪ White Bean Chili with Eggplant ▪ Stovetop Beans with Sweet Potatoes ▪ White Beans and Kale ▪ Vegetable-and-Bean Burrito ▪ Garlic-Ginger-Bean Cakes ▪ Bean Burgers ▪ Broiled Bean Patties ▪ Tomato-Bean Burgers

❧ Cumin-Cilantro Black Beans ❧

Black beans are cooked with tomatoes, cumin, and black pepper, and flavored with cilantro.

PREPARATION TIME: 15 minutes ▪ *COOKING TIME: 12 minutes* ▪
YIELD: 6 servings

¼ cup low-sodium nonfat chicken
  broth
1 medium onion, diced
1 medium red bell pepper, cored and
  diced
2 cloves garlic, minced
2 cups cooked or low-sodium canned
  black beans, rinsed and drained

2 medium tomatoes, chopped and
  drained
½ teaspoon ground cumin
½ teaspoon ground black pepper
1 teaspoon dried cilantro

1. Heat broth in a large saucepan. Add onion, red bell pepper, and garlic, and sauté until pepper begins to soften, about 5 minutes.
2. Add beans, tomatoes, cumin, and black pepper. Simmer, stirring occasionally, for 7 minutes. Stir in cilantro and serve.

Calories Per Serving: 115
Fat: 1 g
Cholesterol: 0 mg
Protein: 6 g

Carbohydrates: 23 g
Dietary Fiber: 6 g
Sodium: 223 mg

❧ Black Beans and Carrots ❧

Black beans, onion, bell peppers, tomato, jalapeño pepper, and carrots are served over rice in this popular Brazilian dish.

PREPARATION TIME: 15 minutes ▪ *COOKING TIME: 38 minutes* ▪
YIELD: 10 servings

¼ cup low-sodium nonfat chicken broth
1 medium onion, diced

1 medium red bell pepper, cored and
  diced

1 medium green bell pepper, cored and diced
1 medium tomato, diced
1 jalapeño pepper, seeded and minced
4 cloves garlic, minced
2 cups water
2 teaspoons dried thyme
3 cups cooked or low-sodium canned black beans, rinsed and drained
1½ cups diced carrots
¼ cup chopped fresh parsley
5 cups cooked white rice

1. Heat ¼ cup broth in a large saucepan. Add onion, red and green bell peppers, tomato, jalapeño pepper, and garlic, and sauté until bell peppers begin to soften, about 7 minutes.
2. Add water, thyme, beans, and carrots. Bring to a boil, reduce heat, and simmer until carrots are just tender, about 20 minutes. Stir in the parsley and continue to simmer for 5 additional minutes.
3. Divide the rice among individual serving bowls, spoon the vegetables over the rice and serve.

Calories Per Serving: 180
Fat: 0 g
Cholesterol: 0 mg
Protein: 6 g
Carbohydrates: 31 g
Dietary Fiber: 3 g
Sodium: 54 mg

Beans with Orzo

Kidney beans and black beans are combined with orzo in this cool salad. Orzo is tiny rice-shaped pasta that can be substituted for rice.

PREPARATION TIME: 10 minutes plus 2 hours chilling time ▪ *YIELD: 4 servings*

2 cups low-sodium canned kidney beans, rinsed and drained
2 cups cooked or low-sodium canned black beans, rinsed and drained
1 cup cooked orzo
¼ teaspoon hot red pepper flakes
4 scallions, minced
2 tablespoons lime juice
2 tablespoons fresh parsley

1. Combine kidney beans, black beans, orzo, pepper flakes, scallions, lime juice, and parsley. Toss well.
2. Refrigerate for 2 hours before serving.

Calories Per Serving: 280

Fat: 1 g

Cholesterol: 0 mg

Protein: 17 g

Carbohydrates: 52 g

Dietary Fiber: 13 g

Sodium: 13 mg

❧ Black Beans with Pumpkin ❧

This stew is made with beans, corn, tomatoes, and pumpkin.

PREPARATION TIME: 15 minutes • COOKING TIME: 35 minutes •
YIELD: 6 servings

¼ cup low-sodium nonfat chicken broth

1 medium onion, chopped

3 cloves garlic, minced

1½ tablespoons paprika

4 tomatoes, chopped

2 teaspoons dried oregano

½ teaspoon ground black pepper

1 cup cooked or low-sodium canned black beans, rinsed and drained

1½ cups water

2 cups peeled and chopped pumpkin

1 cup fresh or thawed frozen corn kernels

1. Heat broth in a large saucepan. Add onion, garlic, and paprika, and sauté for 4 minutes. Add tomatoes, oregano, and black pepper, and simmer, stirring occasionally, for 10 minutes.
2. Add beans, water, and pumpkin, and simmer until pumpkin is just tender, about 15 minutes. Stir in corn kernels and simmer for an additional 6 minutes.
3. Divide among individual bowls and serve.

Calories Per Serving: 99

Fat: 1 g

Cholesterol: 0 mg

Protein: 5 g

Carbohydrates: 21 g

Dietary Fiber: 5 g

Sodium: 151 mg

❧ *Black Bean–Jalapeño Succotash* ❧

In this dish, black beans stand in for the lima beans in traditional succotash.

PREPARATION TIME: 15 minutes • *COOKING TIME: 12 minutes* •
YIELD: 4 servings

*2 tablespoons low-sodium tomato
 juice*
1 medium onion, chopped
*1 medium red bell pepper, cored and
 diced*
2 cloves garlic, minced
1 jalapeño pepper, seeded and minced

*2 cups fresh or thawed frozen corn
 kernels*
*2 cups cooked or low-sodium canned
 black beans, rinsed and drained*
1 teaspoon dried oregano
½ teaspoon ground black pepper
¼ cup chopped fresh parsley

1. Heat tomato juice in a large saucepan. Add onion, red bell pepper, garlic, and jalapeño, and sauté until onion begins to soften, about 4 minutes.
2. Add corn, beans, oregano, and black pepper. Cook over medium heat, stirring frequently, until all ingredients are heated through, about 8 minutes. Stir in parsley and serve.

Calories Per Serving: 211
Fat: 1 g
Cholesterol: 0 mg
Protein: 11 g

Carbohydrates: 44 g
Dietary Fiber: 9 g
Sodium: 118 mg

❧ *Black Beans with Summer Squash* ❧

A nutritious way to use the bumper crop of zucchini and summer squash.

PREPARATION TIME: 20 minutes • *COOKING TIME: 10 minutes* •
YIELD: 8 servings

1 cup low-sodium nonfat chicken broth	3 cups cooked or low-sodium canned black beans, rinsed and drained
1 medium onion, chopped	¼ cup lime juice
2 cloves garlic, minced	1 teaspoon ground cinnamon
2 medium carrots, scraped and chopped	½ teaspoon ground cumin
2 cups chopped yellow summer squash	½ teaspoon turmeric
	2 teaspoons curry powder
2 cups chopped zucchini	⅛ teaspoon cayenne pepper
	4 cups cooked white rice

1. Heat ¼ cup broth in a large saucepan. Add onion, garlic, and carrots, and sauté until onion is just tender, about 5 minutes.
2. Add yellow squash, zucchini, beans, lime juice, cinnamon, cumin, turmeric, curry powder, cayenne pepper, and remaining broth. Bring to a boil, reduce heat, and simmer until squash is just tender, about 5 minutes.
3. Divide the rice among individual serving bowls, top with the beans, and serve.

Calories Per Serving: 241
Fat: 1 g
Cholesterol: 0 mg
Protein: 10 g

Carbohydrates: 50 g
Dietary Fiber: 6 g
Sodium: 56 mg

❧ Black Beans and Rice ❧

Black beans seasoned with onion, jalapeño, garlic, and cumin are served with rice.

PREPARATION TIME: 15 minutes • COOKING TIME: 40 minutes •
YIELD: 6 servings

¼ cup low-sodium nonfat chicken broth	4 cloves garlic, minced
1 medium onion, chopped	1½ teaspoons ground cumin
1 medium red bell pepper, cored and chopped	1 teaspoon dried thyme
	½ teaspoon ground black pepper
1 medium tomato, chopped	1 jalapeño pepper, seeded and minced

1 cup cooked or low-sodium canned
   black beans, rinsed and drained
1½ cups water

1 tablespoon rice wine vinegar
4 cups cooked white rice
2 tablespoons minced fresh parsley

1. Heat broth in a large saucepan. Add onion and red bell pepper, and sauté until pepper begins to soften, about 5 minutes. Stir in tomato, garlic, cumin, thyme, black pepper, and jalapeño, and simmer for 4 additional minutes.
2. Add beans, water, and vinegar. Bring to a boil, reduce heat, and simmer, stirring occasionally, for 30 minutes.
3. Divide the rice among 6 large bowls, top with bean mixture, garnish with parsley, and serve.

Calories Per Serving: 216
Fat: 0 g
Cholesterol: 0 mg
Protein: 6 g

Carbohydrates: 46 g
Dietary Fiber: 3 g
Sodium: 221 mg

❧ *Black Bean Burritos* ❧

These black bean burritos are made with mild green chiles, jalapeño, tomatoes, and cheese.

PREPARATION TIME: 15 minutes ▪ *COOKING TIME: 50 minutes* ▪
YIELD: 6 servings

3 cloves garlic, left whole and unpeeled
1 teaspoon ground cumin
1 teaspoon dried oregano
2 cups low-sodium canned tomatoes,
   chopped and drained
1 4-ounce can mild green chiles,
   drained

½ jalapeño pepper, seeded and minced
2 cups cooked or low-sodium canned
   black beans, rinsed and drained
6 tortillas, warmed
6 tablespoons grated nonfat cheddar

1. Preheat oven to 400 degrees.
2. Heat garlic cloves in a dry skillet over medium heat, stirring, for 10 minutes. Remove garlic and set aside.

3. Remove skillet from heat, add cumin and oregano, and stir several times around the dry skillet.
4. Combine tomatoes, chiles, and jalapeño in a food processor or blender, and process briefly.
5. When garlic cloves are cool enough to handle, peel them. Add peeled garlic cloves, cumin, and oregano to the blender and process again.
6. Place beans in the skillet. Add tomato sauce and simmer until mixture begins to thicken, about 15 minutes.
7. Divide bean mixture among tortillas and sprinkle each with cheese. Roll tortillas and place them seam side down on a nonstick baking sheet. Bake until burritos are heated through, about 15 minutes.
8. Transfer to individual plates and serve.

Calories Per Serving: 174
Fat: 1 g
Cholesterol: 2 mg
Protein: 10 g

Carbohydrates: 31 g
Dietary Fiber: 5 g
Sodium: 252 mg

❧ *Burritos with Black Bean–* ❧
 Corn–Raisin Stuffing

This chili-flavored filling is a blend of black beans, corn, raisins, garlic, onion, chili powder, and cinnamon.

PREPARATION TIME: 10 minutes • COOKING TIME: 10 minutes •
 YIELD: 4 servings

½ cup low-sodium nonfat chicken broth
¾ cup chopped onion
¾ cup cooked or low-sodium canned black beans, rinsed and drained
½ cup fresh or thawed frozen corn kernels

2 cloves garlic, minced
½ cup raisins
1½ teaspoons chili powder
½ teaspoon ground cinnamon
4 corn tortillas, warmed to soften

1. Bring broth to a boil in a saucepan. Add onion, beans, corn, garlic, raisins, chili powder, and cinnamon. Simmer until liquid evaporates, about 10 minutes.
2. Divide the bean mixture among the tortillas, fold, and serve.

Calories Per Serving: 190	Carbohydrates: 42 g
Fat: 1 g	Dietary Fiber: 4 g
Cholesterol: 0 mg	Sodium: 95 mg
Protein: 3 g	

❧ *Black Bean Chili* ❧

This chili contains tomatoes and sweet potatoes.

PREPARATION TIME: 20 minutes • *COOKING TIME: 35 minutes* •
YIELD: 12 servings

¼ cup low-sodium tomato juice
1 medium onion, diced
2 medium red bell peppers, cored and
   diced
2 stalks celery, chopped
4 cloves garlic, minced
1 jalapeño pepper, seeded and minced
6 medium tomatoes, diced with juice

1 cup cooked or low-sodium canned
   black beans, rinsed and drained
4 cups water
2 cups unpeeled diced sweet potatoes
1 tablespoon chili powder
2 tablespoons chopped fresh parsley
2 teaspoons ground cumin
½ teaspoon ground black pepper
4 scallions, minced

1. Heat tomato juice in a large saucepan. Add onion, red bell peppers, celery, garlic, and jalapeño. Sauté until peppers begin to soften, about 7 minutes.
2. Stir in tomatoes with their juice and cook for 3 additional minutes. Add beans, water, sweet potatoes, chili powder, parsley, cumin, black pepper, and scallions. Simmer for 25 minutes.
3. Transfer to individual bowls and serve.

Calories Per Serving: 103

Fat: 1 g

Cholesterol: 0 mg

Protein: 10 g

Carbohydrates: 22 g

Dietary Fiber: 4 g

Sodium: 215 mg

✤ *Microwave Black Bean Chili* ✤ with Cornbread Topping

This black bean chili is made with tomatoes and broccoli, and topped with a cornmeal crust.

PREPARATION TIME: 20 minutes • *COOKING TIME: 16 minutes* •
YIELD: 6 servings

2 medium tomatoes, diced

2 cups cooked or low-sodium canned black beans, rinsed and drained

1 cup fresh, canned (drained), or thawed frozen corn kernels

3 cloves garlic, minced

1 cup chopped broccoli stems

½ cup low-sodium tomato sauce

1 tablespoon low-sodium tomato paste

½ teaspoon ground cumin

1 teaspoon chili powder

1 teaspoon dried oregano

¾ cup cornmeal

2 cups water

4 egg whites

1. Combine tomatoes, beans, corn, garlic, and broccoli in a large microwave-safe casserole.
2. Mix together in another bowl tomato sauce, tomato paste, cumin, chili powder, and oregano. Stir into the bean mixture.
3. Place cornmeal and water in microwave-safe bowl and microwave on HIGH for 6 minutes. Remove from microwave, stir well, then stir in egg whites.
4. Spread cornmeal mixture over the bean mixture, cover, and microwave on HIGH for 10 minutes.
5. Transfer to individual bowls and serve immediately.

Calories Per Serving: 177

Fat: 1 g

Cholesterol: 0 mg

Protein: 10 g

Carbohydrates: 34 g

Dietary Fiber: 6 g

Sodium: 215 mg

❧ *Curried Chickpeas and Potatoes* ❧

Chickpeas are mixed with gingerroot, chiles, and potatoes, and served with yogurt. Chiles contain vitamins A and C.

PREPARATION TIME: 15 minutes • *COOKING TIME: 40 minutes* •
YIELD: 6 servings

*¼ cup low-sodium nonfat chicken
   broth
2 tablespoons minced fresh gingerroot
2 medium onions, sliced
½ cup chopped mild green chiles
2 cups low-sodium canned chickpeas,
   undrained*

*1 teaspoon ground cumin
2 medium potatoes, coarsely chopped
¼ cup low-sodium tomato paste
½ teaspoon ground black pepper
½ cup nonfat plain yogurt
½ cup minced fresh parsley*

1. Heat broth in a large saucepan. Add gingerroot and sauté for 1 minute. Add onions and sauté for 4 additional minutes.
2. Add chiles, chickpeas with their liquid, cumin, and potatoes. Bring to a simmer, cover, and cook, stirring several times, for 20 minutes. Add tomato paste and simmer for 10 more minutes.
3. Stir in black pepper. Transfer to individual bowls, top with yogurt and parsley, and serve.

Calories Per Serving: 231
Fat: 1 g
Cholesterol: 0 mg
Protein: 10 g

Carbohydrates: 48 g
Dietary Fiber: 8 g
Sodium: 130 mg

❧ *Spicy Chickpeas* ❧

A curry made from chickpeas and tomatoes is served on rice and topped with yogurt. Chickpeas have a firm texture and a nutlike flavor.

PREPARATION TIME: 15 minutes • *COOKING TIME: 20 minutes* •
YIELD: 4 servings

2 cups water
1 cup uncooked white rice
1 cup cooked or low-sodium canned chickpeas, rinsed and drained
2 cups low-sodium canned tomatoes, with juice

2 teaspoons curry powder
¼ teaspoon cayenne pepper
¼ teaspoon ground black pepper
¼ cup nonfat plain yogurt
¼ cup mango chutney (see page 309)

1. Bring water to a boil in a saucepan. Add rice. Cover, reduce heat, and simmer until water is absorbed and rice is just tender, about 15 minutes.
2. Place chickpeas, tomatoes with their juice, curry powder, cayenne pepper, and black pepper in a large skillet. Bring to a boil, reduce heat, and simmer until all ingredients are heated through, about 5 minutes.
3. Serve on beds of rice, topped with yogurt and chutney.

Calories Per Serving: 308
Fat: 1 g
Cholesterol: 0 mg
Protein: 9 g

Carbohydrates: 66 g
Dietary Fiber: 5 g
Sodium: 37 mg

৩ *Curried Lentils and Rice* ৩

Lentils are cooked with onions, rice, and curry powder. Prepared curry powder is available in 2 varieties: standard and madras, which is spicier.

PREPARATION TIME: 10 minutes • COOKING TIME: 43 minutes •
YIELD: 5 servings

2 cups water
2¼ cups low-sodium nonfat chicken broth
1 cup dried lentils
2 medium onions, thinly sliced

¼ teaspoon ground black pepper
½ cup uncooked white rice
2 teaspoons curry powder
2 tablespoons minced fresh parsley

1. Bring water and 2 cups broth to a boil in a large saucepan. Add lentils, return to a boil, reduce heat, and simmer for 20 minutes.
2. Heat remaining broth in a skillet. Add onions and sauté until they are soft, about 5 minutes.

3. Add onions, black pepper, rice, and curry powder to the lentils. Cover and simmer, stirring occasionally, until rice is just tender, about 15 minutes.
4. Transfer to individual serving bowls, sprinkle with parsley, and serve.

Calories Per Serving: 125   Carbohydrates: 26 g
Fat: 1 g   Dietary Fiber: 3 g
Cholesterol: 0 mg   Sodium: 175 mg
Protein: 6 g

❧ *Lentils with Paprika* ❧

Lentils and onion are flavored with paprika, ginger, and garlic.

PREPARATION TIME: 20 minutes ▪ *COOKING TIME: 28 minutes* ▪
YIELD: 4 servings

¼ cup low-sodium nonfat chicken   3 tablespoons low-sodium tomato
  broth   paste
1 medium onion, chopped   1 teaspoon paprika
1 medium green bell pepper, cored ½ teaspoon ground ginger
  and chopped   ¼ teaspoon ground black pepper
3 cloves garlic, minced   2 cups dried lentils
3 cups water

1. Heat broth in a large saucepan. Add onions, green bell pepper, and garlic, and sauté until onion softens, about 3 minutes.
2. Stir in water, tomato paste, paprika, ginger, and black pepper. Bring to a boil. Add lentils. Return to a boil, reduce heat, cover, and simmer until lentils are tender, about 25 minutes.
3. Remove from heat, drain, and serve at once.

Calories Per Serving: 364   Carbohydrates: 64 g
Fat: 1 g   Dietary Fiber: 31 g
Cholesterol: 0 mg   Sodium: 36 mg
Protein: 28 g

❧ *Tomato-Garlic Lentils* ❧

This contains garlic, lemon juice, and lentils.

PREPARATION TIME: 15 minutes　•　COOKING TIME: 36 minutes　•
YIELD: 4 servings

2 tablespoons low-sodium tomato juice	3½ cups water
5 cloves garlic, minced	2 cups dried lentils
2 medium tomatoes, finely chopped	1 tablespoon lemon juice

1. Heat tomato juice in a large saucepan. Add garlic and sauté for 1 minute. Add tomatoes and sauté until they begin to thicken, about 5 minutes.
2. Stir in the water and lentils. Bring to a boil, reduce heat, cover, and simmer for 30 minutes. Stir in lemon juice and serve.

Calories Per Serving: 61	Carbohydrates: 13 g
Fat: 0 g	Dietary Fiber: 4 g
Cholesterol: 0 mg	Sodium: 22 mg
Protein: 4 g	

❧ *Lentil–Chickpea–Kidney Bean Chili* ❧

Lentils contain calcium, vitamins A and B, and iron.

PREPARATION TIME: 20 minutes　•　COOKING TIME: 45 minutes　•
YIELD: 12 servings

¼ cup low-sodium nonfat chicken broth	1 medium green bell pepper, cored and chopped
1 medium onion, chopped	1 medium red bell pepper, cored and chopped
2 cloves garlic, minced	
1 medium carrot, scraped and chopped	2½ cups low-sodium canned kidney beans, rinsed and drained
7 cups water	1 cup cooked or low-sodium canned chickpeas, rinsed and drained
⅓ cup low-sodium tomato paste	
2 cups dried lentils	

3 cups crushed low-sodium canned
   tomatoes
2 tablespoons chili powder

1 teaspoon ground cumin
¼ teaspoon ground black pepper

1. Heat broth in a large saucepan. Add onion, garlic, and carrot, and sauté until onion is tender, about 5 minutes.
2. Stir in the water, tomato paste, lentils, green and red bell peppers, beans, chickpeas, tomatoes, chili powder, cumin, and black pepper. Bring to a boil, reduce heat, cover, and simmer until lentils are just tender, about 40 minutes.

Calories Per Serving: 98
Fat: 1 g
Cholesterol: 0 mg
Protein: 6 g

Carbohydrates: 19 g
Dietary Fiber: 5 g
Sodium: 45 mg

❧ *Lentil-Vegetable Stew* ❧

Lentils, red peppers, carrots, celery, and jalapeño are the featured ingredients in this hearty stew.

PREPARATION TIME: *20 minutes* • COOKING TIME: *46 minutes* •
YIELD: *10 servings*

¼ cup low-sodium nonfat chicken
   broth
1 medium onion, chopped
1 medium red bell pepper, cored and
   chopped
2 medium carrots, scraped and diced
2 stalks celery, chopped
3 cloves garlic, minced
1 jalapeño pepper, seeded and minced

6 cups water
2 cups dried lentils
2 medium potatoes, diced
2 tablespoons chili powder
1 tablespoon dried oregano
1 teaspoon ground cumin
½ teaspoon ground black pepper
4 cups chopped low-sodium canned
   tomatoes, with juice

1. Heat broth in a large saucepan. Add onion, red bell pepper, carrots, celery, garlic, and jalapeño. Sauté for 6 minutes.

2. Add water, lentils, potatoes, chili powder, oregano, cumin, and black pepper. Bring to a boil, reduce heat, and simmer, stirring several times, for 20 minutes. Stir in tomatoes with their juice, and continue to simmer until lentils are tender, about 20 minutes.

3. Transfer soup to individual bowls and serve immediately.

Calories Per Serving: 85   Carbohydrates: 18 g
Fat: 1 g   Dietary Fiber: 4 g
Cholesterol: 0 mg   Sodium: 100 mg
Protein: 4 g

❧ *Pumpkin—Pinto Bean Stew* ❧

This Chilean stew contains onion, garlic, jalapeño pepper, corn, pinto beans, and pumpkin. Fresh pumpkins are available in the fall and winter.

PREPARATION TIME: *15 minutes* • COOKING TIME: *48 minutes* •
YIELD: *8 servings*

¼ cup low-sodium nonfat chicken broth
1 medium onion, diced
3 cloves garlic, minced
1 jalapeño pepper, seeded and minced
3 cups chopped low-sodium canned tomatoes
1 teaspoon paprika
1 tablespoon dried oregano

1 tablespoon dried parsley
1 teaspoon ground cumin
4 cups peeled and diced pumpkin
2 cups water
2 cups fresh or thawed frozen corn kernels
2 cups cooked or low-sodium canned pinto beans, rinsed and drained

1. Heat the broth in a large saucepan. Add the onion, garlic, and jalapeño pepper. Sauté until onion begins to soften, about 5 minutes. Add tomatoes, paprika, oregano, parsley, and cumin, and sauté for 3 additional minutes.

2. Add pumpkin and water. Bring to a boil, reduce heat, and simmer until pumpkin is tender, about 30 minutes. Stir in corn and pinto beans and simmer for an additional 10 minutes.

3. Transfer to individual bowls and serve at once.

Calories Per Serving: 129
Fat: 1 g
Cholesterol: 0 mg
Protein: 7 g

Carbohydrates: 27 g
Dietary Fiber: 6 g
Sodium: 69 mg

❧ *Pinto Beans and Potatoes* ❧

Onion, garlic, jalapeño, parsley, cumin, and paprika are the seasonings for this dish.

PREPARATION TIME: *15 minutes* • COOKING TIME: *25 minutes* •
YIELD: *4 servings*

3 cups water
2 cups unpeeled diced potatoes
¼ cup low-sodium nonfat chicken broth
1 medium onion, diced
2 cloves garlic, minced

1 jalapeño pepper, seeded and minced
2 cups cooked or low-sodium canned pinto beans, rinsed and drained
2 tablespoons fresh parsley, minced
1 teaspoon ground cumin
1 teaspoon paprika

1. Bring water to a boil in a saucepan. Add potatoes and cook until just tender, about 15 minutes. Drain.
2. Heat broth in another saucepan. Add onion, garlic, and jalapeño, and sauté until onion begins to soften, about 4 minutes.
3. Add potatoes, beans, parsley, cumin, and paprika. Reduce heat to low and cook, stirring several times, for 6 minutes. Serve at once.

Calories Per Serving: 204
Fat: 1 g
Cholesterol: 0 mg
Protein: 4 g

Carbohydrates: 46 g
Dietary Fiber: 6 g
Sodium: 144 mg

❧ *Hominy and Vegetables* ❧

A traditional Native American stew is the inspiration for this hearty, flavor-filled combination.

PREPARATION TIME: 20 minutes plus 10 minutes standing time •
COOKING TIME: 36 minutes • *YIELD: 10 servings*

¼ cup low-sodium nonfat chicken broth

1 medium onion, diced

1 medium green bell pepper, cored and diced

1 medium zucchini, diced

2 cloves garlic, minced

6 cups water

1 cup diced potato

2 cups canned hominy, rinsed and drained

½ teaspoon ground black pepper

1 jalapeño pepper, seeded and minced

1 cup cooked or low-sodium canned pinto beans, rinsed and drained

2 cups chopped spinach

¼ cup low-sodium tomato paste

1. Heat broth in a large saucepan. Add onion, green bell pepper, zucchini, and garlic, and sauté until onion is tender, about 6 minutes.
2. Stir in water, potato, hominy, and black pepper. Add jalapeño pepper. Bring to a boil, reduce heat, and simmer, stirring occasionally, for 20 minutes.
3. Add beans, spinach, and tomato paste, and simmer for 10 more minutes. Allow to stand for 10 minutes and serve.

Calories Per Serving: 71
Fat: 1 g
Cholesterol: 0 mg
Protein: 2 g

Carbohydrates: 15 g
Dietary Fiber: 3 g
Sodium: 93 mg

❧ *Red Beans and Rice* ❧

A variation of the popular Louisiana favorite.

PREPARATION TIME: 15 minutes • *COOKING TIME: 20 minutes* •
YIELD: 4 servings

¼ cup low-sodium nonfat chicken
broth
1 medium onion, chopped
2 cloves garlic, minced
1 medium yellow bell pepper, cored
and chopped
1 stalk celery, chopped

1½ teaspoons dried thyme
½ teaspoon cayenne pepper
3 cups water
1 cup uncooked white rice
2 cups low-sodium canned kidney
beans, rinsed and drained
¼ teaspoon ground black pepper

1. Heat broth in a large saucepan. Add onion, garlic, yellow bell pepper, celery, thyme, and cayenne pepper. Sauté until bell pepper begins to soften, about 5 minutes.
2. Add water and rice. Bring to a boil, reduce heat, cover, and simmer until rice is just tender, about 15 minutes.
3. Stir in beans and black pepper. Heat through and serve.

Calories Per Serving: 319
Fat: 1 g
Cholesterol: 0 mg
Protein: 12 g

Carbohydrates: 66 g
Dietary Fiber: 8 g
Sodium: 42 mg

❧ *Bean Pot* ❧

This dish, with navy and kidney beans, is prepared on top of the stove.

PREPARATION TIME: 15 minutes · *COOKING TIME: 20 minutes* ·
YIELD: 6 servings

¼ cup low-sodium nonfat chicken
broth
1¼ cups chopped onion
1 medium green bell pepper, cored
and chopped
2 cloves garlic, minced
1 cup low-sodium ketchup
¼ cup brown sugar

¼ cup maple syrup
2 tablespoons Worcestershire sauce
2 teaspoons Dijon mustard
2 cups low-sodium canned red kidney
beans, rinsed and drained
2 cups low-sodium canned navy
beans, rinsed and drained

1. Heat broth in a saucepan. Add onion, green bell pepper, and garlic. Sauté until bell pepper begins to soften, about 4 minutes.
2. Stir in ketchup, brown sugar, syrup, Worcestershire sauce, mustard, kidney beans, and navy beans. Reduce heat and simmer, stirring several times, for 15 minutes. Serve at once.

Calories Per Serving: 291
Fat: 1 g
Cholesterol: 0 mg
Protein: 12 g

Carbohydrates: 62 g
Dietary Fiber: 10 g
Sodium: 138 mg

❧ *Kidney Bean Chili* ❧

Sun-dried tomatoes are combined with red bell pepper, kidney beans, and spinach.

PREPARATION TIME: 20 minutes plus 30 minutes tomato soaking time ▪
COOKING TIME: 36 minutes ▪ *YIELD: 10 servings*

1 cup sun-dried tomatoes
¼ cup low-sodium nonfat chicken broth
1 medium onion, diced
1 medium red bell pepper, cored and diced
1 cup diced celery

3½ cups crushed low-sodium canned tomatoes
2 cups low-sodium canned kidney beans, rinsed and drained
1 tablespoon chili powder
1½ teaspoon ground cumin
½ teaspoon ground black pepper
2 cups chopped spinach

1. Cover the sun-dried tomatoes with water and allow them to stand for 30 minutes. Drain well and chop coarsely.
2. Heat the broth in a large saucepan. Add onion, red bell pepper, and celery, and sauté until pepper just begins to become tender, about 6 minutes.
3. Stir in the sun-dried tomatoes, the crushed tomatoes, beans, chili powder, cumin, and black pepper. Simmer, stirring occasionally, for 20 minutes.
4. Stir in spinach and continue to simmer for 10 additional minutes. Transfer to individual serving bowls and serve at once.

Calories Per Serving: 144
Fat: 1g
Cholesterol: 0 mg
Protein: 8 g

Carbohydrates: 31 g
Dietary Fiber: 6 g
Sodium: 83 mg

❧ *Red Bean and Vegetable Stew* ❧

This stew, made with squash, turnips, onion, carrot, kidney beans, corn, and broccoli, is a perfect winter meal.

PREPARATION TIME: 20 minutes • *COOKING TIME: 44 minutes* •
YIELD: 12 servings

¼ cup low-sodium tomato juice
1 cup chopped celery
1 medium onion, chopped
3 cloves garlic, minced
2 medium tomatoes, chopped
2 cups peeled and diced butternut
*   squash*
2 cups peeled and diced turnips

1 medium carrot, scraped and diced
6 cups water
1 cup low-sodium canned kidney
*   beans, rinsed and drained*
1 cup fresh, canned (drained), or
*   thawed frozen corn kernels*
2 cups chopped broccoli

1. Heat the tomato juice in a large saucepan. Add celery, onion, and garlic, and sauté until onion is just tender, about 3 minutes. Add tomatoes and simmer, stirring frequently, for 5 minutes.
2. Add the squash, turnips, carrot, and water. Bring to a boil, reduce heat, and simmer, stirring occasionally, until turnips are just tender, about 30 minutes.
3. Add beans, corn, and broccoli, and continue to simmer until broccoli is tender-crisp, about 6 minutes. Serve immediately.

Calories Per Serving: 72
Fat: 0 g
Cholesterol: 0 mg
Protein: 4 g

Carbohydrates: 16 g
Dietary Fiber: 4 g
Sodium: 47 mg

❧ *New Year's Black-eyed Peas* ❧

Traditionally eaten on New Year's Day in the South for good luck, black-eyed peas are cooked with tomatoes, bell pepper, and rice.

PREPARATION TIME: 10 minutes   •   COOKING TIME: 20 minutes   •
YIELD: 4 servings

*¼ cup low-sodium nonfat chicken
  broth*
4 cloves garlic, minced
*1 medium green bell pepper, cored
  and chopped*
*2 cups chopped low-sodium canned
  tomatoes, with juice*

*1 cup low-sodium canned black-eyed
  peas, rinsed and drained*
½ cup uncooked white rice
¾ cup water
1 teaspoon dried thyme
¼ teaspoon ground black pepper

1. Heat broth in a large skillet. Add garlic and green bell pepper, and sauté until pepper begins to soften, about 5 minutes.
2. Add tomatoes, black-eyed peas, rice, water, thyme, and black pepper. Bring to a boil, reduce heat, cover, and simmer until rice is just tender, about 15 minutes. Serve at once.

Calories Per Serving: 203
Fat: 1 g
Cholesterol: 3 mg
Protein: 12 g

Carbohydrates: 38 g
Dietary Fiber: 5 g
Sodium: 143 mg

❧ *Spicy Black-eyed Peas* ❧

Black-eyed peas are simmered in a sauce of vinegar, sugar, Worcestershire sauce, chili powder, and black pepper.

PREPARATION TIME: 15 minutes   •   COOKING TIME: 20 minutes   •
YIELD: 6 servings

*¼ cup low-sodium nonfat chicken
  broth*

1 medium onion, chopped
1 medium carrot, scraped and diced

1 stalk celery, sliced
4 cups low-sodium canned black-eyed
    peas, rinsed and drained
½ cup low-sodium tomato paste
¼ cup Worcestershire sauce

2 tablespoons vinegar
3 tablespoons brown sugar
2 teaspoon chili powder
1 teaspoon ground black pepper

1. Heat broth in a large skillet. Add onion, carrot, and celery, and sauté until onion begins to soften, about 5 minutes.
2. Stir in black-eyed peas, tomato paste, Worcestershire sauce, vinegar, brown sugar, chili powder, and black pepper. Bring to a boil, reduce heat, and simmer for 15 minutes. Serve immediately.

Calories Per Serving: 216
Fat: 1 g
Cholesterol: 0 mg
Protein: 12 g

Carbohydrates: 42 g
Dietary Fiber: 10 g
Sodium: 177 mg

❧ *Black-eyed Peas and Spinach* ❧

Black-eyed peas are served with spinach, bulgur, onion, and black pepper.

PREPARATION TIME: *15 minutes plus 15 minutes standing time*   •
COOKING TIME: *10 minutes*   •   YIELD: *6 servings*

2½ cups water
4 cups chopped fresh spinach
2 cups low-sodium canned black-eyed
    peas, rinsed and drained
1 cup bulgur

½ teaspoon ground black pepper
¼ cup low-sodium nonfat chicken
    broth
1 large onion, sliced

1. Bring water to a boil in a large saucepan. Add spinach and black-eyed peas, and cook for 5 minutes. Stir in bulgur and black pepper. Remove from heat, cover, and allow to stand for 15 minutes.
2. Heat broth in another saucepan, add onion, and sauté until onion begins to brown, about 5 minutes.

3. Drain any liquid remaining in the bulgur mixture. Divide bulgur among individual serving bowls, top each with onion slices, and serve.

Calories Per Serving: 176
Fat: 1 g
Cholesterol: 0 mg
Protein: 9 g

Carbohydrates: 36 g
Dietary Fiber: 12 g
Sodium: 154 mg

❧ *Black-eyed Pea Stew* ❧

In this stew, eggplant and black-eyed peas are combined with tomatoes, onion, bell pepper, and garlic.

Preparation Time: 20 minutes plus 15 minutes standing time ▪
Cooking Time: 37 minutes ▪ Yield: 12 servings

¼ cup low-sodium nonfat chicken
  broth
4 cups diced eggplant
4 medium tomatoes, diced, with juice
1 medium onion, diced
1 medium red bell pepper, cored and
  diced

4 cloves garlic, minced
3 cups water
1 tablespoon dried oregano
½ teaspoon ground black pepper
¼ teaspoon cayenne pepper
1½ cups low-sodium canned black-
  eyed peas, rinsed and drained

1. Heat broth in a large saucepan. Add eggplant, tomatoes, onion, red bell pepper, and garlic, and sauté for 7 minutes.
2. Add water, oregano, black pepper, and cayenne pepper. Bring to a boil, reduce heat, and simmer for 25 minutes.
3. Add black-eyed peas and simmer for 5 additional minutes. Remove from heat and allow to stand for 15 minutes before serving.

Calories Per Serving: 60
Fat: 0 g
Cholesterol: 0 mg
Protein: 3 g

Carbohydrates: 12 g
Dietary Fiber: 2 g
Sodium: 17 mg

❧ *Carrot-Lentil Stew* ❧

This dish uses pearl barley, a grain that has had the bran removed.

PREPARATION TIME: *15 minutes* ▪ COOKING TIME: *1 hour, 15 minutes* ▪
YIELD: *10 servings*

¼ cup low-sodium nonfat chicken broth	½ cup pearl barley
1 medium onion, diced	3 cups diced sweet potatoes
2 stalks celery, sliced	2 tablespoons dried parsley
2 medium carrots, scraped and diced	½ teaspoon dried thyme
4 cloves garlic, minced	1 teaspoon dried oregano
6 cups water	½ teaspoon ground black pepper
1 cup dried lentils	2 cups chopped spinach

1. Heat broth in a large saucepan. Add onion, celery, carrots, and garlic, and sauté until carrots begin to soften, about 7 minutes.
2. Stir in water, lentils, barley, sweet potatoes, parsley, thyme, oregano, and black pepper. Bring to a boil, reduce heat, and simmer, stirring occasionally, until lentils are tender, about 1 hour.
3. Add the spinach and continue to simmer for another 8 minutes. Serve immediately.

Calories Per Serving: 224	Carbohydrates: 46 g
Fat: 1 g	Dietary Fiber: 6 g
Cholesterol: 0 mg	Sodium: 64 mg
Protein: 11 g	

❧ *Cannellini Beans, Tomatoes, and Rice* ❧

This simple dish contains cannellini beans, tomatoes, rice, garlic, and black pepper. Cannellini beans are large, white Italian kidney beans.

PREPARATION TIME: *10 minutes* ▪ COOKING TIME: *12 minutes* ▪
YIELD: *4 servings*

*¼ cup low-sodium nonfat chicken
   broth*

2 cloves garlic, minced

*2 cups low-sodium canned tomatoes,
   chopped, with their juice*

*2 cups low-sodium cannellini beans,
   rinsed and drained*

1½ cups cooked white rice

¼ teaspoon ground black pepper

1. Heat broth in a large saucepan. Add garlic and sauté for 2 minutes.
2. Add tomatoes with juice, beans, rice, and black pepper. Simmer until all ingredients are heated through, about 10 minutes. Serve at once.

Calories Per Serving: 233
Fat: 1 g
Cholesterol: 0 mg
Protein: 11 g

Carbohydrates: 47 g
Dietary Fiber: 7 g
Sodium: 42 mg

❧ *Cannellini Beans and Red Peppers* ❧

Cannellini beans are cooked with bell peppers, tomatoes, and celery.

PREPARATION TIME: 20 minutes • *COOKING TIME: 40 minutes* •
YIELD: 8 servings

*¼ cup low-sodium nonfat chicken
   broth*

1 medium onion, chopped

*2 medium red bell peppers, cored and
   chopped*

2 stalks celery, chopped

3 cloves garlic, minced

1 jalapeño pepper, seeded and minced

*3½ cups chopped low-sodium canned
   tomatoes, with their juice*

*2 cups low-sodium canned cannellini
   beans, rinsed and drained*

1 teaspoon paprika

½ teaspoon ground black pepper

1. Heat broth in a large skillet. Add onion, bell peppers, celery, garlic, and jalapeño. Sauté until peppers begin to soften, about 7 minutes.
2. Stir in tomatoes with their juices, beans, paprika, and black pepper. Simmer, stirring several times, for 30 minutes.
3. Transfer to individual serving bowls and serve immediately.

Calories Per Serving: 100

Fat: 1 g

Cholesterol: 0 mg

Protein: 6 g

Carbohydrates: 19 g

Dietary Fiber: 5 g

Sodium: 102 mg

❧ *Cannellini Beans with Shells and Sage* ❧

Cannellini beans are cooked with pasta shells, onion, and sage. Dried sage should be stored in a cool, dark place and lasts no more than 6 months.

PREPARATION TIME: 15 minutes • COOKING TIME: 13 minutes •
YIELD: 6 servings

¼ cup low-sodium nonfat chicken broth

1 medium onion, chopped

3 cloves garlic, minced

4 cups low-sodium canned cannellini beans, with their liquid

1 teaspoon ground black pepper

1 teaspoon dried sage

¼ teaspoon cayenne pepper

1 cup water

2 cups cooked small pasta shells

1. Heat broth in a large skillet. Add onion and garlic, and sauté until onion just begins to become tender, about 3 minutes.
2. Add beans with their liquid, black pepper, sage, cayenne pepper, water, and pasta. Bring to a boil, reduce heat, and simmer for 10 minutes. Serve at once.

Calories Per Serving: 280

Fat: 1 g

Cholesterol: 0 mg

Protein: 16 g

Carbohydrates: 53 g

Dietary Fiber: 1 g

Sodium: 21 mg

❧ *Baked Wild Rice and Cannellini Beans* ❧

Wild rice and cannellini beans are baked with onion, bell pepper, zucchini, mushrooms, carrots, and peas.

PREPARATION TIME: 20 minutes • COOKING TIME: 58 minutes •
YIELD: 8 servings

¼ cup low-sodium nonfat chicken
  broth
1 medium onion, chopped
1 medium red bell pepper, cored and
  chopped
1 medium zucchini, chopped
12 mushrooms, sliced
4 cloves garlic, minced
2½ cups water

2 cups low-sodium canned cannellini
  beans, rinsed and drained
2 medium carrots, scraped and diced
1 cup fresh or frozen green peas
¾ cup uncooked white rice
¼ cup uncooked wild rice
1 teaspoon dried thyme
1 teaspoon ground black pepper

1. Preheat oven to 350 degrees.
2. Heat broth in a large ovenproof casserole. Add onion, red bell pepper, zucchini, mushrooms, and garlic, and sauté until pepper begins to soften, about 7 minutes.
3. Add water, beans, carrots, peas, rices, thyme, and black pepper. Cover and bake until water is absorbed and rice is done, about 50 minutes. Serve at once.

Calories Per Serving: 225
Fat: 1 g
Cholesterol: 0 mg
Protein: 9 g

Carbohydrates: 46 g
Dietary Fiber: 5 g
Sodium: 26 mg

❧ "Baked" Beans ❧

Canned beans have a rich, sweet taste when served with onion, tomatoes, maple syrup, vinegar, parsley, mustard, ginger, and black pepper.

*PREPARATION TIME: 15 minutes • COOKING TIME: 18 minutes •
YIELD: 8 servings*

¼ cup water
1 medium onion, chopped
2 medium tomatoes, chopped
2 tablespoons maple syrup
1 tablespoon vinegar
1 tablespoon dried parsley

1½ teaspoons dry mustard
½ teaspoon ground ginger
¼ teaspoon ground black pepper
5 cups low-sodium canned Great
  Northern beans, rinsed and
  drained

1. Heat water in a large saucepan. Add onion and sauté until onion becomes tender, about 3 minutes. Add tomatoes, maple syrup, vinegar, parsley, mustard, ginger, and black pepper.
2. Add beans and simmer for at least 10 minutes to allow flavors to be absorbed. Serve at once.

Calories Per Serving: 217   Carbohydrates: 41 g
Fat: 1 g   Dietary Fiber: 1 g
Cholesterol: 0 mg   Sodium: 77 mg
Protein: 12 g

❧ *Acorn Squash, Rice, and Tomatoes* ❧

Beans are cooked with rice, corn, tomatoes, and acorn squash. Acorn squash is a winter squash with a ribbed, dark green skin and orange flesh.

PREPARATION TIME: 15 minutes • *COOKING TIME: 45 minutes* •
YIELD: 10 servings

3 cups low-sodium nonfat chicken broth
1 medium onion, chopped
3 cloves garlic, minced
2 medium green bell peppers, cored and chopped
1 jalapeño pepper, seeded and minced
2 medium tomatoes, chopped

2 cups peeled and chopped acorn squash
1 cup uncooked white rice
2 cups low-sodium canned Great Northern beans, rinsed and drained
½ cup thawed frozen corn kernels
¼ cup chopped fresh parsley

1. Heat ¼ cup broth in a large saucepan. Add onion, garlic, green bell pepper, and jalapeño pepper, and sauté until bell peppers begin to soften, about 5 minutes.
2. Add the remaining broth, tomatoes, squash, and rice. Return to a boil, reduce heat, cover, and simmer until rice is tender, about 35 minutes.
3. Stir in beans, corn, and parsley, and continue to simmer until all ingredients are heated through, about 5 minutes. Serve at once.

Calories Per Serving: 256

Fat: 1 g

Cholesterol: 0 mg

Protein: 10 g

Carbohydrates: 53 g

Dietary Fiber: 2 g

Sodium: 102 mg

❧ *Great Northern Bean—Vegetable Curry* ❧

Turnips and sweet potatoes are cooked in a tomato-ginger sauce. Sweet potatoes are high in vitamins A and C.

PREPARATION TIME: 20 minutes   •   COOKING TIME: 48 minutes   •
YIELD: 6 servings

¼ cup low-sodium tomato juice
1 medium onion, finely chopped
2 cloves garlic, minced
1 tablespoon minced fresh gingerroot
2 medium tomatoes, finely chopped
1 tablespoon curry powder
1 teaspoon ground cumin
1 teaspoon coriander

¼ teaspoon cayenne pepper
2 turnips, peeled and chopped
2 medium sweet potatoes, chopped
2 cups water
1 cup low-sodium canned Great
*   Northern beans, rinsed and*
*   drained*

1. Heat the tomato juice in a large saucepan. Add onion, garlic, and gingerroot, and sauté until onion begins to soften, about 3 minutes.
2. Add tomatoes, curry powder, cumin, coriander, and cayenne, and sauté for an additional 4 minutes.
3. Add turnips, potatoes, and water. Bring to a boil, reduce heat, and simmer, stirring frequently, until turnips are just tender, about 30 minutes. Stir in the beans and continue to simmer until all ingredients are heated through, about 5 minutes. Serve at once.

Calories Per Serving: 134

Fat: 1 g

Cholesterol: 0 mg

Protein: 6 g

Carbohydrates: 28 g

Dietary Fiber: 5 g

Sodium: 43 mg

❧ *Bean-Potato Scramble* ❧

This egg dish contains artichokes, potatoes, and white beans.

PREPARATION TIME: 15 minutes • *COOKING TIME: 30 minutes* •
YIELD: 6 servings

3 cups water
2 cups diced potatoes
¼ cup low-sodium nonfat chicken
    broth
1 medium onion, diced
1 medium red bell pepper, cored and
    diced
1 cup canned artichoke hearts, well
    rinsed, drained, and coarsely
    chopped

2 cups low-sodium canned Great
    Northern beans, rinsed and
    drained
2 tablespoons chopped fresh parsley
1 teaspoon dried oregano
6 egg whites, lightly beaten
½ cup shredded nonfat Swiss
¼ teaspoon ground black pepper

1. Bring water to a boil in a saucepan. Add potatoes and cook until tender, about 15 minutes.
2. Heat the broth in a large saucepan over medium heat. Add onion and bell pepper, and sauté until pepper begins to soften, about 5 minutes.
3. Stir in potatoes, artichokes, beans, parsley, and oregano. Reduce heat.
4. Pour egg whites over vegetables. Stir.
5. Cook until egg whites are firm, about 3 minutes.
6. Sprinkle with cheese and black pepper before serving.

Calories Per Serving: 206
Fat: 1 g
Cholesterol: 2 mg
Protein: 14 g

Carbohydrates: 38 g
Dietary Fiber: 7 g
Sodium: 250 mg

❧ *White Bean Pilaf* ❧

Vermicelli is a strand pasta thinner than spaghetti. In this recipe, it is sautéed in nonfat chicken broth and combined with white beans, vegetables, and rice.

PREPARATION TIME: 15 minutes   •   COOKING TIME: 32 minutes   •
YIELD: 8 servings

*6 tablespoons low-sodium nonfat
    chicken broth*
*8 ounces uncooked vermicelli, broken
    into pieces about 1 inch long*
1 medium onion, minced
*1 medium yellow summer squash,
    finely chopped*
*1 medium green bell pepper, cored
    and diced*

4 cups water
1½ cups uncooked white rice
*2 cups low-sodium canned Great
    Northern beans, rinsed and
    drained*
½ teaspoon turmeric
½ teaspoon ground black pepper
½ teaspoon ground cumin

1. Heat 2 tablespoons broth in a saucepan. Add vermicelli and sauté until softened, about 5 minutes. Remove from heat and drain any excess liquid. Set aside.
2. Heat remaining broth in a large saucepan. Add onion, yellow squash, and green bell pepper, and sauté until onion begins to soften, about 7 minutes.
3. Stir in water, rice, beans, turmeric, black pepper, cumin, and vermicelli. Bring to a boil, reduce heat, cover, and simmer until rice is tender and liquid is absorbed, about 20 minutes. Serve at once.

Calories Per Serving: 309
Fat: 1 g
Cholesterol: 0 mg
Protein: 11 g

Carbohydrates: 64 g
Dietary Fiber: 4 g
Sodium: 26 mg

❧ White Bean Chili with Eggplant ❧

This unique chili recipe contains white beans, corn, and eggplant. Great Northern beans are a specific variety of white beans that are grown in the Midwest.

PREPARATION TIME: 20 minutes • *COOKING TIME: 30 minutes* • *YIELD: 10 servings*

¼ cup low-sodium nonfat chicken broth
1 medium onion, diced
1 medium red bell pepper, cored and diced
2 cups diced eggplant
2 cloves garlic, minced
2 cups fresh, canned (drained), or thawed frozen corn kernels

2 cups low-sodium canned Great Northern beans, rinsed and drained
2 medium tomatoes, chopped
¼ cup chopped fresh parsley
1 tablespoon dried oregano
½ teaspoon ground black pepper

1. Heat broth in a large saucepan. Add onion, red bell pepper, eggplant, and garlic, and sauté until pepper begins to soften, about 10 minutes.
2. Add corn kernels, beans, tomatoes, parsley, oregano, and black pepper. Simmer, stirring occasionally, for 20 minutes. Serve at once.

Calories Per Serving: 121
Fat: 0 g
Cholesterol: 2 mg
Protein: 9 g

Carbohydrates: 23 g
Dietary Fiber: 1 g
Sodium: 73 mg

❧ Stovetop Beans with Sweet Potatoes ❧

These beans and sweet potatoes are flavored with chutney, molasses, Worcestershire sauce, chili powder, cumin, hot sauce, and black pepper. Sweet potatoes are high in vitamins A and C.

PREPARATION TIME: 15 minutes • *COOKING TIME: 32 minutes* • *YIELD: 6 servings*

3 cups water	⅓ cup molasses
2 cups diced unpeeled sweet potatoes	3 tablespoons Worcestershire sauce
¼ cup low-sodium nonfat chicken broth	2 teaspoons chili powder
1 medium onion, chopped	1 teaspoon ground cumin
1 medium red bell pepper, cored and chopped	1 teaspoon hot pepper sauce
3 cloves garlic, minced	½ teaspoon ground black pepper
½ cup mango chutney (see page 309)	2 cups low-sodium canned Great Northern beans, rinsed and drained

1. Bring water to a boil in a saucepan. Add potatoes, return to a boil, reduce heat, and cook until potatoes are just tender, about 12 minutes. Drain and set potatoes aside.

2. Heat broth in a saucepan. Add onion, red bell pepper, and garlic. Sauté until pepper just begins to soften, about 7 minutes. Stir in chutney, molasses, Worcestershire sauce, chili powder, cumin, hot pepper sauce, and black pepper. Cook for an additional 3 minutes.

3. Add beans and sweet potatoes and simmer, stirring several times, for 10 minutes. Serve immediately.

Calories Per Serving: 309
Fat: 1 g
Cholesterol: 0 mg
Protein: 8 g

Carbohydrates: 69
Dietary Fiber: 9 g
Sodium: 159 mg

❧ White Beans and Kale ❧

This warming dish is a great source of dietary fiber.

PREPARATION TIME: 15 minutes • COOKING TIME: 44 minutes •
YIELD: 8 servings

6 cups low-sodium nonfat chicken broth	3 cups low-sodium canned Great Northern beans, with their liquid
1 medium onion, chopped	¾ cup low-sodium tomato paste
4 cloves garlic, minced	½ teaspoon ground sage

½ teaspoon hot red pepper flakes
4 cups chopped fresh kale
½ cup cornmeal

½ cup water
2 tablespoons lemon juice
¼ teaspoon ground black pepper

1. Heat ¼ cup broth in a large saucepan. Add onion and garlic, and sauté until onion begins to soften, about 4 minutes.
2. Puree 1½ cups beans in a food processor or blender.
3. Combine remaining broth, pureed beans, whole beans, tomato paste, sage, red pepper flakes, and kale with the onion and garlic. Bring to a boil, reduce heat, and simmer until the kale is just tender, about 30 minutes.
4. Mix the cornmeal, water, and lemon juice into a paste and slowly stir it into the stew. Continue to simmer for 10 minutes. Stir in black pepper and serve.

Calories Per Serving: 167
Fat: 1 g
Cholesterol: 0 mg
Protein: 8 g

Carbohydrates: 34 g
Dietary Fiber: 10 g
Sodium: 56 mg

✨ *Vegetable-and-Bean Burrito* ✨

These burritos are made with pinto beans, zucchini, mushrooms, broccoli, corn, and bell pepper.

PREPARATION TIME: 15 minutes • COOKING TIME: 8 minutes •
YIELD: 4 servings

¼ cup low-sodium nonfat chicken broth
1 cup diced zucchini
1 cup sliced mushrooms
1 cup chopped broccoli
1 medium red bell pepper, cored and chopped

1 cup low-sodium canned pinto beans, rinsed and drained
½ cup fresh or thawed frozen corn kernels
1 teaspoon ground cumin
4 corn tortillas, warmed
½ cup shredded nonfat cheddar

1. Heat broth in a large saucepan. Add zucchini, mushrooms, broccoli, and red bell pepper. Sauté until pepper begins to soften, about 5 minutes.

2. Add beans, corn, and cumin. Reduce heat and cook for 3 additional minutes.

3. Place each tortilla on an individual serving plate, divide the bean mixture among the tortillas, and sprinkle with cheese. Roll up each tortilla and serve immediately.

Calories Per Serving: 162

Fat: 1 g

Cholesterol: 3 mg

Protein: 12 g

Carbohydrates: 29 g

Dietary Fiber: 4 g

Sodium: 372 mg

❧ *Garlic-Ginger-Bean Cakes* ❧

These bean cakes are made with soy sauce, sesame oil, egg white, kidney beans, bread crumbs, garlic, and gingerroot.

PREPARATION TIME: 15 minutes • COOKING TIME: 9 minutes •
YIELD: 4 servings, 2 bean cakes each

1 teaspoon reduced-sodium soy sauce
½ teaspoon sesame oil
1 teaspoon minced fresh gingerroot
3 cloves garlic, minced
¼ teaspoon ground black pepper
2 cups low-sodium canned dark red
kidney beans, rinsed and drained
and mashed into a puree

¼ cup all-purpose flour
1 egg white
2 tablespoons water
½ cup dry bread crumbs

1. Heat soy sauce and sesame oil in a small nonstick skillet. Add gingerroot and garlic, and sauté for 1 minute.

2. Combine gingerroot-garlic mixture and black pepper with the pureed beans. Form into 8 patties.

3. Dredge patties in flour.

4. Whisk together the egg white and water.

5. Dip each patty in the egg white mixture, then in bread crumbs.

6. Lightly spray a nonstick skillet with cooking oil spray. Place bean cakes in the skillet and cook until lightly brown, about 4 minutes on each side. Serve at once.

Calories Per Serving: 105
Fat: 1 g
Cholesterol: 0 mg
Protein: 6 g

Carbohydrates: 19 g
Dietary Fiber: 3 g
Sodium: 90 mg

✌ *Bean Burgers* ✌

These burger patties are formed out of canned butter beans, barley, bulgur, and oatmeal, and are flavored with soy sauce, celery, onion, and garlic. Butter beans are another name for dried lima beans and contain protein, phosphorus, potassium, and iron.

PREPARATION TIME: *15 minutes* • COOKING TIME: *10 minutes* •
YIELD: *6 servings*

1 cup low-sodium canned butter
  beans, rinsed and drained
¾ cup cooked barley
¾ cup cooked bulgur
½ cup uncooked quick oats

1½ tablespoons reduced-sodium soy
  sauce
1 stalk celery, finely chopped
1 medium onion, finely chopped
2 cloves garlic, minced

1. Preheat broiler.
2. Gently mash the beans with a fork. Add the barley, bulgur, oats, soy sauce, celery, onion, and garlic. Mix well.
3. Form the mixture into patties and broil until browned, about 5 minutes per side. Serve immediately.

Calories Per Serving: 122
Fat: 1 g
Cholesterol: 0 mg
Protein: 5 g

Carbohydrates: 24 g
Dietary Fiber: 5 g
Sodium: 142 mg

❧ *Broiled Bean Patties* ❧

Here's a delectable vegetarian alternative to the all-American hamburger.

PREPARATION TIME: 10 minutes • COOKING TIME: 8 minutes •
YIELD: 4 servings

2 cups low-sodium canned kidney
    beans, rinsed and drained
½ cup whole-grain bread crumbs
1 scallion, minced
2 teaspoons Worcestershire sauce
¼ teaspoon ground black pepper

1 egg white
8 slices nonfat bread, lightly toasted
2 tablespoons nonfat Parmesan
4 slices tomato
4 romaine lettuce leaves

1. Preheat broiler.
2. Mash beans in a bowl. Add bread crumbs, scallion, Worcestershire
   sauce, black pepper, and egg white. Mix well.
3. Form bean mixture into patties, place on a nonstick baking sheet, and
   broil until lightly browned, about 4 minutes on each side.
4. Serve on bread, topped with Parmesan, tomato, and lettuce.

Calories Per Serving: 333
Fat: 1 g
Cholesterol: 1 mg
Protein: 17 g

Carbohydrates: 60 g
Dietary Fiber: 7 g
Sodium: 410 mg

❧ *Tomato-Bean Burgers* ❧

Pinto beans, bread crumbs, onion, tomato sauce, basil, and cayenne pepper
are the ingredients of these big-flavored burgers.

PREPARATION TIME: 20 minutes • COOKING TIME: 8 minutes •
YIELD: 12 servings

2 cups cooked or low-sodium canned
    pinto beans, rinsed and drained
½ cup bread crumbs

½ cup minced onion
2 cloves garlic, minced
½ cup low-sodium tomato sauce

¼ teaspoon cayenne pepper   *1 tablespoon minced fresh parsley*
½ teaspoon dried basil

1. Preheat broiler.
2. Mash beans in a bowl. Add bread crumbs, onion, garlic, tomato sauce, cayenne pepper, basil, and parsley, and mix thoroughly.
3. Shape into 12 patties, place on a nonstick cookie sheet, and broil, turning once, until browned, about 4 minutes each side. Serve immediately.

Calories Per Serving: 75   Carbohydrates: 14 g
Fat: 0 g   Dietary Fiber: 3 g
Cholesterol: 0 mg   Sodium: 48 mg
Protein: 4 g

DRESSINGS, SAUCES, AND RELISHES

೬౨

Balsamic Dressing • Sweet-and-Tangy Sour Cream Dressing •
Tomato and Onion Salsa • Salsa-Yogurt Dressing • Apple-
Honey Dressing • Chili-Cilantro Dressing • Mixed Fruit
Chutney • Tropical Chutney • Mango Chutney Sauce •
Peach-Raisin Chutney • Sweet-and-Spicy Tomato Chutney •
Cinnamon-Vanilla Yogurt Sauce • Apricot Sauce • Scallion-
and-Dill Sauce • Lemon-Horseradish Sauce • Horseradish-
Chive Sauce • Lemon-Pepper Sauce • Honey-Mustard Sauce •
Portobello Sauce • Cucumber-Mint Sauce • Vegetable Raita
• Cucumber Raita • Ginger-Carrot-Orange Sauce • Jalapeño
Relish • Jicama Relish • Apple-Strawberry Sauce • Vanilla-
Maple Topping • Very Berry Topping • Spiced Yogurt Topping
• Spicy Fruit Topping

❦ *Balsamic Dressing* ❦

Here is a quick, exciting dressing. It is rich with the distinctive flavor of balsamic vinegar.

PREPARATION TIME: 5 minutes • *YIELD: 12 servings*

¼ cup water
1 cup balsamic vinegar
¼ cup lemon juice
1 teaspoon honey
2 tablespoons Dijon mustard
1 tablespoon minced scallion

3 cloves garlic, minced
1 teaspoon dried oregano
½ teaspoon dried basil
½ teaspoon ground black pepper
2 tablespoons minced fresh parsley

1. Whisk together the water, vinegar, lemon juice, honey, mustard, scallion, garlic, oregano, basil, black pepper, and parsley.

Calories Per Serving: 125
Fat: 0 g
Cholesterol: 0 mg
Protein: 0 g

Carbohydrates: 27 g
Dietary Fiber: 0 g
Sodium: 32 mg

❦ *Sweet-and-Tangy Sour Cream Dressing* ❦

Sour cream, mayonnaise, yogurt, mustard, and honey are blended in this creamy dressing. Serve with a combination of red and green leaf lettuce, cucumbers, scallions, and Italian plum tomatoes.

PREPARATION TIME: 5 minutes plus 3 hours chilling time • *YIELD: 12 servings*

¼ cup nonfat sour cream
¼ cup nonfat mayonnaise
½ cup nonfat plain yogurt

¼ cup Dijon mustard
3 tablespoons honey
2 tablespoons skim milk

1. Mix the sour cream, mayonnaise, yogurt, mustard, and honey in a bowl. Stir in the milk.
2. Cover and refrigerate for 3 hours before serving.

Calories Per Serving: 38
Fat: 0 g
Cholesterol: 0 mg
Protein: 1 g

Carbohydrates: 8 g
Dietary Fiber: 0 g
Sodium: 77 mg

❧ *Tomato and Onion Salsa* ❧

Red onion and yellow bell pepper contribute to this colorful salsa.

PREPARATION TIME: 15 minutes • *YIELD: 24 servings*

1½ cups minced red onion
2 tablespoons dried cilantro
3 medium tomatoes, minced
1 cup minced fresh parsley
¾ teaspoon ground black pepper

¼ teaspoon cayenne pepper
1 medium yellow bell pepper, cored
  and minced
2 teaspoons brown sugar

1. Combine onion, cilantro, tomatoes, parsley, black pepper, cayenne pepper, yellow bell pepper, and brown sugar. Mix thoroughly.
2. Serve with nonfat corn chips, nonfat potato chips, or fresh raw vegetables.

Calories Per Serving: 15
Fat: 0 g
Cholesterol: 0 mg
Protein: 0 g

Carbohydrates: 3 g
Dietary Fiber: 1 g
Sodium: 4 mg

❧ *Salsa-Yogurt Dressing* ❧

Use this salsa-flavored yogurt dressing on salads for a Tex-Mex meal. Unopened commercial salsa can be stored at room temperature for up to 6 months. Once open, it can be stored in the refrigerator for up to a month.

PREPARATION TIME: 5 minutes plus 3 hours chilling time • *YIELD: 8 servings*

½ cup nonfat plain yogurt

¼ cup nonfat mayonnaise

½ cup prepared chunky salsa

1. Mix yogurt and mayonnaise. Stir in salsa, cover, and chill for 3 hours before serving.

Calories Per Serving: 14

Fat: 0 g

Cholesterol: 0 mg

Protein: 2 g

Carbohydrates: 2 g

Dietary Fiber: 0 g

Sodium: 184 mg

❧ *Apple-Honey Dressing* ❧

This honey-mustard–accented dressing works well on a mixed salad of bitter greens like arugula and radicchio.

PREPARATION TIME: 5 minutes • *YIELD: 8 servings*

½ cup unsweetened apple juice

½ teaspoon ground thyme leaves

2 teaspoons Dijon mustard

2 tablespoons honey

1. Whisk together the apple juice, thyme, mustard, and honey.

Calories Per Serving: 29

Fat: 0 g

Cholesterol: 0 mg

Protein: 1 g

Carbohydrates: 7 g

Dietary Fiber: 2 g

Sodium: 22 mg

❧ *Chili-Cilantro Dressing* ❧

The next time you're serving chili, top a mixed green salad with this spicy ranch dressing made with cilantro, chili powder, and hot sauce.

PREPARATION TIME: 10 minutes • *YIELD: 10 servings*

1 cup nonfat buttermilk
2 teaspoons corn syrup
2 tablespoons lemon juice
2 tablespoons chopped fresh cilantro

1 teaspoon chili powder
¼ teaspoon ground white pepper
4 drops hot pepper sauce

1. Whisk together the buttermilk, corn syrup, lemon juice, cilantro, chili powder, white pepper, and hot sauce.

Calories Per Serving: 15
Fat: 0 g
Cholesterol: 1 mg
Protein: 1 g

Carbohydrates: 3 g
Dietary Fiber: 0 g
Sodium: 30 mg

❧ *Mixed Fruit Chutney* ❧

Cranberries are cooked with pears, onion, gingerroot, apricots, and raisins. Serve with curried rice dishes.

PREPARATION TIME: *15 minutes plus 30 minutes cooling time* ▪
COOKING TIME: *20 minutes* ▪ YIELD: *10 servings*

3 cups whole cranberries
2 large pears, cored and diced
1 medium onion, diced
4 cloves garlic, minced
1 tablespoon grated fresh gingerroot
¾ cup sugar
½ cup raisins

½ cup chopped dried apricots
1½ cups red wine vinegar
1 cup unsweetened apple juice
½ teaspoon ground black pepper
¼ teaspoon ground cloves
¼ teaspoon ground nutmeg

1. Combine all the ingredients in a large aluminum saucepan.
2. Simmer, stirring several times, until mixture thickens, about 20 minutes. Allow to cool to room temperature before serving.

Calories Per Serving: 147
Fat: 0 g
Cholesterol: 0 mg
Protein: 1 g

Carbohydrates: 37 g
Dietary Fiber: 4 g
Sodium: 10 mg

❧ *Tropical Chutney* ☙

In this chutney, papaya and pineapple chunks are simmered with apple, raisins, orange juice, gingerroot, jalapeño pepper, and cloves.

PREPARATION TIME: 20 minutes plus 10 minutes standing time •
COOKING TIME: 20 minutes • *YIELD: 16 servings*

1 medium papaya, peeled, pitted,
  and chopped
2 cups water-packed canned pineapple chunks, drained
1 medium apple, cored and diced
½ cup raisins
½ cup brown sugar
½ cup orange juice

1 cup red wine vinegar
1 medium onion, diced
1 tablespoon grated fresh gingerroot
4 cloves garlic, minced
1 jalapeño pepper, seeded and minced
½ teaspoon ground cumin
½ teaspoon ground cloves

1. Combine all the ingredients in a large aluminum saucepan.
2. Simmer until mixture thickens, about 20 minutes. Allow to stand for 10 minutes before serving. The chutney can be served warm or at room temperature.

Calories Per Serving: 161
Fat: 0 g
Cholesterol: 0 mg
Protein: 1 g

Carbohydrates: 41 g
Dietary Fiber: 3 g
Sodium: 37 mg

❧ *Mango Chutney Sauce* ☙

This tropical chutney can be served with curried vegetables and rice.

PREPARATION TIME: 15 minutes • *COOKING TIME: 20 minutes* •
YIELD: 6 servings

1 medium onion, chopped	½ cup orange juice
1 medium carrot, scraped and diced	1 cup red wine vinegar
2 cloves garlic, minced	2 tablespoons Worcestershire sauce
1 jalapeño pepper, seeded and minced	⅓ cup sugar
1 medium mango, peeled, pitted, and chopped	¼ teaspoon ground allspice

1. Combine all the ingredients in a large aluminum saucepan.
2. Simmer, stirring several times, until mixture thickens, about 20 minutes. The chutney can be served warm or at room temperature.

Calories Per Serving: 131	Carbohydrates: 34 g
Fat: 0 g	Dietary Fiber: 2 g
Cholesterol: 0 mg	Sodium: 132 mg
Protein: 1 g	

❧ *Peach-Raisin Chutney* ❧

Dried peaches are the key ingredient in this chutney, which is a wonderful condiment on warm curried fruit dishes.

PREPARATION TIME: *15 minutes plus 40 minutes standing time and 1 hour chilling time* ▪ COOKING TIME: *1 hour* ▪ YIELD: *16 servings*

2 cups water	1 teaspoon minced fresh gingerroot
1 cup chopped dried peaches	½ cup red wine vinegar
½ cup raisins	¾ cup brown sugar
5 cloves garlic, minced	⅛ teaspoon cayenne pepper

1. Bring water to a boil. Place dried peaches in a saucepan and pour boiling water over them. Allow to stand for 30 minutes.
2. Stir in raisins, garlic, gingerroot, vinegar, sugar, and cayenne pepper. Bring to a boil, reduce heat, and simmer, stirring several times, until mixture begins to thicken, about 1 hour.
3. Remove from heat and allow to stand for 10 minutes.
4. Refrigerate for 1 hour before serving.

Calories Per Serving: 77
Fat: 0 g
Cholesterol: 0 mg
Protein: 1 g

Carbohydrates: 20 g
Dietary Fiber: 0 g
Sodium: 3 mg

❧ *Sweet-and-Spicy Tomato Chutney* ❧

Try tossing this chutney, which features plum tomatoes, with leftover pasta.

PREPARATION TIME: 10 minutes plus 10 minutes standing time •
COOKING TIME: 2 hours • *YIELD: 12 servings*

12 plum tomatoes, chopped
½ cup raisins
6 cloves garlic, minced
1 tablespoon minced fresh gingerroot

½ cup brown sugar
¼ teaspoon ground cinnamon
⅛ teaspoon cayenne pepper
½ cup red wine vinegar

1. Combine all the ingredients in a saucepan. Bring to a boil, reduce heat, and gently simmer, stirring frequently, until mixture thickens, about 2 hours.
2. Remove from heat and allow to stand for 10 minutes.

Calories Per Serving: 56
Fat: 0 g
Cholesterol: 0 mg
Protein: 1 g

Carbohydrates: 14 g
Dietary Fiber: 1 g
Sodium: 6 mg

❧ *Cinnamon-Vanilla Yogurt Sauce* ❧

This simple, sweet, and spicy yogurt sauce, flavored with nutmeg, cinnamon, and vanilla extract, can be served with fat-free pound cake. Vanilla extract can be stored indefinitely sealed airtight and kept in a dark, cool place.

PREPARATION TIME: 5 minutes • *YIELD: 4 servings*

1 cup nonfat plain yogurt
1 tablespoon honey
⅛ teaspoon vanilla extract

⅛ teaspoon ground nutmeg
⅛ teaspoon ground cinnamon

1. Combine yogurt, honey, vanilla, nutmeg, and cinnamon. Stir until well blended and serve.

Calories Per Serving: 50
Fat: 0 g
Cholesterol: 1 mg
Protein: 3 g

Carbohydrates: 10 g
Dietary Fiber: 0 g
Sodium: 47 mg

❧ *Apricot Sauce* ❧

Apricot jam, dry mustard, soy sauce, and white vinegar are combined in this easy sauce, which gives a sweet-and-sour accent to vegetable dishes.

PREPARATION TIME: 10 minutes • *YIELD: 3 servings*

6 tablespoons sugarless apricot all-fruit jam
½ teaspoon dry mustard

1½ teaspoons reduced-sodium soy sauce
1½ teaspoons vinegar
1 teaspoon water

1. Combine jam, mustard, soy sauce, vinegar, and water. Whisk together all ingredients.
2. Store in the refrigerator until used.

Calories Per Serving: 74
Fat: 0 g
Cholesterol: 0 mg
Protein: 0 g

Carbohydrates: 18 g
Dietary Fiber: 0 g
Sodium: 100 mg

❧ *Scallion-and-Dill Sauce* ❧

Yogurt is blended with scallion, dillweed, mustard, and lemon peel. Store scallions wrapped in a plastic bag in the vegetable section of the refrigerator for up to 5 days.

PREPARATION TIME: 5 minutes • *YIELD: 3 servings*

¼ cup nonfat plain yogurt
1 tablespoon nonfat mayonnaise
1 scallion, minced

½ teaspoon dried dill
1 teaspoon Dijon mustard
1 tablespoon minced lemon peel

1. Combine yogurt, mayonnaise, scallion, dill, mustard, and lemon peel.
2. Chill until ready to use.

Calories Per Serving: 16
Fat: 0 g
Cholesterol: 0 mg
Protein: 2 g

Carbohydrates: 2 g
Dietary Fiber: 0 g
Sodium: 76 mg

❧ *Lemon-Horseradish Sauce* ❧

Horseradish has been widely used in food preparation for thousands of years. When fresh horseradish is available, grate your own for a sharp taste treat.

PREPARATION TIME: 5 minutes • *YIELD: 8 servings*

1 cup nonfat plain yogurt
2 tablespoons prepared horseradish

1 tablespoon lemon juice
½ teaspoon ground black pepper

1. Combine yogurt, horseradish, lemon juice, and black pepper, and mix thoroughly.

Calories Per Serving: 26
Fat: 1 g
Cholesterol: 2 mg
Protein: 2 g

Carbohydrates: 3 g
Dietary Fiber: 0 g
Sodium: 35 mg

❧ *Horseradish-Chive Sauce* ❧

Horseradish is mixed with lemon juice, yogurt, sour cream, and herbs.

PREPARATION TIME: 5 minutes • YIELD: 6 servings

1 tablespoon prepared horseradish
1 tablespoon lemon juice
⅓ cup nonfat plain yogurt
⅓ cup nonfat sour cream

2 tablespoons minced fresh parsley
1 teaspoon dried chives
½ teaspoon grated lemon peel

1. Combine horseradish, lemon juice, yogurt, sour cream, parsley, chives, and lemon peel.
2. Chill until ready to use.

Calories Per Serving: 30
Fat: 0 g
Cholesterol: 1 mg
Protein: 4 g

Carbohydrates: 4 g
Dietary Fiber: 0 g
Sodium: 60 mg

❧ *Lemon-Pepper Sauce* ❧

Lemon juice and white pepper accent this nonfat variation of an old standard.

PREPARATION TIME: 10 minutes • COOKING TIME: 3 minutes •
YIELD: 8 servings

2 tablespoons nonfat mayonnaise
2 tablespoons nonfat sour cream
¼ cup nonfat plain yogurt
1½ tablespoons water

1 tablespoon lemon juice
¼ teaspoon ground white pepper
1 tablespoon dried dill

1. Combine mayonnaise, sour cream, yogurt, water, lemon juice, and white pepper in a saucepan.
2. Stir over medium heat for 3 minutes.
3. Remove from heat and stir in dill.

Calories Per Serving: 9
Fat: 0 g
Cholesterol: 0 mg
Protein: 1 g

Carbohydrates: 2 g
Dietary Fiber: 0 g
Sodium: 54 mg

❧ *Honey-Mustard Sauce* ❧

Lemon juice, honey, and mustard are featured in this super-quick, zesty, nonfat sauce.

PREPARATION TIME: 10 minutes • *COOKING TIME: 3 minutes* •
YIELD: 8 servings

1½ tablespoons honey
3 tablespoons Dijon mustard
½ cup nonfat plain yogurt

¼ cup nonfat mayonnaise
3 tablespoons lemon juice

1. Combine honey, mustard, yogurt, mayonnaise, and lemon juice in a saucepan.
2. Stir over medium heat for 3 minutes.

Calories Per Serving: 33
Fat: 0 g
Cholesterol: 0 mg
Protein: 1 g

Carbohydrates: 6 g
Dietary Fiber: 0 g
Sodium: 223 mg

❧ *Portobello Sauce* ❧

Sun-dried tomatoes and portobello mushrooms are the essential ingredients of this wonderful sauce. Serve it over vegetables or pasta.

PREPARATION TIME: 15 minutes plus 30 minutes soaking time •
COOKING TIME: 48 minutes • *YIELD: 4 servings*

1 cup water

½ cup sun-dried tomatoes

2 tablespoons low-sodium nonfat chicken broth

5 cloves garlic, minced

1 medium onion, chopped

½ cup fresh parsley, chopped

1 jalapeño pepper, seeded and minced

3 large portobello mushrooms, chopped

3½ cups low-sodium canned tomatoes, drained and chopped

1 teaspoon sugar

½ teaspoon dried oregano

½ teaspoon dried basil

½ teaspoon ground black pepper

1 tablespoon nonfat Parmesan

1. Place sun-dried tomatoes in a bowl, cover them with water, and allow to soak for 30 minutes. Drain tomatoes and chop.
2. Heat broth in a large saucepan. Add garlic and onion, and sauté until onion begins to soften, about 3 minutes. Add sun-dried tomatoes, parsley, jalapeño, portobello mushrooms, canned tomatoes, sugar, oregano, basil, and black pepper. Simmer slowly for 45 minutes.
3. Remove from heat and stir in Parmesan before serving.

Calories Per Serving: 171

Fat: 1 g

Cholesterol: 0 mg

Protein: 7 g

Carbohydrates: 40 g

Dietary Fiber: 5 g

Sodium: 183 mg

❧ *Cucumber-Mint Sauce* ❧

This yogurt-based sauce is flavored with lemon juice and mint. Cucumbers can be stored in a plastic bag in the refrigerator for up to 10 days.

PREPARATION TIME: 10 minutes plus 1 hour chilling time ▪ *YIELD: 10 servings*

2 cups minced cucumber

2 cups nonfat plain yogurt

1 tablespoon lemon juice

1 teaspoon dried mint leaves

1. Combine cucumber, yogurt, lemon juice, and mint.
2. Chill for 1 hour before serving.

Calories Per Serving: 17

Carbohydrates: 3 g

Fat: 0 g

Dietary Fiber: 0 g

Cholesterol: 0 mg

Sodium: 19 mg

Protein: 1 g

✌ *Vegetable Raita* ✌

Used in Indian cuisine as salad, raitas are made with yogurt. This one has roasted eggplant and yellow bell peppers.

PREPARATION TIME: 10 minutes   ·   COOKING TIME: 10 minutes   ·
YIELD: 8 servings

2 eggplants, cut in half lengthwise
1 medium yellow bell pepper, cut in
*   half lengthwise and seeded*
2 cups nonfat plain yogurt
2 scallions, minced

2 tablespoons minced fresh cilantro
¼ teaspoon ground cumin
¼ teaspoon coriander
¼ teaspoon cayenne pepper

1. Preheat broiler.
2. Prick the eggplant skin with a fork. Place eggplant and bell pepper halves cut sides down on a shallow baking dish and broil until skin is charred, about 10 minutes. Cool to room temperature.
3. Combine yogurt, scallions, cilantro, cumin, coriander, and cayenne pepper in a mixing bowl.
4. Remove the charred skin off the eggplant and peppers, and discard.
5. Chop the eggplant and yellow pepper.
6. Blend the vegetables into the yogurt, and serve.

Calories Per Serving: 23

Carbohydrates: 4 g

Fat: 0 g

Dietary Fiber: 0 g

Cholesterol: 1 mg

Sodium: 23 mg

Protein: 2 g

❧ *Cucumber Raita* ❧

This combination of cucumber, tomato, and onion can be served with vegetable main dishes.

PREPARATION TIME: 10 minutes plus 2 hours chilling time   ·   YIELD: 6 servings

1 cup nonfat plain yogurt	¼ teaspoon ground black pepper
1 teaspoon dried mint leaves	⅔ cup shredded cucumber
½ teaspoon ground cumin	1 medium tomato, chopped
¼ teaspoon chili powder	1 tablespoon minced scallion

1. Combine yogurt, mint, cumin, chili powder, and black pepper.
2. Stir in cucumber, tomato, and scallion, and mix thoroughly. Chill for 2 hours before serving.

Calories Per Serving: 42	Carbohydrates: 8 g
Fat: 0 g	Dietary Fiber: 0 g
Cholesterol: 1 mg	Sodium: 28 mg
Protein: 2 g	

❧ *Ginger-Carrot-Orange Sauce* ❧

In this chunky, zesty sauce, carrot juice is combined with orange juice, gingerroot, cayenne, and cilantro. Serve over rice and mixed vegetables.

PREPARATION TIME: 10 minutes   ·   COOKING TIME: 3 minutes   ·
YIELD: 8 servings

2 cups carrot juice	3 teaspoons water
1 tablespoon orange juice	⅛ teaspoon cayenne pepper
1 teaspoon minced fresh gingerroot	1 tablespoon chopped fresh cilantro
2 teaspoons cornstarch	

1. Mix carrot juice, orange juice, and gingerroot in a sauce pan. Bring to a simmer, about 1 minute.

2. Whisk together the cornstarch and water.

3. Remove the carrot-orange mixture from the heat and stir in the cornstarch mixture. Return to heat and cook, stirring, until sauce begins to bubble, about 1 minute.

4. Stir in the cayenne and cilantro, and simmer for 1 additional minute. Serve at once.

Calories Per Serving: 76	Carbohydrates: 18 g
Fat: 0 g	Dietary Fiber: 5 g
Cholesterol: 0 mg	Sodium: 59 mg
Protein: 2 g	

❧ *Jalapeño Relish* ☙

Tomato, jalapeño, curry powder, onion, garlic, and lime juice are simmered together in this relish.

PREPARATION TIME: 10 minutes • *COOKING TIME: 10 minutes* •
YIELD: 10 servings

2 tablespoons low-sodium nonfat
   chicken broth
½ cup chopped onion
2 cloves garlic, minced
2 medium tomatoes, chopped

1 teaspoon curry powder
2 jalapeño peppers, seeded and
   minced
¼ teaspoon ground black pepper
1 tablespoon lime juice

1. Heat broth in a saucepan. Add onion and garlic, and sauté until onion begins to soften, about 3 minutes.

2. Stir in tomatoes, curry powder, and jalapeño peppers, and simmer until tomatoes are softened, about 7 minutes.

3. Remove from heat. Stir in black pepper and lime juice.

Calories Per Serving: 11	Carbohydrates: 2 g
Fat: 0 g	Dietary Fiber: 1 g
Cholesterol: 0 mg	Sodium: 68 mg
Protein: 1 g	

❧ *Jicama Relish* ❧

Serve this relish with tacos, burgers, or as a dip for raw vegetables.

PREPARATION TIME: 15 minutes ▪ *YIELD: 3 servings*

1 cup minced onion
½ cup minced jicama
3 cloves garlic, minced
2 medium tomatoes, finely chopped

1 cup finely chopped fresh parsley
1 jalapeño pepper, seeded and minced
¼ teaspoon ground black pepper
⅛ teaspoon salt

1. Combine onion, jicama, garlic, tomatoes, parsley, jalapeño, black pepper, and salt. Mix thoroughly.

Calories Per Serving: 123
Fat: 0 g
Cholesterol: 0 mg
Protein: 1 g

Carbohydrates: 7 g
Dietary Fiber: 2 g
Sodium: 154 mg

❧ *Apple-Strawberry Sauce* ❧

This warm strawberry sauce takes only 10 minutes to make and is a perfect topping for vanilla frozen yogurt or slices of angel food cake.

PREPARATION TIME: 5 minutes ▪ *COOKING TIME: 10 minutes* ▪
YIELD: 12 servings

¼ cup sugar
1 tablespoon cornstarch
¾ cup unsweetened apple juice

2 cups sliced fresh or frozen, thawed
    strawberries

1. Combine the sugar and cornstarch.
2. Place the apple juice in a saucepan. Slowly stir the sugar-cornstarch mixture into the apple juice. Bring to a boil, stirring constantly.
3. Add strawberries, return to a boil and reduce heat. Simmer, stirring frequently, for 5 minutes or until the sauce begins to thicken.

Calories Per Serving: 33   Carbohydrates: 8 g
Fat: 0 g   Dietary Fiber: 0 g
Cholesterol: 0 mg   Sodium: 1 mg
Protein: 0 g

❧ *Vanilla-Maple Topping* ❧

Skim milk, maple syrup, and vanilla are whipped together in this delightful dessert topping. Serve with warm baked apples.

Preparation Time: 10 minutes plus 45 minutes chilling time •
Yield: 4 servings

¾ cup evaporated skim milk   1 teaspoon vanilla extract
2 tablespoons maple syrup

1. Chill evaporated milk and electric mixer beaters in the freezer for 45 minutes.
2. Combine milk, maple syrup, and vanilla extract, and beat on high in an electric mixer until mixture becomes stiff, about 5 minutes. Serve immediately.

Calories Per Serving: 53   Carbohydrates: 10 g
Fat: 0 g   Dietary Fiber: 0 g
Cholesterol: 1 mg   Sodium: 38 mg
Protein: 2 g

❧ *Very Berry Topping* ❧

Strawberries, blueberries, and lemon juice are combined in this lively berry sauce, which can be served over angel food cake. Fresh strawberries are available year round but at their peak from April to June.

Preparation Time: 5 minutes • Yield: 6 servings

¼ cup sliced fresh or frozen, thawed
   strawberries
¼ cup fresh or frozen, thawed blueberries

½ teaspoon lemon juice
1½ tablespoons powdered sugar

1. Combine strawberries, blueberries, lemon juice, and powdered sugar in
   a blender and process until pureed.

Calories Per Serving: 22
Fat: 0 g
Cholesterol: 0 mg
Protein: 0 g

Carbohydrates: 5 g
Dietary Fiber: 1 g
Sodium: 1 mg

❧ Spiced Yogurt Topping ❧

Cinnamon, allspice, and nutmeg accent this sweet topping.

PREPARATION TIME: 10 minutes plus 45 minutes chilling time   ▪
YIELD: 6 servings

¼ cup evaporated skim milk
½ cup nonfat vanilla yogurt
¼ teaspoon ground cinnamon

⅛ teaspoon ground allspice
⅛ teaspoon ground nutmeg
2 tablespoons powdered sugar

1. Place evaporated milk and electric mixer blades in the freezer for 45
   minutes.
2. Combine evaporated milk, yogurt, cinnamon, allspice, and nutmeg in
   the bowl of an electric mixer and beat for 1 minute. Continue to beat as
   you gradually add the powdered sugar. Continue beating until soft peaks
   form. Serve immediately.

Calories Per Serving: 36
Fat: 0 g
Cholesterol: 0 mg
Protein: 2 g

Carbohydrates: 7 g
Dietary Fiber: 0 g
Sodium: 26 mg

ꙮ *Spicy Fruit Topping* ꙮ

Navel oranges and blueberries are spiced with cinnamon. This topping is used for nonfat vanilla ice cream.

PREPARATION TIME: 15 minutes plus 2 hours chilling time •
COOKING TIME: 15 minutes • *YIELD: 6 servings*

½ cup orange juice
3 tablespoons honey
1 teaspoon ground nutmeg

1 teaspoon ground cinnamon
3 navel oranges, peeled and sectioned
2 cups blueberries

1. Combine orange juice, honey, nutmeg, and cinnamon in a small saucepan.
2. Bring to a boil over medium heat. Reduce heat and simmer, uncovered, for 5 minutes.
3. Combine orange sections and blueberries in a bowl.
4. Stir orange sauce into fruit and chill for 2 hours.

Calories Per Serving: 93
Fat: 0 g
Cholesterol: 0 mg
Protein: 1 g

Carbohydrates: 23 g
Dietary Fiber: 6 g
Sodium: 2 mg

BREAKFAST DISHES

◦◦

Good-for-You French Toast ▪ Strawberry Pancakes ▪ Pear-
Oatmeal Pancakes ▪ Applesauce-Vanilla Waffles ▪ Applesauce-
Apple Muffins ▪ Apricot Muffins ▪ Maple-Raisin-Bran Muffins
▪ Carrot-Oat Muffins ▪ Down-Home Maple-Corn Muffins ▪
Peach Muffins ▪ Peach-Ginger Muffins ▪ Pear Muffins ▪
Raspberry Muffins ▪ Strawberry Muffins ▪ Good-Morning
Zucchini Muffins ▪ Pan-Baked Corn Cake ▪ Broiled Potato
Cakes ▪ Back Bay Brown Bread

❧ *Good-for-You French Toast* ❧ ✓

This healthy french toast recipe uses whole-grain bread and egg whites, and is flavored with maple syrup, cinnamon, and nutmeg.

PREPARATION TIME: *10 minutes* • COOKING TIME: *4 minutes* •
YIELD: *4 servings*

1 cup skim milk	*1 teaspoon vanilla extract*
4 egg whites	*¼ teaspoon ground cinnamon*
1 tablespoon maple syrup	*8 slices nonfat whole-grain bread*
1 tablespoon sugar	

1. Combine the milk, egg whites, syrup, sugar, vanilla extract, and cinnamon. Stir vigorously.
2. Heat a nonstick skillet. Dip each slice of bread in the batter and cook until lightly brown on each side, about 4 minutes total. Serve hot.

Calories Per Serving: 99	Carbohydrates: 16 g
Fat: 0 g	Dietary Fiber: 1 g
Cholesterol: 1 mg	Sodium: 147 mg
Protein: 8 g	

❧ *Strawberry Pancakes* ❧

These strawberry pancakes are easy to make. Turning a pancake more than once during cooking toughens it.

PREPARATION TIME: *10 minutes* • COOKING TIME: *8 minutes* •
YIELD: *4 servings*

¾ cup unbleached pastry flour	*1¼ cups nonfat buttermilk*
¾ cup cornmeal	*2 egg whites*
1 tablespoon sugar	*1½ cups fresh or frozen, thawed*
1 teaspoon baking soda	*strawberries*

1. Mix flour, cornmeal, sugar, and baking soda in a bowl.
2. Stir in the buttermilk and egg whites, and mix thoroughly.

3. Fold in the strawberries.

4. Heat a nonstick skillet and spoon out ¼ cup batter for each pancake. Cook until bubbles appear and edges begin to become dry. Then flip over and cook until second side is lightly browned, about 4 minutes. Serve hot.

Calories Per Serving: 69
Fat: 0 g
Cholesterol: 0 mg
Protein: 3 g

Carbohydrates: 14 g
Dietary Fiber: 1 g
Sodium: 107 mg

❧ *Pear-Oatmeal Pancakes* ❧

These pear-oatmeal pancakes take less than a half hour to make. Leftover pancakes can be frozen in a freezerproof container for up to 3 months.

PREPARATION TIME: *10 minutes* • COOKING TIME: *8 minutes* •
YIELD: *4 servings*

¾ cup quick-cooking rolled oats
2¼ cups nonfat buttermilk
1¼ cups whole-wheat flour
1 tablespoon brown sugar

1 teaspoon baking soda
¼ teaspoon ground cinnamon
4 egg whites
2 cups peeled chopped pear

1. Combine oats and buttermilk, mix well, and set aside.

2. Mix flour, brown sugar, baking soda, and cinnamon, and set aside

3. Stir the egg whites into the oat mixture. Stir in the flour mixture, add the pears, and blend thoroughly.

4. Heat a nonstick skillet and spoon out ¼ cup batter for each pancake. Cook until bubbles appear and edges begin to become dry. Then turn and cook until second side is lightly browned, about 4 minutes. Serve hot.

Calories Per Serving: 98
Fat: 1 g
Cholesterol: 1 mg
Protein: 4 g

Carbohydrates: 11 g
Dietary Fiber: 2 g
Sodium: 111 mg

❧ *Applesauce-Vanilla Waffles* ❧

These waffles are flavored with applesauce. Use a fork to lift them off the waffle iron.

PREPARATION TIME: 15 minutes ▪ COOKING TIME: 5 minutes per waffle ▪
YIELD: 4 waffles

3 egg whites
1 cup all-purpose flour
1 teaspoon low-sodium baking
  powder

½ teaspoon brown sugar
1 cup skim milk
3 tablespoons unsweetened applesauce
½ teaspoon vanilla extract

1. Preheat nonstick waffle iron.
2. Beat egg whites until they form peaks. Beat in flour, baking powder, brown sugar, milk, applesauce, and vanilla extract.
3. Pour batter onto the hot waffle iron and bake until steaming stops, about 5 minutes. Serve hot.

Calories Per Serving: 155
Fat: 0 g
Cholesterol: 1 mg
Protein: 8 g

Carbohydrates: 29 g
Dietary Fiber: 1 g
Sodium: 187 mg

❧ *Applesauce-Apple Muffins* ❧

These apple muffins are made with honey, vanilla, and applesauce. If the baked muffins should stick to the tin pan, set the hot muffin tin on a wet towel for 2 minutes.

PREPARATION TIME: 20 minutes ▪ COOKING TIME: 20 minutes ▪
YIELD: 12 muffins

1 cup all-purpose flour
¾ cup quick-cooking rolled oats
½ cup oat bran

¾ teaspoon low-sodium baking powder
½ teaspoon cinnamon
¾ cup unsweetened applesauce

½ cup honey

1 teaspoon vanilla extract

½ cup skim milk

3 egg whites, lightly beaten

1 medium apple, peeled, cored, and
chopped

1. Preheat oven to 350 degrees.
2. Combine flour, oats, and oat bran in a blender and process for 10 seconds. Mix flour mixture with baking powder and cinnamon.
3. Mix applesauce, honey, vanilla extract, and milk. Stir into the flour mixture. Stir in the beaten egg whites.
4. Stir the apple into the batter. Spoon batter into 12 nonstick muffin cups and bake until done, about 20 minutes. Serve warm.

Calories Per Serving: 132

Fat: 1 g

Cholesterol: 0 mg

Protein: 4 g

Carbohydrates: 30 g

Dietary Fiber: 2 g

Sodium: 100 mg

❧ *Apricot Muffins* ❧

These muffins are studded with dried apricots and minced orange peel. Leftover muffins should be stored in a tightly sealed plastic bag at room temperature for up to 3 days.

PREPARATION TIME: *20 minutes plus 30 minutes standing time* •
COOKING TIME: *28 minutes* • YIELD: *12 muffins*

2 cups chopped dried apricots

1½ cups water

2 tablespoons corn syrup

1 cup brown sugar

2 egg whites

1 teaspoon vanilla extract

1 teaspoon minced orange peel

2½ cups all-purpose flour

1 teaspoon salt (optional)

1 teaspoon baking soda

1 teaspoon low-sodium baking
powder

1. Preheat oven to 350 degrees.
2. Combine apricots and water in a saucepan. Bring to a simmer, cover, and simmer for 3 minutes. Remove from heat and allow to stand for 30 minutes.

3. Mix cooled apricots, corn syrup, brown sugar, egg whites, vanilla, and orange peel.
4. Combine flour, salt, baking soda, and baking powder. Stir apricot mixture into flour and mix well.
5. Spoon batter into 12 nonstick muffin cups and bake until done, about 25 minutes. Serve warm.

Calories Per Serving: 221
Fat: 0 g
Cholesterol: 0 mg
Protein: 4 g

Carbohydrates: 52 g
Dietary Fiber: 1 g
Sodium: 128 mg

❧ *Maple-Raisin-Bran Muffins* ❧

All-Bran cereal is a key ingredient in these raisin bran muffins. Bran is a good source of calcium, phosphorus, and fiber.

PREPARATION TIME: *20 minutes plus 45 minutes standing time* •
COOKING TIME: *25 minutes* • YIELD: *12 muffins*

1½ cups All-Bran cereal
1 cup raisins
2 cups skim milk
1½ cups all-purpose flour
*1 teaspoon low-sodium baking
   powder*

½ teaspoon salt (optional)
1 cup sugar
2 teaspoons vanilla extract
2 egg whites
¼ cup maple syrup

1. Preheat oven to 350 degrees.
2. Combine cereal and raisins in a large bowl. Heat 1½ cups milk (do not boil) and stir into the cereal.
3. Combine flour, baking powder, salt, and sugar. Stir in remaining milk, vanilla extract, egg whites, and maple syrup. Let batter stand for 45 minutes.
4. Spoon batter into 12 nonstick muffin cups and bake about 25 minutes. Serve warm.

Calories Per Serving: 212

Fat: 0 g

Cholesterol: 1 mg

Protein: 5 g

Carbohydrates: 51 g

Dietary Fiber: 4 g

Sodium: 117 mg

ও *Carrot-Oat Muffins* ও

These muffins are made with oat bran, shredded carrot, orange juice, maple syrup, and raisins. To reheat leftover muffins, loosely wrap in foil and place in a 325-degree oven for 10 minutes.

PREPARATION TIME: *20 minutes* ▪ COOKING TIME: *25 minutes* ▪
YIELD: *12 muffins*

3½ cups all-purpose flour
*2½ teaspoons low-sodium baking
   powder*
1 teaspoon baking soda
¼ teaspoon salt (optional)
¾ teaspoon ground cinnamon
¾ cup honey

1½ cups orange juice
¾ cup oat bran
¼ cup nonfat buttermilk
¼ cup maple syrup
¾ cup shredded carrot
¾ cup raisins
¼ cup nonfat plain yogurt

1. Preheat oven to 350 degrees.
2. Sift the flour, baking powder, baking soda, salt, and cinnamon together.
3. Combine honey and orange juice, and stir vigorously to blend. Stir in the oat bran and mix thoroughly.
4. Mix buttermilk and maple syrup in a large bowl, add the shredded carrot, and stir in the oat bran mixture.
5. Add the raisins to the flour mixture and stir in the buttermilk-oat bran mixture and the yogurt.
6. Spoon the batter into 12 nonstick muffin cups and bake until done, about 25 minutes. Serve warm.

Calories Per Serving: 254

Fat: 1 g

Cholesterol: 0 mg

Protein: 5 g

Carbohydrates: 57 g

Dietary Fiber: 2 g

Sodium: 123

❧ *Down-Home Maple-Corn Muffins* ❧

Pure maple syrup and cornmeal are key ingredients in these muffins. Pure maple syrup should be refrigerated after opening.

PREPARATION TIME: 20 minutes • *COOKING TIME: 25 minutes* •
YIELD: 12 muffins

1½ cups all-purpose flour	½ cup sugar
½ cup cornmeal	1 teaspoon vanilla extract
2 teaspoons low-sodium baking powder	2 egg whites
	1 cup skim milk
1 teaspoon salt (optional)	½ cup pure maple syrup

1. Preheat oven to 350 degrees.
2. Combine flour, cornmeal, baking powder, and salt in a mixing bowl and mix well.
3. In another bowl, combine sugar, vanilla extract, egg whites, milk, and maple syrup, and mix well.
4. Stir flour mixture into the maple syrup mixture and mix until all ingredients are moistened.
5. Spoon the batter into 12 nonstick muffin cups and bake until done, about 25 minutes.

Calories Per Serving: 149	Carbohydrates: 33 mg
Fat: 0 g	Dietary Fiber: 0 g
Cholesterol: 0 mg	Sodium: 100 mg
Protein: 3 g	

❧ *Peach Muffins* ❧

These muffins are flavored with brown sugar and cinnamon.

PREPARATION TIME: 20 minutes • *COOKING TIME: 25 minutes* •
YIELD: 12 muffins

2 cups all-purpose flour
½ cup powdered sugar
1 teaspoon low-sodium baking
    powder
½ teaspoon salt (optional)
1 teaspoon ground cinnamon

1 cup brown sugar
1 teaspoon vanilla extract
1 cup skim milk
2 cups fresh or juice-packed canned
    peaches, drained and diced

1. Preheat oven to 350 degrees.
2. Combine flour, powdered sugar, baking powder, salt, and cinnamon, and mix thoroughly.
3. Stir in brown sugar, vanilla extract, and milk. Fold in peaches.
4. Spoon batter into 12 nonstick muffin cups and bake for 25 minutes, or until done. Serve warm.

Calories Per Serving: 187
Fat: 0 g
Cholesterol: 0 mg
Protein: 3 g

Carbohydrates: 44 g
Dietary Fiber: 1 g
Sodium: 50 mg

❧ Peach-Ginger Muffins ❧

Dried peaches and candied ginger are paired in these muffins. Candied ginger is ginger that has been cooked in sugar syrup and coated with coarse sugar.

PREPARATION TIME: 20 minutes • COOKING TIME: 25 minutes •
YIELD: 12 muffins

2 cups all-purpose flour
3 tablespoons brown sugar
1 tablespoon low-sodium baking
    powder
½ teaspoon salt (optional)
½ teaspoon ground nutmeg
½ teaspoon ground cloves

2 egg whites
1 cup skim milk
¼ cup unsweetened applesauce
1 teaspoon vanilla extract
1 cup diced dried peaches
2 tablespoons minced candied ginger

1. Preheat oven to 350 degrees.
2. Combine flour, brown sugar, baking powder, salt, nutmeg, and cloves in a mixing bowl.
3. In another bowl, combine egg whites, milk, applesauce, and vanilla. Stir briskly until smooth. Combine with the flour mixture and stir just until all ingredients are moistened.
4. Fold in peaches and ginger. Spoon the batter into 12 nonstick muffin cups, and bake until done, about 25 minutes. Serve warm.

Calories Per Serving: 58
Fat: 0 g
Cholesterol: 0 mg
Protein: 2 g

Carbohydrates: 13 g
Dietary Fiber: 1 g
Sodium: 56 mg

✎ *Pear Muffins* ✎

These muffins are made with dried pears and minced orange peel.

PREPARATION TIME: 20 minutes plus 30 minutes standing time ▪
COOKING TIME: 28 minutes ▪ *YIELD: 12 muffins*

2 cups chopped dried pears
1½ cups water
2 tablespoons corn syrup
1 cup sugar
2 egg whites
1 teaspoon vanilla extract

2½ cups all-purpose flour
1 teaspoon salt (optional)
1 teaspoon low-sodium baking powder
1 teaspoon baking soda

1. Preheat oven to 350 degrees.
2. Combine pears and water in a saucepan. Bring to a simmer, cover, and simmer for 3 minutes. Remove from heat and allow to stand for 30 minutes.
3. Mix together cooled pears, corn syrup, sugar, egg whites, and vanilla extract.
4. Combine flour, salt, baking soda, and baking powder.
5. Stir pear mixture into dry ingredients.

6. Spoon the batter into 12 nonstick muffin cups and bake for 25 minutes, or until done. Serve warm.

Calories Per Serving: 221
Fat: 0 g
Cholesterol: 0 mg
Protein: 4 g

Carbohydrates: 52 g
Dietary Fiber: 1 g
Sodium: 128 mg

❧ *Raspberry Muffins* ❧

These raspberry muffins are made with skim milk and applesauce. Muffins can be frozen for up to 3 months.

PREPARATION TIME: 20 minutes • COOKING TIME: 25 minutes •
YIELD: 12 muffins

2 cups all-purpose flour
3 tablespoons sugar
1 tablespoon low-sodium baking
    powder
½ teaspoon salt (optional)
1 teaspoon ground cinnamon

2 egg whites
1 cup skim milk
¼ cup unsweetened applesauce
1 teaspoon vanilla extract
1 cup fresh or frozen, thawed raspber-
    ries

1. Preheat oven to 350 degrees.
2. Combine flour, sugar, baking powder, salt, and cinnamon in a mixing bowl. Stir well.
3. In another bowl, combine egg whites, milk, applesauce, and vanilla extract.
4. Combine egg mixture with the flour mixture and stir just until all ingredients are moistened.
5. Fold in raspberries. Spoon the batter into 12 nonstick muffin cups, and bake until done, about 25 minutes. Serve warm.

Calories Per Serving: 58
Fat: 0 g
Cholesterol: 0 mg
Protein: 5 g

Carbohydrates: 13 g
Dietary Fiber: 1 g
Sodium: 56 mg

❧ *Strawberry Muffins* ❧

These strawberry muffins take less than an hour to make. Muffins can be frozen for up to 3 months.

PREPARATION TIME: 20 minutes • COOKING TIME: 25 minutes •
YIELD: 12 muffins

1 cup all-purpose flour
1 cup whole-wheat flour
3 tablespoons sugar
1 tablespoon low-sodium baking
powder
½ teaspoon salt (optional)
½ teaspoon ground nutmeg

½ teaspoon ground cinnamon
2 egg whites
1 cup skim milk
¼ cup unsweetened applesauce
1 teaspoon vanilla extract
1 cup sliced fresh strawberries

1. Preheat oven to 350 degrees.
2. Combine all-purpose flour, whole-wheat flour, sugar, baking powder, salt, nutmeg, and cinnamon in a mixing bowl. Stir well.
3. In another bowl, combine egg whites, milk, applesauce, and vanilla extract. Stir briskly until smooth. Combine with the flour mixture and stir just until all ingredients are moistened.
4. Fold in strawberries. Spoon the batter into 12 nonstick muffin cups, and bake until done, about 25 minutes. Serve warm.

Calories Per Serving: 58
Fat: 0 g
Cholesterol: 0 mg
Protein: 2 g

Carbohydrates: 13 g
Dietary Fiber: 1 g
Sodium: 56 mg

❧ *Good-Morning Zucchini Muffins* ❧

These unique muffins are made with zucchini and raisins. When baking, check muffins by inserting a toothpick in the center. If the toothpick is clean, the muffins are done.

PREPARATION TIME: 20 minutes • COOKING TIME: 25 minutes •
YIELD: 12 muffins

2 cups all-purpose flour

2 teaspoons low-sodium baking powder

¼ teaspoon baking soda

½ teaspoon salt (optional)

3 egg whites, lightly beaten

1 teaspoon minced orange peel

½ cup corn syrup

6 tablespoons brown sugar

½ teaspoon ground allspice

1¼ teaspoons ground cinnamon

¼ teaspoon ground cloves

1 cup shredded zucchini

½ cup raisins

1. Preheat oven to 350 degrees.
2. Sift the flour, baking powder, baking soda, and salt together.
3. Whisk together the beaten egg whites, orange peel, and corn syrup. Whisk in the brown sugar, allspice, cinnamon, and cloves. Stir in the zucchini and raisins.
4. Combine the flour mixture and the liquid ingredients and stir until well blended.
5. Spoon the batter into 12 nonstick muffin cups and bake until done, about 25 minutes.

Calories Per Serving: 155

Fat: 0 g

Cholesterol: 0 mg

Protein: 3 g

Carbohydrates: 36 g

Dietary Fiber: 1 g

Sodium: 110 mg

❧ *Pan-Baked Corn Cake* ❧

This corn cake, tightly wrapped, can be frozen for up to 3 months.

PREPARATION TIME: 15 minutes • *COOKING TIME: 15 minutes* •
YIELD: 10 servings

1½ cups cornmeal

⅔ cup all-purpose flour

1 teaspoon low-sodium baking powder

1 teaspoon baking soda

1 teaspoon salt (optional)

1½ cups nonfat buttermilk

¼ cup corn syrup

2 tablespoons skim milk

5 tablespoons nonfat plain yogurt

2 egg whites, beaten lightly

1. Preheat oven to 450 degrees. Place an ovenproof, nonstick skillet in the oven for 4 minutes.
2. Sift cornmeal, flour, baking powder, baking soda, and salt together in a large bowl.
3. Combine buttermilk and corn syrup, and whisk vigorously. Add milk and yogurt, and continue to whisk until yogurt is dissolved.
4. Stir the buttermilk mixture into the flour mixture. Fold in the egg whites.
5. Pour the batter into the heated skillet, and bake for 15 minutes, or until the edges of the cornbread are brown. Serve at once.

Calories Per Serving: 141
Fat: 1 g
Cholesterol: 1 mg
Protein: 5 g

Carbohydrates: 28 g
Dietary Fiber: 0 g
Sodium: 481 mg

❧ *Broiled Potato Cakes* ❧

These potato cakes work well as a side dish or a breakfast treat.

PREPARATION TIME: *15 minutes* • COOKING TIME: *6 minutes* •
YIELD: *4 servings*

½ cup grated onion
3 cups grated potato
1 clove garlic, minced
⅓ cup whole-wheat flour

¼ teaspoon ground black pepper
¼ cup low-sodium nonfat chicken
   broth

1. Preheat broiler.
2. Combine onion, potato, garlic, flour, pepper, and chicken broth in a mixing bowl. Mix well.
3. Form the mixture into patties and broil, turning once, until heated through and lightly browned, about 3 minutes on each side. Serve hot.

Calories Per Serving: 220
Fat: 0 g
Cholesterol: 0 mg
Protein: 5 g

Carbohydrates: 51 g
Dietary Fiber: 7 g
Sodium: 29 mg

❧ *Back Bay Brown Bread* ❧

A low-fat version of the traditional accompaniment to Boston baked beans.

PREPARATION TIME: 20 minutes plus 5 minutes cooling time   •
COOKING TIME: 55 minutes   •   YIELD: 10 servings

2 cups cornmeal
1 cup rye flour
1 teaspoon low-sodium baking
   powder
1½ teaspoons baking soda

⅔ cup molasses
2 cups nonfat buttermilk
¼ teaspoon ground ginger
1 cup raisins

1. Preheat oven to 350 degrees.
2. Combine cornmeal, flour, baking powder, and baking soda in a bowl.
3. Mix molasses, buttermilk, ginger, and raisins. Stir molasses mixture into the flour mixture and stir just until all ingredients are moistened.
4. Transfer batter to a 9 × 5-inch nonstick loaf pan and bake for 55 minutes, or until done. Allow to cool for 5 minutes before serving.

Calories Per Serving: 252
Fat: 1 g
Cholesterol: 1 mg
Protein: 6 g

Carbohydrates: 56 g
Dietary Fiber: 2 g
Sodium: 174 mg

SNACKS

❦

Steamed Vegetable Dumplings ▪ Broccoli–Red Pepper Steamed
Dumplings ▪ Dumpling Dipping Sauce ▪ Spinach-Topped
Crostini ▪ Garlic Bread ▪ Roasted Garlic Bread ▪ Bean-
Stuffed Eggs ▪ Tomato Toasts ▪ Tortilla-Bean Wedges ▪
Sweet Tortilla Bites ▪ Broccoli-Chili Dip ▪ Spiced Tofu Spread
▪ Sherried Mushroom Spread ▪ Black Bean–Pinto Bean Dip ▪
Black Bean–Bell Pepper Dip ▪ Great Northern Bean Spread
▪ Spicy Black-eyed Pea Dip ▪ Red Pepper–Cumin Dip ▪
Cottage Cheese–Roasted Red Pepper Dip ▪ Garlic-Spinach Dip
▪ Classic Fresh Tomato Salsa ▪ Two Tomato Salsa ▪ Black
Bean–Tomato Salsa ▪ Roasted Fresh Tomato Salsa ▪ Jalapeño-
Mango Salsa ▪ Mango-Yogurt Dip ▪ Cherry-Yogurt Dip ▪
Peaches and Cream Dip

❧ *Steamed Vegetable Dumplings* ❧

These vegetarian dumplings feature minced spinach and shiitake mushrooms.

PREPARATION TIME: 20 minutes • COOKING TIME: 10 minutes •
YIELD: 10 servings

2 cups minced shiitake mushrooms	1 tablespoon sherry
½ cup minced onion	2 egg whites, lightly beaten
1 cup minced fresh spinach	2 teaspoons reduced-sodium soy sauce
3 cloves garlic, minced	½ teaspoon cayenne pepper
1 tablespoon minced fresh gingerroot	60 wonton wrappers
1 teaspoon curry powder	4 large lettuce, kale, or spinach leaves

1. Combine mushrooms, onion, spinach, garlic, gingerroot, curry powder, sherry, egg whites, soy sauce, and cayenne pepper in a large bowl. Mix thoroughly.
2. Place a generous tablespoon of the mixture in the center of a wonton wrapper, raise the corners of the wrapper, and pinch them together, leaving a small opening for steam to escape.
3. Line the bottom of a steamer basket with lettuce, kale, or spinach leaves, place a layer of dumplings in the steamer, and steam until dumplings are done, about 10 minutes. Serve hot.

Calories Per Serving: 164	Carbohydrates: 32 g
Fat: 1 g	Dietary Fiber: 1 g
Cholesterol: 0 mg	Sodium: 326 mg
Protein: 6 g	

❧ *Broccoli–Red Pepper Steamed Dumplings* ❧

These steamed dumplings are filled with minced onion, broccoli, bell pepper, potatoes, and an array of spices.

PREPARATION TIME: 20 minutes plus potato boiling time •
COOKING TIME: 12 minutes • YIELD: 8 servings

¼ cup low-sodium nonfat chicken
   broth
1 medium onion, minced
3 cloves garlic, minced
2 jalapeño peppers, seeded and
   minced
1 teaspoon ground cumin
1 teaspoon curry powder
½ teaspoon ground ginger
½ teaspoon turmeric

1 cup minced broccoli stems
1 medium red bell pepper, cored and
   minced
1 cup peeled, boiled potatoes, mashed
¼ cup minced fresh parsley
2 tablespoons lime juice
2 tablespoons nonfat plain yogurt
¼ teaspoon cayenne pepper
48 wonton wrappers
romaine lettuce leaves

1. Heat broth in a large skillet. Add onion and garlic, and sauté until onion begins to soften, about 3 minutes. Stir in jalapeño, cumin, curry powder, ginger, and turmeric, and sauté for 1 additional minute.
2. Add broccoli and red bell pepper, and sauté until pepper begins to soften, about 3 minutes. Remove from heat and add mashed potatoes, parsley, lime juice, yogurt, and cayenne. Mix thoroughly.
3. Place a generous tablespoon of the mixture in the center of a wonton wrapper, raise the corners of the wrapper, and pinch them together, leaving a small opening for steam to escape during the cooking process.
4. Line the bottom of a steamer basket with lettuce leaves, place a layer of dumplings in the steamer, cover, and steam until dumplings are heated through, about 5 minutes. Serve hot.

Calories Per Serving: 182
Fat: 1 g
Cholesterol: 6 mg
Protein: 6 g

Carbohydrates: 37 g
Dietary Fiber: 1 g
Sodium: 332 mg

✢ *Dumpling Dipping Sauce* ✢

This sauce is an excellent accompaniment for steamed dumplings.

PREPARATION TIME: 5 minutes ▪ *YIELD: 12 servings 2 teaspoons each*

*2 tablespoons reduced-sodium soy
    sauce*
1 tablespoon chili oil

2 tablespoons grated fresh gingerroot
3 tablespoons vinegar
1 teaspoon honey

1. Whisk together the soy sauce, chile oil, gingerroot, vinegar, and honey.
2. Serve with steamed dumplings.

Calories Per Serving: 13
Fat: 1 g
Cholesterol: 0 mg
Protein: 0 g

Carbohydrates: 1 g
Dietary Fiber: 0 g
Sodium: 93 mg

❧ *Spinach-Topped Crostini* ❧

Toasted Italian bread is topped with spinach, sun-dried tomatoes, and cayenne pepper.

PREPARATION TIME: 10 minutes plus 1 hour tomato soaking time ▪
COOKING TIME: 4 minutes ▪ *YIELD: 8 servings*

½ cup sun-dried tomatoes
*¼ cup low-sodium nonfat chicken
    broth*
2 cloves garlic, minced

4 cups chopped fresh spinach leaves
¼ teaspoon cayenne pepper
8 slices toasted Italian bread
2 tablespoons chopped fresh parsley

1. Cover the tomatoes with warm water and allow to stand for 1 hour. Remove from water and coarsely chop.
2. Heat broth in a skillet. Add garlic and sauté for 2 minutes. Add tomatoes, spinach, and cayenne, and continue to sauté until spinach wilts, about 2 minutes.
3. Divide the spinach mixture among the bread slices, sprinkle with parsley, and serve at once.

Calories Per Serving: 78
Fat: 0 g
Cholesterol: 0 mg
Protein: 3 g

Carbohydrates: 15 g
Dietary Fiber: 2 g
Sodium: 181 mg

❧ *Garlic Bread* ❧

The topping for this fat-free garlic bread is a blend of garlic, red wine vinegar, oregano, basil, and black pepper.

PREPARATION TIME: *10 minutes* • COOKING TIME: *6 minutes* •
YIELD: *12 servings*

3 tablespoons red wine vinegar
¼ teaspoon dried oregano
¼ teaspoon dried basil
¼ teaspoon ground black pepper

3 cloves garlic, minced
1 loaf Italian bread, halved lengthwise

1. Preheat broiler.
2. Whisk together the vinegar, oregano, basil, black pepper, and garlic.
3. Brush the cut sides of the bread with the dressing and broil until crisp, about 3 minutes each side. Serve hot.

Calories Per Serving: 62
Fat: 0 g
Cholesterol: 0 mg
Protein: 3 g

Carbohydrates: 14 g
Dietary Fiber: 0 g
Sodium: 155 mg

❧ *Roasted Garlic Bread* ❧

A sliced French baguette spread with roasted garlic is deliciously simple.

PREPARATION TIME: *10 minutes* • COOKING TIME: *45 minutes* •
YIELD: *9 servings*

1 whole bulb of garlic

1 French bread baguette

1. Preheat oven to 400 degrees.
2. Slice off the end of the head of garlic to expose the cloves. Wrap the garlic tightly in aluminum foil and bake until soft, about 40 minutes.
3. Slice the bread into 1-inch-thick slices. Toast the bread in the oven until golden, about 5 minutes.

4. Separate the garlic bulb into individual cloves, squeeze the garlic from the cloves, and spread it on the toasted bread. Serve immediately.

Calories Per Serving: 146 Carbohydrates: 28 g
Fat: 0 g   Dietary Fiber: 2 g
Cholesterol: 0 mg   Sodium: 305 mg
Protein: 5 g

❧ Bean-Stuffed Eggs ❧

These deviled eggs are stuffed with beans, mustard, garlic, and onion instead of high-cholesterol egg yolks. Eggs should be refrigerated and stored in the container they came in.

PREPARATION TIME: 15 minutes • YIELD: 8 servings

8 whole hard-boiled eggs   4 teaspoons Dijon mustard
2 cups low-sodium canned Great   2 cloves garlic, minced
    Northern beans, rinsed and   ¼ teaspoon ground black pepper
    drained   2 scallions, minced
¼ cup water   ½ teaspoon paprika
¼ cup chopped fresh parsley

1. Remove shells from eggs and halve lengthwise. Discard egg yolks.
2. Place beans, water, parsley, mustard, garlic, and black pepper in a food processor or blender, and process until smooth.
3. Combine pureed beans and scallions.
4. Fill egg whites with pureed bean mixture, sprinkle with paprika, and serve.

Calories Per Serving: 28   Carbohydrates: 1 g
Fat: 0 g   Dietary Fiber: 0 g
Cholesterol: 0 mg   Sodium: 214 mg
Protein: 4 g

❧ *Tomato Toasts* ❧

Toasted slices of French baguettes are topped with tomatoes, basil, garlic, and black pepper. Choose tomatoes that are free from blemishes, heavy for their size, and give slightly to palm pressure. When fresh basil is available, substitute ¼ cup chopped fresh basil leaves for the dried basil.

PREPARATION TIME: 15 minutes plus 30 minutes standing time ·
COOKING TIME: 5 minutes · YIELD: 8 servings

2 cups finely chopped tomatoes
1 tablespoon dried basil
3 cloves garlic, minced

¼ teaspoon ground black pepper
16 slices French baguettes
2 tablespoons nonfat Parmesan

1. Preheat broiler.
2. Combine tomatoes, basil, garlic, and black pepper in a bowl. Mix well and allow to stand for half an hour.
3. Place bread slices on a baking sheet and broil until lightly brown.
4. Top each bread slice with a tablespoon of the tomato mixture, sprinkle with the Parmesan, and serve.

Calories Per Serving: 61
Fat: 0 g
Cholesterol: 0 mg
Protein: 3 g

Carbohydrates: 14 g
Dietary Fiber: 1 g
Sodium: 122 mg

❧ *Tortilla-Bean Wedges* ❧

Corn tortillas are topped with scallions, pinto beans, and yellow bell pepper.

PREPARATION TIME: 15 minutes · COOKING TIME: 8 minutes ·
YIELD: 8 servings

2 scallions, finely chopped
2 cloves garlic, minced

2 cups low-sodium canned pinto
beans, rinsed and drained

1 teaspoon vinegar
1½ teaspoons chili powder
½ teaspoon dried oregano

4 corn tortillas
½ cup minced yellow bell pepper

1. Preheat oven to 400 degrees.
2. Combine scallions, garlic, beans, vinegar, chili powder, and oregano in a food processor or blender, and process until smooth.
3. Cut each tortilla into 8 wedges. Arrange in a single layer on a shallow baking dish and bake until crisp, about 8 minutes.
4. Top the wedges with the bean mixture, sprinkle with yellow pepper, and serve.

Calories Per Serving: 93
Fat: 1 g
Cholesterol: 0 mg
Protein: 5 g

Carbohydrates: 18 g
Dietary Fiber: 3 g
Sodium: 26 mg

❧ Sweet Tortilla Bites ❧

Tortilla pieces are topped with honey, cinnamon, and sugar. Honey can be stored tightly sealed in a cool, dry place for up to a year.

PREPARATION TIME: 10 minutes • COOKING TIME: 8 minutes •
YIELD: 12 servings

6 corn tortillas, each cut into 6
    wedge-shaped pieces
1 tablespoon powdered sugar

1½ teaspoons ground cinnamon
3 tablespoons honey

1. Preheat oven to 400 degrees.
2. Arrange tortilla pieces on a baking sheet and bake until crispy, about 8 minutes.
3. Combine sugar and cinnamon.
4. Top each tortilla piece with about ¼ teaspoon honey, sprinkle with the sugar mixture, and serve at once.

Calories Per Serving: 46

Fat: 0 g

Cholesterol: 0 mg

Protein: 1 g

Carbohydrates: 11 g

Dietary Fiber: 0 g

Sodium: 20 mg

❧ *Broccoli-Chili Dip* ☙

Serve this dip of broccoli, lemon juice, cumin, and garlic with sticks of carrot and celery.

PREPARATION TIME: 15 minutes plus 1 hour chilling time • *YIELD: 8 servings*

1½ cups chopped cooked broccoli
   stems and florets
1 tablespoon lemon juice
¼ teaspoon ground cumin

2 cloves garlic, minced
1 medium tomato, chopped
½ cup canned mild green chiles

1. Combine broccoli, lemon juice, cumin, and garlic in a food processor or blender, and process until smooth.
2. Transfer broccoli puree to a bowl. Stir in tomato and chiles. Refrigerate for 1 hour before serving.

Calories Per Serving: 16

Fat: 0 g

Cholesterol: 0 mg

Protein: 1 g

Carbohydrates: 3 g

Dietary Fiber: 1 g

Sodium: 50 mg

❧ *Spiced Tofu Spread* ☙

Tofu, which is a rich source of iron and protein, has been a staple of Asian cooking for centuries. It is now widely available in supermarkets.

PREPARATION TIME: 10 minutes • *YIELD: 12 servings, 3 tablespoons each*

2 cups "lite" tofu, drained
¼ cup nonfat plain yogurt
3 tablespoons Dijon mustard
2 teaspoons reduced-sodium soy sauce
½ teaspoon turmeric
3 scallions, minced
¼ cup minced celery

1. Place tofu in a bowl and mash with the back of a large spoon. Stir in yogurt, mustard, soy sauce, and turmeric. Mix thoroughly.
2. Add scallions and celery.

Calories Per Serving: 33
Fat: 1 g
Cholesterol: 0 mg
Protein: 3 g

Carbohydrates: 3 g
Dietary Fiber: 1 g
Sodium: 90 mg

❧ Sherried Mushroom Spread ❧

Mushrooms are blended with onion and garlic, then combined with lemon juice and sherry. To clean mushrooms, rinse them briefly with cold water and dry thoroughly. They should never be soaked, because they absorb water.

PREPARATION TIME: 15 minutes plus 2 hours chilling time ·
COOKING TIME: 5 minutes · YIELD: 16 servings

2 tablespoons low-sodium nonfat
chicken broth
4 cups sliced mushrooms
1 medium onion, finely chopped
2 cloves garlic, minced
2 tablespoons lemon juice
2 tablespoons sherry
¼ teaspoon ground black pepper

1. Heat broth in a skillet. Add mushrooms, onion, and garlic, and sauté until onion begins to soften, about 5 minutes.
2. Transfer mushroom mixture to a food processor or blender and process until mixture is finely chopped.
3. Combine processed mushrooms, lemon juice, sherry, and black pepper. Mix well and refrigerate for 2 hours before serving.

Calories Per Serving: 10

Carbohydrates: 2 g

Fat: 0 g

Dietary Fiber: 0 g

Cholesterol: 0 mg

Sodium: 2 mg

Protein: 1 g

❧ *Black Bean–Pinto Bean Dip* ❦

The sharp flavors of lemon, jalapeño, and garlic are combined with pinto beans and black beans.

PREPARATION TIME: 10 minutes ▪ *YIELD: 10 servings*

1 cup low-sodium canned black
   beans, rinsed and drained

1 cup low-sodium pinto beans, rinsed
   and drained

3 tablespoons lemon juice

1 jalapeño pepper, seeded and minced

3 cloves garlic, minced

¼ teaspoon ground black pepper

2 tablespoons white wine

1. Combine black beans, pinto beans, lemon juice, jalapeño pepper, garlic, and black pepper in a blender or food processor and puree.
2. Stir wine into bean puree and serve.

Calories Per Serving: 49

Carbohydrates: 9 g

Fat: 0 g

Dietary Fiber: 3 g

Cholesterol: 0 mg

Sodium: 31 mg

Protein: 3 g

❧ *Black Bean–Bell Pepper Dip* ❦

Black beans are blended with onion, bell pepper, cumin, garlic, and oregano. Serve with fat-free corn chips.

PREPARATION TIME: 10 minutes plus 3 hours chilling time ▪ *YIELD: 12 servings*

2 cups cooked or low-sodium canned
    black beans, rinsed and drained
½ cup minced onion
1 medium green bell pepper, cored
    and minced
2 cloves garlic, minced

1 teaspoon red wine vinegar
2 teaspoons lemon juice
1½ teaspoons ground cumin
¼ teaspoon dried oregano
¼ teaspoon ground black pepper

1. Puree beans in a food processor or blender.
2. Combine pureed beans with onion, bell pepper, garlic, vinegar, lemon juice, cumin, oregano, and black pepper. Mix thoroughly.
3. Refrigerate for 3 hours before serving.

Calories Per Serving: 45
Fat: 0 g
Cholesterol: 0 mg
Protein: 3 g

Carbohydrates: 8 g
Dietary Fiber: 2 g
Sodium: 5 mg

❧ Great Northern Bean Spread ❧

Great Northern beans are blended with garlic, basil, vinegar, and black pepper. Dried basil can be stored in a cool, dark place for up to 6 months.

PREPARATION TIME: 10 minutes plus 2 hours chilling time   ▪   YIELD: 12 servings

2 cups low-sodium Great Northern
    beans, rinsed and drained
2 cloves garlic, minced

2 teaspoons dried basil
2 teaspoons red wine vinegar
¼ teaspoon ground black pepper

1. Combine beans, garlic, basil, vinegar, and black pepper in a food processor or blender and process briefly.
2. Transfer to a serving bowl and refrigerate for 2 hours before serving.

Calories Per Serving: 40
Fat: 0 g
Cholesterol: 0 mg
Protein: 3 g

Carbohydrates: 7 g
Dietary Fiber: 2 g
Sodium: 2 mg

❧ *Spicy Black-eyed Pea Dip* ❧

Black-eyed peas, tomatoes, bell pepper, and scallions are combined with jalapeño, lime juice, and chili powder.

PREPARATION TIME: 15 minutes • YIELD: 20 servings

2 cups low-sodium, low-fat canned
   black-eyed peas, rinsed and
   drained
1 medium green bell pepper, cored
   and diced
2 medium tomatoes, diced
3 scallions, chopped

1 jalapeño pepper, seeded and minced
3 cloves garlic, minced
2 tablespoons lime juice
1 teaspoon chili powder
½ teaspoon ground black pepper
¼ cup fresh chopped parsley

1. Combine black-eyed peas, bell pepper, tomatoes, scallions, jalapeño, and garlic in a bowl.
2. Mix lime juice, chili powder, and black pepper. Add dressing and parsley to the vegetable mixture, and toss to coat all ingredients.
3. Serve with fat-free crackers or corn chips.

Calories Per Servings: 29
Fat: 0 g
Cholesterol: 0 mg
Protein: 2 g

Carbohydrates: 6 g
Dietary Fiber: 2 g
Sodium: 25 mg

❧ *Red Pepper–Cumin Dip* ❧

This spicy Mexican dip is made with canned roasted red peppers and sour cream.

PREPARATION TIME: 20 minutes plus 2 hours chilling time •
COOKING TIME: 5 minutes • YIELD: 12 servings

¼ cup low-sodium nonfat chicken
  broth
1 medium onion, chopped
2 cloves garlic, minced
1 teaspoon ground cumin
1 teaspoon chili powder

¼ teaspoon ground black pepper
2 tablespoons lime juice
1 cup canned roasted red peppers,
  drained
¼ cup whole-grain bread crumbs
¼ cup nonfat sour cream

1. Heat broth in a skillet. Add onion, garlic, cumin, chili powder, and black pepper. Sauté until the onion begins to soften, about 5 minutes.
2. Combine lime juice, red peppers, and bread crumbs in a food processor or blender. Add onion mixture and blend until smooth.
3. Stir in sour cream and chill for 2 hours before serving.

Calories Per Serving: 30
Fat: 0 g
Cholesterol: 0 mg
Protein: 1 g

Carbohydrates: 6 g
Dietary Fiber: 0 g
Sodium: 31 mg

❧ Cottage Cheese–Roasted Red Pepper Dip ❧

In this tasty dip, red bell peppers are roasted and combined with cottage cheese and anchovies.

PREPARATION TIME: 15 minutes ▪ COOKING TIME: 10 minutes ▪
YIELD: 6 servings

2 medium red bell peppers
1 cup nonfat cottage cheese
3 anchovy fillets, drained

2 teaspoons lemon juice
2 cloves garlic, minced
⅛ teaspoon cayenne pepper

1. Preheat broiler.
2. Cut red bell peppers in half lengthwise. Remove seeds and place cut side down on a shallow baking dish.
3. Broil until skin is charred, about 10 minutes. Remove from heat and cool. Remove the skins and chop the flesh.

4. Combine peppers, cottage cheese, anchovies, lemon juice, garlic, and cayenne pepper in a food processor or blender, and process until smooth.
5. Refrigerate until ready to serve.

Calories Per Serving: 39	Carbohydrates: 3 g
Fat: 0 g	Dietary Fiber: 0 g
Cholesterol: 2 mg	Sodium: 198 mg
Protein: 6 g	

❧ *Garlic-Spinach Dip* ❧

This spinach dip is made with cottage cheese, basil, garlic, onion, black pepper, and Parmesan cheese. Serve with fresh vegetable dippers.

PREPARATION TIME: 10 minutes plus 2 hours chilling time • YIELD: 9 servings

1 cup nonfat cottage cheese	*1 tablespoon minced onion*
½ cup chopped fresh spinach leaves	*1 tablespoon nonfat Parmesan*
1 tablespoon dried basil leaves	*¼ teaspoon ground black pepper*
2 cloves garlic, minced	

1. Combine cottage cheese, spinach, basil, garlic, onion, Parmesan, and black pepper in a food processor or blender and process until smooth.
2. Transfer to a serving bowl and chill for 2 hours before serving.

Calories Per Serving: 27	Carbohydrates: 1 g
Fat: 0 g	Dietary Fiber: 0 g
Cholesterol: 3 mg	Sodium: 58 mg
Protein: 5 g	

❧ *Classic Fresh Tomato Salsa* ❧

This bright spicy-sweet salsa is flavored with scallions, green bell pepper, jalapeño, oregano, lemon juice, and sugar.

PREPARATION TIME: 15 minutes plus 2 hours chilling time • YIELD: 10 servings

3 medium tomatoes, chopped

3 scallions, chopped

¼ cup finely chopped green bell pepper

1 jalapeño pepper, seeded and minced

2 cloves garlic, minced

2 teaspoons lemon juice

1 teaspoon sugar

¾ teaspoon dried oregano

½ teaspoon ground black pepper

1. Combine all ingredients.
2. Mix thoroughly and chill for 2 hours before serving.

Calories Per Serving: 16

Fat: 0 g

Cholesterol: 0 mg

Protein: 1 g

Carbohydrates: 3 g

Dietary Fiber: 1 g

Sodium: 35 mg

❧ *Two Tomato Salsa* ❧

This salsa is made with fresh and canned tomatoes, yellow bell pepper, onion, garlic, cilantro, oregano, black pepper, and cayenne pepper. Use it as a dip or try it as a low-calorie dressing with greens.

PREPARATION TIME: 15 minutes plus 2 hours chilling time • *YIELD: 12 servings*

2 medium tomatoes, chopped

1 medium yellow bell pepper, cored and chopped

1 medium onion, chopped

2 cloves garlic, minced

1 jalapeño pepper, seeded and minced

1 tablespoon dried cilantro

2 teaspoons lime juice

1 teaspoon chili powder

1 teaspoon dried oregano

¼ teaspoon ground black pepper

⅛ teaspoon cayenne pepper

2 cups crushed low-sodium canned tomatoes

1. Place the fresh tomatoes, yellow bell pepper, onion, garlic, jalapeño, cilantro, lime juice, chili powder, oregano, black pepper, and cayenne pepper in a food processor. Process briefly. Salsa should stay chunky.
2. Stir the crushed tomatoes into the salsa, cover, and refrigerate for 2 hours before serving.

Calories Per Serving: 34
Fat: 0 g
Cholesterol: 0 mg
Protein: 1 g

Carbohydrates: 7 g
Dietary Fiber: 1 g
Sodium: 116 mg

᭝ *Black Bean–Tomato Salsa* ᭡

This tangy salsa is made with tomatoes, black beans, corn, green bell pepper, garlic, honey, and black pepper. Serve with baked blue corn chips.

PREPARATION TIME: 15 minutes plus 2 hours chilling time • YIELD: 12 servings

4 cups chopped fresh or low-sodium
  canned tomatoes
2 cups cooked or low-sodium canned
  black beans, rinsed and drained
1 cup frozen, thawed, or low-sodium
  canned corn kernels
¼ cup minced onion

¼ cup finely chopped green bell
  pepper
2 cloves garlic, minced
1 jalapeño pepper, seeded and minced
1 tablespoon red wine vinegar
2 teaspoons honey
1 teaspoon chili powder
¼ teaspoon ground black pepper

1. Combine all ingredients.
2. Refrigerate for 2 hours before serving.

Calories Per Serving: 76
Fat: 1 g
Cholesterol: 0 mg
Protein: 4 g

Carbohydrates: 16 g
Dietary Fiber: 3 g
Sodium: 65 mg

᭝ *Roasted Fresh Tomato Salsa* ᭡

Here is a salsa with the deep flavor of roasted tomatoes, bell pepper, and onion.

*PREPARATION TIME: 15 minutes plus 20 minutes cooling time •
COOKING TIME: 15 minutes • YIELD: 4 servings*

4 medium fresh tomatoes
1 medium green bell pepper, halved
    and cored
1 medium onion, peeled and halved
2 whole garlic cloves
1 jalapeño pepper, halved and seeded

¼ cup minced fresh parsley
1 tablespoon lemon juice
½ teaspoon ground cumin
1 teaspoon dried oregano
½ teaspoon ground black pepper

1. Preheat oven to 375 degrees.
2. Place tomatoes, bell pepper, onion, garlic, and jalapeño in a shallow baking dish and bake until vegetables are just tender, about 15 minutes. Remove from oven and allow to cool sufficiently to handle.
3. Crush the tomatoes in a mixing bowl with the back of a large spoon. Chop the bell pepper and onion, mince the garlic and jalapeño, and add these to the tomatoes.
4. Stir in the parsley, lemon juice, cumin, oregano, and black pepper. Toss to mix well and serve at once.

Calories Per Serving: 36
Fat: 0 g
Cholesterol: 0 mg
Protein: 1 g

Carbohydrates: 8 g
Dietary Fiber: 2 g
Sodium: 79 mg

❧ Jalapeño-Mango Salsa ❧

This mango salsa, with red bell pepper, basil, vinegar, and jalapeño pepper can be refrigerated tightly covered for up to 5 days. Serve with chunks of honeydew melon for dipping.

PREPARATION TIME: 15 minutes plus 1 hour chilling time • YIELD: 5 servings

1 mango, peeled, pitted, and chopped
¼ cup chopped red bell pepper
1 teaspoon dried basil
1½ teaspoons red wine vinegar

2 teaspoons lime juice
½ teaspoon sugar
1 jalapeño pepper, seeded and minced

1. Combine mango, red bell pepper, basil, vinegar, lime juice, sugar, and jalapeño pepper. Mix thoroughly.
2. Chill for 1 hour before serving.

Calories Per Serving: 41
Fat: 0 g
Cholesterol: 0 mg
Protein: 0 g
Carbohydrates: 11 g
Dietary Fiber: 1 g
Sodium: 105 mg

Mango-Yogurt Dip

Mango, in season between May and September, is blended with lime juice and yogurt and flavored with allspice. Serve with fresh pineapple.

Preparation Time: 10 minutes plus 2 hours chilling time ▪ *Yield: 8 servings*

1 mango, peeled, pitted, and chopped
1½ teaspoons brown sugar
1 teaspoon lime juice
½ cup nonfat plain yogurt
¼ teaspoon ground allspice

1. Combine mango, brown sugar, and lime juice in a blender or food processor and process until smooth.
2. Add yogurt and allspice to the mango mixture. Chill for 2 hours.

Calories Per Serving: 32
Fat: 0 g
Cholesterol: 0 mg
Protein: 1 g
Carbohydrates: 7 g
Dietary Fiber: 1 g
Sodium: 10 mg

Cherry-Yogurt Dip

Serve this instant cherry dip with fresh peach slices.

Preparation Time: 5 minutes ▪ *Yield: 6 servings*

½ cup nonfat plain yogurt   ¼ cup cherry sugarless all-fruit jam

1. Combine yogurt and jam and mix thoroughly.

Calories Per Serving: 36   Carbohydrates: 8 g
Fat: 0 g   Dietary Fiber: 0 g
Cholesterol: 0 mg   Sodium: 16 mg
Protein: 1 g

❧ *Peaches and Cream Dip* ❧

A simple, quick, sweet favorite.

PREPARATION TIME: 10 minutes plus 2 hours chilling time • *YIELD: 6 servings*

¼ cup nonfat sour cream   1 tablespoon brown sugar
¾ cup nonfat plain yogurt   1 teaspoon lime juice
½ cup sugarless peach all-fruit jam

1. Combine sour cream, yogurt, jam, brown sugar, and lime juice. Mix thoroughly.
2. Cover and refrigerate for 2 hours before serving.

Calories Per Serving: 89   Carbohydrates: 20 g
Fat: 0 g   Dietary Fiber: 0 g
Cholesterol: 2 mg   Sodium: 30 mg
Protein: 2 g

BAKED DESSERTS

❧

Applesauce-Carrot Bread • Applesauce-Corn Bread • Buttermilk-Banana Quick Bread • Cinnamon Quick Bread • Cranberry-Molasses Quick Bread • Raisin-Applesauce Quick Bread • Pear-Ginger Quick Bread • Pumpkin–Golden Raisin Bread • Cinnamon-Molasses Cookies • Chewy Golden Raisin–Oatmeal Cookies • Honey–Whole Wheat–Oatmeal Cookies • Strawberry Jam Cookies • Almond-Vanilla Cake • Apple-Raisin Cake • Molasses Cake • Oranges Caramel • Peach Buckle • Peach Cake • Pear Cake • Pear-Apple-Buttermilk Cake • Maple-Pineapple Upside-down Cake • Strawberry Cake • Pumpkin-Applesauce Squares • Maple-Date Squares • Apple-Bread Pudding • Maple-Cornmeal Indian Pudding • Maple Custard

❧ *Applesauce-Carrot Bread* ❧

This moist bread is made with applesauce, chopped dried apricots, and shredded carrot.

PREPARATION TIME: 15 minutes • *COOKING TIME: 45 minutes* • *YIELD: 12 servings*

1¼ cups all-purpose flour
1 teaspoon low-sodium baking
    powder
¼ teaspoon baking soda
2 egg whites, lightly beaten

½ cup sugar
⅔ cup unsweetened applesauce
⅓ cup chopped dried apricots
½ cup shredded carrot

1. Preheat oven to 350 degrees.
2. Sift together flour, baking powder, and baking soda in a large bowl.
3. Mix egg whites, sugar, applesauce, apricots, and carrot. Gradually add to the flour mixture, stirring only enough to moisten all ingredients.
4. Transfer batter to a nonstick loaf pan sprayed with vegetable spray and bake until done, about 45 minutes. Remove from oven and allow to cool thoroughly before serving.

Calories Per Serving: 112
Fat: 0 g
Cholesterol: 0 mg
Protein: 2 g

Carbohydrates: 26 g
Dietary Fiber: 1 g
Sodium: 32 mg

❧ *Applesauce-Corn Bread* ❧

Applesauce replaces fat in this corn-bread batter.

PREPARATION TIME: 15 minutes • *COOKING TIME: 20 minutes* • *YIELD: 9 servings*

1¼ cups cornmeal
¾ cup all-purpose flour
1 tablespoon sugar

2 teaspoons low-sodium baking
    powder
½ teaspoon salt (optional)

1 cup skim milk   *2 egg whites*
¼ cup unsweetened applesauce

1. Preheat oven to 425 degrees. Heat an ovenproof nonstick skillet in the oven while mixing the batter.
2. Combine cornmeal, flour, sugar, baking powder, and salt in a small bowl.
3. Mix together the milk, applesauce, and egg whites in a large bowl. Stir the flour mixture into the liquid ingredients until just blended.
4. Transfer batter to the heated skillet and bake until lightly browned, about 20 minutes. Serve hot.

Calories Per Serving: 130   Carbohydrates: 27 g
Fat: 0 g   Dietary Fiber: 2 g
Cholesterol: 0 mg   Sodium: 28 mg
Protein: 4 g

❧ *Buttermilk-Banana Quick Bread* ❧

Bananas, cinnamon, nutmeg, and lemon juice are the featured ingredients in this easy quick bread.

PREPARATION TIME: 15 minutes · COOKING TIME: 1 hour, 15 minutes ·
YIELD: 12 servings

2 cups all-purpose flour   *½ teaspoon ground nutmeg*
¾ cup powdered sugar   *3 ripe bananas*
1 teaspoon low-sodium baking   *1 tablespoon lemon juice*
  powder   *1 cup brown sugar*
½ teaspoon salt (optional)   *1 cup nonfat buttermilk*
½ teaspoon ground cinnamon

1. Preheat oven to 325 degrees.
2. Combine flour, powdered sugar, baking powder, salt, cinnamon, and nutmeg in a bowl, and mix thoroughly.
3. Mash the bananas and mix in lemon juice, brown sugar, and buttermilk in another bowl.

4. Stir flour mixture into banana mixture and mix thoroughly.
5. Pour batter into a nonstick loaf pan sprayed with vegetable spray and bake until done, about 1 hour and 15 minutes. Serve immediately.

Calories Per Serving: 189
Fat: 0 g
Cholesterol: 0 mg
Protein: 3 g

Carbohydrates: 43 g
Dietary Fiber: 1 g
Sodium: 56 mg

❧ Cinnamon Quick Bread ❧

This easy bread is made with yogurt, sour cream, and egg whites and flavored with cinnamon and nutmeg.

*PREPARATION TIME: 15 minutes   •   COOKING TIME: 40 minutes   •
YIELD: 6 servings*

*1½ cups all-purpose flour
1 teaspoon low-sodium baking
   powder
½ teaspoon baking soda
¼ teaspoon ground nutmeg*

*¼ teaspoon ground cinnamon
½ cup nonfat sour cream
½ cup nonfat plain yogurt
¾ cup sugar
4 egg whites*

1. Preheat oven to 350 degrees.
2. Combine flour, baking powder, baking soda, nutmeg, and cinnamon in a large bowl.
3. Mix sour cream, yogurt, sugar, and egg whites in another bowl.
4. Stir sour cream mixture into dry ingredients and mix well.
5. Lightly spray an 8 × 8 × 1½-inch nonstick baking dish with vegetable spray. Transfer batter to baking dish and bake until done, about 40 minutes. Serve immediately.

Calories Per Serving: 247
Fat: 0 g
Cholesterol: 0 mg
Protein: 5 g

Carbohydrates: 56 g
Dietary Fiber: 1 g
Sodium: 143 mg

❧ *Cranberry-Molasses Quick Bread* ❧

This quick bread is made with fresh cranberries, orange juice, and vanilla. The peak season for fresh cranberries is October through December.

PREPARATION TIME: 15 minutes • *COOKING TIME: 45 minutes* •
YIELD: 10 servings

2 cups all-purpose flour
½ teaspoon low-sodium baking
   powder
½ teaspoon baking soda
2 egg whites
1½ cups sugar

2 teaspoons vanilla extract
½ cup orange juice
2 tablespoons molasses
1½ cups fresh whole cranberries,
   rinsed, drained, and chopped

1. Preheat oven to 325 degrees.
2. Combine flour, baking powder, and baking soda in a bowl.
3. Mix egg whites, sugar, vanilla extract, orange juice, and molasses in another bowl.
4. Stir the flour mixture into the orange juice mixture and mix thoroughly.
5. Fold in the cranberries and transfer to a nonstick loaf pan sprayed with vegetable spray. Bake until done, about 45 minutes. Serve immediately.

Calories Per Serving: 243
Fat: 0 g
Cholesterol: 0 mg
Protein: 3 g

Carbohydrates: 57 g
Dietary Fiber: 2 g
Sodium: 93 mg

❧ *Raisin-Applesauce Quick Bread* ❧

This bread contains iron-rich raisins.

PREPARATION TIME: 15 minutes • *COOKING TIME: 1 hour, 23 minutes* •
YIELD: 10 servings

2 cups raisins

1 cup water

2 cups all-purpose flour

2 teaspoons low-sodium baking
  powder

1½ cups sugar

2 egg whites

½ cup unsweetened applesauce

1. Preheat oven to 300 degrees.
2. Combine raisins and water in a saucepan. Bring to a boil, reduce heat, cover, and simmer for 3 minutes. Remove from heat.
3. Mix flour and baking powder in a bowl.
4. Combine sugar, egg whites, and applesauce in a separate large bowl. Stir in flour mixture and mix thoroughly.
5. Add raisin mixture and stir to blend. Transfer batter to nonstick loaf pan sprayed with vegetable spray and bake until done, about 1 hour and 20 minutes. Serve immediately.

Calories Per Serving: 346

Fat: 0 g

Cholesterol: 0 mg

Protein: 4 g

Carbohydrates: 85 g

Dietary Fiber: 4 g

Sodium: 86 mg

❧ Pear-Ginger Quick Bread ❧

This sweet gingerbread is flavored with molasses, cinnamon, and vanilla.

PREPARATION TIME: *15 minutes plus 20 minutes cooling time* •
COOKING TIME: *35 minutes* • YIELD: *12 servings*

1⅔ cups all-purpose flour

½ teaspoon low-sodium baking
  powder

1½ teaspoons ground ginger

¾ teaspoon ground cinnamon

2 egg whites

½ cup sugar

1 cup molasses

⅓ cup nonfat plain yogurt

1 teaspoon vanilla extract

2 cups chopped fresh or juice-packed
  canned pears, drained

2 tablespoons powdered sugar

1. Preheat oven to 325 degrees.
2. Combine flour, baking powder, ginger, and cinnamon in a bowl.
3. Combine the egg whites, sugar, molasses, yogurt, and vanilla extract in another large bowl. Mix thoroughly. Stir flour mixture into the molasses mixture and mix well. Fold chopped pears into the batter.
4. Transfer to a 13 × 9-inch nonstick baking dish sprayed with vegetable spray and bake until done, about 35 minutes. Allow cake to cool to room temperature, dust with powdered sugar, and serve.

Calories Per Serving: 195
Fat: 0 g
Cholesterol: 0 mg
Protein: 3 g

Carbohydrates: 46 g
Dietary Fiber: 1 g
Sodium: 90 mg

✎ *Pumpkin–Golden Raisin Bread* ✎

After baking this pumpkin-raisin bread, it will be easier to handle if you leave it in the pan for 10 minutes to allow it to cool and set.

PREPARATION TIME: 15 minutes plus 10 minutes cooling time •
COOKING TIME: 1 hour, 10 minutes • *YIELD: 12 servings*

2 cups all-purpose flour
1½ tablespoons quick-cooking rolled oats
2½ teaspoons low-sodium baking powder
1 teaspoon baking soda
½ teaspoon salt (optional)
1 teaspoon ground cinnamon

½ teaspoon ground nutmeg
1 cup sugar
¼ cup brown sugar
1¼ cups skim milk
2 cups canned pumpkin
2 egg whites
1 teaspoon vanilla extract
1 cup golden raisins

1. Preheat oven to 325 degrees.
2. Combine flour, oats, baking powder, baking soda, salt, cinnamon, and nutmeg in a bowl and mix thoroughly.

3. Mix sugar, brown sugar, milk, pumpkin, egg whites, and vanilla extract in another bowl.
4. Stir flour mixture into liquid and mix thoroughly. Stir in raisins.
5. Pour batter into a nonstick loaf pan sprayed with vegetable spray and bake until done, about 1 hour, 10 minutes. Let the bread cool for 10 minutes before serving.

Calories Per Serving: 222   Carbohydrates: 52 g
Fat: 0 g   Dietary Fiber: 2 g
Cholesterol: 0 mg   Sodium: 168 mg
Protein: 5 g

◖ *Cinnamon-Molasses Cookies* ◗

These soft and chewy molasses cookies are made with prune puree and flavored with cinnamon and ginger.

PREPARATION TIME: 15 minutes   ·   COOKING TIME: 12 minutes   ·
YIELD: 18 servings

1 cup pastry flour   1 teaspoon ground cinnamon
1 cup all-purpose flour   ¾ teaspoon ground ginger
½ cup sugar   6 tablespoons prune puree
1 teaspoon low-sodium baking   6 tablespoons molasses
  powder   2 egg whites

1. Preheat oven to 325 degrees.
2. Combine pastry flour, all-purpose flour, sugar, baking powder, cinnamon, and ginger in a large bowl. Mix well.
3. Combine prune puree, molasses, and egg whites in another bowl. Stir the prune mixture into the dry ingredients and mix until moistened.
4. Drop generous tablespoons of batter onto a nonstick baking sheet. Flatten the cookies slightly with the back of a wet spoon. Place in the oven and bake until golden, about 12 minutes.
5. Remove cookies from the oven and allow to cool on rack before serving.

Calories Per Serving: 93
Fat: 0 g
Cholesterol: 0 mg
Protein: 2 g

Carbohydrates: 21 g
Dietary Fiber: 1 g
Sodium: 13 mg

❧ *Chewy Golden Raisin–Oatmeal Cookies* ❧

To keep these chewy oatmeal cookies soft, add 1 or 2 apple quarters to the storage container, cover tightly, and let stand for 2 days, then remove the apples.

PREPARATION TIME: 15 minutes • *COOKING TIME: 15 minutes* •
YIELD: 10 servings

¾ cup quick-cooking rolled oats
1¾ cups all-purpose flour
½ teaspoon low-sodium baking
    powder
½ teaspoon baking soda
½ teaspoon salt (optional)
¾ cup unsweetened applesauce

¼ cup corn syrup
½ cup brown sugar
1 egg white, beaten
1 teaspoon vanilla extract
¾ teaspoon ground cinnamon
1 cup golden raisins

1. Preheat oven to 350 degrees.
2. Combine the oats, flour, baking powder, baking soda, and salt in a large bowl, and mix thoroughly.
3. In another bowl mix applesauce and corn syrup. Stir in the brown sugar and mix until sugar is dissolved. Add the beaten egg white and vanilla extract. Stir in the cinnamon and the oat mixture and mix until all ingredients are moistened. Fold in the raisins.
4. Drop large spoonfuls of the batter onto a nonstick cookie sheet, flatten slightly, and bake until the edges begin to turn brown, about 15 minutes. Serve warm.

Calories Per Serving: 216
Fat: 1 g
Cholesterol: 0 mg
Protein: 4 g

Carbohydrates: 50 g
Dietary Fiber: 2 g
Sodium: 85 mg

❧ *Honey–Whole Wheat–Oatmeal Cookies* ❧

These oatmeal-raisin cookies take less than an hour to make and are a great portable fat free snack.

PREPARATION TIME: 15 minutes • COOKING TIME: 12 minutes •
YIELD: 15 servings

3 cups whole-wheat pastry flour
1 cup quick-cooking rolled oats
2 teaspoons baking soda
1¾ teaspoons ground cinnamon
¼ teaspoon ground nutmeg
¼ teaspoon ground allspice

3 egg whites
¾ cup honey
½ cup thawed apple juice concentrate
¼ cup unsweetened applesauce
2 teaspoons vanilla extract
¾ cup raisins

1. Preheat oven to 350 degrees.
2. Mix flour, oats, baking soda, cinnamon, nutmeg, and allspice in a large bowl.
3. Lightly beat the egg whites.
4. Mix honey, juice concentrate, applesauce, vanilla extract, raisins, and beaten egg whites in another bowl.
5. Stir the honey-egg mixture into the flour mixture and mix to just moisten dry ingredients.
6. Drop teaspoonfuls of batter onto a nonstick baking sheet, flatten slightly, and bake until done, about 12 minutes. Serve warm.

Calories Per Serving: 182
Fat: 1 g
Cholesterol: 0 mg
Protein: 4 g

Carbohydrates: 42 g
Dietary Fiber: 1 g
Sodium: 172 mg

❧ *Strawberry Jam Cookies* ❧

These cookies are baked with strawberry jam in the middle.

PREPARATION TIME: 15 minutes • COOKING TIME: 15 minutes •
YIELD: 18 servings

2⅔ cups all-purpose flour
½ teaspoon low-sodium baking
   powder
1 cup nonfat plain yogurt
1½ cups sugar

3 tablespoons corn syrup
2 teaspoons vanilla extract
2 egg whites
1 cup sugarless all-fruit strawberry
   jam

1. Preheat oven to 325 degrees.
2. Combine flour and baking powder in a bowl. Mix thoroughly.
3. Place yogurt, sugar, syrup, vanilla extract, and egg whites in a separate large bowl, and mix thoroughly. Stir flour mixture into yogurt mixture and mix until all ingredients are moistened.
4. Drop heaping tablespoons of dough onto a nonstick baking sheet, create a small depression in the center of each, fill with ½ teaspoon jam, and bake until golden, about 15 minutes. Serve warm.

Calories Per Serving: 179
Fat: 0 g
Cholesterol: 0 mg
Protein: 3 g

Carbohydrates: 42 g
Dietary Fiber: 1 g
Sodium: 28 g

❧ *Almond-Vanilla Cake* ❧

Serve this simple cake with fresh fruit slices.

PREPARATION TIME: 15 minutes plus 5 minutes standing time and 20 minutes cooling time · COOKING TIME: 1 hour · YIELD: 10 servings

3 cups all-purpose flour
1½ cups powdered sugar
½ teaspoon low-sodium baking
   powder
1 teaspoon salt (optional)
½ cup nonfat plain yogurt

2 cups sugar
2 egg whites
1 cup skim milk
2 teaspoons vanilla extract
1 teaspoon almond extract

1. Preheat oven to 350 degrees.
2. Combine flour, powdered sugar, baking powder, and salt in a bowl. Mix thoroughly.

3. Mix yogurt, sugar, egg whites, milk, vanilla extract, and almond extract in a separate large bowl.

4. Stir flour mixture into yogurt mixture and blend thoroughly.

5. Transfer to a nonstick loaf pan sprayed with vegetable spray and bake until done, about 1 hour. Remove from oven and allow to stand for 5 minutes before removing from pan. Cool to room temperature before slicing.

Calories Per Serving: 384
Fat: 0 g
Cholesterol: 1 mg
Protein: 6 g

Carbohydrates: 89 g
Dietary Fiber: 1 g
Sodium: 51 mg

✢ *Apple-Raisin Cake* ✢

This sweet spice cake is studded with dried apples and raisins. The fat has been replaced with applesauce and prune puree.

PREPARATION TIME: 20 minutes • COOKING TIME: 40 minutes •
YIELD: 12 servings

2½ cups whole-wheat pastry flour
1 teaspoon low-sodium baking powder
½ teaspoon baking soda
1½ teaspoons cream of tartar
1 teaspoon ground cinnamon
1 teaspoon ground cloves
1 teaspoon ground nutmeg

1½ cups honey
⅓ cup orange juice
1 teaspoon vanilla extract
4 egg whites
⅓ cup unsweetened applesauce
½ cup prune puree (see glossary)
½ cup raisins
1¼ cups chopped dried apples

1. Preheat oven to 350 degrees.

2. Combine flour, baking powder, baking soda, cream of tartar, cinnamon, cloves, and nutmeg in a large bowl.

3. Mix honey, orange juice, vanilla extract, 2 egg whites, applesauce, prune puree, raisins, and apples in a separate bowl. Stir into flour mixture and

mix just until all ingredients are moistened. Beat the remaining 2 egg whites until soft peaks form and fold them into the batter mixture.

4. Transfer batter to 2 round 9-inch nonstick cake pans and bake until done, about 40 minutes. Cool to room temperature before slicing.

Calories Per Serving: 352 Carbohydrates: 87 g
Fat: 0 g Dietary Fiber: 3 g
Cholesterol: 0 mg Sodium: 224 mg
Protein: 5 g

✤ *Molasses Cake* ✤

Serve this hearty cake with cups of hot cider.

PREPARATION TIME: 20 minutes plus 30 minutes cooling time ▪
COOKING TIME: 25 minutes ▪ *YIELD: 9 servings*

⅓ cup nonfat plain yogurt
⅓ cup nonfat sour cream
⅓ cup unsweetened applesauce
3 egg whites
3 tablespoons brown sugar
2 tablespoons molasses
¾ cup whole-wheat flour

¾ cup all-purpose flour
1½ tablespoons ground ginger
1 teaspoon cinnamon
½ teaspoon ground cloves
1 teaspoon low-sodium baking powder
1 teaspoon baking soda

1. Preheat oven to 350 degrees.
2. Combine yogurt, sour cream, applesauce, egg whites, brown sugar, and molasses in a large bowl. Stir until blended.
3. Sift together the whole-wheat flour, all-purpose flour, ginger, cinnamon, cloves, baking powder, and baking soda in another bowl. Stir flour mixture into the yogurt mixture and mix just until all ingredients are moistened.
4. Transfer batter to an 8 × 8-inch nonstick baking dish sprayed with vegetable spray and bake until done, about 25 minutes.
5. Allow to cool for 30 minutes before serving.

Calories Per Serving: 127
Fat: 0 g
Cholesterol: 0 mg
Protein: 5 g

Carbohydrates: 27 g
Dietary Fiber: 2 g
Sodium: 178 mg

❧ Oranges Caramel ❧

An elegant way to finish a special meal for a special occasion.

PREPARATION TIME: 10 minutes • COOKING TIME: 3 minutes •
YIELD: 4 servings

4 navel oranges, peeled and sectioned
⅓ cup brown sugar
3 tablespoons maple syrup

2 tablespoons lemon juice
2 tablespoons water

1. Divide the oranges among individual serving dishes.
2. Combine brown sugar, syrup, lemon juice, and water in a small saucepan. Bring to a boil, reduce heat, and simmer until mixture begins to thicken, about 3 minutes. Pour the sauce over the oranges and serve at once.

Calories Per Serving: 168
Fat: 0 g
Cholesterol: 0 mg
Protein: 1 g

Carbohydrates: 43 g
Dietary Fiber: 3 g
Sodium: 10 mg

❧ Peach Buckle ❧

Peaches are baked under a thick crust. This recipe works well with a variety of fresh fruits.

PREPARATION TIME: 20 minutes • COOKING TIME: 30 minutes •
YIELD: 8 servings

⅓ cup sugar

4 cups fresh or juice-packed canned
   sliced peaches, drained

6 tablespoons skim milk

3 egg whites

¾ cup all-purpose flour

¾ teaspoon low-sodium baking
   powder

1. Preheat oven to 400 degrees.
2. Toss 2 teaspoons sugar with the peaches.
3. Whisk together the milk and egg whites in a large bowl. Combine remaining sugar, flour, and baking powder in a separate bowl. Add flour mixture to the milk–egg mixture and stir to blend.
4. Put peaches in a 9-inch nonstick baking dish. Pour the batter over the peaches and bake until topping is browned, about 30 minutes. Serve hot.

Calories Per Serving: 114

Fat: 0 g

Cholesterol: 0 mg

Protein: 3 g

Carbohydrates: 25 g

Dietary Fiber: 1 g

Sodium: 61 mg

❧ *Peach Cake* ❧

Peaches are baked into a cake flavored with orange juice and cinnamon.

PREPARATION TIME: *15 minutes* • COOKING TIME: *1 hour, 30 minutes* •
YIELD: *12 servings*

2 cups fresh or juice-packed canned
   peaches, drained and chopped

2 teaspoons ground cinnamon

3 cups all-purpose flour

2 teaspoons low-sodium baking
   powder

2 cups sugar

4 egg whites

½ cup skim milk

½ cup light corn syrup

1 tablespoon thawed orange juice concentrate

2 teaspoons vanilla extract

1. Preheat oven to 300 degrees.
2. Toss chopped peaches with cinnamon in a mixing bowl.

3. Combine flour and baking powder in a separate bowl.

4. Combine sugar, egg whites, milk, corn syrup, orange juice concentrate, and vanilla extract in another large bowl, and mix thoroughly. Stir in flour mixture and fold in peaches.

5. Transfer batter to a nonstick loaf pan sprayed with vegetable spray and bake until done, about 1 hour and 30 minutes.

Calories Per Serving: 379   Carbohydrates: 90 g
Fat: 0 g   Dietary Fiber: 2 g
Cholesterol: 0 mg   Sodium: 95 mg
Protein: 5 g

❧ *Pear Cake* ❧

This spiced pear cake contains honey and raisins. Before baking, be sure the rack is in the center of the oven.

PREPARATION TIME: 20 minutes   •   COOKING TIME: 40 minutes   •
YIELD: 12 servings

2½ cups whole-wheat pastry flour   *½ teaspoon vanilla extract*
1 teaspoon low-sodium baking   *½ cup unsweetened applesauce*
* powder*   *½ cup prune puree*
½ teaspoon baking soda   *⅓ cup apple juice*
1½ teaspoons cream of tartar   *4 egg whites*
2 teaspoons ground cinnamon   *2½ cups chopped pear*
¾ teaspoon ground cloves   *½ cup golden raisins*
1½ cups honey

1. Preheat oven to 325 degrees.

2. Combine flour, baking powder, baking soda, cream of tartar, cinnamon, and cloves in a large bowl.

3. Mix honey, vanilla extract, applesauce, prune puree, apple juice, and 2 egg whites in another bowl. Stir in pear and raisins. Stir into flour mixture and mix just until all ingredients are moistened. Beat the remaining 2 egg whites until soft peaks form and fold them into the batter.

4. Transfer batter to 2 round 9 × 1½-inch nonstick baking pans sprayed with vegetable spray and bake until done, about 40 minutes.

Calories Per Serving: 293
Fat: 0 g
Cholesterol: 0 mg
Protein: 4 g

Carbohydrates: 72 g
Dietary Fiber: 2 g
Sodium: 87 mg

❧ *Pear-Apple-Buttermilk Cake* ❧

Pear and apple are baked with a buttermilk-applesauce batter.

PREPARATION TIME: 20 minutes plus 15 minutes cooling time •
COOKING TIME: 45 minutes • *YIELD: 10 servings*

¼ cup honey
¼ cup brown sugar
1 large apple, peeled, cored, and
    thinly sliced
1 large pear, cored and thinly sliced
¾ cup sugar
½ cup corn syrup
1 egg white

1 cup unsweetened applesauce
½ cup nonfat buttermilk
1 teaspoon low-sodium baking
    powder
1½ teaspoons ground cinnamon
½ teaspoon salt (optional)
2½ cups all-purpose flour

1. Heat honey and brown sugar in a saucepan over low heat. Simmer and stir until sugar is dissolved, about 5 minutes. Add apple and pear slices and continue to simmer until fruit begins to soften.
2. Pour apple mixture into a 9-inch nonstick cake pan.
3. Combine sugar and corn syrup in an electric mixer and beat until well mixed. Add the egg white and beat at high speed until smooth. Stir in the applesauce and buttermilk, and beat for 1 more minute.
4. Mix baking powder, cinnamon, salt, and flour, and stir into the sugar-syrup mixture. Continue mixing until batter is free of lumps.
5. Spoon the batter over the apple mixture in the cake pan and bake until done, about 40 minutes.
6. Remove from the oven and cool for 15 minutes before serving.

Calories Per Serving: 167

Fat: 1 g

Cholesterol: 1 mg

Protein: 5 g

Carbohydrates: 35 g

Dietary Fiber: 1 g

Sodium: 217 mg

❧ *Maple-Pineapple Upside-down Cake* ☙

This moist cake is flavored with maple syrup and vanilla. Pineapple is traditionally the most popular flavor of upside-down cakes.

PREPARATION TIME: 20 minutes plus 10 minutes cooling time ▪
COOKING TIME: 35 minutes ▪ *YIELD: 12 servings*

1 cup brown sugar

¼ cup maple syrup

½ cup skim milk

*10 water-packed canned pineapple
slices, drained, ½ cup liquid
reserved*

1 cup sugar

2 egg whites

2 teaspoons vanilla extract

1½ cups all-purpose flour

*½ teaspoon low-sodium baking
powder*

1. Preheat oven to 325 degrees.
2. Mix brown sugar, maple syrup, and ¼ cup milk, and spread mixture on the bottom of a 9 × 13-inch nonstick baking dish.
3. Cut pineapple slices in half and arrange them in a single layer on top of the brown sugar mixture.
4. Combine reserved pineapple liquid, sugar, egg whites, vanilla extract, and remaining milk, and mix thoroughly. Mix flour and baking powder, and stir mixture into the egg white mixture until dry ingredients are completely incorporated.
5. Pour batter over the pineapple slices in the baking dish and bake until done, about 35 minutes.
6. Allow to cool for 10 minutes, turn out onto a plate, and serve.

Calories Per Serving: 247

Fat: 0 g

Cholesterol: 0 mg

Protein: 3 g

Carbohydrates: 60 g

Dietary Fiber: 1 g

Sodium: 37 mg

❧ *Strawberry Cake* ❧

Strawberries are flavored with vanilla in this classic cake.

PREPARATION TIME: 15 minutes plus 20 minutes cooling time •
COOKING TIME: 50 minutes • *YIELD: 12 servings*

3 cups all-purpose flour
2 teaspoons low-sodium baking
   powder
2 cups sugar
1½ cups skim milk

2 teaspoons vanilla extract
2 egg whites
1 cup fresh or frozen, thawed strawberries, hulled and sliced

1. Preheat oven to 300 degrees.
2. Combine flour and baking powder in a bowl and mix well.
3. Combine sugar, milk, vanilla extract, and egg whites in a separate large bowl. Stir flour mixture into egg white mixture and mix thoroughly. Fold in strawberries, transfer to a nonstick loaf pan sprayed with vegetable spray, and bake until done, about 50 minutes.
4. Allow to cool before serving.

Calories Per Serving: 290
Fat: 0 g
Cholesterol: 1 mg
Protein: 6 g

Carbohydrates: 66 g
Dietary Fiber: 1 g
Sodium: 27 mg

❧ *Pumpkin-Applesauce Squares* ❧

These squares are spiced with cinnamon, ginger, cloves, and allspice—just like pumpkin pie.

PREPARATION TIME: 15 minutes plus 10 minutes cooling time •
COOKING TIME: 20 minutes • *YIELD: 24 servings*

6 egg whites

1 cup unsweetened applesauce

1½ cups sugar

2 cups canned pumpkin

2 cups all-purpose flour

3 teaspoons low-sodium baking
  powder

2 teaspoons ground cinnamon

½ teaspoon ground ginger

¼ teaspoon ground cloves

½ teaspoon allspice

1. Preheat oven to 375 degrees.
2. Combine egg whites, applesauce, sugar, and pumpkin in a large bowl,
   and mix thoroughly.
3. Mix flour, baking powder, cinnamon, ginger, cloves, and allspice in a
   separate bowl.
4. Combine flour mixture and applesauce–pumpkin mixture. Stir just until
   all ingredients are moistened.
5. Transfer to an 8 × 8-inch nonstick baking dish sprayed with vegetable
   spray and bake until lightly browned, about 20 minutes. Allow to cool
   before serving.

Calories Per Serving: 101

Fat: 0 g

Cholesterol: 0 mg

Protein: 2 g

Carbohydrates: 24 g

Dietary Fiber: 1 g

Sodium: 20 mg

❧ *Maple-Date Squares* ❧

These chewy bars are made with dates and cinnamon. Fresh dates can be
stored in a plastic bag in the refrigerator for up to 2 weeks.

PREPARATION TIME: 15 minutes plus 15 minutes cooling time •
COOKING TIME: 30 minutes • *YIELD: 12 servings*

1 cup all-purpose flour

½ teaspoon low-sodium baking
  powder

½ teaspoon ground cinnamon

2 tablespoons maple syrup

1 cup brown sugar

6 egg whites

2 teaspoons vanilla extract

2 cups chopped dates

1. Preheat oven to 300 degrees.
2. Sift together flour, baking powder, and cinnamon in a bowl.
3. Combine maple syrup, brown sugar, egg whites, and vanilla extract in a large bowl. Stir flour mixture into egg white mixture and mix well.
4. Fold in dates. Transfer batter to an 8 × 8-inch nonstick baking dish sprayed with vegetable spray and bake until done, about 30 minutes. Remove from oven, allow to cool to room temperature, and cut into squares to serve.

Calories Per Serving: 186
Fat: 0 g
Cholesterol: 0 mg
Protein: 3 g

Carbohydrates: 45 g
Dietary Fiber: 3 g
Sodium: 49 mg

✑ *Apple-Bread Pudding* ✒

Apples, maple syrup, cinnamon, vanilla, and raisins are the main ingredients in this variation on the classic bread pudding.

PREPARATION TIME: 20 minutes plus 25 minutes standing time •
COOKING TIME: 40 minutes • *YIELD: 6 servings*

2 tablespoons lemon juice
3 medium tart apples, peeled, cored,
   and finely chopped
1½ cups skim milk
2 egg whites
½ cup maple syrup

2 teaspoons ground cinnamon
1 teaspoon ground nutmeg
¼ teaspoon vanilla extract
4 cups cubed nonfat bread
½ cup raisins

1. Preheat oven to 325 degrees.
2. Sprinkle lemon juice on apples and toss to coat.
3. Combine milk, egg whites, maple syrup, 1 teaspoon cinnamon, nutmeg, and vanilla extract in a bowl. Mix well.
4. Place one half of the bread in the bottom of a 9 × 9 × 2-inch baking dish; cover with half the raisins and half the apples. Pour one third of the liquid mixture over the apples. Repeat the layers: half the bread, half the raisins, half the apples, and one third of the liquid. Pour the remaining

one third of the liquid over the top and sprinkle with the remaining teaspoon of cinnamon.

5. Allow the pudding to stand for 15 minutes, cover, and bake for 40 minutes.

6. Remove from the oven and allow to stand for 10 minutes before serving.

Calories Per Serving: 177   Carbohydrates: 39 g
Fat: 0 g   Dietary Fiber: 2 g
Cholesterol: 1 mg   Sodium: 154 mg
Protein: 5 g

❧ *Maple-Cornmeal Indian Pudding* ❧

This pudding is flavored with molasses and cinnamon.

PREPARATION TIME: *15 minutes plus 5 minutes standing time* •
COOKING TIME: *15 minutes* • YIELD: *6 servings*

1 cup cornmeal   *2 cups water*
⅓ cup brown sugar   *2 teaspoons molasses*
¾ teaspoon ground cinnamon   *⅓ cup raisins*
1½ cups skim milk

1. Combine cornmeal, brown sugar, and cinnamon in a saucepan. Stir in milk.

2. Stir in water, molasses, and raisins. Bring to a boil, reduce heat, and simmer, stirring frequently, until mixture begins to thicken, about 15 minutes. Remove from heat.

3. Transfer to individual bowls and allow to stand for 5 minutes before serving.

Calories Per Serving: 177   Carbohydrates: 40 g
Fat: 1 g   Dietary Fiber: 2 g
Cholesterol: 1 mg   Sodium: 32 mg
Protein: 4 g

❧ *Maple Custard* ❧

Maple syrup and lemon top individual egg-white custard cups. Custards require slow cooking and gentle heat in order to prevent separation.

PREPARATION TIME: 15 minutes plus 10 minutes cooling time and 2 hours chilling time • COOKING TIME: 45 minutes • YIELD: 4 servings

1½ cups evaporated skim milk
4 egg whites
⅓ cup sugar
2 teaspoons fresh minced lemon peel

1 teaspoon vanilla extract
4 teaspoons maple syrup
¼ teaspoon lemon extract

1. Mix the evaporated milk, egg whites, sugar, lemon peel, and vanilla extract. Whisk briskly and divide mixture among 4 custard cups.
2. Place custard cups in a large baking pan and surround the cups with 1½ inches of hot water. Transfer to the oven and bake until the custard is set, about 45 minutes.
3. Remove from oven and allow to cool for several minutes, then chill in the refrigerator for 2 hours. Mix the syrup and the lemon extract, and top each custard before serving.

Calories Per Serving: 173
Fat: 0 g
Cholesterol: 3 mg
Protein: 11 g

Carbohydrates: 32 g
Dietary Fiber: 0 g
Sodium: 167 mg

FROZEN DESSERTS AND DRINKS

❧

Apricot Freeze ▪ Blueberry Ice ▪ Blueberry Cream ▪
Grapefruit Sorbet ▪ Kiwi Freeze ▪ Melon-Mango Freeze ▪
Papaya Sorbet ▪ Ginger-Pear Freeze ▪ Pineapple Sorbet ▪
Frozen Yogurt with Raspberry Sauce ▪ Strawberry Sorbet
▪ Lemon-Blueberry Sorbet ▪ Orange Shake ▪ Cranberry-
Lemon Spritzer ▪ Ginger-Fruit Punch ▪ Ginger Ale Punch ▪
Honeyed Orange-Blueberry Shake ▪ Peach Shake ▪ Strawberry
Iced Tea Spritzer ▪ Strawberry Shake ▪ Morning Honey-
Banana Shake

❧ *Apricot Freeze* ❧

Other fruits and flavors of jam can be substituted in this quick and easy frozen dessert.

PREPARATION TIME: 10 minutes plus 30 minutes freezing time •
YIELD: 4 servings

2 cups fresh or water-packed canned
   apricots
3 tablespoons sugarless all-fruit apricot jam

3 cups nonfat plain yogurt
½ teaspoon vanilla extract

1. Combine apricots, apricot jam, yogurt, and vanilla extract in a blender or food processor. Blend until smooth.
2. Transfer to a plastic container and place in the freezer for 30 minutes before serving.

Calories Per Serving: 139
Fat: 0 g
Cholesterol: 4 mg
Protein: 11 g

Carbohydrates: 26 g
Dietary Fiber: 1 g
Sodium: 124 mg

❧ *Blueberry Ice* ❧

This delectable frozen dessert is made with fresh blueberries and apple juice and spiced with nutmeg.

PREPARATION TIME: 15 minutes plus 1 hour chilling time and additional freezing time • *COOKING TIME: 2 minutes* • *YIELD: 8 servings*

2 cups fresh blueberries
1 cup apple juice
5 tablespoons sugarless all-fruit blueberry jam

3 tablespoons sugar
3 cups evaporated skim milk, chilled
½ teaspoon vanilla extract
¼ teaspoon nutmeg

1. Place blueberries and apple juice in a saucepan. Bring to a boil, reduce heat, and simmer for 2 minutes. Stir in blueberry jam and sugar, and chill for 1 hour.
2. Combine blueberry mixture, milk, vanilla extract, and nutmeg. Transfer to an ice cream maker and process according to manufacturer's instructions.

Calories Per Serving: 135

Fat: 0 g

Cholesterol: 3 mg

Protein: 7 g

Carbohydrates: 26 g

Dietary Fiber: 1 g

Sodium: 123 mg

❧ *Blueberry Cream* ❧

Blueberries, lemon juice, and yogurt are pureed with egg white and frozen.

PREPARATION TIME: 10 minutes plus freezing time • YIELD: 4 servings

1 cup fresh blueberries
¼ cup honey
1 teaspoon lemon juice

2 cups nonfat plain yogurt
1 egg white, lightly beaten

1. Combine blueberries, honey, and lemon juice in a blender or food processor, and puree.
2. Mix blueberry puree and yogurt, and place in the freezer until edges begin to harden. Fold in the egg white and return to the freezer until frozen.

Calories Per Serving: 159

Fat: 0 g

Cholesterol: 0 mg

Protein: 7 g

Carbohydrates: 33 g

Dietary Fiber: 1 g

Sodium: 112 mg

❧ *Grapefruit Sorbet* ❧

Grapefruit and honey are united in this light, delicious dessert.

PREPARATION TIME: *10 minutes plus 2 hours freezing time* • YIELD: *4 servings*

4 medium grapefruits, peeled, sectioned, and chopped	*2 cups water*
3 tablespoons honey	*½ teaspoon ground cinnamon*
	½ teaspoon ground nutmeg

1. Combine grapefruit, honey, water, cinnamon, and nutmeg in a blender or food processor, and process until smooth.
2. Transfer to a plastic container and place in the freezer until the edges of the mixture begin to harden.
3. Stir until mixture is smooth, return to the freezer, and freeze until creamy.

Calories Per Serving: 123
Fat: 0 g
Cholesterol: 0 mg
Protein: 1 g

Carbohydrates: 32 g
Dietary Fiber: 3 g
Sodium: 4 mg

❧ *Kiwi Freeze* ❧

Kiwifruit and orange juice are blended, then frozen. Ripe kiwis can be stored in the refrigerator up to 3 weeks.

PREPARATION TIME: *15 minutes plus freezing time* • YIELD: *4 servings*

4 kiwifruits, peeled and cut into chunks	*3 cups orange juice*

1. Place kiwi chunks in a blender or food processor and blend until smooth.
2. Combine kiwi puree and orange juice. Mix well, cover, and place in the freezer until almost firm.
3. Remove from freezer, stir until smooth, and return to freezer until firm.

Calories Per Serving: 130
Fat: 1 g
Cholesterol: 0 mg
Protein: 2 g

Carbohydrates: 31 g
Dietary Fiber: 4 g
Sodium: 5 mg

❧ *Melon-Mango Freeze* ❧

The mango is mixed with melon and sweetened with brown sugar and maple syrup to produce this light, flavorful dish.

PREPARATION TIME: 15 minutes plus freezing time • *YIELD: 8 servings*

3 cups chopped mango
1 cup chopped honeydew melon
¼ cup maple syrup

1 tablespoon brown sugar
½ cup water
2 tablespoons lemon juice

1. Combine mango, honeydew, maple syrup, brown sugar, water, and lemon juice in a blender or food processor, and process until smooth.
2. Pour into a shallow plastic container and place in the freezer. When the mixture begins to freeze around the edges, stir well and return to the freezer until sorbet reaches the desired consistency.

Calories Per Serving: 98
Fat: 0 g
Cholesterol: 0 mg
Protein: 1 g

Carbohydrates: 25 g
Dietary Fiber: 2 g
Sodium: 7 mg

❧ *Papaya Sorbet* ❧

Papaya and lemon juice are pureed to create this tangy sorbet. Sorbet, unlike sherbet, never contains milk.

PREPARATION TIME: 10 minutes plus freezing time •
COOKING TIME: 3 minutes • *YIELD: 8 servings*

½ cup water
½ cup sugar

4 papayas, peeled, seeded, and diced
¼ cup lemon juice

1. Combine water and sugar in a saucepan and simmer, stirring occasionally, until sugar is dissolved, about 3 minutes. Remove from heat and allow to cool to room temperature.
2. Place the papayas in a blender or food processor and puree. Add the sugar syrup and lemon juice, and mix well.
3. Transfer to an ice cream maker and process according to the manufacturer's instructions.

Calories Per Serving: 118	Carbohydrates: 31 g
Fat: 0 g	Dietary Fiber: 2 g
Cholesterol: 0 mg	Sodium: 3 mg
Protein: 1 g	

೨ *Ginger-Pear Freeze* ೮

Pears, ginger, and orange juice are combined in this frozen dessert.

PREPARATION TIME: *10 minutes plus 30 minutes freezing time* •
YIELD: *4 servings*

4 cups water-packed canned pear halves, drained and cut into chunks

6 slices candied ginger
½ cup orange juice

1. Place pears, 2 slices ginger, and the orange juice in a blender or food processor, and puree.
2. Transfer to a freezerproof container and place in the freezer for 30 minutes.
3. Remove, stir to blend, and serve garnished with remaining ginger.

Calories Per Serving: 144	Carbohydrates: 37 g
Fat: 0 g	Dietary Fiber: 5 g
Cholesterol: 0 mg	Sodium: 11 mg
Protein: 1 g	

❧ *Pineapple Sorbet* ❧

This sorbet not only is delicious but is also a good source of vitamin C.

PREPARATION TIME: 10 minutes plus freezing time • *YIELD: 6 servings*

*4 cups crushed water-packed canned
pineapple, drained*

2 cups pineapple juice
¼ cup sugar

1. Puree pineapple in a blender or food processor.
2. Combine the pineapple puree, pineapple juice, and sugar, and mix until sugar is dissolved.
3. Transfer mixture to an ice cream maker and process according to the manufacturer's instructions.

Calories Per Serving: 137
Fat: 0 g
Cholesterol: 0 mg
Protein: 1 g

Carbohydrates: 30 g
Dietary Fiber: 2 g
Sodium: 2 mg

❧ *Frozen Yogurt with Raspberry Sauce* ❧

Raspberries are blended with sugar and skim milk to create a wonderful sauce for frozen yogurt.

PREPARATION TIME: 10 minutes plus 30 minutes chilling time •
YIELD: 6 servings

¾ cup fresh raspberries
3 tablespoons skim milk

1 tablespoon brown sugar
4 cups nonfat vanilla frozen yogurt

1. Place berries, milk, and brown sugar in a blender or food processor. Blend until smooth. Transfer to a bowl, cover, and chill for 30 minutes.
2. Spoon over yogurt and serve.

Calories Per Serving: 138 Carbohydrates: 28 g
Fat: 0 g Dietary Fiber: 1 g
Cholesterol: 3 mg Sodium: 97 mg
Protein: 8 g

❧ *Strawberry Sorbet* ❧

Because this dessert is made from frozen strawberries, it is a perfect choice for a winter dessert when fresh berries are hard to find.

PREPARATION TIME: 10 minutes plus cooling time and freezing time ▪
COOKING TIME: 3 minutes ▪ *YIELD: 6 servings*

½ cup water 2½ cups frozen strawberries, partially
½ cup sugar thawed
  3 tablespoons lemon juice

1. Combine water and sugar in a saucepan and simmer, stirring occasionally, until sugar is dissolved, about 3 minutes. Remove from heat and allow to cool to room temperature.
2. Place partially thawed strawberries, with their juice, in a food processor or blender. Add sugar syrup and lemon juice, and blend until smooth.
3. Transfer mixture to an ice cream maker and process according to the manufacturer's instructions.

Calories Per Serving: 168 Carbohydrates: 45 g
Fat: 0 g Dietary Fiber: 8 g
Cholesterol: 0 mg Sodium: 4 mg
Protein: 1 g

❧ *Lemon-Blueberry Sorbet* ❧

A refreshing blend of seltzer and lemon juice brighten the fresh blueberries in this quick and easy dessert.

PREPARATION TIME: 15 minutes plus freezing time ▪ *YIELD: 6 servings*

4 cups seltzer water, chilled   *½ cup sugar*
2 cups fresh blueberries   *¼ cup lemon juice*

1. Combine seltzer water, blueberries, sugar, and lemon juice in a blender or food processor, and blend until smooth. Transfer to a plastic container, cover, and place in the freezer until almost firm.
2. Remove, stir vigorously until smooth, and return to freezer until firm.

Calories Per Serving: 94   Carbohydrates: 24 g
Fat: 0 g   Dietary Fiber: 1 g
Cholesterol: 0 mg   Sodium: 5 mg
Protein: 0 g

❧ *Orange Shake* ☙

Orange juice, skim milk, and vanilla are combined in this creamy orange shake.

PREPARATION TIME: 5 minutes • *YIELD: 6 servings*

12 ice cubes   *1 cup skim milk*
½ cup sugar   *1 teaspoon vanilla extract*
1 cup water   *2 cups orange juice*

1. Combine ice cubes, sugar, water, skim milk, vanilla extract, and orange juice in a blender or food processor. Blend until smooth.
2. Pour into individual glasses and serve.

Calories Per Serving: 118   Carbohydrates: 28 g
Fat: 0 g   Dietary Fiber: 1 g
Cholesterol: 1 mg   Sodium: 23 mg
Protein: 2 g

❧ *Cranberry-Lemon Spritzer* ❧

This fat-free, low-sodium combination of frozen lemonade, cranberry juice, and seltzer is a quick and refreshing way to cool off on a summer day.

PREPARATION TIME: 5 minutes • *YIELD: 6 servings*

1 6-ounce can frozen lemonade con-
    centrate
2¼ cups water

1½ cups cranberry juice
1 12-ounce can seltzer water
lime wedges

1. Combine lemonade concentrate, water, and cranberry juice. Chill thoroughly.
2. Stir in seltzer water and serve over ice. Garnish with lime wedges.

Calories Per Serving: 108
Fat: 0 g
Cholesterol: 0 mg
Protein: 0 g

Carbohydrates: 28 g
Dietary Fiber: 0 g
Sodium: 6 mg

❧ *Ginger-Fruit Punch* ❧

This combination of four fruit juices makes a great party drink and is quick and easy to prepare.

PREPARATION TIME: 10 minutes • *YIELD: 30 servings*

3 cups apple juice, chilled
1½ cups orange juice, chilled
6 cups cranberry juice, chilled
½ cup lime juice, chilled

1 medium lime, thinly sliced
1 navel orange, thinly sliced
2 28-ounce bottles diet ginger ale,
    chilled

1. Combine apple, orange, cranberry, and lime juices in punch bowl.
2. Add lime and orange slices, stir in ginger ale, and serve.

Calories Per Serving: 40

Carbohydrates: 15 g

Fat: 0 g

Dietary Fiber: 0 g

Cholesterol: 0 mg

Sodium: 5 mg

Protein: 0 g

❧ *Ginger Ale Punch* ❧

This punch gets added zing from fruit-flavored frozen sherbet and diet ginger ale.

PREPARATION TIME: 5 minutes • YIELD: 8 servings

1 cup orange juice, chilled

½ cup sugar

½ cup lemon juice, chilled

1 pint nonfat orange sherbet

2 cups cranberry juice, chilled

4 cups diet ginger ale, chilled

1. Combine orange juice, lemon juice, cranberry juice, and sugar in a large serving bowl.
2. Scoop sherbet into punch. Pour in ginger ale, stir, and serve.

Calories Per Serving: 197

Carbohydrates: 48 g

Fat: 0 g

Dietary Fiber: 0 g

Cholesterol: 0 mg

Sodium: 39 mg

Protein: 2 g

❧ *Honeyed Orange-Blueberry Shake* ❧

This shake is a nutritious and delicious snack in a glass.

PREPARATION TIME: 5 minutes • YIELD: 4 servings

1 cup blueberries, hulled and sliced

1 cup orange juice

1 medium banana, peeled and cut
   into chunks

2 tablespoons honey

¼ teaspoon vanilla extract

1 cup nonfat plain yogurt

12 ice cubes

1. Combine blueberries, banana, yogurt, orange juice, honey, vanilla extract, and 6 ice cubes in a blender or food processor, and process until smooth.
2. Add remaining ice and continue to process until smooth. Serve at once.

Calories Per Serving: 142
Fat: 0 g
Cholesterol: 1 mg
Protein: 4 g

Carbohydrates: 33 g
Dietary Fiber: 2 g
Sodium: 37 mg

❧ *Peach Shake* ❧

Peaches and yogurt are blended in this vanilla–accented shake.

PREPARATION TIME: 5 minutes ▪ YIELD: 6 servings

*4 fresh peaches, peeled, pitted, and
  quartered
1 cup nonfat plain yogurt*

*½ teaspoon vanilla extract
10 ice cubes*

1. Combine peaches, yogurt, and vanilla extract in a blender or food processor. Process until smooth.
2. Continue to process while you add ice cubes, a couple at a time. Serve at once.

Calories Per Serving: 46
Fat: 0 g
Cholesterol: 1 mg
Protein: 3 g

Carbohydrates: 10 g
Dietary Fiber: 1 g
Sodium: 29 mg

❧ *Strawberry Iced Tea Spritzer* ❧

Americans started drinking iced tea at the St. Louis World's Fair in 1904. This variation features strawberries and frozen lemonade concentrate.

*PREPARATION TIME: 10 minutes plus 5 minutes tea steeping and 1 hour
chilling time ▪ YIELD: 8 servings*

2 cups strawberries, hulled and sliced
½ cup sugar
5 cups boiling water
4 tea bags

1 12-ounce can frozen lemonade con-
centrate, thawed
1 quart seltzer water, chilled

1. Combine strawberries and sugar in a pitcher.
2. Pour boiling water over tea bags and allow to steep for 5 minutes. Discard tea bags and allow tea to cool to room temperature.
3. Combine tea and lemonade concentrate. Add liquid to strawberries and chill in the refrigerator for 1 hour.
4. Add seltzer water to strawberry-tea mixture, pour over ice cubes, and serve.

Calories Per Serving: 102
Fat: 0 g
Cholesterol: 0 mg
Protein: 1 g

Carbohydrates: 25 g
Dietary Fiber: 1 g
Sodium: 6 mg

❧ *Strawberry Shake* ❧

A healthful, low-fat variation of the old favorite.

PREPARATION TIME: 10 minutes   •   YIELD: 4 servings

3 cups nonfat vanilla frozen yogurt
2 cups strawberries, hulled and halved
¼ cup skim milk

1 tablespoon sugar
4 springs fresh mint

1. Place yogurt, strawberries, milk, and sugar in a blender or food processor, and blend until smooth.
2. Garnish with a sprig of mint and serve at once.

Calories Per Serving: 92
Fat: 1 g
Cholesterol: 2 mg
Protein: 2 g

Carbohydrates: 19 g
Dietary Fiber: 1 g
Sodium: 57 mg

❧ *Morning Honey-Banana Shake* ❧

This breakfast drink is healthy, delicious, and quick.

PREPARATION TIME: 5 minutes   •   *YIELD: 2 servings*

2 cups skim milk
1 banana
½ cup nonfat plain yogurt

1 teaspoon lemon juice
1 tablespoon honey

1. Combine milk, banana, yogurt, lemon juice, and honey in a blender or
   food processor and blend until smooth. Serve at once.

Calories Per Serving: 193
Fat: 1 g
Cholesterol: 4 mg
Protein: 12 g

Carbohydrates: 37 g
Dietary Fiber: 1 g
Sodium: 174 mg

INDEX

ABOUT THE AUTHOR

SARAH SCHLESINGER is the author of the bestselling *500 Fat-Free Recipes; 500 Low-Fat and Fat-Free Appetizers, Snacks, and Hors d'Oeuvres; 500 Low-Fat Fruit and Vegetable Recipes,* and *500 (Practically) Fat-Free Pasta Recipes.* She is the co-author of *The Low-Cholesterol Olive Oil Cookbook, The Low-Cholesterol Oat Plan,* and *The Pointe Book.* She is also a lyricist-librettist who, with her collaborator Mike Reid, has recently written *Different Fields,* an opera about football in contemporary life commissioned by the Metropolitan Opera Guild, and a musical based on the film *The Ballad of Little Jo.* She is the chair of the Graduate Musical Theatre Writing Program at New York University's Tisch School of the Arts. She and her husband, Sam Gossage, live in Greenwich Village and in Lewes, Delaware.